BRITAIN'S BLACK POPULATION

Dedicated to my late mother Amarjit K Luthra who
devoted her life to public service

Britain's Black Population

Social change, public policy and agenda

Mohan Luthra

arena

Published by
Arena
Ashgate Publishing Limited
Gower House
Croft Road
Aldershot
Hants GU11 3HR
England

Ashgate Publishing Company
Old Post Road
Brookfield
Vermont 05036
USA

British Library Cataloguing in Publication Data

Luthra, Manmohan
    Britain's black population
    1. Blacks – Great Britain
    I. Title
    305.8'96'041

Library of Congress Catalog Card Number: 96-85880

ISBN 1 85742 189 2 (paperback)
ISBN 1 85742 041 1 (hardback)

Printed and bound in Great Britain by Hartnolls Limited, Bodmin, Cornwall

Contents

Section II Law and Society

Section III Social Policy

Section IV Housing, Enterprise and Urban Policy

List of tables

List of charts

Foreword

This book is the third in the series of *Britain's Black Population*. The first edition of this book was a collective effort between several authors associated with Radical Statistics: the main focus was on the presentation of relevant data in an accessible form. The second in the series, edited by one member of Radical Statistics together with two community activists, moved away from strictly quantitative/ statistical focus and included more of a story about the data. This book continues that trend towards interpretation and away from quantification. Whilst there are some who will regret the opportunity to present and analyse trends given the publication of detailed data from the 1991 census, this move towards theoretical contextualisation and interpretation is, in general, to be welcomed as the descriptive analysis of data is covered by recent OPCS texts on ethnicity and the census.

Mohan Luthra, who has been a practitioner and an academic, sets out to explore the implications of social and economic change over the last decade, both within and outside ethnic minority communities, for social and urban policies concerning those communities. Where evidence is addressed in previous books it tends to be statistical, but that is not the predominant focus in this edition. Instead, Luthra has drawn together a wide range of evidence from the law, social and urban policy, education and health sectors, combining them with OPCS data to provide a story about what has happened to the ethnic minority communities over the last ten years. In particular, he shows how the experience of minority groups has to be understood on the framework of what has happened in the wider society. Of course, given the contentious nature of many of the issues, his choice of evidence will also be contentious; but the review is an essential backdrop for anyone hoping to understand the conflicts and problems facing Britain's black population as we approach the millennium.

Roy Carr-Hill

Preface

At the end of the millennium it will be a quarter of a century since the Race Relations Act 1976 was passed. The Act heralded a tradition of state intervention aimed at tackling discrimination and disadvantage inspired by the Civil Rights movement in the USA Since then a lot of changes have taken place, including the rise and demise of the antiracist movement and a number of inner city uprisings. Britain has joined the European Union and Euroracism has been put on the agenda. The old established ethnic minorities communities have also been joined by the new migrant communities. Sadly there has been little success in making a major dent in the prevalence of racism in Britain and the rest of the Europe is just beginning to acknowledge the issue.

In this book, aimed at students and practitioners alike, I have endeavoured not only to chart changes which flow from public policy or from within black and ethnic minorities communities, but also to explore some relevant agendas, options and discourses as we embark upon a journey into the next century.

Acknowledgements

Writing books on a solo basis when working full time can be a very frustrating task and can in some circumstances lead to serious demoralisation I am grateful to a number of friends and colleagues who have assisted me with moral and practical support to enable me to complete this book

I would particularly like to thank Jacqueline Burns and Synolda Butler for their assistance in both typing and editing my drafts as well as being patient with me I would also like to thank Anjuna who assisted and offered moral support and encouragement throughout the project. Acknowledgements are also due to Mr Godfrey Cremer the Director of the Ealing Racial Equality for institutional support and help with computer problems

Finally I would like to thank Keith Davis who finally helped to convert the whole book into its current presentable form .All errors, flaws and drawbacks however the readers might notice are entirely mine

The author

Mohan (Manmohan S Luthra)Luthra was born and educated in the city of Amritsar in Punjab and received his higher education in the UK. During his career he has held many different posts in local government including that of a Community Relations Officer, Housing Officer, Head of Race Equality and a Senior Education Officer . He has also been research fellow at Brunel University, a visiting fellow at the Institute of Education and is currently a Principal Lecturer at Southbank University.

Introduction

The purpose of this introduction is threefold. First, to provide the context to this book insofar as its place in the series is concerned. Second, to provide background information to the reader to establish the context pertaining to the content of the book and finally, to provide guidance on the structure of the book.

The series and the book

This book is third in part of the series *Britain's Black Population* launched in 1974. The first two books in the series were essentially an analysis of the statistical trends. And the main area of focus was Britain. In this book the emphasis is on the social and economic changes over the last decade both within and outside ethnic minority communities. The book endeavours to explore the relationship of and implications of these changes for social and urban policy and the emerging challenges and options to ethnic minorities. In charting this terrain the book takes into account many changes over the last decade, i.e. the further development of the European union, the arrival of new managerialism and quality assurance within the framework of contract culture as well as current debates about citizenship, postmodernism, communitarianism and challenges to eurocentricism. In so doing I have attempted to link the specific analysis in each chapter with such wider contemporary narratives, unlike previous books in this series. Wherever possible I have attempted to integrate the observations and findings about communities which have established themselves recently, i.e. the Somali and the West African communities, although I am somewhat hampered by the availability of adequate data on such communities..

Background

Historically, European experience with in-migration is different from that of other major immigrant nations such as Australia and the United States. In the last century Europe, and in particular Britain, exported a huge amount of labour to other 'immigrant nations'[1], while in the post-war period it switched from exporting humans to importing them, often to the benefit of economies. Recently even Italy, traditionally an out-migrating nation, has experienced in-migration from Africa and Eastern Europe[2] along with migrants from other European countries, partly instigated by political upheaval and partly by the attraction of economic opportunities in developed nations in Europe. This must be set against the fact that more people leave Britain than enter and the British birth-rate has remained low for a number of years[3]. Popular projections in the realm of folklore often tend to exaggerate the number of ethnic minorities, a distortion in perception which the majority of European populations suffer from[4]. Historically ethnic minority population estimates stood at 74,000 in 1951, 336,000 in 1961, 1.3 million in 1971, 2.2 million in 1981 and just over 3 million in 1991 consisting 5.9% of the population, expected to stabilize at around 8% in the year 2000. Currently some first generation settlers in some communities are returning in significant numbers to their country of origin.

In most countries of Europe at the end of the eighties the intake of asylum seekers went up from a poor base to be curtailed severely in the nineties[5]. One significant feature of the time of arrival of recent migrants and refugees has been the way it has coincided with the European debate about the welfare state and citizenship and in particular in Britain[6] Furthermore, the European integration debate has pushed the issue of national identity on the European agenda, an issue about which the British have agonised much more than other European nations. In a minority context, European born second-generation immigrants franchised and empowered to different extents in different nations have experienced the implications of such debates.

Historically, unlike the United States, Canada and Australia, Europe (including Britain) has limited experience of receiving and accommodating people with religious, cultural, and ethnic characteristics that diverge sharply from its own and the myth of British tolerance has been questioned [7]. The movement of people and ideas within Europe and their influx from outside has contributed to the development of both European capitalism and culture. This contribution is often underplayed by defining Europe in a restrictive way as Graeco-Judaeo-Christian civilisation[8], a notion recently challenged by Bernal and others[9] who have highlighted the evidence of the North African civilisation's contribution to European classical culture.

In Britain the social and economic contribution of ancestors of the present ethnic minorities to empire capitalism as subjects, slaves, soldiers and residents[10] is well documented, and there has been fierce debate about the role of immigration as a catalyst of post-war capitalism or as an inhibitor of modernisation [11]. More recently in Germany some research has been carried out to show the impact of immigration on trade links, in this case with Turkey, although similar studies do not exist within the context of the UK [12].

Terminology

Throughout the book the terms black and ethnic minorities or ethnic minorities have been used to represent the spectrum of ethnic minority groups in Britain. This terminology is flawed and inadequate in representing the ethnic and genetic diversity of Britain's population. The use of the term white to represent a spectrum of ethnicities is problematic to say the least.

Nevertheless social science analysis requires the use of categories and broad generalisations and some form of 'grossing-up' to build a picture. Hence in addition to the above we have used the term Asian for Indian, Pakistani and Bangladeshi. While the term Chinese has been used to represent South East Asians including Vietnamese. The term black embraces both African and Caribbeans and has been used interchangeably with African-Caribbeans. Somalis are measured as a specific group, being now a major group amongst the Africans. The term visible minorities has been used in Chapter 2, to make a distinction between immigrants who migrate within Europe and those from outside Europe.

Historically Britain has been one country where the new arrivals in this century have held different and sometimes overlapping status as subjects, aliens, residents, nationals etc.,[13]. The colonial relationship between Britain and the Commonwealth, along with other historical factors, has meant that unlike most European migrants the British New Commonwealth settlers had voting and residential rights including rights of access to welfare provision. Furthermore access to British citizenship, by virtue of ordinary residence and on the basis of birth, had been historically maintained in contrast to other European countries. Despite these rights, systemic resistance, discrimination and exclusions have interacted with cultural and social disadvantages to produce differential outcomes for different ethnic minority communities.

Structure of the book

The first chapter (Chapter 1) explores major changes within the communities as well as systemic changes over the last two decades. The focus of the chapter is on two well established communities, the Asian and the Caribbeans communities. The chapter endeavours to delineate trends discernible from evidence available from a variety of resources within the context of changes, social and economic, with a focus on first generation immigrants and their children. In the absence of good data split by three generations, I have endeavoured to delineate trends as far as possible. As this chapter is rather large and divided into three major sections, it comprises the whole of Section I of the book.

Section II of the book is comprised of three chapters broadly dealing with the issue of the role of conventions, constitutions and the law and its implications for the rights of ethnic minorities and their well being in relation to diversity and race equality both in a British and a wider European context. While Chapter 2 endeavours to develop an evaluative overview of provision of anti-discrimination law in Europe. Chapter 3 is a case study of the British experience of use of the Race Relations Act (1976) by the individual complainants. This is followed by Chapter 4 which is a compilation of case studies of state responses to key legal issues for black and ethnic minorities over the last decade - i.e. racial violence, cultural diversity and contract compliance.

Section III is comprised of two chapters, Chapters 5 and 6 are both aimed primarily at British social policy developments and its implication for race equality and ethnic minorities at large. We have taken cognisance of the fact that the education and training debates continue to converge. Similarly the professional collaboration between health and social services is increasing rapidly, catalysed by statutory changes.

In Section IV, the focus of the book shifts to British urban policy. The theme of enterprise and owner-occupation, two main planks of government policy, as well as its implications for employment of ethnic minorities are explored in Chapters 7 and 8. The final chapter (Chapter 9) these themes are distilled to explore projections and possible avenues of action as well as extending the debate of these themes to link with contemporary debates. The chapter also updates some of the earlier observations.

A number of contemporary issues such as crime and race equality, or issues and themes related to the arts, crime and the media have not been dealt with in this book, although some of these have been touched upon in Chapter 1. The reader is guided to the previous volume of *Britain's Black Population* for analysis of some of these areas.

References

1 Here I refer to America and Canada, see Hobsbawm E. (1994) *The Age of Empires*, Penguin.
2 See Chapter 2
3 *Social Indicators* (1995) Central Statistical Office. HMSO
4 Various surveys over the years have shown this, and I have often asked this question in various training programmes to find extreme overestimations.
5 Smelser N. (1994) *Sociology*, Sage.
6 See Chapter 2.
7 Holmes C. (1991) *A Tolerant Country, Immigrant Refugees and Minorities in Britain*, Faber.
8 Mrs Thatcher speech to the Synod in 1988 referred to this notion acknowledging Jewish contribution to English civilisation.
9 Bernal M. (1993) *Black Athena*, Free Association Press, London.
10 Friar P. (1984) *Staying Power*, Pluto. Holmes (Op. Cit.).
11 For a wide view, see Bohning W.R. and Castles S. and Kosack G. in Brahm P. (Ed.) Rhodes K. and Pearn M. (Ed.), *Discrimination and Disadvantage in Employment*, Harper Row.
12 Paper presented by Dr Hakki Keskin Kraiplinwey, 2000, Hamburg 76, at Birmingham - an evaluation of the latest racist attacks on foreigners in Germany. Conference on Race Equality in Europe, 1992, Birmingham City Council.

SECTION I

Identity and
Society

1 Social change, identity and the state

An overview of continuity and change amongst British ethnic minority communities

This chapter charts the major social changes and developments within ethnic minority communities with a particular focus on the last decade with reference to first and second generation. The first part charts social changes and trends in community development and electoral affiliations and is followed by a section which examines the nature and processes at work in stratification and social mobility. The final part of the chapter develops an overview of systemic changes in state, private and local government apparatus and its implications for integration of ethnic minorities into the mainstream. The central thrust of the chapter is to explore the theme of continuity and change and the nature of challenges ethnic minorities face because of major systemic changes which have taken place over the last decade.

Post-war community development: black identity and the emergence of anti-racism

In Britain the presence of ethnic minority enclaves (Liverpool Eight,

Liverpool and Bute Town in Wales, and China towns in Manchester and Gerrard Street in London) and prominent political contributions of individuals from ethnic minority groups can be traced back to the pre-war era[1]. The only post war ethnic minority community to have a pre-war economic nucleus in Britain were the Chinese[2]. Pre-war settlers from New Commonwealth groups were far more likely to marry local women, being single or simply alone. Consequently they integrated phenotypically and socially to become part of the local communities under assimilationist pressures over a period of time.

In the fifties the Caribbeans arrived followed by Asians from the Indian subcontinent by invitation of the government subsequent to the failed attempts to recruit European labour. Pre-war community development was essentially rooted in nationalist and student protests as well as self-help traditions leading to the formation of cultural and welfare associations parallel to the establishment of handful religious institutions[3]. The Asian communities produced three MPs at the turn of the century, one for each of the three main parties[4].

Early-post-war migrants were joined by their dependants in the sixties and seventies. Political refugees from Kenya in 1968 and Uganda in 1972 who were relatively better off also joined. The early seventies also saw a chain migration of Bangladeshis, as well as student-based Malaysian immigration. African immigration rooted historically in student intake increased in the eighties as did immigration from Hong Kong and the New Territories for both political and economic reasons. Political refugees from Vietnam, Somalia, the Middle East, Lebanon and Eastern Europe all added to the existing British diversity in the last two decades. Of these arrivals, the Vietnamese and the Bangladeshis were particularly disadvantaged economically. Average length of residence of different ethnic minority communities varies according to the time of arrival with some communities such as the Indians and West Indians being more established in terms of time than others[5].

According to Ward, apart from ideology, the early eighties saw a wide measure of agreement on the broad dimensions of an analysis of the developing context of race relations in Britain. The main points identified by him[6] were as follows:

1   Between 1945 and 1965 there was an unfilled demand for labour, mainly to do poorly paid and unpleasant jobs. A replacement labour force was provided by migrant workers from the New Commonwealth (mainly India, Pakistan and the Caribbean), who aspired initially to better the living standards of their families in their country of origin.

2   Such employment was most frequently found in sectors where there was a continuing demand for a replacement labour force to carry out jobs which were a well-established part of the local economy - e.g. metal manufacturing, textiles industries and work in public utilities[7].

3   Immigration was abruptly curtailed in 1962 by legislation[8] leaving very limited scope mainly for immigration, in the main only for dependants to join. In the late sixties and early seventies, New Commonwealth migrants were joined by East African Asians who were under severe pressure to leave Kenya, and a bit later Uganda. Despite coming from a more privileged, middle-class background, they were (at least initially) obliged to fit into a similar niche to that occupied by their predecessors from South Asia. Attempts by the government to resettle them in areas away from existing ethnic minority concentrations were not particularly successful[9] as they were attracted to areas where jobs and social links were available, although often characterised by housing shortage.

4   In the early period of settlement at least, they were usually without residential qualifications for a council house or sufficient income to qualify for a mortgage. In addition, attitudes to black and ethnic minority people derived from the colonial period, reinforced the tendency to practise racial discrimination, reducing the opportunities open to them. In consequence, their typical housing situation in the early years

11

consisted of renting furnished rooms, often by landlords of the same group, in run-down areas. Their concentration in such areas had serious consequences for the education of their children and hence for the levels of employment they were likely to achieve[10]. In most cases the gradual settlement and consolidation of black and ethnic minority populations including their institutions in white-working-class residential areas was accelerated by existing white residents who were moving out to seek better housing. Some ethnic minorities, mostly professionals, were able to escape to the suburbs. In consequence, large areas of unimproved terraced houses in the inner city outside the belt of slum clearance were available to Asians and West Indians to buy and occupy as a replacement residential population, while West Indians finally made their way on to the council 'problem' estates[11].

Ward concludes that the resulting situation was one of structural discontinuity between the white, and black and ethnic minority working class: at work or in terms of residential space. The settlers attempts to move into more attractive and lucrative employment areas have been fiercely resisted. Many of those who still identified themselves primarily as West Indians, Indians and Pakistanis were reasonably satisfied with what is objectively a considerable improvement in their standard of living compared with their situation in their countries of origin. But some of their children who have been brought up in Britain and were developing higher aspirations, found the opportunities open to them, particularly at work, inadequate.

Several observations are needed to update this scenario in the nineties. Firstly, the above perspective is imbued with victimology in which little credit is given to the victim for taking control or altering his destiny. Secondly, the uniformity of situation across ethnic minority groups is questionable. Chapters 6 and 7 show how the economic and social progression as well as strategic accommodation of different ethnic minority groups varies a great

deal. Thirdly, the labour replacement theory does not hold very well
in the regions such as Scotland or London, neither is the housing
replacement theory as valid as it was then[12]. Fourthly, there has been
the emergence of the middle classes, as business and house
ownership have developed to a significant extent within some of the
ethnic minority communities. Some groups including newly-arrived
Africans, the Chinese and earlier Indians and refugee East-Africans
have become economically and educationally well established.

  Finally, there has been total destruction of some of the traditional
industries, particularly manufacturing, which employed first-
generation immigrants in the seventies including ethnic minority
women. In the early eighties the recession hit minorities
disproportionately. The situation in terms of unemployment levels
has not been dissimilar for minorities in the second recession at the
end of the eighties, although some ethnic minority groups such as the
Chinese and the Indians have been slightly better protected because
of their expanding ethnic cultural enterprise sector and partly due to
having a large proportion of people with higher educational
qualifications[13].

Community development up to the eighties: a brief overview

Early-post-war community and race relations organisations were
ethnically mixed and fell into four major categories. One group was
often led by white liberals such as church leaders and trade
unionists[14], while a second group were minority-led cultural and
welfare organisations. The former group was to develop into
Community Relations Councils which were funded by the Home
Office in the late-sixties. A third group of organisations were rooted
in the experience of the nationalist struggle with left-wing leanings.
One example would be the Indian Workers Associations (IWAs)[15]
which partly assisted ethnic minority newcomers in relation to
immigration advice, education, sending money to the country of
origin, nationality papers and passports. They also took up issues
such as the bussing of ethnic minority children to schools outside of

13

their residential area [16]. A fourth group developed as an independent sector of travel agents, financiers, job brokers[17], 'partners clubs' as well as cinema clubs were also developed in the case of some communities, aided by the banks usually belonging to their country of origin[18], and community leaders.

Places of worship have historically been important to settlers of different origins in the initial phase of settlement. The West Indian immigrants developed their own Pentecostal church, while in the case of Asians, initially houses and later old churches were converted into temples and mosques[19].

The civil rights debate in the USA together with the emergence of independent Caribbean states contributed to the development of Black Power groups in 1969[20], further influenced by Garvey's ideology and the black nationalist movement in the USA. Groups in Britain such as the Black Panthers and Black Unity were often in a state of tension with the more cosmopolitan left-wing groups such as the Race Today collective or even the IWAS[21]. By the end of the sixties, the government had acknowledged the ineffectiveness of the 1968 Race Relations Act, and had also passed the Local Government Act 1966 which made financial provision under section 11 to fund local councils with a certain percentage of NCWP population[22] in their catchment areas.. In addition to this provision, the urban programme was to be used for the development of projects to counter the disadvantages experienced by ethnic minorities.

By the early seventies some of these ethnic-minority organisations had formed umbrella groups leading to the development of standing conferences such as the West Indian Standing Conference (WISC), while the IWAs were already being co-ordinated nationally[23]. These organisations were to come together with the Pakistani Welfare Association (PWA) and the National Federation of Pakistanis Associations (NFPA) to form Campaign Against Racial Discrimination (CARD) in 1965 and to form Black Peoples Alliances in 1968. Their position of advocating constructive engagement was somewhat different from the exclusionary, often confrontational and ethnic-nationalist position taken by Black

Power, Black Unity and RAAS who are influenced by the ideas of Malcolm X.

The availability of some state funding under the urban programme and Section 11 programme strengthened some of the service and advice provision groups. The early seventies also saw the strengthening of the base of the religious organisations. The Muslims established the United Muslim Organisations (UMO) in 1973 and the Muslim Education Council (aimed at tackling the secular curriculum) in 1974 with Saudi resources. And by the mid-seventies there were already some sixty mosques in Britain[24]. The Sikhs had won a battle over the turban issue, and the Asian left was able to use its Gurdwaras as a base to mobilise Sikhs in many campaigns against discrimination and immigration law[25].

The passing of the Race Relations Act 1976 and the increase in funding of both section 11 and urban aid programmes led to further establishment of a state-aided voluntary sector further assisted by the aid programme provided by the newly formed CRE, which was allowed to fund organisations as well as finance the Community Relations Councils[26]. Ethnic minority groups were also developing compensatory provisions such as the supplementary schools (see Chapter 6). They also confronted much government legislation on immigration during this period. Some multiracial organisations such as JCWI (established on a multi-funded basis) showed how the use of casework strategy, coupled with legal mobilisation can mount successful campaigns on immigration[27].

The mid-seventies also saw Asians flexing their industrial muscle by effectively using their community ties in industrial action in Mansfield (1972), Imperial Typewriters (1974), Grunwick (1976) and Quaker Oats (1974). These struggles sharpened class divide as well countered the myth of a compliant immigrant workforce. Simultaneously, skinhead attacks in Southall and London's East End increased, followed by other killings in Southall (Chaggers 1976, Peach 1979), culminating in the development of many youth organisations. These included the Southall Youth Movement (SYM), the Bengali Housing Action Group, the Bengali Youth League in the

East End and the Asian Youth Movement (AYM) in Bradford. All of these groups challenged the constructive engagement and intermediary leadership model of incremental gains followed by the liberals and minority leaders of that generation at the time. In contrast many of the new youth organisations launched self-defence campaigns or took direct action supported by the Caribbean youth[28]. Some of these organisations enabled the young with limited education, who in many cases had a brush with the law, to engage with political issues. Such organisations opposed the influence of the liberal organisations such as the National Association of Asian Youth, which played an important role in community development and provided national platforms for debates. The late-seventies also saw the development of a popular movement, the ANL (Anti-Nazi League), supported by the organisations such as CARD (Campaign Against Racial Discrimination) and the student unions of the broad-left, as well as the development of anti-discrimination-law campaigns.

The eighties: municipal left and the black identity

The early eighties also saw a shift in the debate from community relations to race equality as the inner-city disturbances shook the urban policy-makers. This was symbolised in the mushrooming of anti-racist organisations and the change in the name of the Community Relations Councils to the Council for Racial Equality. Supplied by the US terminology, the term 'black' was used mainly by activists to symbolise the common experience of exclusion, a history of colonial oppression and racism. The idea of celebrating diversity was linked to the notion of equality. Out of this emerged the anti-racist movement led by the municipal socialists in the GLC who were to ally themselves with black activists to take forward the anti-racist ideology[29]. The GLC also engaged in considerable resource politics leading to the proliferation of groups in London, in some cases supported by the funding from other sources such as the

Manpower Services Commission (MSC) or Sports Council [30.]

This led to one analysis that central-government-funded organisations such as the renamed Councils for Racial Equality (previously Community Relations Councils) were not needed due to the growth of significant ethnic minority voluntary sectors[31]. In addition, other movements such as the emerging law centre movement provided an opportunity for many black activists to integrate in a collective culture to take on the local state with the backdrop of the welfare rights movement[32]. Sadly the experiment failed to realise its full potential due to too many rifts and the obsession of the movement with collective management. The demise of the GLC, the rate-capping of local authorities and the shift away from multiculturalism to integration in central government funding policy, e.g. Section 11 funding, and the death of the urban programme meant that the black and ethnic minority organisations were severely hit, curtailing the base of the ethnic minorities voluntary sector by the end of the eighties[33]. The decline of the law centre movement[34] also affected the minority communities leaving the RECs holding the ground on their own in the inner cities in the period of recession in the early-nineties[35.].

Some community groups were having to adapt to the changing conditions. For instance, the Asian-left came to terms with the changing world, and the two (Maoist and Leninists) IWAs which had split in the fifties came together, having spent a lot of time in Britain fighting the ethnic-right in the eighties. While the Asian-left had barely survived the global demise of the left, there had been a considerable explosion in the number of religious organisations and places of worship often built by the contributions of local people, and in some cases with contributions from abroad[36], often attracting members of the expanding commercial clergy class in the subcontinent. The Rushdie affair gave birth to the Islamic party and the Muslim parliament and brought the Muslim community into conflict with the British state. Yet the new Muslim ethnic-right failed to make any major electoral gains in the last election despite polls suggesting that 66% of Muslims would rely on the Sharia in the case of conflict between British and Islamic law[37]. There has been considerable fission in the Muslim leadership - perhaps more so than other groups - leading to increasing religious and cultural demands quite often at the expense of race equality campaigns[38].

The ageing of ethnic minority populations (particularly the middle-class) who feel the need to contribute to the community as well as to establish status is probably a key factor explaining the increasing number of religious, cultural and leisure organisations. Some of these organisations are state funded[39]. The local state, often unclear about its policy on secularism, in some cases has encouraged exclusionary and segregationist tendencies by funding separate provision, even when it is not cost effective[40].

Nevertheless some weaker groups did benefit from such state sponsorship in the eighties. For instance, the GLC gave a particular impetus to ethnic-minority women's community development who felt increasingly confident to develop organisations against the backdrop of a strong feminist movement[41]. It was an Asian women's group who took on the task of challenging the ethnic-right and orthodox perspectives in the wake of the Rushdie affair. Some of these women's organisations are cultural and recreational while others focus on social issues[42]. Women's activist groups such as the Southall Black Sisters (SBS) make an effective case against violence against women, but have been accused of being confrontational. Conciliation organisations such as Relate have failed to emerge as yet, partly because the divorce rate in ethnic minorities communities remains still relatively low, with the exception of African and Caribbean communities[43]. This picture, however, is changing rapidly amongst the young across the board. Many of the women's groups which developed in the eighties appear to have petered away in the nineties, although those providing a service or advice are more likely to survive. Significantly no major women's national groups have emerged despite much debate about ethnic minority women and their rights.

Some government-assisted national initiatives established in the late eighties, such as the Black Housing Association movement supported by the Federation of Black Housing Associations (FBHO), developed slowly and benefited from the switch in government funding to the Housing Corporation. Nevertheless in overall terms there are some 12 Black Housing Associations supporting some 7,000 properties[44]. Another major government initiative in the eighties and early nineties has led to the proliferation of a number of very small health projects[45] including mental health organisations, often on short-term funding[46].

The nineties: from anti-racism to equal opportunities

The re-emergence of the anti-racist movement as the Anti-Racist Alliance and the Anti-Nazi League (ANL)in the early nineties, both of which are broad based coalitions, was welcomed. However their failure to emerge as one organisation was regrettable[47]. The ARAs policy of black-only leadership brought it into confrontation with the left-wing IWA and of the liberal ANL[48]. The IWA has had difficulties with the notion of the formation of separate black sections in the trade unions and in the labour party - the latter falling foul of the labour party conference because of the demand for black-only candidates. Some of the current debates mirror the debates between CARLD and RAAS in the early sixties. The black nationalists in the race equality movement, although still on the scene, on the whole are now marginalised, yet seem to survive in pockets within the labour party.

Overall, in the eighties national organisations in areas such as legal mobilisation, racial harassment or urban regeneration and training have failed to emerge over the last decade. On the positive side some organisations such as the National Association of Multi-Cultural Education (NAME), the Joint Council for Welfare of Immigrants (JCWI), and the Federation of Black Housing Associations (FBHO), have managed to survive as indeed have the IWAs, but the overall picture seems less optimistic. Attempts to establish national organisations such as Project Full Employ (three years), Community

Roots College (two years), Legal Defence Fund (3 months) have been fruitful only in the short-term and have eventually died. Other setbacks included the inability to set up a national help-line on racial harassment or a conciliation service for women mooted by Asian lawyers[49]. At local level many useful organisations have emerged and developed and there has been a considerable growth in cultural centres. In contrast the reduction in funding of legal advice groups has meant that they have had to rely on legal aid to survive - i.e. they have become captives of the network of barristers and solicitors they support[50].

Another feature of the past decade has been the failure on the part of most organisations to switch over to addressing issues relevant to a younger constituency. The IWA (GB) has made some attempt to engage with local issues but has failed to attract younger membership[51]. Having discouraged the young from taking part in electoral politics for two decades thay are having difficulty finding people who will now come forward. In the wake of the Rushdie affair, Muslim organisations have been more successful in recruiting the young. In parallel with the case of women, major national or regional youth organisations have failed to develop.

The early eighties gave birth to a new language for equality discourse in which the term black at least came to represent all ethnic groups in lobbying circles. By the late eighties the term 'black and ethnic minorities', had been developed to accommodate the cultural diversity and resistance of some communities to the use of the term black to describe them. Gilroy (1994) described the end of this period as also being 'the end of anti-racism' from which point minorities did not simply want to define themselves as anti something. As we show later on anti-racism and race equality were beginning to be subsumed in the technocratic and human resourcing framework.

Some major trends in the past decade: stratification, social mobility and exoticism

Some of the earlier social trends over the past two decades have been accentuated while some new ones have emerged. These include: feminisation of labour* and poverty[52], contractualisation of marriages[53], individualisation of culture and families[54], the much contested notion of secularisation and the increasing gap between the rich and the poor[55]. In systemic terms there has been an increase in the distance between the centre and periphery as well as the disappearance of the pyramid structure of the labour market[56] in which the base is not only shrinking but it also being casualised. The impact of the systemic changes on minorities is explored in the final part of this chapter. In this section we explore major trends related to social change under the following broad headings.

Secularisation, westernisation and the family

Beckford (1992) in his analysis of Britain put forward the notion of 'believing without belonging', and argued that the decline in attendance or changing rituals of worship does not mean a decline in faith, that is *within* the context of faith there is continuity and change[57]. Indeed the attendance rates of Mormons and Jehovah's Witness and Seventh-Day Adventists have increased when other Christian groups have been declining. Beckford explores the implicit aspects of life - folk or custom - which harbour faith, a process through which the Jewish community has gone.

Historically some minority groups have been more prone to assimilation and secularisation than other groups. For instance, Jews and Hindus have been less successful in retaining their identity than other groups such as the Muslims[58]. Current evidence suggests that British Hindus and Sikhs are more prone to secularisation and westernisation than other groups originating from the sub-continent[59]. In most cases it is likely to be tactful accommodation

*This became restricted to single parents in the nineties

21

particularly in the case of the young, leading to the notion of being culturally a Hindu or a Sikh, i.e. believing and belonging to the majority culture to a deliberate extent depending upon the situation.

Relying on traditional social science terminology, some groups such as the Caribbeans are relatively more secularised and westernised as they have been historically closer to these traditions[60]. Nevertheless their first generation has retained their churches while the second generation is bifurcated amongst those who are secular and those who are practising, including those who are joining groups such as Jehovah's Witness in large numbers along with Africans[61]. Overall the evidence suggests that island identity has become a lesser component of self-identity in the case of Caribbeans, leading to pan-Caribbeanism, than is the case with Asians. Although Butler suggested that amongst second-generation Muslims, nationality has been substituted by an Islamic component[62].

Acquiring a western education, particularly higher education, is an indicator of the extent to which a group embraces the rationalist culture of the west. The influence and exposure to such education on the social customs of a group has historically varied from one group to another. Western education, despite the economic mobility it is able to offer, is in some groups perceived as a threat to the culture of a minority group. In many cases it is also seen as loss of the person (i.e. a child), to what is seen as a rationalist, arrogant and highly individualistic type of education, emphasising enablement rather than ennoblement. It is this fear which has led some well-to-do parents to send their children for long holidays or to public schools on the subcontinent.

The erosion of the patriarchal family is perceived as another indicator of westernisation as indeed its nuclearisation. These have led to the emergence of a new kind of family, historically found in the Caribbean, albeit less extended than the Caribbean version. This together with a similar development amongst the white communities has led to a division of British ethnic minority communities into those who are perceived to be secular and autonomous with a non-conservative way of life, in contrast to a collective (or patriarchal) familistic and conservative model. Research by Heath et al (1992) based on census analysis suggests that with patterns of family structure in both the case of Asians and Caribbeans, the picture remains that of continuity for different ethnic minority communities rather than change. (See Table 1.1 and Table 1.2.)

Table 1.1 Cohabiting rates by ethnicity, age groups and generation (%)

Age	16-20		21-24		25-29		30-35	
Generation	1st	2nd	1st	2nd	1st	2nd	1st	2nd
White	4	6	13	17	17	14	8	9
Black	8	2	7	7	9	12	6	7
Asian	4	0	1	2	2	4	1	-

Source: Heath et al (1994) OPCS Monitor 4.

The cohabiting rate appears to follow traditional patterns for both Asian and Caribbean communities going up very little in the case of 16-20 year old Asian women (Table 1.2). The cohabitation phenomenon is significant for Asian women who are qualified or living with men of other ethnic groups. Regardless of age, Asian women are more likely to be married than other groups followed by white and Caribbean women. Second generation black women are less likely to be married than their first generation counterparts. This change has sparked a fierce debate about autonomy, single-parenthood and the emerging relationship gulf between Caribbean men and women and to a lesser extent amongst Africans[63].

Table 1.2 Lone parents and married couples with children by ethnicity (%)

Age	16-20		21-24		25-29		30-35	
Single parents or married with children	S	M	S	M	S	M	S	M
White	2.3	1.2	7.9	12.0	9.8	34.5	10.3	57.7
Black	5.4	0.3	17.2	3.5	28.4	13.8	32.2	30.8
Asian	0.6	2.2	1.9	21.9	21.1	50.4	5.7	75.5

S = single parents
M = married with children
Source: Heath et al (1994) OPCS Monitor 4.

The notion of continuity amongst Asian youth is further supported by observation of Drewery that amongst 16-20 year old Sikh girls, 34% were very positive about facilitated marriages[64]. Heath et al[65] suggests that second generation Asian women in their twenties have very similar marriage rates to their white counterparts and higher education appears to delay that marriage. Furthermore, the tendency of Asian women to live with their husband's families continues to be higher than observed for other groups. Overall they tend to stay at home until they get married and then stay with their in-laws. Consequently, as shown in Table 1.2, teenage pregnancy leading to single parenthood remains a rare phenomenon, partly aided by the relatively late start of sexual activity amongst Asian girls and boys[66].

Insofar as sustaining marriage is concerned, the confidence of the Asian community in its own form of facilitated marriage is borne out by very low divorce rates and the approval of the young for such arrangements[67]. It is likely that a different kind of 'vertically' extended-family is emerging from the horizontal *and* vertically extended-families observed in the past, as only a quarter of the Asian household population now live in such families. Like urbanisation and industrialisation in India, exposure of Asians to a multi-tasking work environment, shopping spaces and experience of being destatused all have eroded caste barriers. Although some caste-consciousness survives amongst the second generation, as shown by Madood et el (1995) it has decreasing relevance to the second and third generation Asians, particularly to those born in the UK.

Ashrafisation

The arrival of further members of Muslim communities from Africa and Somalia who have been attracted to the established Asian areas of settlement in areas such as Tower Hamlets and Southall[68] added to the pool of established Muslim communities from the New Commonwealth. An important consequence of this development has been the growing realisation on the part of Caribbeans that they cannot afford to perceive Islam as a Middle Eastern or Asian phenomenon any more.This process has been aided by Nationalist Separatist Muslim leaders like Louis Farakhon in the USA who have visited Britain. The Rushdie affair in Britain, the war with Iraq, the debate about wearing the *Hijab*[69] have all clearly catalysed the process of Ashrafisation (normally restricted to lower middle income/middle aged people) as a way of enhancing status through symbols of dress and modes of worship[70], and in some cases swapping their regional identities for religious ones. This could partly be attributed to the global, and prophetic nature of Islam which has similar ideological shades and appeal as Marxism; and partly to the tussle between Iranian and Saudis to control their sphere of influence in Europe[71]. One view is that Islam now represents the only remaining global force against secular capitalism, whilst others see it as a counter-force to Western WASP nationalism in the absence of a global left-wing force[72].

The development of an imported clergy-class amongst some ethnic minority group has further accelerated the process of Ashrafisation, exploiting the Rushdie affair in the case of Muslims, and the Khalistan movement in the Punjab in the case of Sikhs[73]. The new clergy in international and commercial circles are often supported by the petty commercial classes and the less educated members of society. They tend to politicise the faith of the masses and push religion into the public domain in order to retain a political hold on the ethnic minority population. The use of temples and mosques for teaching ethnic minority languages to young people has increased the sphere of influence of the new clergy in education. Poorly defined multiculturalism (without any emphasis on secularism or multifaithism) has been abused for the purposes of catalysing Ashrafisation, giving more power to the clergy, who seek to create a segregated private domain from which common notions of basic human rights[74] and informed choice are excluded, much to the detriment of historically disempowered sub-groups within ethnic minority communities.

Conversely Ashrafisation has at the same time, given personal strength and a sense of empowerment to some women who have joined the so-called 'fundamentalist (or what I have called ethnic-right) movements'. In a paper entitled *The Second Generation of Muslim women in Bradford* Spivac[75] has depicted it as "constructing constriction in choice"[76]. Yet Knott (1992) et al have shown how young Muslim women synthesise identities as a spectrum with open channels to their own and the majority communities while Butler (1995) has shown that young educated Muslim women are now making a distinction between culture and religion to enable them to utilise what they regard as egalitarian and liberating aspects of Islam[77]

Ashrafisation may well have delayed the secularisation process amongst young Muslims as evident from the apparent lack of major differences in opinions about some contentious issues between the young Muslims and their parents (Table 1.3) although according to Anwar (1994) Muslim parents have also moved a little to adopt liberal attitudes in the last decade.

Table 1.3: Differences between the views of young Muslims and their parents

	Agree %	Disagree %
Asian girls wearing western clothes	+9	-10
Facilitated marriage in country of origin	-6	+7
Endogamy	-12 [10]	-
Single sex schools for daughters	-8 (-3)	+4

[ ] = 1983   ( ) = 1975
Source: M Luthra, developed from Anwar M. (1994) Muslim Youth in Britain, The Islamic Foundation

There is some evidence that a politicised version of Islam, Hinduism and Sikhism are being peddled to the young [78.] The Rushdie affair affected young Muslim people deeply and the very weak liberal-lobby within the Muslim community failed to stand up to the very distorted debate being put forward by the ethnic-right[79]. This is in contrast to the challenge the coalition of Sikhs and Hindu-Panjabi-secular-left has been able to present to the right-wing Khallistanis in Britain[80]. This is not to say that Ashrafisation has been an exclusively ethnic minority phenomenon. Christian evangelism including state evangelism in school curricula has been on the rise with demands for the establishment of evangelical schools from some conservative quarters[81].

Yet another aspect of Ashrafisation, which could be described as language Ashrafisation, is where some ethnic minority groups foist classical languages on to their children to enhance their own and their children's status and identity. For instance, historical denial by Pakistani Punjabis of their own mother tongue has been transferred to the UK. This led to parental demands to teach Urdu or Hindi as a mother tongue on the grounds of imagined affiliation of these languages with religion[82]. Ashrafisation encouraged by forces outside the UK is also apparent on British university campuses.

Sanskritisation

Sanskritisation, as observed by Srinivas, is a phenomenon of lower-caste Indian groups who acquire features of higher castes to upgrade their status[83]. Studies on Sanskritisation in Britain are generally lacking and there is little evidence of caste-awareness amongst young Asians although they appear to be endogamous mostly under parental pressure. In addition the lower castes groups have established their own temples and organisations in the UK as an expression of their new found economic and political autonomy in a relatively affluent setting [84]. This could be described as group Sanskritisation. Having escaped the caste oppression of the subcontinent such an act uplifts the self-esteem of the settler and is a liberating experience even in a racist society. At the other end, well-to-do members of ostensibly egalitarian groups are now adding caste or tribal names to their religious names. For instance Muslims use names such as Khan-Cheema, which is a relatively recent development on similar lines to the Sikhs. Overall this process affects first- and some second- generation ethnic minority groups.

Towards cosmopolitanisation: composite, fluid and situational identities

The young, although influenced and steered by the above trends to some extent, are also charting their own social course. Over the decade, Milner (1973) has shown that the phenonomen of mis-identification of self-identity in terms of skin colour amongst the ethnic minority young people in school, has disappeared[85]. From an earlier age children tend to prefer their own ethnic group[86] although they have some multiracial-friendships which tend to decline after the age of 12 or 13.

Another significant phenomenon apparent amongst the young is the extent to which black American and black Caribbean culture has permeated mainstream youth culture, not only of the majority community but also that of other ethnic communities. The language of many young Asians in Southall and Birmingham is a cross between the local dialect, black-American language and Caribbean patois. Caribbean youth are developing a growing awareness of multiple pan-Caribbean identity with consciousness of their roots in pan-African identity[87]. Yet like the situations between the Asians sub-group, tensions remain with black Africans[88]. To what extent the attraction of black youth culture should be regarded as a product of the masculine black and to a lesser extent Caribbean, culture is a matter of debate. One suspects that the success of TV shows from the United States such as *The Cosby Show* and films such as *Beverly Hills Cop* and *Malcolm X,* and the relative success of young blacks on the music and sports scene, have all played a crucial role in creating a new Anglo-American youth culture and language with a substantive black dimension.

In contrast the profile of Asian youth remains marginal with little emergence of role models in sports and the leisure industry. As conformity has been the norm, the Asian young remain relatively pragmatic and accommodating. They appear still to accept facilitated marriages as an alternative to finding someone for themselves, and quite enjoy the exoticism of their own culture. Haleh (1989) has suggested that the recession and discrimination have further catalysed this process in which even educated young Asian women voluntarily withdraw from the labour market to take care of the family or accept marriages[89]. Perceived from a non-ethnocentric point of view, one could argue that affinity for or access to the labour market is calculated by these women in terms of its implications for being the pivot of the family and the alternative (i.e., being a unit of production in the labour market) status of being married. The demise of the older industries such as textiles and manufacturing has catalysed the withdrawal of Asian women who are over fifty, from the labour market, partly because their children have started earning [90].

Asian youth, although still on the margins of the mainstream British youth culture, are finding increasing confidence in relation to their own culture. For instance, 80% of young women in Stoppes Roe survey had worn their own dress[91]. This is partly because mainstream white culture has borrowed a great deal over the last two decades from the subcontinent in terms of design and fashion. This trend which began in the sixties, was catalysed by the Festival of India in the early eighties and now lives on through the Asian cultural enterprise. Asian youth have also evolved their own local sub-culture by developing initiatives such as day-discos, Asian charts and music groups[92], some of which integrate western, Caribbean and Asian traditions. Recognition by the majority community is more important to these groups than was the case with their parents[93]. Small but increasing numbers of young Asians are marrying across caste, religion and nationalities. This mirrors the trend in urban centres of India, which have brought together Indians of different states, religions and caste. These are likely to be the first major integration hurdles for Asian youth rather than marrying across into majority communities or into other ethnic groups.

Woolett (1991) has argued that the fluidity of Asian identity defies notions such as westernisation and modernisation and is not a function of length of residence which terms like acculturation imply, while Brah (1991) pointed out that the difference (with other groups) is constructed differently within various discourses[94]. In broad terms one can agree with these statements, but nevertheless changes in manifested cultural patterns, however fluid they may be, need recording.

Caribbean youth, on the other hand, are leading the youth-culture bandwagon in terms of recreation, sport and art as the attraction of a Rastafarian way of life has declined[95]. As indicative from census responses, the most popular notions of black self-identity[96] amongst

Caribbean youth probably are now identities based on the notion of being black in the USA, and in some cases incorporating ideas of having an African heritage. These contrast with the island identity preferred by the first-generation Caribbeans. There is likely to be a tussle between the African identity, and the notion of being black on the one hand, and the rapid phenotypical integration of Caribbean community (leading to the fear of its disappearance) on the other[97]. At a collective and discoursive level, it remains to be mooted if this is an attempt at enhancing social mobility and status on American lines. In the US the light-skinned elite have had traditionally better access to power and privilege than their black counterparts. Alternatively, this integration could be perceived as a manifestation of the failure to convincingly embrace the African identity. The Caribbean youth, having resisted integration politically, are now leading the way on phenotypical and social integration.

At a broader level of generality, the young in ethnic minority communities, having grown up with the local population, increasingly see their primary identity more so in regional (London in particular), or pan-group terms, than do the young people of previous decades. There is impressionistic evidence of a shift from the earlier position[98] where Asian youth saw their identity, first and foremost in religious (particularly Muslim), and secondly in cultural terms. If unsure they resorted to a negative identity i.e., defining what they are not[99]. At the peak of the Rushdie affair, young Muslim Asians began to refer to themselves as British Muslims[100], although on the whole during the OPCS census test pilots Asians resisted the hyphenated identity[101] . The Rushdie affair has left a small militant and politicised crusading section amongst the Muslim youth, lurking partly in Islamic societies at the universities and at the fringe of community development. The Ashrafisation of some of these young people is expressed in terms of dress and organisation. On the whole, however, the majority of the Muslim young people remain middle-of-the-road, pragmatically imbued with self-development values.

In this respect there is now a marked difference between the confidence and the drive for self-development aided by the educational expansion amongst the young ethnic minority in marked contrast to the first generation. The arrival of European multilingualism has helped to create an affinity for learning their ancestral languages, although it is a losing battle due to lack of state support[102]. The decline of faith in social structures and[103] emerging post-modern scepticism about rationality has also forced the ethnic minority young to reflect on the strength of resilience of their own culture and value of their community's support[104].

Yet at the same time a small section of Asian youth in the East End of London or Bradford and Southall are emulating gang formation on similar lines to their white counterparts and occasionally creating no-go areas. In some cases there is ethnically-mixed gang formation involving Caribbean youth who harass Asians[105]. These groups are beyond the influence of the accommodation model of the elders or the personal self-development route taken by their contemporaries. Arguably such groups are in the same mould as the Caribbean groups who offered 'resistance through rituals' and tend to be very wary of police and authority[106]. As evident from recent events in Bradford, police harassment leading to a youth reaction is no longer a phenomenon restricted to Caribbean youth.

Overall, the ethnic minority young appear to be healthily divided between the religious, pragmatic and rationalists, quite often happy to hold on to the multiple identities of being an Asian, a Caribbean, a Muslim or a Briton depending upon the situation they find themselves in[107]. Those born here tend to have strong regional identities[108]. The term 'Asian' coined in East Africa has been appropriated by the Asian youth and is well used to maintain links between Asian sub-groups. This removes the necessity then for sub-groups to have to debate about their religious and national origins when they interact with each other. The same applies to the term black within a Caribbean or African context. Madood et al's (1995) analysis of five groups, namely Black Caribbeans, Punjabi Sikhs, Gujerati Hindus, Pakistani Muslims and Bangladeshi Muslims, confirmed the above and made further observations. The difficulties with such predefined groupings is that this can influence outcomes, nevertheless their observations included:

- Religion was less important to Sikh and Caribbean youth than others.
- Trial marriage and cross-cultural marriages were supported by Indian and Caribbean youth, whilst young Muslim youth were firmly against it.
- Sikh and Hindu through the Indian heritage link, Pakistani and Bangladeshi youth through the Islamic awareness link, and Caribbeans because of their commonality of colour, felt close to each other. The latter also felt unreciprocated commonality with the white community.

The British education system has contributed very little in shaping these identities. It has failed to provide the intellectual tools to the young to analyse and locate diversity in a comprehensible and meaningful framework. While parents can help in terms of passing on folk culture, their own lack of education in many cases does not help the much-needed transmission of values in a rational framework. In the context of diversity, black, Asian and even the white young in the inner cities are demanding education, couched in terms of diversity and equality[109], yet the government ideology has been to promulgate a uniform and static nationalist identity, which relies on the imperial past.

Ethnic minority groups which have historically been perceived to be somewhat close knit are undergoing change. In a recent study Stopes-Roe and R. Cochrane (1990)* noted that there was little support for segregated schools amongst Asians. They are more likely to have close white friends than before, yet at the same time they sustain links with their country of origin through visits[110]. Of all the Asian youth, the Muslims were the least assimilated and were twice as likely to retain customs related to food and dress, and ten times less likely than average (30%) to consider inter-marriage with other groups[111]. Yet there was agreement on women being able to

* See also Mahood T. et al who came to the same conclusion

33

work across the spectrum of ethnic groups.

On the issue of education Stopes noted that 67% of Asian youth were in agreement with their parents about the need to learn about their religion, but thought it to belong to the personal domain unlike their parents. Although only 6% preferred to speak another language other than English yet 66% of parents and young people thought that school was the place for teaching community language, while religion was thought to be the parents' responsibility[112]. A section of the third generation is beginning to 'get back to their roots', with increasing appreciation for aspects of their culture as they see the institutions of the west falling victim to individualistic rationalism. Similar convergence has been noted in relation to Caribbean youth in relation to the authoritarianism of their parents[113]. Asian youth tend to be highly polarised between those who are in agreement with their parents and those who dissent, unlike their white counterparts who appear to fall more in the middle (see Table 1.4). At the same time, *in practice* they are also slightly more likely to be compromising about individualism versus familyism kind of tensions[114].

Table 1.4 Agreement between Asian and white young people and their parents (%)

	Agree	More Traditional than their Parents	Less traditional than their Parents
Asian	33.3	10.0	56.7
British	35.0	25.0	32.5

Source: Stopes M. and Cochrane (1992), *Citizen of this Country - Multilingual Matters,* Cleverdon.

New exoticism and consumerisation of minority ethnicity

Outsiders often see the diversity of British major cities in terms of music, leisure and culture as a factor which should put the ethnic minority young at ease. The fact that the UK now boasts arguably the best Indian restaurants[115], with Indian food almost a statutory phenomenon after a beer binge, does not mean the consumption of some aspects of culture leads to better understanding or tolerance of a wider cultural context. There is considerable evidence that while people will eat the so-called 'ethnic foods', sing or dance to Reggae, it makes little or marginal difference to the level of racism, they harbour or practise. Having a Chinese, or an Indian take-away on the high street near the house may be deemed an amenity, but at the same time the workers who work in these restaurants are held in contempt[116] by some white customers, and they are not always acceptable as neighbours.

Such a consumption pattern is not restricted only to food. Following a recent survey by the *Asian Babes* magazine, the director pointed out that most of the demand for and consumption of the pornographic magazine originated from white men (*The Guardian*, 26 April 1995) and a lot of white men seek Asian brides. It would appear that some aspects of minority cultures have acquired a new dimension from being a subject either of exotic admiration or racial hatred whilst at the same time being consumed as a product. While diversity is now recognised as an asset in the corporate sector[117], the national and local public sector are becoming reluctant supporters, having previously been enthusiastic. Nevertheless, black and ethnic minority workers are used to dealing with clients of similar ethnic groups, while the public relations skills of Asian women are used to ghettoise them in reception work in banks. This commodification of culture continues simultaneously with the exclusion and intimidation of bearers and producers of culture.

Stratification and fragmentation

Most groups when they arrive as immigrants suffer downward mobility initially but improve their standing later. Current data on social mobility suggests relatively poor mobility amongst some ethnic minorities such as established Caribbeans and recently arrived Bangladeshis[118]. Within the context of relatively newly established communities, the Africans are advantaged in comparison with Somalis and Bangladeshis although their higher than average level of qualifications do not protect them from unemployment[119]. Comparison between generations within ethnic groups are difficult to make because of wide variations in factors such as the age of individuals on arrival and the period in which they arrived in Britain. Nevertheless, some broad observations can be made from Table 1.5.

The first-generation gender gap in terms of economic inactivity and poor access to education is being passed down in some groups to the next generation, particularly groups such as Bangladeshis and to a lesser extent Pakistanis. There has however been some improvement in women's economic activity and education level over the last decade. Overall (as shown below) however both economic activity and education of black and ethnic minority women have improved with free educational facilities[120].

While Caribbeans have developed a public-sector elite and an elite in the entertainment and leisure industry, the development of the Asian and African elite has been more broad-based. As we have shown in Chapter 8, there is a caste dimension to economic prosperity with upper castes still retaining a larger share of the wealth and expanding their economic base with links to India[121]. A similar domination of businesses, albeit to a lesser extent, exists in relation to Pakistani elites although there are examples of rags to riches in the north of England and Scotland[122].

The extent to which the elite is capable of influencing government policy on behalf of the rest of the commercial community or the whole community is questionable, although there is emerging evidence of the establishment of several chambers of commerce across

Table 1.5 Education: comparison of respondents in 16-24 age group with 35-60 age group (%)

	White	African Caribbean	Asian African	Indian	Pakistani	Bangla-deshi	Chinese	African
No qualifications (16-24) (Male)	22	26	13	22	34	45	[15]	54
No qualifications (16-24) (Female)	18(36)	16(31)	21(35)	22(45)	58(69)	63(76)	46[15]	20(22)
Employment Activity (Female)	74(71)	70(76)	66(69)	50(57)	34(23)	31(23)	37(55)	61(54)
Employment Activity (male)	86(89)	78(85)	78(89)	62(84)	64(77)	55(79)	77(73)	72(49)
In Education (Male)	836	39	75	35	64	41	-	-
In Education (Female)	40	48	56	61	45	-	-	-
In further and higher Education (Male)	26	31.3	-	42.3	36.7	32.3	77.9	64.3

( ) Figures for 35-60 age group
[ ] Average for all used as gender element not separated
Source: Luthra, M. complied from Labour Force Survey 1988-1990 and OPCS 1991.

ethic and national lines[123].

Insofar as financial contribution is concerned, these elites prefer to donate resources for medical or main stream projects rather than donating money to race relations causes[124]. Gradually they seem to prefer religious causes to egalitarian causes. Part of this could be attributed to the tradition of charity through religious institutions and part of it is based on the notion that no one goes hungry in this country. The self-made origins of the Asian elite further undermines their notion of collective assistance. Indeed unlike their black counterparts, the Asians private sector elite detests the notion of positive action and feels that it under-rates their achievement and undermines meritocracy[125].

There is some evidence that a middle class consciousness is emerging amongst upper income and professional black and ethnic minority people. In Dye's sample, 56% of African-Caribbean professionals felt themselves to be middle class, negating the left-wing notion that being external to British class structure they could not generate such consciousness amongst ethnic minorities[126]. Of these, only 15% actually voted Conservative[127].

Asian big business, particularly business people born overseas, courted both the SDP and the Conservatives in the eighties although small businesses have returned to the Labour fold recently having seen non-action on small business by the Tories accompanied by the lack of action in relation to the collapse of BCCI[128]. Nevertheless only 18% of Asians and 12% of Caribbeans in class ABC1/2 are likely to vote Tory as compared to 44% of white people[129]. This small and gradual tilt towards the right amongst Asians is also evident from the fact that trade union membership amongst minorities has declined in line with overall decline, although still higher than the indigenous population. The centre left was found to be slightly more attractive than the Labour-left politics amongst younger people in the 18-35 age group[130]. Overall, ethnic minority access to politics became slightly easier generally, as both communities have moved away from conservative and centre-right affiliation over the last three years. Selection of an ethnic minority candidate was noted to be a liability only where the majority was less than 1,000, a major change over the last decade[131].

   Although large sections of some communities, for instance the Indian community, have moved into UK suburbia to a higher extent than others[132], there is little evidence that it has adversely affected those who are left behind. In Britain this could be because it is a small island and the fact that those who leave do not gain a high enough status to disconnect from those who are left behind in the original areas of concentration. Generally the network of Asian and Caribbean and African communities remain quite robust although a recent *Panorama* programme argued that lack of education, orthodoxy, together with drug links was creating an underclass culture amongst the young Muslim Asians in Bradford[133]. The link between religion, ethnicity and underclass is not empirically established. This is not to suggest that there is no criminalisation or deviancy of a section of ethnic minority youth. The new deviant and gang youth culture is increasingly more ethnically mixed[134]. On the whole it would appear that - at least in comparison with their country of origin in sound economic terms - the young are less stratified, having had the benefit of state comprehensive education. Unlike the first generation, they also have many more role models in the UK to aspire to.

The death of activism: political integration

First generation immigrants evolved many organisations. The role of the West Indian Standing Conference (WISC) and the IWAs is well documented[135]. The latter has somewhat failed to affect the young with continuous observation of the politics of the subculture. It has, however, played a crucial role in terms of challenging the rise of fundamentalism in the Indian community and challenged the take-over of schools by religious factions in some areas[136]. There is little evidence of the existence of a left amongst Pakistani communities, and liberal views are rarely expressed openly in collective terms.

The Indian-left has, however, a dwindling membership, partly due to loss of some of its members as they become owner-managers[137] or by the lack of its capacity to attract Asian youth.

Much of the militant leadership which led the anti-racist movement at a national level, for instance Darcus Howe, Farukh Dhondy, Ranjit Sondhi (Birmingham), Tariq Ali and Dorothy Kuya in Liverpool, have been co-opted into the establishment. They have left behind a space which has not been filled by the next generation of activists. This could partly be attributed to dwindling funding and the current preoccupation of ethnic minority organisations with survival. Furthermore, activism has gone out of fashion. As regards the electoral domain of politics, the picture of disengagement on part of the young is shown in Table 1.6 with one-fifth of Asian and whites and a quarter of Caribbeans not wanting to vote. Most of the energy of the older co-opted activist has gone into constructive engagement within organisations such as the local councils and in sustaining some of the gains made in the early eighties [138]. Local electoral politics have also absorbed many of these activists [139]. Local authorities which lagged behind, often replicated the resource politics of the GLC leading to the proliferation of separatist, religious and nationalist groups undermining political alliances between Caribbeans and Asians and the broad alliances between Asian subgroups, though the emergence of the ethnic right and the politics of identity have further catalysed this process of fission.

Table 1.6 Not likely to vote by ethnicity and age (%)

Age Group	18-34	All
Asian	16	13
Carribean	28	22
White	18	11

Source: Amin K. & Richardson (1991) *Politics for All*, Runnymede Trust.

Younger people, with the exception of Asian youth are less likely to vote than other groups. Although, as Bhavani has pointed out, the disengagement from party politics amongst the young should not necessarily be construed as non-political[141]. Race relations may not feature high on the agenda of adults but they appear to be quite important to both ethnic minority and white youth[142]. Here the first important point is to what extent organised campaigning of the eighties has been replaced by personal engagement with issues within the system in the nineties. Second, to what extent the minority communities can build infrastructural capacity relying on cross-community alliances between the young. And finally, to what extent the rate the equality debate has been linked to other issues closer to the heart of young people at large, i.e., environmentalism.

Institutional and systemic changes

Over the past decade, both local and central government and the private sector have undergone radical changes which have had serious implications for the integration of black and ethnic minority groups in the system. Such an integration has implications for service provision to ethnic minority groups, availability of role models, networks and support facilities.

Population projections suggest that by the year 2000, most of the labour would be provided by the ethnic minority communities in major cities such as London, Brighton, Bradford and Leicester. At the same time there would be a growing number of black and ethnic elderly who need to be cared for. These changes raise issues about having enough black and ethnic minority people including bilingual people in the institutions to provide good caring service. Yet in proportional terms there remains a shortage of black and ethnic minority teachers, social workers and nurses.

Local government

The eighties saw the emergence of the new right and, some say in response to and replicating the populism of the right, the new left. Most of the radical change took place under the premiership of Mrs Thatcher in the period after 1984. Apart from her own agenda there were other forces at work. These included growth in expenditure of the local government in the seventies from 9% of the GDP in 1950 to approximately 12% in 1983[143]*. Added to this was considerable borrowing from both central government and the private sector. Secondly, emerging assertiveness among local government trade unions, the lack of customer care and inefficiency in some areas, together with local government scandals, gave central government an excuse to undermine the base of local centre-left politics [144].

The Thatcher super-agenda embraced a number of issues, including the then Secretary of State for the Environment, Nicholas Ridley's scheme, leaked to the *Economist*, 27 May, 1978, which put monetarism firmly at the centre of government policy. Notions of contract culture and minimal government, developed by the new right in the USA, shaped these ideas in the early eighties and merged with the 'good housekeeping' economics of Mrs Thatcher.

To reduce the PSBR, cuts in local government expenditure were sought as it was projected as suffering from rapid expansion and bedrock of socialism, particularly when the GLC was successfully promulgating the notion of local socialism. It was part of the government's attempt to leapfrog over the liberal and left establishment to connect with the common prejudices of people. Ironically at the time of this conflict over the abolition of the GLC, Ken Livingstone was able to convey to the public the importance of local government[145]. The government abolished the GLC and the metropolitan counties despite having lost the political argument[146]. At the same time it embarked upon the restructuring of the health service. The marketisation of local government and health service has undermined some of the recruitment gains in terms of ethnic minority representation made by pioneering urban authorities[147].

* Although this was reducing at the time.

Both the EOC study and casework in the spate of so-called restructurings and marketisation, suggest that the proportion of ethnic minority employees in local government has not increased in the last four years (with the exception of a handful of authorities)[148].

Another feature of this change has been the loss of race relations units and advisers as well as committees in local government and their merger with women's units to establishing equal opportunity units in local government has had many consequences. Firstly, it has removed the 'outcome' element from the debate and has refocussed the debate on opportunity at a time when government is pushing the notion of targets within the context of accountability through charters and performance indicators. Secondly, it has depoliticised the debate and relocated it in a comfortable managerial personnel discourse on equal opportunities.

Thirdly, it has restricted the focus of the race equality development on employment, leaving the equality in service delivery to the 'customer care' debate. The removal of the separation between race equality and gender equality concepts has added to the tendency to interpret the equal opportunity debate in terms of gender rather than race[149]. In the world of cloak and dagger and the pub politics of local government there are a few left to champion the cause of racial equality. And there is little evidence that the emerging white female managerial class is likely to be fairer to minorities compared with their male counterparts. Furthermore, being deprived of the experience of a new criteria of appointments (knowledge CCT, redundancy management, budget management, coupled with less emphasis on qualifications), has meant upward mobility within structures is often hindered by lack of sponsorship[150]. Use of private agencies and head hunting together with psychometric testing for recruitment have all made ethnic minority access to the labour markets difficult at a time when there is so much pressure to discriminate in the market[151].

Nonetheless there are now a number of black and ethnic minority leadership-led local authorities and there is some visibility of minorities at chief officer level in boroughs such as Haringey,

Lewisham, Leicester, Hackney. The number of ethnic minority councillors has doubled over the decade, although far removed from representational figures, and there are very few ethnic minority chairs of committees[152]. In some areas such as Waltham Forest, Bradford and Ealing, there remains a religious and village kinship dimension to the electoral process often at odds with the more detached individualistic and trade union type of politics of the left[153].

Overall the weakening and fragmentation of local government has not only weakened local civic leadership[154] but also undermined minority gains. The new managerial contract culture is likely to short-change minorities in terms of business and employment opportunities and in terms of the slice of cake available to the very underdeveloped ethnic minority voluntary sector[155]. The small burst of political dialogue and engagement with ethnic minorities created during the GLC period has been destroyed[156] although the ideas created by GLC continue to live on in the main stream. Another sad feature of the demise of local government is the drastic reduction in youth provision which historically was already weak in engaging ethnic minority youth. This has further eroded the opportunities to maintain a dialogue with the ethnic minority young, and has left them vulnerable to youth work of the ethnic right. Marginalisation of ethnic minority activists and the demise of activism has not been compensated by political integration of the ethnic minority young in mainstream politics. The ethnic minority young have worked hard, in most cases gained qualifications, yet they feel hemmed in and stripped of their dignity in urban areas which offer little hope or an escape route.

The atomisation of central government

Insofar as central government as an employer is concerned, it has historically excluded minorities from the civil service both in the UK as well as the civil service in the Empire[157]. Nevertheless ethnic minorities, particularly 'A'* voucher-holders and East-Africans in a post-war period, were allowed some entry to the civil service at a

* Those who were invited to join professions such as nursing or teaching.

time when it was expanding and there was a shortage of clerical assistants/officers and executive officers, particularly in the Inland Revenue and the DHSS[158]. From the evidence available, much of the level of entry of different groups into the civil service correlates well with qualifications (see Chapter 5) and with the length of residence. There is also evidence that the entry of minorities across the board and middle ranking positions has improved. Yet this explanation is unlikely to account for poor upward mobility and high exit rates[159], and unlikely to rectify historical imbalances.

Overall, the splitting-up of the Civil Service into agencies is likely to create some limited opportunities for new ethnic minority entrants, although if the Training and Enterprise Councils' (TECs) experience is anything to go by, progress is likely to be extremely slow, by virtue of ring-fencing of jobs and secondments[160].

The independent and quango sector

The independent sector, boosted in size by the contract culture of the eighties, has excluded ethnic minority groups as they do not belong to the network of patronage. Thus bodies such as TECs, and hospital trusts tend to exclude ethnic minorities, both at decision-making and administrative levels[161]. Housing Associations tend to be an exception to this rule, being well-rooted in the public sector ethos. Currently the law enforcement sector can only boast two black high court judges, seven QCs and less than 1% of black and ethnic minority solicitors although there is good representation amongst magistrates[162]. Solicitor and barrister trainees of ethnic minority origin have 30/40 times more difficulty getting articles and pupilages, and black barristers have little chance of getting into mainstream chambers[163]. The proportion of ethnic minority officers in the police has remained less than 2% and there are only six officers above the rank of a superintendent. The same applies to the army and air force[164].

The underrepresentation of ethnic minorities, particularly Asians, continues in some sectors such as social work, teaching and many other caring professions[165]. Ethnic minorities are also under-represented in higher education, particularly the administration of. The sectorial orientations of the young also creates underrepresentation. While some Caribbean youth are more likely to seek qualifications and jobs in teaching, social work and in law, the Asian orientation is towards business, management, administration and medicine[166]. The move away from health, and nursing in particular, even amongst Caribbean communities, is likely to present a serious problem as the population ages[167]. The traditionally negative views about nursing and the low status of social work (Asians) and police (Asians and Caribbeans) have been reinforced by the unpleasant experience of those who joined the service and encountered barriers to occupational integration in these sectors. Overall the ethnic minority representation on local government has improved over the last decade but is not likely to improve further.

In the world of finance there are still no home-grown ethnic minority banks and the scope for minorities participating in the contract culture seems limited. Furthermore the unaccountable and closed culture of the quangos is likely to hinder the entrance of ethnic minorities into the atomised local state marginalising them further. In this sense Jacobs' optimism[168] on privatisation of initiative and the decentralisation of funding of a plethora of organisations has not so far been realised[69]. The community work focus has had to shift from radical pragmatism* and campaigning to patchwork quilt development based on short-term funding in an area increasingly dominated by unaccountable quangos (see Chapter 8). Cross-sector programmes such as City Challenge, Single Regeneration budgets remain driven by deadlines, dominated by presentation ethos and controlled by technocrats drawn from the well financed large institutions amongst which ethnic minorities are under-represented (see Chapter 8).

The demise of activism and the loss of race units has left the marketised local authorities and the quango sector totally unchallenged and unmonitored enabling them to continue the exclusion of minorities. The rise of contract culture on the one hand

* Pragmatism underpinned by radical thinking.

offers opportunities for business development for ethnic minorities, while at the same time in the public sector or voluntary sector, ethnic minorities are likely to be short-changed due to lack of development in this area. With regard to the effectiveness of the voluntary sector, Gutch (1993), has pointed out that contractualising the relationship with the local or central state makes independent agencies insecure and compromises them while at the same time it enables government to make cuts without talking responsibility[170]. In the tension between the market aspect of the local government and the redistributive aspect, race equality has been squeezed out or passed on to the increasingly fragmented and conservative personnel sections out of the influence of the corporate centre.

Overall the British-born black and ethnic minority groups face a society in which institutions are highly marketised and inclined towards a closed culture, dominated by new managerialism with increasing commitment to efficiency devoid of notions of equality and public service. Unlike their parents and grandparents they face a more fragmented, casualised and marketised spectrum of institutions as well as a system endowed with magistracy, networks and patronage in which gaining of qualifications appears to offer little protection from discrimination. Large cross-sector programmes in the community regeneration domain are further likely to marginalise ethnic minorities and hinder capacity development (see Chapter 8). To what extent westernisation and strategic accommodation will assist black and ethnic minority youth participation in such structures remains a moot point given the experience of Caribbean youth.

The discourse of diversity and equal opportunities is a comfortable discourse in managerial terms, but it is sadly also utilised as a cloak for non action in relation to tackling continuing discrimination and spending resources on affirmative action[171]. Increasingly the equal opportunity is seen as a gender issue particularly due to the domination of human resource departments by white women.

Conclusions, issues and challenges

Organisations which developed during the early community development phase appear to have failed to involve young people. And large-issue based regional or national organisations are not emerging. As our survey shows, ethnic minority community development in the late eighties is characterised by the lack of national independent agencies. Part of the problem lies in the fact that the government and charity funding structures are biased against district level small-scale projects, a process further catalysed by quangoisation and emphasis on the new contract culture on favouring established large players. Emerging large ethnic minority business class has failed to fund projects pertaining to race equality or large scale community development partly as their meritocratic orientation and partly as they do not see association with ethnicity as beneficial. They want to be seen as mainstream business giving money and support to mainstream causes and are much in line with the very non-giving corporate culture of Britain. The Asian elite have nevertheless, established links with almost all the parties although the extent to which these can be used well for community gain remains a moot point in the wake of BCCI. Capacity building aspect of community development is lacking and the energy and skills of many first generation settlers have not been harnessed for community development. Under-representation in both local and parliamentary politics continues with the parties creating obstacles to ethnic minorities advancement.

Overall, as shown in section II black and ethnic minority youth are better educated and more confident than their parents although their access to the labour market, remains very poor as compared to their white peers and even their parents. Furthermore education offers little protection from discrimination. Amongst ethnic minority women, Caribbean women particularly are in a better position in terms of education and access to jobs than their male counterparts. The relative economic and educational success of black women has unleashed a lot of talent and has generated an interesting debate about its link with single parenthood and autonomy. This individualistic model of development is somewhat different from the model of pragmatic accommodation being pursued by young Asian women who may perceive family support and their traditions as genuine alternatives to the oppression of the labour market. They tend to stay with their own parents longer than other groups and then move in with the parents of their husbands. Clearly for a small proportion this arrangement can be very stressful and even lethal[172]. The extent to which this choice is exercised depends upon a variety of social and cultural factors, including class, and differs for different groups.

Although Ashrafisation and group Sanskritisation have fragmented the Asian collective struggle particularly in the case of the first generation, at the same time the notion of being an Asian amongst the Asian young is well established albeit in conjunction with other identities (Hindu, Indian/Pakistani), except in the case of Muslim youth who are some what more likely to give prominence to their religious identity. Overall Asian youth tend to see the issue of nationality in the context of history and increasingly see religion as a matter to be confined to the personal domain with the exception of fringe groups of Islamic radicals. Aspects of these composite identities are highlighted to connect with people according to time, place and company. This wider Asian identity label is helpful and is well appropriated by the majority of younger Asians for the purposes of communicating and relating with each other.

The Caribbean youth use the term' black' to describe themselves in a similar way. Emphasis on regional identities also helps to escape the colonial connection. This is likely to be the dominant way of resolving value conflicts both in generations as well as within the context of minority/majority relations. In the nineties this process of managing the fluid and composite aspect of identity has become easier as the new urban culture is more conducive to it. Some people have proposed the idea of a hyphenated identity to be promulgated on American lines, i.e. British-Asians, British-Caribbeans which appears to be a preferred way of resolving conflict of identity[173]. In fact while origins of terminology related to self-identity needs thorough examination as new groups join, established groups modify their identity, and generally ethnic and religious identities become increasingly important. Furthermore self-identity and ethnicity are somewhat poor variables for epidemiological research which heads a uniform genetic pool as a variable for reference and analysis. The notions of genetic and cultural and even possibly religious heritage need to be explored to reflect the multiplicity of identities.

Authors such as Lyotard (1988) have argued that during the course of this post-modernism a de-differentiation of traditional race, class and gender boundaries is taking place. Within the context of ethnic minority identities what is in fact happening is that this de-differentiation is manifesting itself in the form of multiple and fluid identities[174]. This wider process of formation of new cosmopolitan culture is in conflict with emerging council estate tribalism in some cases in which gang and patch loyalties are mixed with a cocktail of folk tales and racism[175]. Furthermore in the expanding global urban western culture, different ethnic minority groups are located at different points of proximity to mainstream western culture with black culture much closer to the mainstream which also explains the rapid integration of the black Caribbean community.

Overall it would appear that British urban young are weaving a collective urban culture in which blackness is closer to the centre of the spectrum of youth culture, while Asian identity still remains at the margins yet gradually moving towards the centre. With one third of Caribbean young people now involved in a relationship with a white partner, black nationalist, Pan-African and ethnic-nationalist ideological perspectives continue to survive although increasingly under threat from the demographic and integrationist tide. To what extent this could be attributed to push factors such as the emerging autonomous culture amongst black women, the crises of their relationships with black men or pull factors such as the increased social mobility through integration remains a moot point. One thing, however, is clear, that the notion held strongly in the early eighties of how one can integrate with something, i.e. the system, which rejects and alienates you, is rarely heard.

Over the next decade, unless there is a major change, Caribbean integration will accelerate further adding to the number of mixed-race children, some of whom will hold on to their black identity. Others are likely to choose their mixed heritage as a key component rather than their race and colour. The first generation is holding on to the West Indian or Trinidadian identity in contrast to the Africans who tend to emphasise their African origins rather than their national origins.

In the case of Asians the forces of westernisation and secularisation on the one hand and Sanskritisation and Ashrafisation are all impinging on the young indirectly if not directly shaping a fluid spectrum of identities. Broadly at one end of such a fluid spectrum of identity labels lies pan or umbrella identity labels such as 'Asian' or 'black' or 'Chinese' while at the other end lies the individual identity with religious, national and caste identities located somewhere in the middle. The young move along this spectrum to communicate in different settings and with different groups i.e., the identities are not only fluid they are also situational.

It is very likely that groups which will be able to create a cohesive organisational structures to mirror the pan-ethnic identity are likely to be more successful in negotiating with the local and central state. Indeed some European countries such as France and Belgium already encourage such formations (see Chapter 2) to develop intermediaries which they find easier to negotiate with.

Yet westernisation at an individual level and Sanskritisation for first generation immigrants in some cases has been a liberating experience from the oppression of their own societies. The former can be very relevant in challenging patriarchal oppression which emanates from the recent feudal past of some ethnic minority groups. Ashrafisation can clearly be an attractive vehicle for enhancing self-preservation of status for ethnic minority young in a society which is exclusionist and promulgates derogatory images of their culture. It also allows young people to feel secure and close to the first generation and enjoy a sense of cohesion. Yet at the same time

51

Ashrafisation in a non-Christian context in Britain can add to disadvantage making the young very prone to cultural and religious discrimination in what can be described as a *de facto* Christian or a secular society.

Given the current legitimation crises in the moral and economic domain, the continuity of parental culture remains an important element as a source of strength and certainty for the young as well as being a catalyst in retaining a sense of integrity. The bifurcation of the public and personal domain in the minds of Asian youth points towards a kind of reformation in which religion is being increasingly confined to the personal domain. This is likely to be a key factor for the integration of ethnic minority young in Britain i.e., it will enable them to integrate on their own terms. Yet in the absence of youth work provision and educational support to underpin and consolidate such reformation, sectarianism is breeding amongst the young in some areas, such as Southall, Birmingham and Leicester.

The young are clearly vulnerable in the nineties from a variety of post-modern forces, relative lack of faith in the political establishment, and the demise of notions such as progress and rationality has further added to their uncertainty. Increasing individualisation means that they carry a greater burden in terms of having to make sense of the post-modern world themselves and so are at a greater risk than their forebearers. In this context they feel drawn towards contradictory forces of religion, individualised 'life styles' and the consumerist culture. The diminishing influence of the school and of the secular community institutions including the local state means that they have to rely on themselves to give meaning to their existence. This void is particularly large for young Asians who do not see the clergy or the first generation leaders as their role models. Continuity and fluidity serve them well in their survival strategies and well being in the social and moral domain even though they may have to pay a price in terms of social and economic exclusion by the majority community. The overall picture of community links and identity changes is shown in Charts 1.1 and 1.2.

It would be wrong to see the phenotypical and cultural integration of the Caribbean community as well as the polarisation (orthodox militancy and westernisation being the two ends of a spectrum) of the Asian community as being internally driven. Both systemic factors and forces including discrimination have been crucial factors in shaping these responses.

In this respect Swidlers (1986) notion of culture as a tool kit for individuals to deal with certain situations and ecological constraints has partial ring of truth[176]. In this sense it remains to be seen to what extent the desire on the part of the Muslim community to be identified as a separate entity from the Asian community is driven by ecological factors or emanates from an agenda located outside the UK. Above all, whether or not it is likely to be beneficial for the 'British Muslim community', particularly for the young Muslims, remains a moot point.

The discourse on post-modernism by virtue of its non-essentialist nature has created an intellectual space in which the superiority of one culture over the other and the notion of purity and singularity of identity are all being questioned creating some scope for a dialogue between cultures. Yet at the same time the Anglo-American discourse on post-modernism which is anti-essentialist and counter grand narrative has become essentialist and a narrative in itself, and its relevance is confined to the West.

As I have argued earlier in this chapter given the atomisation of the local and central state, the economic integration of ethnic minorities will depend partly upon the stereotype which various gatekeepers of the system hold of them, and partly upon the extent to which they can be seen to be appproximating to the 'acceptable' image. It is likely that members of those ethnic groups which are perceived to be integrating in the public domain are more likely to be co-opted into the system. Others who resist will retain the benefits of continuity of culture at the expense of economic and social opportunities.

Institutions need to look beyond demonisation of young black and ethnic minority youth (more recently the Muslim youth) and do more than simply make pious statements about diversity and equal

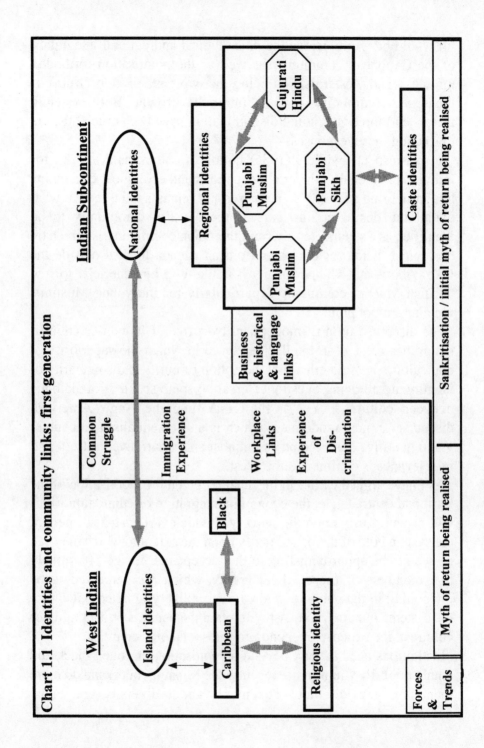

Chart 1.1 Identities and community links: first generation

Indian Subcontinent

National identities

Regional identities

Gujurati Hindu

Punjabi Muslim

Punjabi Sikh

Punjabi Muslim

Caste identities

Sankritisation / initial myth of return being realised

Business & historical & language links

Common Struggle

Immigration Experience

Workplace Links

Experience of Dis-crimination

Myth of return being realised

West Indian

Island identities

Black

Caribbean

Religious identity

Forces & Trends

54

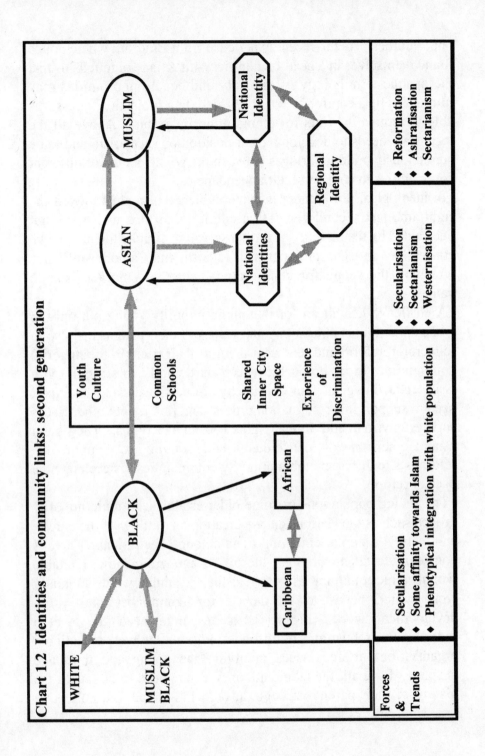

Chart 1.2 Identities and community links: second generation

		Forces & Trends
◆ Secularisation	◆ Secularisation	◆ Reformation
◆ Some affinity towards Islam	◆ Sectarianism	◆ Ashrafisation
◆ Phenotypical integration with white population	◆ Westernisation	◆ Sectarianism

opportunities. As the recent experience from Bradford where police found themselves in a head-on conflict with Asian youth tells us that the opaque terminology of diversity and equal opportunities may turn out to be a comfortable and self-deluding projection unless it is able to remove barriers for ethnic minority young. Above all the local state needs to develop a clear position on secularism and to be continuously building bridges between the young people of different communities to counter sectarian tendencies.

In ideological terms there is some evidence of a shift toward the right amongst second generation ethnic minorities which has not been aided by the inability of the conservative establishment to make concessions to Islam on a par with Judaism and Catholicism[177] thus widening the scope for conservative values to embrace Islamic values.

A challenge lies ahead for the ethnic minority young not only to grasp the religious philosophy and values of their parents but also to reinterpret, reform and represent them to their peers in the majority community. In so doing they need particularly to struggle with issues related to gender and patriarchy. Educationalists for their part need to support this reformation process and link it with other issues such as environment, animal rights and human rights. The liberal establishment needs consciously and actively to support the reformists in different ethnic minority communities to accelerate the pace of reform.

The ageing populations of some older established ethnic minority groups such as the Caribbeans are creating an outflow of the elderly and there is a similar emerging trend amongst the Asians. There is considerable talent amongst the 50-70 age group now available within ethnic communities as well as their leaning towards voluntary work which needs to be tapped for community and youth development work. There is a desperate need to develop independent, robust and multifunded regional as well as national organisations around issues involving the young and third age people. Above all, the ethnic minority young need to be taught the history of their parents struggle at both individual and collective community action level to inspire an active political life.

References

1   See Fryer P. (1984) *Staying Power,* Pluto, although its focus is on the Caribbean community. For earlier African networks before the war, see Green J. *New Community,* vol. XIII, no. 2, Winter 1986.

2   Choo, N (1970), *Chinese in London*, Oxford University Press

3   Many Gurdwaras and Mosques were converted houses in the beginning and catered for earlier nucleus settlements .

4   See Desai, R. (1988) *Indian Immigrants in Britain,* Oxford University Press.

5   Jones, T. (1992) *Britain's Ethnic Minorities*, PSI.

6   Ward, R. (1978) 'Race Relations in Britain', *British Journal of Sociology,* vol. 29 , no. 4, pp 464-80.

7   Ward argued that spatial variation in employment did not make a difference to settlement patterns. (Ibid.).

8   Immigration Act 1962, HMSO.

9   See Chapter 7. Ugandan Settlement Board's attempt to disperse Ugandan refugees failed.

10   See Brooks, D and Singh, K (1978) 'Aspirations of Asian Youth', Warwick University. In reality educational disadvantage was primarily and still remains a major issue for Caribbeans.

11   See Chapter 7

13   Affinity for owner occupation is an over-riding force amongst some groups such as the Asians. Some regions of the metropolis are first rung of the ladder for a variety of settler groups as accommodation tends to be cheaper there. See Luthra, M. (1988) in Bhat et al, *Britain's Black Population*, Gower, Aldershot.

13   See Chapter 7

14   See Hiro (1971) *Black British, White British,* Spottiswoode

15   (Ibid.). See also Dewit, J. (1966) *I was in Britain.* Cf Hiro.

16   I am indebted to Professor Kogan for a copy of the paper on segregation in Southall.

17   See Hiro (op.cit.)

18   These included Bank of India, Bank of China and Bank of Pakistan and more recently BCCI.

19   Hiro (op.cit.)

20   Ibid.

21   Ibid.

22   See Race Relations Board report 1968-1974. See also Street Report. cf.

Rose et al. Local Government Act 1966, Section 11.

23   It was thought that this was done on the suggestion of Mr Nehru, the Indian Prime Minister.

24   Hiro (op.cit.) p.133. There were some 60 mosques already by this time. The current figure is 600.

25   This is based on personal experience. Coachloads were sent from Gurdwaras.

26   This was a very small budget (£20,000 - 30,000) as compared to the budget of £1/2 Million which was spent on CRCS.

27   See Martin, I. in Dhavan, R. and Cooper (1984) *Public Interest Law*, Sweet & Maxwell. *The Struggle of Asian Workers in Britain* (1993), Race Today Collective.

28   James, W. in James, W. and Morris, C. (eds) (1993) *Inside Babylon*, Verso.

29   Ousley, H.in Boddy, M. and Fudge, C. (1984) *Local Socialism*, Macmillian, Basingstoke .

30   Very inexperienced workers were appointed to manage such a large budget. Their knowledge of different ethnic groups was very sparse and there was little policy formulation for funding.

31   A paper called Yellow Peril was produced by a group of senior CROs and Dev Sharma (the Regional Principal) in 1982 Senior Director (now) CRE which took this position.

32   For a debate on campaigning in the context of Community Development, see Greer, J. and Chapman, A. (1992) *Community Development Journal*, vol. 27, no. 3 July.

33   Urban Programme was quietly terminated in 1992 while Section 11 Programme has been severely curtailed and funding was absorbed into SRB

34   The number of law centres has declined significantly since 1986-1994. (Law Centre Federation Reports 1988-1992.)

35   In areas such as Ealing the devastation was quite significant. EREC Annual Report 1993.

36   Saudis have contributed to the building of some of the most beautiful mosques in the UK. Samud, Y. (1992) 'Book burning and race relations', *New Community,* vol. 18.

38   Amin, K. and Richardson, A. (1993) *Politics For All*, Runnymead Trust, p. 35. According to Lewis P, the support for the Muslim manifesto was very limited within the Muslim community. (1994) *Islamic Britain*, Tauris and Co., London.

38   Hiro (op.cit.) p. 21.

39   In West London, for instance, many such organisations exist which support gatherings, dancing, music and other services. Similar analysis of lists of organisations in 1988-1994 for Glasgow showed considerable increase in the number of cultural and leisure organisations.

40 I faced this dilemma myself as a Head of Race Equality in the London Borough of Greenwich. Anwari Din in Strathclyde Regional Council felt the same, but changed her position to support the funding of a Pakistani Centre.

41 See GLC's Women's Committee Reports 1983-1986.

42 In Glasgow the number of such organisations increased fourfold during 1986-1993.

43 OPCS (1981)

44 The Federation of Black Housing Associations was established in the early eighties.

45 I acquired a list of projects from the Kings Fund, most of the projects were 1-2 year funding.

46 Feminisation of disadvantage and poverty. This term was quite popular in the mid eighties in describing poverty in the USA although it no longer holds true as much as in the nineties.

47 There were several reasons for this. For an overview of the issue from a left perspective see Lalker (Punjabi): debate on anti-racisim and anti-racist movement, March, April 1992.

48 I am grateful to Dev Sharma, the Deputy Chief Executive of CRE, for articulating this argument.

49 One example of this is Southall Rights in Southall, West London.

50 Interview with Charan Athwal, Chair of IWA (GB), Greenwich. This was decided in 1988 after much debate.

51 Ref. 46.

52 For an overview of research, see the speech written by Civil Service for Lord Young of Darlington at the first ESCR annual lecture. The future of the family.

53 Ibid.

54 Institute of Fiscal Affairs Report, December 1994 and Rowntree Report, February 1995.

55 West London Training and Enterprise Council Business plan (1994) made this point in the context on West London.

56 Leger, H. et al (1992) *La Religione degli Europei. Fedi, cultura religiosa e modernita in Francia, Italia, Spagna, Gran Bretagna, Germania, Ungheria, Turin Adzione*, Edizioni della Fondazione Giovanni Agnelli.

57 Parekh, B. (1994) 'The Hindu Diaspora', *New Community* July, no. 4.

58 Tomlinson, S. and Smith, D.J. (1991) *The School Effect*, PSI. See also Modood, T., Beishan, S. and Virdee, S. et al (1995) *Changing Ethnic Identities*, PSI.

59 James, W. (op.cit.)

60 Personal observation based on membership of Jehovah's Witness church in Ealing. See also Williams, O.L. (1988) who refers to the attraction of the Black Church for young blacks (p.69) in *Partial Surrender: Race and*

resistance in youth service, Falmer Press, Brighton.

61   James, W. et al (1993) *Inside Babylon* (op.cit.). For Asians see Butler et al *Religious Conformity and Cultural Diversity,* BSA, Leicester University

62   See *The Independent* for single black attitude revisited and as many reasons as people, *The Independent* 8/2/95 .

63   Drurey, B. (1991) 'Sikh girls in Coventry', *New Community* vol.17, no.3 pp387-99.

64   Heath et al (1994) OPCS monitor Autumn.

65   See Chapter 6.

66   OPCS data compiled by Centre for Ethnic Relations, Warwick University, for CRE. See also Madood et al (op.cit.).

67   Fanzi, C. (1991) 'Somalis in the East End', *New Community,* vol. 17, July.

68   The scarf issue revolved around the problem of admitting religious symbols in secular state schools in France. Similar instances have been cited by Raza, M, *Islam in Britain*, Volcano Press Ltd.

69   Jeffrey, P. (1970) 'Pakistani families and their networks', PhD Bristol University.

70   Stone, M. (1985) *Racial Conflict in Society*, Harvard University Press.

71   Samad, Y. (1992) 'Book burning and race relations', *New Community*, vol. 18, no. 4, July.

72   This led to many criminal court proceedings reported in the Panjabi press. See Des Pardes and Panjab Times 1988-1992.

73   One optimistic view is that human rights aspects common to all religions could be welded together. Morrison, J. (1994) *Human Rights and Religion*, The University Centre for Human Values, Princeton University, USA

74   Afsher, H. (1989) 'Gender roles and moral economy of kin amongst Pakistani women in West Yorkshire', *New Community*, vol. 15, no. 2. Brah, A. and Shaw, S. (1992) 'Working choices of South Asian Muslim Women', Employment Department Research Paper No 91, DE.

75   Spivac, G. (1994) 'Reflections on cultural societies in post-colonial conjencture', *Critical Studies,* vol. 3, no. 1, pp.61-78. Special Issue on Cultural Studies.

76   Knott, K. et al. (1993) 'Religion and ethnic identity amongst young women in Bradford', *New Community,* vol. 19 .

77   Seminars and studies circles around Islam, Sikhim or Hinduism are held paid for often by middle class participants. See Raza, M. (1991) on petrodollar leadership and sectarianism in Chapter 4.

78   Muslim liberals tend to exercise restraint in going public on their own liberalism. One exception was the challenge posed to the Muslim parliament by Muslim Forum and Labour party Muslim councillors. For the role of the Saudis, see Samud, Y. (op. cit.). See also Kaye, R. (1993) 'The politics of religious slaughter of animals', *New Community,* vol. 19, no. 2, pp.235-50.

See also Raza and Lewis (op.cit.).

79 See various reports in Lalkar. (IWA - GB) paper.

80 Lady Blach asked for Evangelical school to be established.

81 Census of Pakistan 1981 showed that only 16% of Panjabis in Pakistan spoke Urdu.

82 Srinivas, M. (1995) *Social Change in Modern India*,Longman.

83 Nisbett, E. (1990) 'Religious identity and the Valmiky Community in Coventry', *New Community*, vol. 16, no. 2, pp.261-74.

84 Davy c.f. Milner, D. (1990) *Children and Race - 10 Years On*, Ward Lock Educational p.161. Clark 1984 c.f. Tizzard and Phoney (p.30). For a critique of this, see Foster-Carter (1986) 'Insider, outsiders anomalies; A review of identity', *New Community,* vol. 11, no 2.

85 c.f. Milner (op.cit.), p. 126.

86 James (op.cit.), p.257.

87 Ibid. p.258

88 Haleh (op. cit.)

89 OPCS 1991

90 Stopes, M. and Cochrane R. (1992) 'Citizens of this Country', *Multilingual Matters*, Clevedon.

91 These include Bali Sagoo, Alapp, Hira and many others.

92 Ackland, T. (1989) 'Integration and segregation in an Asian community', *New Community*, vol. 15, July.

93 Brah, A. (1991) 'Diversity and Differentiation', *International Review of Sociology* , no. 2, pp56-72. See Woolett, A.

94 The taking of Ganja has permeated mainstream culture as a relaxant, so much so that police have argued for its legislation. See 'So are the kids alright', *The Independent,* January 1995.

95 OPCS (1991).

96 30% of the Afro-Caribbeans (16-35) are married to white people. OPCS (1991).

97 Hutnik, N. (1985) 'Aspects of identity in a multiethnic society', *New Community*, vol. XII, no. 2.

98 Ibid.

99 The term 'British Muslim' was coined when 'Muslim' became a word of abuse. See Hiro (op.cit.)

100 Madood, T. (1988) 'Black identity and racial equality', *New Community, v*ol. XIV, spring.

101 Hobswam, E. (1992) lecture at Institute of Education. He argued that a language in a foreign land could not be sustained for a long period

102 See *The Independent* series on youth, June 1995. Various polls suggest the young are disengaged from party politics. (17th October News S.A.M. M. Power launched to recruit the young on electoral register), BBC

103 The overall impressions from various references and surveys mentioned in this chapter as well as my experiences of education officers suggest that young people take a sanguine stance on western values.

104 See Hewitt, R (1990) *Sagaland,* London Borough of Greenwich with Institute of Education. See Cohen, P. *Monstrous Images and Perverse Reasons,* CMCE, p. 11.

105 Cohen (1992) *Resistance Through Rituals,* Hutchinson

106 Black, L. (1993) 'Race identity and nation within an adolescent community in London', *New Community,* January

107 Black, L. (op.cit.).

108 Stopes, M., pp. 94, 110.

109 Ibid. p.149.

110 Ibid. p.104.

111 Ibid.

112 Personal experience.

113 Stopes (op.cit.).

114 It is estimated that Britain has 7,000 Asian restaurants.

115 See Home Office study (1989) *Racial Harassment of Asian Shopkeepers,* HMSO. See also Parker, D. (1994) *Encounters Across the Counter.* 'Young Chinese People in Britain', *New Community,* vol. 20, July 1992.

116 Kandola, D. and Fullerton, J. (1994) *Managing the Mosaic Diversity in Action,* IPD. Also Hernot, D. and Pemberton, C. (1994), *Gaining Competitive Advantage from Diversity.* Cf. Kandola, D. et al.

117 Balarajan, R. and Luthra, M. (forthcoming.) Earlier immigrants worked as post office workers, as bus conductors, factory hands, even though they were better qualified.

118 LFS data (1988-1990)

119 Daye, S. (1994) *The Black Middle Class,* Macmillan, Basingstoke.

120 Luthra, (op.cit.)

121 See *Ethnic Minorities in Scotland* (1990), Scottish Office. Edinburgh Asians have produced disproportionate number of self employed owners.

122 Bradford is one example. I am indebted to Mohan De Silva of Bradford City Council for this comment.

123 I am grateful to Dev Sharma Dep. Chief executive CRE for this comment.

124 Comments from Dev Sharma.

125 Daye (op.cit.)

126 Ibid.

127 The Asian businesses raised £7 million for the conservative party. There are many clubs such as the Darbar which raise funding for the Tories. See also Amin et al (1994) *Politics for All,* Runnymede Trust, Table 17 for Asian Conservative support.

128 Ibid. p.26.

129 Ibid. p.24.
130 Ibid. p.21.
131 See debate on underclass in Robinson, F. and Gregson, N. *Critical Social Policy*. We had such a situation in Southall.
132 'Underclass in Purdah', *Panorama,* BBC, 25 March 1993.
133 Black (op. cit.). Hewitt (op. cit.).
134 Dewitt (op. cit.).
135 Hiro (op.cit.).
136 Many IWA members have set up shops and have done very well.
137 See Boddy, M. (op.cit.).
138 Anwar, M. (op.cit.)
139 James, W. (op. cit.) refers to this conflict.
140 Bhavani, K. (1991) *Talking Politics; A psychological framing of views from youth in Britain,* Cambridge University Press, Amin et al (op.cit.).
141 CRE (1992) Survey showed that race appeared low on the agenda. Several youth surveys show that the young regard racism as an important phenomenon.
142 Duncan, S. and Goodwin, M. (1988) 'Local state and uneven development behind the local government crisis', *Daily Press* p.99.
143 For the evidence of Town Halls painted as "loony left", see *Searchlight* issues 1988-1990.
144 Much of the credit for 77% of Londoners supporting the GLC prior to its abolition went to Ken Livingstone.
145 Ibid.
146 At the EREC we have received a large number of cases against the Council and Local Health Authority.
147 Haringey Report by the Equal Opportunities Advisor - 25 March 1993.
148 Women constitute more than 70% of personnel officers.
149 See *Local Government and Race Equality*. The case of Ajit Singh - v. - London Borough of Ealing, March 1995, illustrates the point.
150 Psychometric testing has become prevalent over the last five years.
151 Anwar, M. (1994) 'Race and elections', Economic and Social Research Council, Centre for Research in Ethnic Relations. No. 9.
152 This has led to disputes with the Labour Party in areas such as Southall, Waltham Forest and the Midlands.
153 Donnison, D., 'Muscle and Muddle', *The Guardian*, April 21, 1993.
155 According to the CRE, of the SRB application in Aug 1995, only 19% of the projects had some ethnic minority dimension. Information re SRB by the CRE (1995). Both CRE and EOC analysis of employers suggest that private sector agencies are less concerned with equal opportunities issues. See reference 7, Chapter 3.
155 Race and ethnic minority forums initiated by urban local government

including race committees have been abolished.

156 Asians were not allowed to sit the British Civil Service exams for almost 100 years.

157 Many Asians were recruited into the DHSS and Inland Revenue in junior positions in the sixties and seventies.

158 See Equal Opportunities in the Civil Service report, Cabinet Office (1992-1993), HMSO. The proportion of ethnic minority staff is around 5.2 in the Civil Service.

159 Most Training and Enterprise Councils (TECs) inherited their mostly white staff from the Department of Employment Civil Service - no jobs were advertised.

160 'No equal opportunity in the TEC', *The Guardian*, 8 September 1992.

161 I am grateful to CRE for this information.

162 Race Relations Sub-committee reports of the Bar (1990-1995).

163 The Navy and the Army all have less than 2% of ethnic minority members, Ministry of Defence.

164 Under-represented in white collar public service except the Civil Service (op. cit.)

165 UCCA (1994) report on ethnic monitoring.

166 See reference 113 in Chapter 6.

167 Jacobs, D. (1981) 'Private initiative and community responsibility', *Public Administration,* vol.63, 1983, pp309-25.

168 Luthra, M. (1988) 'Local government and race equality', unpublished paper, LB Greenwich Race Committee.

169 Gutch, R. (1994) 'Contracting in the USA', NCVO News, September 1994

170 This is evident from the recent CRE survey, 'Do the right thing'. The survey, of 168 British private-secotor companies, concluded that only 15% had progressed to any action beyond policy statements.

171 Suicide rates are high amongst young Asian women. See Chapter 6.

172 Carrington, B. and Short, B. (1995) 'What makes a person British? Children's perception of their national culture', *Educational Studies,* vol. 21, no. 2.

173 Lyotard, J. (1984) *Postmodernist Condition,* University of Minnesota, Minnesota.

174 Luthra, M. (1987) 'Kept in the dark on racism', *The Guardian,* 7th September 1988. Hewitt, R. (1992) *Sagaland,* London Borough of Greenwich.

175 Swidler, A. (1986) 'Culture in action; attitudes and stratigies', *American Sociological Review,* vol. 51, from Butler et al (op.cit)

176 Malcolm, G., 'Votes to be found in the footsteps of the prophet', *Daily Telegraph,* 16th March 1995.

SECTION II

Law and Society

2 Racial discrimination, diversity and the law in Europe

An overview of anti-discrimination and cultural aspects of law

Increasingly, European law and the development of European institutions are making inroads into the lives of British people including ethnic minorities. In this chapter we turn to the legislative framework in the European Union to develop an overview of changes over the last decade and the likely developments in the near future.

An estimated 8.5 million people in the European Union fall into categories of either residents with a full work permit of non-EU origin, or the third country national category who stay in a country on a time-limited basis and require revocable permission to work[1]. Historically various facets of racism rooted in Aryanism[2], slavery[3], or the imperial past[4] of different European nations, have all contributed to the:

Discriminatory ethnocentricity in Europe which not only prevents the recognition and integration of outsiders but also operates within society grading the aliens according to their country of origin[5].

Its subsequent manifestations, including varying degrees of exclusion, to which different countries subject their ethnic minorities, depends upon a variety of factors including the historical relationship between the host and the migrant/settling communities and the religious affiliations of the groups.

The demarcation between victim and perpetrator of exclusion is not a clear cut one. In Luxembourg the Portuguese are ostracised, while in Portugal, Cape Verdeans are treated as ethnic minorities. Colour and religion play an important overrider to the graded citizenship accorded to ethnic minorities in which new Commonwealth, Middle Eastern and Chinese are likely to be at the bottom of the pile. Scaremongering about immigration and welfare benefit abuse does not change the fact that immigration to most countries in Europe is difficult, benefit payments which are often dependent upon historical welfare contributions for the period of settlement are not easy to access. Furthermore despite unemployment levels remaining above 10% in most EU countries, the local communities need immigrants in the expanding service sector, particularly in the secondary labour market. The European discourse in both research and policy circles is trapped in the language of 'foreigners and aliens', which is then reflected in the range of hurdles which the states erect to stop generations of migrants acquiring full citizenship[6]. The erosion of these rights has serious implications for ethnic minorities across nation states in terms of access to welfare and to labour markets. There is also increasing evidence that discrimination in Europe is increasingly taking on a violent, ideological form and is organised [7].

In response to this the international community and non-governmental organisations have invoked a range of agreements and treaties to encourage the European Union to take on broad anti-discrimination issues. First the International Convention on the Elimination of all Forms of Discrimination (CERD 1965), by the UN, has been ratified by all EU states except Ireland, placing obligations (Art. 1-6) on states to take statutory and systemic development measures to eliminate discrimination in all forms[8]. Forbes (1992) takes the view that this provision embraces indirect discrimination, including public and private employers, even though it is not mentioned explicitly, and covers both public and private employers[9]. Second, the International Labour Organisation (ILO) Convention, ratified by nine EU countries (excluding Ireland, Luxembourg and the UK), has a wording similar to the above, except it is unlikely to cover indirect discrimination. Finally the EC Human Rights Article 14 reads:

The enjoyment of the rights and freedoms set forth in Convention shall be secured without discrimination on any grounds such as race, sex, colour, language and religion, political or other opinion, national or social origin, association with national minority, property, birth or other status[10].

Protection against racial discrimination is available only through the state's ratification of the UN Convention (except where there is automatic ratification such as that in Greece). In practical terms, this protection is usually weak in the provision of any of the basic human rights guaranteed in the European Convention of Human Rights. The remedy here is much stronger than that under the UN Convention, as an individual is entitled to seek a ruling from the Strasbourg Court against a government, and that government must comply. Unfortunately the scope of the Convention is limited as it does not cover discrimination in housing, employment, education and the provision of services and is restricted only to the right to family life, and to due process of law. In the event of a failure by the state to incorporate international conventions into domestic law, proceedings can, in theory, be instituted against the state. And in the case of ICERD it can be heard by the Committee on Elimination of Racial Discrimination [11].

In addition to the above international and European conventions, the Treaty of Rome, Article 4, offers limited protection against discrimination on the basis of nationality restricted only to the nationals of member States[12]. Its other provisions, such as those in Article U8 restricts this protection in an employment context to the

69

private sector[13]. However the Treaty does enable the EU to introduce articles, directives and regulations on anti-discrimination should it want to[14]. Currently there is no community law offering protection against race discrimination and its introduction would require amendment to the Treaty under Article 236 (14) - a matter we return to later.

All the EU states except the UK have written constitutions guaranteeing certain rights to their citizens. In some cases, certain rights are specified for religious or ethnic groups within the citizen body. But the general picture shows little protection for ethnic minority residents except in certain respects. Protection is accorded by Community Law to aliens who are Community Nationals, not against racial discrimination as such, but against treatment of workers and their families if that treatment is less favourable than that of citizens of the country. This applies particularly in the context of employment opportunity and access to welfare services[15]. In some countries such as Germany or Portugal the constitutional responsibility not to discriminate is restricted only to public employers.

Protection under national laws specifically dealing with racial discrimination varies greatly from one country to another in its scope and effectiveness. This will be described below. One major difficulty is that in some cases protection is only accorded to a fully-fledged citizen. Much of the debate in Europe is likely to hinge around the definition of citizenship and nationality, as only some countries including the UK offer full citizenship on birth and through naturalisation after some years' residence or via marriage. As we show, while all countries have introduced specific anti-sex-discrimination legislation in the wake of various EU directives, and despite the fact it is enshrined in the constitution (as indeed is race or colour anti-discrimination), countries vary considerably in their current provision in terms of the advocacy, support provision and the breadth of their specific anti-race discrimination, civil or criminal legislation, as well as enshrined scope for positive action and contract compliance[16].

A number of other contextual issues need to be borne in mind before we embark upon this overview. Firstly, the language and discourse on continental Europe is imbued with the 'outsider' and exclusionary ideology[17]. Secondly, there is general agreement that a variety of factors, including German unification and economic problems and anti-Islamic fervour, have all contributed to increasing hostility to migrants, often and increasingly manifested in violent terms[18]. Thirdly, unemployment rates of ethnic minorities and their participation in the 'alternative economy' are very high as compared to the indigenous population, pushing many minorities below minimum-wage levels. This obviously hastens the trend towards the formation of an increasingly bifurcated European labour market. Finally, politicians have made 'illegal' synonymous with 'clandestine' and 'undesirable' despite the economic importance of migrant labour and the negative implications of the 'stop immigration' debate[19].

On the legal front two features are notable in regard to the anti-discrimination law. First, both the private domain of the individual in all cases and the private sector in many cases tend to be free of the rigours of anti-discrimination law. Secondly, the emphasis in the continental legal processes is on collaborative adjudication. Finally, much of the non-UK European anti-race discrimination law has a strong criminal dimension, and often a weak civil dimension, with over-reliance on civil and judicial officers to take action rather than individuals themselves.

Belgium

There has been a total ban on immigration in Belgium since 1974 (except in the case of family reunification). A person born in Belgium has no automatic right to citizenship, nor do his Belgian-born children although a recent concession has given grandchildren this right. This has explicit ramifications in the public sector labour market, where even 'simple, ordinary posts' are the exclusive reserve of Belgian nationals[20] although Belgian civil servants are required not to discriminate.

Municipal authorities are lately encouraged to employ 'integrated' migrants. The segregation issues also come to the fore as municipal authorities in Brussels have been refusing to allow immigrants to live in certain quarters of the city and there appears to be an active dispersal policy. Reports from Belgium identify Turks, Moroccans, Algerians and Zairians, who constitute less than 2.5% of the population, as the main victims of exclusion and oppression, followed by citizens from Spain and Italy[21]. In comparison, Jews and persons of Chinese origin with Belgian nationality are said by the authorities to be 'well integrated'.

The Belgian Constitution states that all Belgians are equal before the law (Article 6), and Belgium ratified ILO III in 1977 and CERD in 1975. The law of 30 July 1981 enacted in pursuance of CERD debated whether legal protection against discrimination in employment should be granted. It was on the grounds of this backlash ('foreigners' were thought to be better protected) and the difficulty of proving intent, that a criminal law test, aimed at offering statutory protection in the area of employment was excluded[22]. The current criminal law makes provision for punishing certain deeds motivated by racism or xenophobia. It forbids incitement to discrimination, hatred or violence against a person or group because of their race, colour, national or ethnic origin, and anyone publicly resolved to practise racial discrimination. Participation in racist propaganda groups is also forbidden under this law. Law is also in place to prevent officials from arbitrarily denying a person their rights for racist reasons.

To some extent hitherto the lack of protection on discrimination in employment is in line with the National Labour Agreement No 38 which also forbids most types of discrimination including that on grounds of nationality but *not* on grounds of race or ethnicity. According to Forbes[23], the Employment Contract Act applying to both the public and private sectors gives the right of termination without notice to judges if there is a serious reason for doing so.

Obviously the ILO III agreement has not been followed in terms of enactment of explicit employment legislation although a bill was presented in 1994 to have civil sanctions in the areas of employment and housing. Given that a tiny minority of people of non-Belgian origin are allowed to become citizens, the scope for using the constitution as a shield is an academic issue. Insofar as the use of current 1981 law, in 1987, of the 93 complaints only three resulted in prosecution. In 1988 there was one prosecution out of 83, and this was that of an African who called a politician 'racist' [24].

Unlike the UK, the law in Belgium also empowers registered anti-racist organisations to bring an action under the above headings instead of leaving it to the public prosecutor to do so. The procedures, however, are entirely in the criminal law domain. Hitherto the public prosecutor has been reluctant to pursue cases. Furthermore, the requirement that a victim must give prior consent to lodging the case for trial in order to participate in legal action has hampered the complaints rate [25].

As yet, there is no specific legislation covering racial discrimination in employment. One view is that terms of dismissal from employment and the legislation on termination of contracts would appear to render unlawful a dismissal on grounds of race, although this is not expressly provided for[26]. The provisions which do exist on discrimination in employment cover a wide variety of types of discrimination (such as sex, marital status, nationality), but race and colour are not yet included. The recent collective agreement by the National Labour Council, when it becomes law, will outlaw a discriminatory stance on the basis of race, colour and national or ethnic origin by all employers. This involves an obligation on the part of employers to check discrimination, but is not a readily enforceable right on the part of workers.

In May 1988 the Belgian government instituted a policy of 'harmonious co-existence', similar to UK integration policy, i.e. restrict immigration and improve measures for cultural integration. A Royal Commission on Immigrant Policy was appointed to make proposals on policy directly to the Prime Minister. The Commission has suggested giving access to public sector employment to non-Belgians, and removing the nationality condition to access minimum wage protection[27]. The integrationist policies of the government remain a contentious issue as they are seen as assimilative and somewhat hostile to Islam, applying tests which are not applied to the indigenous population[28].

The report of the Royal Commission has led to setting up a national centre for the integration of immigrant communities and against discrimination, similar to the CRE in the UK with a restrictive focus on tackling skin-colour-based discrimination[29]. The historical absence of specific law, the paucity of case-law, and the infancy of policy measures designed to counter discrimination in employment practices, means that historically very little progress has been made in state-of-the-art or innovative approaches. For instance, hitherto there is little evidence of the development of structures to monitor policy or to undertake positive action and introduce codes of practice. Indeed racial discrimination has frequently been practised openly, and is often viewed as not abnormal behaviour. Discrimination has been however challenged by some 30 advisory councils the key ones being Mouvement Centre Racisme et Xenophobia (MRAX), ADDE and VOCOM - all assist ethnic minorities.

As regards multiculturalism, Article 117 of the Belgian Constitution which enables the state to fund churches has been extended to Islam, creating scope for state-funded Muslim organisations on a provincial basis[30] overseen by a state-supported Islamic Cultural Centre. This could be described as churchification of Islam, which may have unintended consequences[31]. The Belgian state has also given strong acknowledgement to ethnicity albeit in a segregationist context. It has enacted policies to create tripartite partnership government in some areas - for instance, in education where Walloon and the Flemish minorities have their own education ministers and there is strong acknowledgement of religious identity constitutionally although Muslim schools and institutions are not encouraged on par with Catholics[32]. There appears to be a strong policy theme emerging which involves giving some rights to immigrants in a pluralist framework while at the same time emphasising responsibilities and applying various tests of integration.

France

In France, Algerians constitute 1.5% of the population, Portuguese and Moroccans 1% each, followed by smaller proportions of Turks, Cambodians, Vietnamese and Tunisians all making up 4% of the ethnic minority population. Like Germany, the terminology of aliens and foreigners is quite prevalent in France[33]. French law in many ways offers wider scope than Belgian law, it is also complicated and diverse. The preamble to the 1958 Constitution affirms the Rights of Man, applicable to everyone in the jurisdiction, and is expressly secular[34] in nature completely de-linking the state and the church. Article 2 of the French Constitution states that:

France is a Republic, indivisible, secular, democratic and social. It shall ensure the equality of all citizens before the law, without distinction of origin, race or religion. It shall respect all beliefs.

The preamble makes a specific reference to employment. The indivisibility of the constitutional French identity presents a particular problem for France in terms of both countering and monitoring discrimination.

France has ratified CERD and ILO III, which is therefore part of the law of France. In pursuance of the ratification, an anti-racism domestic law of July 1972 laid down penalties for discrimination on grounds of religious belief or of racial, ethnic or national origin. Defamation, abuse, incitement and apologies for war crimes against humanity are all covered. Under the Penal Code, racial discrimination in the provision of any goods or services is forbidden, so are racially-motivated dismissals, refusals to recruit, and economic boycotts. Anyone in a position of public authority is explicitly forbidden to discriminate on grounds of race, ethnicity or religion. Anti-racist organisations also have the facility to sue in the civil courts for damages in respect of certain (racial and discriminatory) offences against the Penal Code[35].

Unfortunately the implementation of these laws depends heavily on the initiative of public prosecutors. They have been repeatedly circularised by the chancellery with requests to pursue race offences. Somewhat inadequate statistics on the implementation of the law suggest that between 1975-1984 there were 160 convictions dealt by the ministry of justice for racial offences[36]. These figures escalated to a figure of over next seven years of which 40% to 60% were instigated by the public prosecutors criticised often for concentrating on the little people.

In employment the figure for discrimination cases did not exceed two for the year 1987 due partly to the heavy burden of proof and the fact that courts are very lenient towards 'material facts' kind of explanations. In 1981, additional provisions were introduced into labour law to protect employees from wage discrimination as well as to protect job security (Labour Code 113-5). Section 416-3 of the French Criminal Code states that an offence has been committed by 'a person whose trade, occupation or profession necessitates his employing (on his own account or on behalf of or for another) one or more employees, agents or subordinates' if such a person:

Without justification valid in law, refuses to take into his service or dismisses any person on account of his origin, or the fact that he belongs or does not belong to a specific racial group, nationality, race or religion, or who makes an offer of employment subject to a condition based on the applicant's origin or the fact that he does or does not belong to a specific ethnic group, nationality, race or religion[37].

Contravention of this provision renders the employer liable to penalties of imprisonment or fine.

French law, like the UK, has no separate provision for racial violence and the motive of an act is not indictable, i.e. to constitute specific offences racism and discrimination must be explicit. There is some evidence to suggest violence increased against minorities in the late eighties was declining a little in 1992[38]. In addition to this between 1980 and 1992 some 1667 people were convicted for either threats or violence against ethnic minorities with around 50% against the Maghrebians who formed the majority of the victims (25 killed , 289 wounded) during the same period (Costa Lascoux). In addition to the criminal sanction, the authorities can use some administrative powers against racism within the framework of civil law.

Two other provisions of the Penal Code warrant mention. First, Section 187-1, introduced by the same Act of 1972, offers remedy if any public servant or person in charge of a public service knowingly denies the benefit of a right to a person because of origin, ethnic group, nationality or religion. After 1981 new provisions were introduced into labour law in particular[39]. The second new section of the Labour Code provides that shop rules cannot contain provisions differentiating between employees for reasons, *inter alia*, of origin, ethnicity, nationality or race[40]. Further, it provides that:

> No employee can be punished or dismissed because of his origin, ethnicity, nationality or race [41].

In addition, the Collective Bargaining Act of November 1982 established the principle of equal treatment for French and foreign wage earners[42], although it does not deal with denial or hiring, transfers, demotion or promotion.

Immigrants now have some right of association (which they lacked until about a decade ago) and can vote and participate in trade union elections. At the same time, they have lost the automatic right to citizenship by birth. This has to be applied for at the age of 18 and is acquired only at the discretion of the Ministry. Marrying a French citizen does not assist the settlement process either[43]. In 1987 a

French MP, Michael Hannoun, drew up a report suggesting 52 measures for combating racism more effectively and he asked for a mandatory annual report on the enforcement of the anti-racism law of 1972[44].

Amendments to legislation in 1990 now disqualify people who engage in discrimination from holding public office or serving on juries[45]. So far there is no evidence that the government has introduced positive action programmes, as required by CERD Article 2(2), to help racially disadvantaged groups. The current provisions do not offer protection against indirect discrimination, despite strong arguments that it is covered by the CERD and ILO III[46]. Commitment to law enforcement is poor hence convictions are extremely rare, partly because the offence is very hard to prove, discouraging the victims of discriminatory practices from lodging a complaint[47]. This is backed up by other research which suggests that shame and fear also add to the general reluctance to pursue complaints[48].

Most complaints are brought about by non-governmental organisations. The declining number of convictions overall suggest that employers are becoming more adept at avoiding the intentions of the legislators, given that the burden of proof rests with the complainant. Improved liaison with government agencies is being considered[49], and in March 1990 the Minister of the Interior urged authorities to take action. Public service employment has now been opened up to migrants and settlers[50] although it still excludes third-country nationals. Most of the assistance to victims is given by licensed organisations: *Mouvement contre le Racisme art pour l'amitreb entre les peuples* (MRAP) and *l'Ordere des Avocates a la de Paris* (LICRA).

The Netherlands

People of Surinamese, Turkish and Moroccan origin constitute less than 11% of the Dutch population, although they constitute around

15% of the population in four major cities[51]. Since 1986, any settler who has been legally resident in the Netherlands for five years may vote in local elections. Insofar as explicit commitment is concerned the Netherlands has ratified both CERD and ILO III on equality in employment and occupation, leading to the amendment of both the Penal Code and the Constitution. The law applies to Dutch and non-Dutch citizens equally unless the law itself makes a distinction and measures giving rights and protection apply to resident 'aliens'. Workers' councils, for instance, are open to all.

The constitution also explicitly forbids racial and religious discrimination. The provision is then elaborated in the Criminal Code, the Civil Code and the labour laws. The Dutch Criminal Code (Art. 137c,d,e) forbids racial insult, incitement to racial hatred, discrimination and violence, participation in or financial support for activities aimed at racial discrimination, and discrimination in the exercise of a profession or trade. Since 1985, jobs in the public sector have been opened to all in theory. There have been a number of prosecutions for incitement (29 in 1986, 24 in 1987, and 54 in 1988), and similar prosecutions of slander acts committed by companies [52].

Under the Civil Code, organisations advocating racial discrimination are illegal and can be dissolved by a court decision. Discriminators can be ordered to pay damages. Discrimination in admissions to bars and discotheques is also against the Penal Code. The civil law route enables individuals to seek compensation[53] and workers council and labour law allows individuals to act against discrimination[54]. Discriminatory collective agreements are not binding in law.

The law on employment came into force in 1986. The overall level of compensation has been very poor under civil law, and the same applies to fines. In 1987 and 1988, there were 22 cases with five convictions in the employment area[55]. Overall, however, the law against discrimination has been given greater impetus over the last ten years by a series of court decisions. Some local authorities have also been active in developing counter-racism policies, and ethnic minorities are now allowed to enter public sector employment as long as they hold a permit. Dutch law also has scope for positive action which is often funded by local authorities and the Ministry of Social Affairs and Employment.

The *Landetyle Bureau Racisme* (LBR), or National Bureau Against Racism, founded in 1985 by ethnic minority organisations, is largely engaged in legal work on behalf of minorities and is funded by the Department of Justice. Although its action has not been very successful it has been suggested that its strategic case selection approach with an emphasis on common practices is valuable[56]. It has a brief very similar to the CRE in the UK, although being a non-governmental organisation (NGO) it does not have the same powers as the CRE of outreach investigations (i.e. it must have the consent of the person or body being investigated to proceed) nor is it able to issue a notice of non-discrimination. Recently an Equal Treatment Act, mainly a civil law, has been passed which will enable the establishment of the Commission for Equal Treatment with powers similar to the CRE in the UK and with a similar scope to the Race Relations Act covering employment, supply of goods and services and school and vocational information.

Changes in the Constitution in 1993 heralded some gains towards relative equality of treatment of Christian and non-Christians in terms of calls for prayer and protection from blasphemy[57]. Ritual (kosher and halal) slaughter of animals is permitted by special ministerial regulation, but permits are difficult to come by. In education, Holland is experimenting with the idea of incorporating equal opportunity audit as a function of the school inspectorate, in addition to checking that the school's resources for multicultural education is utilised for earmarked purposes including intensive language teaching policies. The Netherlands Scientific Council recommended that minority languages be taught in schools albeit in a voluntary capacity[58]. State funding has been suggested for all religious and cultural groups to treat them on a par in the extracurricular domain and for purposes of establishing denominational schools[59]. They are also considering establishing contract compliance along American lines (see Chapter 4).

Italy

Until recently, Italy had passed no immigration laws since 1931, and entry and stay were scarcely controlled. Currently it has only 924,229 (1.5%) 'legal' migrants and foreign nationals of which one half are from developing countries, mostly Moroccan (98,000), Yugoslavian (47,000), Filipinos (46,000) and Tunisian (44,000). Sengalese, Somalis, Ghanian and Ethiopian constitute 89,000. A figure of 0.5 million has been cited in relation to 'illegal migrants'[60]. Following the Albanian influx the government has clamped down on immigrant entry, particularly from North Africa, and Italy has joined the European Communities Schengen Group[61]. It is not yet clear how effective the new laws can be against Maghrebians and Africans arriving by boat, but the easy-going attitude to entrants without documents has disappeared with the Martelli law passed in 1990, subsequent to amnesty for previous illegal entrants in 1989. The law was passed on the basis of the Schengan Treaty and led to the issue of 50,000 expulsion orders.* No new measures of anti-discrimination law or of integration have been instituted.

Most African immigrants work for very low wages and with no protection from labour law in agriculture in the south. The Italian tomato-growers could not survive without this cheap labour. This is a worry to Italian trade unionists, who want to see foreign workers better protected both in their own interests and in the interests of Italian labour[62]. In recent years, the situation has been changing very rapidly. Although many Africans had been entering the country (often illegally), for a long time up until 1989 there was little public awareness of immigration, and public attitudes to people of varied nationalities was usually relaxed. The anti-racist organisation Italia-Razzismo says there has been a rapid deterioration, with several violent racial incidents including murders and growing activity by racist organisations - some in big northern cities with decaying areas, some in the rural south[63]. At the same time, regional parties like the Lega Lombarda in the north, which play on hatred for southern Italians and Sicilians, have made electoral gains leading to the re-

*Only 10% were implemented, *Financial Times,* 27/3/95.

emergence of a right-wing government.

Italy has ratified both the major conventions on racial discrimination, and in the field of employment has introduced measures pursuant to them. The Constitution guarantees a right to 'equal social status' and 'equality before the law' regardless of race, language and religion. Legal opinion suggests that this provision probably now places obligations upon private as well as public bodies. In 1985 the EPC reported that Italy was noted as one of the countries with the lowest number of racist incidences[64], although the situation has changed recently.

Pursuant to Law No. 943/1986 guaranteeing equality of treatment to all workers legally resident on Italian territory and exactly the same rights as Italian workers, a council was set up to achieve the legislative objectives. Also, a committee within the Ministry of Foreign Affairs was set up to promote and monitor the bilateral and multilateral agreements relating to ILO 143 of 24 June 1975, part of which is concerned with safeguarding the civil, social, economic and cultural rights of immigrant workers and their families.

The 903/1977 law was explicit in relation to protection from sex discrimination and Section 13 forbids racial discrimination. There is also some provision against arbitrary dismissal which could be utilised to seek protection against discrimination[65]. It has been used in the courts only a very few times, mainly as a result of the problems relating to proof. In April 1990, Law No. 125 was passed to make it easier to establish that an instance of unlawful discrimination had occurred. As yet, no cases have been brought under this new provision. It is unlikely that there will be much change in the number of cases brought, since the legal process still presents many impediments[66].

According to Treu, regional legislation, particularly in the Trentino-Alto Adige region, provides for positive action and positive discrimination policies. These include the recognition of linguistic and ethnic minorities and the right to be hired in public posts in accordance with their representation in each area[67]. Generally, enforcement of the existing laws is not rigorous. According to

Forbes, severe limitations are imposed by the practice and perspectives of the courts, which tend to focus on objective evidence that a person has been disadvantaged unfairly, and do not consider subjective evidence on the intention to discriminate[68]. The courts are also reluctant to admit statistical evidence of discrimination[69]. Treu concludes that:

> The problem could be successfully resolved only by giving the judge wider powers to order positive action on the part of the employer[70].

A recent change in immigration law has seen the introduction of quotas for employment for specific categories of immigrants tied to work permits and jobs. This is the only example in Europe of jobs being earmarked for specific ethnic minorities and the only practice which can be described as positively discriminatory in its intent and effect. Yet the overall verdict of the EPC report (1990) is that:

> No laws nor regulations about implementation have been implemented in the last four years [71].

Germany

Migration to Germany is comprised of Turks, Arabs and Poles adding up to 5 million (4%), of which half have been resident for over ten years[72]. German-born 'foreigners' can apply for citizenship. Germany, like Belgium, has been very reluctant to award citizenship and permanent residence to migrant workers although it has transmitted full rights to ethnic Germans and East Germans[73]. The same applies to children of foreigners except in some conditions[74]. Takers tend to be too few because of property links with Turkey, (as acquisition of citizenship leads to the loss of right of ownership) and to the strict cultural tests of acquiring citizenship[75], both of which act as deterrents.

The work permits given to migrant workers nevertheless give standing in terms of permission to work and the right of complaint. Special permission is needed to be self-employed in addition to the fact that there is the eight year residence rule, and foreign qualifications are not recognised The Kohl government has helped to return 180,000 Turks to their country of origin. The situation in relation to treatment of ethnic minority workers has worsened since 1987. The 1990 EPC report recorded a rise in the number of violent racist attacks and the sluggish response of prosecuting authorities[76].

Germany has ratified both CERD and ILO III. However, being a federal state the ratification places the burden on the regional government for implementation, as many of the powers which in other countries belong to central government are in Germany held by the Lander, or regions (e.g. Bavaria, Westphalia). (Within each Land is a lower tier of local authorities, similar to ours.) The Federal Basic Law (Article 3.1 of the Constitution) prohibits racial discrimination in general terms although it has little impact on employers who are covered indirectly by the trade unions and employers agreements. Litigation can be adjudicated in constitutional courts and cases of discrimination can be taken to labour or civil court by individuals. The civil law, however, does not make any provision for compensation[77].

The Penal Code treats incitement to hatred, or violence against minorities, incitement to racial hatred, and defamation, as punishable offences. The federal government primarily regards the overcoming of discrimination as a task for the educational system, which is in the competence of the Lander. Some regions do have well-developed policies on multicultural issues[78].

The country's asylum policy and migration policy in terms of entry of foreigners have both been liberal over a long period, and still so in comparison with other norms in Europe. The German authorities however tend to regard resident foreigners exclusively in economic terms - as temporary and potential workers - irrespective of their length of residence. German officials do not regard Germany as a country of immigration and reject the possibility that it could be a racist country. Racist political parties are seen as something outside of the culture and norms of the country[79]. Anti-immigrant feeling tends to be particularly high among East Germans than the level observed amongst the West Germans[80].

The Germans have an explicit priority of employment for 'native Germans' enshrined in statute in the form of Promotion of Employment Law[81]. In the event of discrimination the first course of action for an aggrieved party is likely to be a trade union and the Workers Constitution Act, which has provision of protection from discrimination including protection from victimisation. The workers' council has a legal obligation to keep the companies free of discrimination. A second route is through the administrative courts, and if the case is proven there is compensation. The Federal Commissioner for the Integration of Workers advises and supports the complaints as well as acting as a pressure group to encourage employers to improve practices. According to Forbes, it is likely that indirect discrimination is not covered by statute[82].

The courts have consistently denied any racial element to have been present in various well-attested incidents of racial violence. Furthermore there are no statistics on racial attacks. Turks, Iranians, Maghreb-country nationals and others suffer severe inequalities at work, in housing and in access to a place of public resort. The 'Foreigners Law' is severely restrictive and there is no security of residence. Discrimination is so well rooted in the constitution that recent attempts by two Lander governments (Hamburg and Schleswig-Holstein) to allow resident foreigners to vote in Land and local elections were struck down as unconstitutional by the Federal Constitutional Court[83].

Church groups, welfare groups and migrants' associations, together with some academics, work against racism with little help from the law. However, the federal government has appointed an official to promote integration of foreign workers and there are government-funded non-govermental organisations to assist with anti-discrimination work.

Greece, Portugal, Spain, Ireland, Denmark and Luxembourg

In this group of countries constitutional protection on grounds of colour and ethnic origin is likely to be absent (particularly Greece, Italy and Portugal). They are also less likely to have ratified Article 14(1) although protection on grounds of language tend to be better in this group.

Greece

Greece, like Germany, denies the possibility that there could be racism on its territory. But gypsies, and the Turkish-descended minority in Thrace, occupy a socially inferior position. The Constitution and Law 927 of 1979 forbid racial discrimination, but there seems to be little implementation[84]. Interestingly, ethnic Greek immigrants from the Black Sea area of the USSR have experienced classic discrimination; hostility, charges of taking jobs and homes from native Greeks, high unemployment and appalling housing. The Greek authorities, who have long complained of Albanian persecution of ethnic Greeks, have nonetheless been sending back ethnic Greek refugees from Albania.

Greece has ratified both of the two main international provisions on racial discrimination. It ratified the CERD in 1972, and the ILO III in 1984 by enacting Law 1429/1984[85]. Anti-racial discrimination Law 927/1979 passed in response to CERD criminalises public incitement of acts of racial discrimination or hatred (Article 1), or expression of ideas which are offensive to other persons because of their racial or national origin (Article 2), and refusal to provide goods or services on the grounds of a person's racial or national origin[86]. This Act requires states to introduce measures to combat incitement to racial hatred and discrimination in the provision of goods and services, although it does not cover refusal of employment on racial grounds. Other laws however do apply to the employment situation:

Law 1264/1982 on the democratisation of the trade union movement and the safeguarding of workers' trade union freedoms is significant in this respect in that it applies in full and on equal terms to foreign nationals who are allowed to belong to trade unions in the normal way. Since then it has been accepted that foreign nationals in Greece are themselves free to form their own associations and unions[87].

As regards access to the courts, civil and criminal courts are available to anyone whose rights have been infringed. Equal treatment in respect of lawsuits and legal proceedings is guaranteed by Article 20 of the Constitution, and the relevant provisions of the Civil Code, especially Articles 62, 63 and 110. Article 62 of the Code of Civil Procedure states that any person who has rights and obligations may be a party to court proceedings. Persons who meet in groups which do not constitute associations, and companies without legal personality, may nevertheless be party to court proceedings. Article 63 states that any person who possesses legal capacity may represent a person in court. Article 110 states that the parties have the same rights and obligations and are equal before the courts. With regard to financial redress to private individuals, Article 914 of the Civil Code states that anyone who is in breach of the law or causes injury to another shall be obliged to pay compensation.

The Greek Human Rights Foundation is the main organisation charged with the responsibility to eradicate racism and advises 'foreigners' and government in respect of social issues[88]. The Greek Commission of International Solidarity does similar work[89].

Portugal

Portugal's concern about racism includes concerns about Portuguese, both black and white, who have emigrated to other EU countries and who suffer discrimination. Nevertheless a small African population of around 0.5% exists. Portugal proscribes fascist organisations and has very heavy penalties (10 to 25 years' imprisonment) for racial murders and serious acts of physical or psychological violence against members of a national, ethnic, racial, religious or social community, committed with the intent to destroy that group entirely or in part. Racist and extreme-right gangs have emerged in Portugal since the mid-nineties; the government's concerns tend to focus on this sort of racism. There is no effective legal coverage of 'day-to-day' discrimination against ethnic minorities. Nevertheless Portugal has both NGOs and the Ombudsman facility for counter-discrimination.

Spain

Has half a million Gypsies (Spanish citizens) who suffer extreme poverty and some suffer discrimination. Government efforts against discrimination tend to concentrate on them[90]. There are now some African migrants (2%), many of them without papers, working for low pay particularly in the construction industry. Spain has constitutional guarantees against racial discrimination but little means of implementation of laws to protect foreigners/immigrants[91]. Spain has ratified CERD and ILO III. The Government of Spain, in their ninth periodic report to the CERD, explicitly link Article 14 of the 1978 Constitution relating to equality before the law and Article 5 of the CERD:

The principle of no discrimination on grounds of race, embodied in the Spanish Constitution, means that the People's Advocate must see to it that, in their activities, all organs of the Public Administration respect and abide by that principle, and he can monitor their activities for that purpose.

Alternatively, the Attorney General's Office is charged with furthering the course of justice in order to protect the rights of citizens, since it is empowered to intervene in all proceedings brought on the grounds of violation of fundamental rights and freedoms[92]. Since most problems are essentially those of residence and citizenship status, most of the legal efforts are made in respect of immigration law rather than labour law and the right not to be discriminated against in employment. There is hardly any developed case law concerning racial discrimination in employment, nor are there any codes of practice.

It is in respect of the Gypsy community that Spain has developed most of its public policy measures of a type that are associated with countering racial discrimination. First there is a recognition of the existence of an ethnic minority; second there is the judgement that this group is disadvantaged; and third there is the political decision to devise and implement programmes to improve the situation of the group in question. In an EPC report (1990) Portugal has recognised violence by skinheads against ethnic minorities[93].

The Workers' Charter of 1980 confers on all employees who are not public servants a right to freedom from discrimination on grounds of race when seeking employment or after having found employment. Separate provision is made for public servants. The Act further provides that regulations and collective agreements must not discriminate on grounds of race or origin. It is unclear whether the provision covers indirect discrimination. However, the Act does allow for positive action by the government to help groups of unemployed workers who have difficulty finding work. The wrong committed by an employer who discriminates is, according to the law, a criminal wrong. The Labour Inspectorate, the constitutional court and the People's Advocate are available to the aggrieved individual in Spain.

Most of the good practice on anti-discrimination has developed in respect of the travelling community, but very little relates to employment thus far. Positive action programmes are clearly allowed, are a functioning part of policy and constitute good practice in some sense. However, such measures and associated coercive action are not uniformly or consistently implemented by the authorities responsible for devising and administering these policies. There are 17 autonomous regions and municipal authorities, and it is inevitable that attitudes and practices vary considerably, with observable differences between urban and non-urban areas.

Ireland

The Republic of Ireland is now the only EU country with net emigration. It has very few ethnic minorities: the main group causing concern are Gypsies, who are Irish citizens, in addition to an emerging settlement of Asians and Chinese (approximately 2%). Ireland is the only member state *not* to have ratified the CERD; neither has it ratified ILO III. There is no domestic legislation to counter racial discrimination in employment although there is a general constitutional provision guaranteeing equality before the law. The Irish law also forbids incitement to racial hatred. In practice this has never been relied upon by anyone. In any case, it could only place obligations upon public employers. However, the unfair dismissal legislation does make an express provision that a dismissal on grounds of race is automatically unfair, as long as the employee has been employed for at least a year by that employer[94]. A case of this kind has yet to come into the public domain.

Industrial tribunals have the ability to deal with racial discrimination, but there have been no cases to date. It is unlikely that the government will introduce legislation on race discrimination as a whole. An *ad hoc* approach is more likely, involving new pieces of legislation to outlaw specific forms of racial discrimination. There are positive action training programmes in place to deal with the educational disadvantage and lack of qualifications of the travelling community wishing to find work.

Denmark

Denmark has just under 2.1% of the population whose origins lie outside the country - mainly in Turkey, Yugoslavia, Pakistan and Africa. All foreign work-permit holders are expected to have employment insurance, often organised by unions, for at least two years. Denmark has the highest unemployment rate amongst migrants in western European nationals[95]. Despite its liberal traditions, disparagement of migrants, particularly Muslim migrants, has been increasing. It has penal laws against incitement to racial hatred and against racial discrimination, but very little government implementation owing to its reliance upon the power of officials like the heads of local government to take action. Over the last decade Denmark has reversed its earlier relatively relaxed policy towards refugees, and public hostility to non-European residents has increased sharply. Unlike some other European states, non-EU citizens in Denmark are not significantly worse off in legal terms in relation to EU-migrants or naturalised migrants[96]. And the obstacles to becoming a full legally accepted citizen are neither numerous, or difficult to negotiate, even though only about 12% of migrants have obtained citizenship since 1978[97].

Denmark has ratified the CERD and ILO III, yet has not introduced employment law legislation pursuant to these instruments, and the constitutional position is that these conventions do not automatically become incorporated into domestic law. There is legislation in the field of racial discrimination, but the coverage extends only to refusal to serve a person in a public place, and incitement to racial hatred. Public sector employers might be under a duty not to exercise administrative discretion unreasonably, although this provides no genuine protection. In terms of treatment within employment, there is a rule that collective bargains cannot distinguish between workers on grounds of race, and any dismissal must be reasonably justified. Even this protection does not extend to all employees.

Denmark seems not to have comprehensive unfair dismissal legislation covering all employees, although Article 413 of 30 August 1971 provides protection for 'salaried workers', and expressly excludes factory workers. Section 2b(1) provides that:

Where the dismissal of a salaried employee who has been continuously employed in the undertaking for at least twelve months is not deemed reasonably justified by the conduct of the employee or the circumstances of the undertaking, the employer shall pay compensation.

91

Once again, it is strongly arguable that dismissal on grounds of race would be rendered unlawful by this provision. The Danish legal system operates in such a way that a treaty validly entered, only acquires the force of national law when it is incorporated into it by legislation[98]. However, it has been pointed out that this does not mean that unincorporated treaties have no effect hence the trend within the courts is to interpret national law in accordance with international obligations within the language of the national law[99].

The Racial Discrimination Act of 1971 allows criminal prosecution in respect of direct but not indirect discrimination in the conduct of a trade or business. The penalty is a fine, simple detention or imprisonment of up to six months. There is little effective provision against discrimination at the point of recruitment. The Public Prosecutor's Office and the Ministry of Justice are also responsible for bringing proceedings in respect of incitement to racial hatred under Section 266b of the Penal Code. The lack of case law and the outcomes of investigation suggest a reluctance to institute such proceedings. The first recorded case was in 1979, and there have been only seven more since then.

Denmark also has an Ombudsman to whom complaints may be made. The principle that all persons are to be treated equally is deemed to apply to all levels of public administration, and that principle could be imposed by the Ombudsman. In practice, complaints tend to be restricted to a concern about lack of action by the appropriate authorities. There has been some pressure placed on the Ministry of Justice by the increasing activity of neo-Nazi groups, and this has led to the Public Prosecutor's Office being urged to be more active. There have been only two cases relating to racial discrimination, and these concerned discrimination in the housing area.

For employment cases another route is to pursue the case via an industrial tribunal. An individual has to prove discrimination rather than the employer having to satisfy the tribunal that the law has been observed. The Labour Ministry and the Labour Exchange provide special language education and vocational courses for immigrant groups. It is indicative of the problems with the law and the level of equal opportunities awareness in Denmark that positive action measures are seen as violating the principle of neutrality[100].

Judgements concerning access to the law are overshadowed by the inadequacy of the law's operation. Criminalising racial discrimination is not proving an effective substitute for a range of policy instruments, and Denmark is only at the beginning of the process of developing good practice in this field. Unlike most North-European countries, organisations which specialise in campaigns on racial discrimination are not much in evidence although there are licensed NGOs which help victims.

Luxembourg

Luxembourg is the smallest of states with 3.7% of its total population belonging to non-EU origins in addition to 13.5% of Portuguese and Italians, all contributing to a large figure of 45% of the workforce which originates from outside the country. Such workers are not allowed to enter white collar public sector employment despite the fact that Luxembourg ratified the CERD in 1977, although it is not signatory to ILO III. The law of 9 August 1980, implements the CERD and supplements the Penal Code by Articles 454 and 455 of the Penal Code[101]. These articles render liable to punishment people who provide goods or services and who refuse to provide them to individuals on the basis of race, colour etc. This Act does not cover discriminatory denial of employment, and there is no provision in its employment legislation to deal with racial discrimination; in this respect it has not fully complied with the requirements of the CERD.

However, there is legislation governing *dismissal* from employment, and as we have discovered with other countries, this is such that it ought to provide protection against discriminatory dismissal. The relevant law is the Act of 1989 on Contracts of Employment. Section 28(1) provides that:

Termination shall be considered wrongful ... where it is not based on serious reasons grounded on fact or related to the capacity or conduct of the employee or on the operating needs of the enterprise, establishment or service.

Section 29 goes on to provide remedies for wrongful termination; these include compensation and, if:

Conditions exist for the continuation or resumption of the employment relationship the tribunal may recommend reinstatement.[102]

It must be stressed that while these provisions would appear to render dismissals on the grounds of race unlawful, it is unclear whether any cases have been brought alleging wrongful termination on these grounds.

Given the fact that the domestic legislation of Luxembourg does not grant all of the rights contained in the Convention even to its own citizens, the issue arises as to how, if at all, the provisions of the Convention can provide protection to victims of racial discrimination in Luxembourg. Forbes speculates that an individual may be able to rely on CERD for public sector breaches of law[103].

The Luxembourg courts regard the direct applicability of treaties as normal procedure. Any provision that either explicitly recognises a right to the advantage of individuals or imposes clear, precise and unconditional obligations on the contracting states is, according to the government, directly applicable. Moreover:

The principle of the primacy of international treaties makes up for the absence of explicit provisions for the application of conventions at national level[104].

However, since no case involving CERD has ever been brought before the Luxembourg courts, the question of the direct applicability of the provisions has not yet arisen. The provisions apply before the judicial court dealing with civil and commercial matters, as well as before the administrative courts dealing with actions of public administration[105]. An aggrieved individual may approach the Conciliation Board which deals with disputes between employers and manual workers.

The Ministry of the Family and Social Solidarity has responsibility for a multilingual information policy to acquaint immigrants of their rights and available resources. Moreover, immigrants have access to a free aid and support service in the same Ministry. However, the 1980 law does not allow associations to bring a civil suit on behalf of, or instead of, an individual. The Luxembourg courts have yet to hear a case of racial discrimination. Moreover, since the Penal Code does not penalise racial discrimination in employment, the claim that it effectively punishes any act of racial discrimination is difficult to sustain.

Recent developments in Europe

There have been some recent developments in Europe which will assist migrants. At the Maastricht Summit a declaration was made against racism and xenophobia to strengthen legal protection for third world country nationals. The European Council at Maastricht in December 1991 asked ministers and the Commission to increase their efforts to combat discrimination and xenophobia. In the famous case of Marshal, the European Court of Justice (1994) decided that there was no limitation to damages in so far as sex discrimination was concerned. This has now been applied to race discrimination[106].

The Union's institutions and their response

At least since the mid-eighties, the European Union's institutions have shown concern about the growth of racism and xenophobia within European Union territory. Parliament endorsed the Evrigenis

95

report of 1986 and the Ford report of 1991. In 1986 the Council, Commission and Parliament issued a joint Declaration, vigorously condemning all forms of intolerance, hostility and use of force against persons or groups of persons on the grounds of racial, religious, cultural, social or national differences. And a further Declaration at Maastricht in 1991 called for member states to act on the issue clearly and unambiguously[107]. The CRE takes the view that this concern springs from anxiety about the growth in support, in certain countries, for parties of the extreme right and the fear that racist propaganda is producing violence and social unrest, irrespective of the activities of political parties[108]. In response, the European Council's Declaration made at Maastricht expressed the conviction that combating discrimination in all its forms was 'vital to the European Union', and asked Ministers and the Commission to increase their efforts to combat discrimination and xenophobia and to strengthen the legal protection for third country nationals in the territories of the member states.

European Union law

European Union law has not been developed to protect people from racial discrimination. There have been reports to the European Parliament in 1985 and 1990 and the Parliament has called for the 'Review and amendment of national legislation against political extremism, racism and racial discrimination.'[109]

European Union law incorporates, as a source of law, rights which are to be found in international human rights conventions to which member states are party. The clearest recognition of this source of Union law is to be found in the judgement of the European Court of Justice in *Defrenne* v *Sabena* 149/77 [1978] ECR 1365[110]. The question was whether, outside Article 119, sex discrimination was prohibited. The answer was that it was not, but only because at that time no rule of community law had been developed. The implication here is that there is competence to develop law relating to fundamental human rights outside the treaty provisions, and that this is not limited to sex discrimination. The Court has repeatedly stated:

> That respect for fundamental personal human rights is one of the general principles of Community Law, the observance of which it has a duty to ensure[111].

The European Convention of Human Rights now has an existence within European Union Law as evident from the *Defrenne* case. It is also referred to in the preamble to the Single European Act. Beyond that, however, the Court will look at other conventions and in the *Defrenne* case it looked to an ILO convention. Freedom from racial discrimination is enshrined in international law, for example, by the UN Convention on the Elimination of All Forms of Racial Discrimination (Art. 2[D]):

> Each State Party shall prohibit and bring to an end, by all appropriate means, including legislation as required by circumstances, racial discrimination by any persons, group, or organisation.

Article 5 obliges states parties to prohibit and to eliminate racial discrimination in all its forms and to guarantee equality in a wide range of situations. The International Convention on Civil and Political Rights (Art. 26):

> The law shall prohibit any discrimination and guarantee to all persons equal and effective protection against discrimination on any grounds such as race, colour, sex, language, religion, political or other opinion, national or social origin, property, birth or other status.

The CRE's view that the principle of racial equality is a source of Union law is reinforced by an article written by Chris Docksey, a member of the Legal Service of the European Commission, writing in a personal capacity in the *Industrial Law Journal* for December

1991[112]. He argues that the right of non-discrimination on grounds of race:

> ... undoubtedly exists in inchoate form at Community level, but specific primary and derived Community legislation only exists at present with regard to equal treatment on grounds of nationality. This does not directly cover discrimination in employment on grounds of race. Race is thus a good example of a fundamental right which may be recognised by the Court, an aspect of the general principle of equality which has not yet been specifically legislated into Community law.

Later in the same article Docksey refers to various developments as:

> ... a trend which may one day result in legislation embodying a new form of the principle of equality, at least with regard to discrimination in employment on grounds of race[113].

An independent group of experts[114] gathered by CRE has argued that Union action is now necessary. The Union has acknowledged the general principles of law, in particular the fundamental human rights and principles on which member states' constitutional law is based and which are stated in the European Convention for the Protection of Human Rights and Fundamental Freedoms, and so the Union must act to prevent the breaches of human rights caused by racism and xenophobia.

In the single European market, unjust discrimination will interfere with the free movement of persons and services by preventing persons who experience discrimination when seeking jobs, housing or services. Variations between national levels of protection will hinder free movement and will interfere with the proper functioning of the single market: on the basis of these arguments, the CRE has proposed the creation of a Community Directive so as to impose a time-limit on member states for producing their own legislation, and to lay down a common pattern of development.

A model for such a Directive already exists in Council Directive 76/207/EEC of 9 February 1976 on the principle of equal treatment for men and women. The preamble to this measure acknowledges that action to achieve equal treatment in respect of access to employment and vocational training and promotion and in respect of other working conditions appears to be necessary. It invokes Article 235 of the EEC Treaty since 'the Treaty does not confer the necessary specific powers for this purpose' and 'equal treatment for male and female workers constitutes one of the objectives of the Community, in so far as the harmonisation of living and working conditions while maintaining their improvement are *inter alia* to be furthered'.

The only doubt that can arise whether racial discrimination could equally well be the subject of a Directive is the question whether equal treatment between persons of different racial/ethnic origins constitutes an objective of the EU, and the wording cited above from 76/207/EEC strongly suggests that it may do so. The furthering of harmonisation of living and working conditions surely applies to all workers and their families. Indeed the preamble to Council Directive 75/117/EEC on equal pay for men and women not only claims the authority of Article 119 but also states that:

It is desirable to reinforce the basic laws by standards aimed at facilitating the practical application of the principle of equality in such a way that all employees in the Community can be protected in these matters .[115]

If EU competence exists to legislate in this field, then there is a further question: can it legislate only for EU nationals and their families, or can it protect all residents in the jurisdiction from unjust discrimination? Or is there EU competence regarding third-country nationals? The CRE conceded that in some respects third-country nationals occupy a different legal position from EU nationals. But it felt that they should at least be protected from racial/ethnic discrimination producing unjust treatment, as they suffer most severely from this type of discrimination.

The breakup of the Kohl-Mitterand team and the ascendency of Chirac in power in France has undermined the progress on strategies for anti-discrimination measures developed by the Kahn Committee based on the Eminent Persons paper. The Cannes summit aimed at this failed to make any progress on this issue, other than to note the need to co-operate and establish a monitoring centre on racism and xenophobia. This is in contrast to the call for 'continued measures of improvement on gender issues'[116]. The Kahn Committee's attempt to establish race discrimination as a community competence under the first pillar (rather than the third pillar) was sabotaged by Baroness Flather of Britain. The British position favours no extension of competence and prefers co-operation, which in effect confines it to the third pillar[117] thus excluding the European Commission, ECJ and other key institutions and restricting the debate to secret meetings between ministers and government officers. Overall it would appear that whilst gender equality has been well located under the first pillar, despite cross-party support to do the same for racial discrimination, there is much delay and many political hurdles.

The role of European human rights and the UN Convention

The European Commission of Human Rights and the Court are endeavouring to make up for the basic failing of the European Convention of Human Rights. The Convention fails to address itself explicitly to the issue of protection from racial discrimination, by failing to recognise that the 'protection from degrading treatment' in Article 3 can also encompass racial discrimination. This need also stems from the fact that explicit reference to discrimination in the Convention is found in Article 14 which simply protects enjoyment of the other rights and freedoms in the Convention which are free from discrimination. It does not grant an independent right to freedom from discrimination. It reads as follows:

The enjoyment of the rights and freedoms set forth in this

Convention shall be secured without discrimination on any ground such as sex, race, colour, language, religion, political or other opinion, national or social origin, association with a national minority, property, birth or other status.

As Van Dijk and Van Hoof say in their leading work, *Theory and Practice of the European Convention of Human Rights*[118]:

It may be said that such a right ought not to be lacking in the Convention ... The Convention thus lags behind the development in the United Nations where the elimination of discrimination has received and still receives a good deal of attention, as has been expressed in a number of conventions.

Mr Bucquiquio, Head of the Central Division of Legal Affairs of the Council of Europe, spoke of the constant evolution of the European Convention of Human Rights, and expressed the opinion that it was possible to envisage in future a new protocol containing a general non-discrimination clause[119]. Again we take the view that this would be all the more likely if there was UK and other government support for the idea.

While the British government recognises the individual's right to pursue matters under the European Convention, it does not recognise the individual's right to petition the UN Committee on the Elimination of All Forms of Racial Discrimination where, obviously, freedom from racial discrimination is explicitly recognised in the Convention. The person who has to rely on the European Convention cannot boldly assert such a freedom, but must construct an argument that the racial discrimination they have suffered is sufficiently serious to be regarded as 'degrading treatment' under Article 3. It may also be possible to use Article 6:

In the determination of his civil rights and obligations ... everyone is entitled to a fair and public hearing within a reasonable time by an independent and impartial tribunal established by law.

The CRE urged the government to recognise the competence of the UN Committee on the Elimination of All Forms of Racial Discrimination:

> ... to receive and consider communications from individuals or groups of individuals within its jurisdiction claiming to be victims of a violation of that State Party of any of the rights set forth in this Convention. (Article 14)[120]

There are two major European Courts capable of dealing with human rights, and they should have full powers in this by explicit legislative texts and not need to feel their way there by the adaptation of non-explicit texts.

The European Parliament in 1993 called for practical measures to combat racial prejudice, develop a directive to strengthen legal instruments and campaign to raise awareness in the parliament (1993). It also called for the establishment of a resident card, a residents' charter and the appointment of a European Union officer for issues of asylum and strict measures against employers who use undeclared labour [121]. Insofar as the link between welfare rights and citizenship is concerned, it is being strengthened even in countries such as the UK, which is increasingly relying on the narrowing definition of ordinary residence and recourse to public funding as restrictive clause to grant benefits with Germans following suit.

As for social policy, apart from the European Social Fund which have over the last two years widened the definition of migrant to include ethnic minorities, little exists by way of targetted consideration in other social policy programmes aimed at ethnic minority groups.

Conclusions, issues and challenges

Three groups of countries can be identified according to their social context. First, there are those countries with relatively large visible minority populations, some of long standing. The Netherlands has the largest visible minority population, followed by Britain, France, Germany and Belgium. Second are those countries with only a low and fairly stable percentage of the population who can be described as visible ethnic minorities from developing countries (less than 2%). These are, in descending order, Ireland, Denmark, Portugal, Luxembourg and Greece. The third group includes those countries which are experiencing significant inflows of visible minorities, on an informal or illegal basis. The main countries in the group are Spain and Italy, with Greece rapidly joining this group.

Broadly, most EU nations have ratified both CERD and ILO III except Britain, Ireland and Luxembourg. Article 14 has been ratified by only Denmark, France, Italy and the Netherlands, giving rights to its citizens to communicate with the Committee of CERD. Analysis of the state of the law, and access to the law and its operation in each of the member states reveals that some countries, such as the Netherlands, Britain, France and Belgium, which have the largest visible ethnic minority populations, also appear to have taken some measures in relation either to race equality or multiculturalism. Of these countries, Britain offers no constitutional protection but offers considerable protection in terms of specific legislation. Of these, the Belgium constitution makes an explicit reference to rights for citizens. Both the Netherlands and Belgium do not offer protection in terms of discrimination on grounds of nationality or ethnic origin.

Most ethnic minorities experience varied levels of discrimination in the labour markets of the member countries. In some countries such as Denmark and France such exclusion can reach extreme levels. The extent of its relationship with spatial concentration is questionable as white/invisible migrants appear to do better. Forbes[122] postulated from his survey of countries that legislation and policy development are linked to a variety of factors, i.e. the size and concentration of ethnic minority population, the duration of citizenship/residence, the nature of citizenship and voting rights for the visible ethnic minorities, and to the level of industrialisation. In my view it is also dependent upon the extent to which social and political discourses of a nation are influenced by the Anglo-American and Canadian discourse on equality and diversity.

According to Forbes, when the member countries are grouped according to the measures that have been taken to deal with racial discrimination, different combinations appear. Britain and the Netherlands, in that order, have moved toward the multicultural approach and are the leaders in terms of legislation and implementation. The second group is headed by France, Germany and Spain, and includes, marginally, Italy, on the basis of some legislation, the ease of access to remedies, and the existence of policies and approaches to overcome disadvantage among visible minorities. The remainder were ranked as follows: Denmark, Ireland, Belgium, Portugal and Greece. These countries have one or more of the following features: an assimilationist approach; a minimal legislative base; and very restricted access to remedies; ineffective implementation. As we have pointed out Belgium is making some interesting progress on this to step out of this group.

An alternative view would be that the nature of legislation and policy development is closely dependent on the history of attitudes of a nation concerning diversity and equality and the awareness of the distinction between disadvantage and discrimination. Assimilationist as well as segregationist and immigrant aid type of approaches are the least conducive to catalysing development of anti-discrimination law and policy, since they are based on a denial that there are differences between people. And that differences can be associated with disadvantage which in turn can perpetuate and indeed catalyse as well as attract discriminatory practices[123]. It is my view that Belgium and the Netherlands have made some interesting progress in terms of developing alternative models of state-supported religious pluralism. Belgium appear to be following a segregationist and assimilative model of pluralism. A typology of these responses could be presented as follows in Chart 2.1.

Chart 2.1 Leading countries' anti-discrimination and cultural policies

Legal Responses Cultural Policy	Social Policies	Domestic Legislation	Positive Action/ discrimination	Implementation of Law
Assimilative Secular	France	Germany		Government funded Agency
Pluralist Defacto Secular	Britain Netherlands	Britain Netherlands	Italy Britain	Netherlands Equal Rights Commission plus LBR Britain (CRE)
Segregationist Assimilative	Belgium	Belgium		Just established a goverment agency

Paradoxically, it is the 'advanced' countries with domestic legislation who are leading the trends towards Fortress-Europe by adopting harsh policies against asylum seekers and reducing the rights of immigrants, particularly in relation to welfare rights[124]. In the area of anti-discrimination law relating to employment, this chapter confirms one of Blanpain's general conclusions concerning equal opportunities law:

The lesson is clear. Equal opportunity legislation, although more than necessary, may not be sufficient for the elimination of inequality between majority and minority groups within the labour force. Legal approaches are limited because they operate only on the demand side of the problem (i.e. employer side) and do little to change supply (i.e. education and training of minorities). Free and equal access to education and professional training is the essential condition for the realisation of the right to work and employment. This suggests the need for supportive policies in education and training, together with continued vigilance[125].

Forbes on the other hand argues that analysis of the application of the conventions, their incorporation into national law, and international remedies demonstrates three things: first, conventions are important only through the *pressure* they place on governments to introduce domestic legislation to prohibit discrimination in employment; second, access to the provisions of conventions is very poor; and third, a prerequisite for effective protection from discrimination in employment is the *actual* introduction of such legislation.

The country reports draw attention to policies and programmes which seek to ameliorate educational disadvantage and the lack of qualifications among ethnic minorities, rarely earmarking significant resources for these issues. In general, measures within individual member countries to combat discrimination are by no means comprehensive or uniformly effective, and in some cases are largely absent. Even where there are provisions given the non-adversarial nature of continental systems, some alternative thinking is necessary rather than to implant a British style system.

Some countries have made racial discrimination a civil *and* criminal offence although the crime aspect is often located in the context of incitement or propaganda which is rooted in the historical European experience of Fascist propaganda. The distinction between direct and indirect discrimination is crucial for effective legislation and implementation as indeed is protection from victimisation. These two elements often tend to be lacking in Europe as is a properly funded and empowered agency to enforce the law, educate the populations and assist in and evaluate implementation. Only Britain, Germany and the Netherlands followed by Belgium have such agencies. In the absence of specific legislation, an ombudsman can make an effective contribution to combating discrimination. Out of the total, five countries - Spain, the

106

Netherlands, Portugal, Germany and Denmark - have made such provision. Minimalist positive action programmes are in existence in eight countries, but not all programmes apply to ethnic minorities. And only Italy has positive discrimination policies. Germany's industrial legislation creates an obligation on employers *and* employees not to discriminate. Contract compliance has been used in Britain and Northern Ireland, with indications of positive outcomes in the past.

European Union law has not yet developed an explicit protection from racial discrimination (save in the limited area where a person is discriminated against on the grounds of nationality if they are a citizen of an EU member country). This contrasts with the position of sex discrimination where there is a developed jurisprudence and a treaty provision (Article 119) dealing with the matter and many countries have pursued enactment of specific anti-sex discrimination law.

As CRE argued, the European Union appears to have legal competence to tackle racial discrimination and the lack of a jurisprudence, therefore, seems to represent a lack of political will. The protection from racial discrimination in the European Convention of Human Rights is only a subsidiary protection coming into play in the exercise of the other convention rights (see Article 14), save in those circumstances where the racial discrimination is so serious that it can be described as degrading treatment for the purposes of Article 3, these aspects remain inexplicit.

As I have shown, the other countries of the European Union are not altogether without protection from racial discrimination. It exists in a variety of constitutional guarantees, provisions of criminal codes and other measures, but it is nowhere so comprehensively dealt with as in Britain, and no country has an enforcement agency equivalent to that of the Commission for Racial Equality. That is not to say that the British Act is as effective as it was meant to be, far from it. But in comparative terms Britain has a better legal framework than elsewhere in Europe with its residents and citizens protected almost to the same extent (and non-residents following very close behind) and with similar rights, e.g. voting rights, access to welfare and public sector employment.

Insofar as mobility is concerned, people coming to the UK from the rest of Europe fall within the protection of UK laws. People going from here to the rest of Europe are not so well protected. One view is that one day a process of harmonisation of laws might lead, not to an improvement in protection from racial discrimination across Europe, but to a reduction to, as it were, the lowest common denominator. That could all be done in the name of free trade. On the other hand, the adoption of CERD by almost all EU countries and strong theoretical egalitarian elements in the constitutions does offer scope for seeking country by country change. This approach is in contrast to seeking a law at European level which warrants political agreement (the UK Conservative government is against it) across the board. The case law on sex discrimination at the ECJ, however, does provide some hope.

The increasing pressure to develop a Eurowide resident card in addition to the proposals by the Trevi group to create a common visa are likely to create a four-tier citizenship (EU citizen, EU residents both with rights of passage and full access to welfare, followed by third country nationals and followed by undeclared workers). This is likely to get tied to the level of welfare provision and political rights available to individuals in each category. The adoption integrating workers in the latter two categories will compete with the pressures generated by nativism and the escalating cost of welfare leading to the temptation of the European states to use the indigenous population (as opposed to foreign labour) as a reserve army of labour in increasingly polarised labour market. This is evident from the expulsion and deportation policies adopted by Italy and Germany. This is despite the fact that demography, including low birth rates in Europe, are likely to create a shortage of carers and skilled workers to run the welfare state. The exclusion of visible ethnic minorities from the public sector employment in many countries, together with use of citizenship papers and ID papers for access to services means that minorities access to social and welfare services, is likely to be problematised by state policies.

In policy terms it poses a dilemma. Should we argue for a UK type arrangement across the board as indeed CRE does or should we be arguing for an incremental notion of citizenship. Taking European nativism into account and assuming that if the Treaty of Rome is amended the EU is likely to take the latter more realistic position. In brief, four options are being pursued simultaneously:

- Amend Article 14 of the ECHR for cases to be heard by the ECHR at Strasbourg and enforced via the Council of Europe. This is unlikely to be area specific.
- Amend the Treaty of Rome leading to direct legislation (on specific areas such employment, education etc.) to be passed by the European Parliament. This could then be heard at ECJ.
- Seek publication of a community directive following amendment of the treaty or without (debatable) asking states to pass laws within a specified period. Access to ECJ can be provided for after local courts have dealt with the matter.
- To argue for CERD to be adopted beyond the four countries to be able to hear individual complaints against the state.

The extent to which each of these options progresses is likely to depend upon the alignment of ideological forces in Europe. Even with correct alignments it is option three which is likely to be less prescriptive and democratically more acceptable to the European populations then the other two. In any case the benefits of the first options are very limited given the overall nature of the convention.

As evident from the experience of Britain and France, it is ethnic minority cultural and often group-based values which are likely to be in conflict with more individualistic secular European values, particularly in the arena of social policy. Three options exist for policy-makers. One is to argue for the creation of a personal domain in which many laws including those relating to family, relationships, education and worship could be left to the individual ethnic communities (an extreme form of the Jewish model of board of

109

deputies). Here the major difficulty is that of protection of weaker groups, such as women and children, within ethnic minorities communities and the fact that many communities are not monolithic and cohesive although many states are trying to make them so.

The second option is to develop segregated provision and give maximum control to various communities (Belgium's segregationist model) in some areas such as education. This presents a long-term problem of perpetuating stereotypes that communities hold of each other and conflicts with the principle that in some areas, such as education, segregation cannot be part of education (see Chapter 5). The third option is to strive for maximum commonality (an agreed charter of human and cultural rights) whilst being pragmatic on case by case approaches (the British approach). In all cases the presence of a legal arena and an arbitration body on religious and cultural affairs at European level would be valuable. Alternatively, competence in nondiscrimination for both race and religion under pillar one will have to be fought for. The Anglo-American notice and theory of equal opportunities involving race, gender disability and religion is clearly having difficulty, with gender making the progress at a higher rate than other elements. Conflicts over subsidiarity, harmonisation between the states and within the communities, the conflict between governments, and above all the absence of community competence, all continue to undermine developments on race equality.

References

1   In Denmark, France and Britain, those who have residency enjoy rights similar to those who are citizens. The term 'third country national' applies to people who are not nationals of any EC country.
2   Poliokov, C. (1964) *The Aryan Myth,* Chatto & Windus.
3   Friar, P. (1990) *Staying Power*, Pluto.
4   For a wider debate see Cain, F. and Hopkins, G. (1990) *British Imperialism: Innovationist Expression,* Miles, R. (1979) *Racism and Migrant Labour,* RKP, Banton, M. (1969) *Race Relations in Britain*, Basic Books.

5   Nijoff, M. (1985) *Human Rights of Aliens in Europe,* Council of Europe. Directorate of Human Rights, pp 93-4.

6   See Raybock, R. (1991) 'Migration and Citizenship', *New Community,* vol. 18, October, for debate on graded citizenship. For a wider debate see Meehan, E. (1993) *Citizenship and European Community,* Sage.

7   The causes of the rise of racism in the eighties remain a matter of debate. See Ford, G. (1992) *Fascist Europe,* and Cheles et al *Neo-fascism in Western Europe.* For an incisive and critical article on causal analysis, see Miles, R. (1994) *A Rise of Racism and Fascism in Contemporary Europe.* Some sceptical reflections on its nature.

8   (i) Racial discrimination is defined in Article 1(1) as meaning:any distinction, exclusion, restriction or preference based on race, colour, descent, or national or ethnic origin which has the purpose or effect of nullifying or impairing the recognition, enjoyment or exercise, on an equal footing, of human rights and fundamental freedoms in the political, economic, social, cultural or any other field of public life. Article 1(2) goes on to state that the Convention does not apply to 'distinctions ... between citizens and non-citizens'. (ii) Article 2(2) places an obligation on States to take:measures to ensure the adequate development and protection of certain racial groups of individuals belonging to them, for the purposes of guaranteeing them the full and equal enjoyment of human rights and fundamental freedoms. (iii) Articles 3 and 4 are concerned with apartheid (Art 3) and propaganda and organisations which incite racial hatred or discrimination (Art 4); these articles are not particularly relevant to the employment context. (iv) In terms of protection against discrimination and remedies for victims of discrimination. Article 6 provides that: State parties shall assure to everyone within their jurisdiction effective protection and remedies, through the competent national tribunals and other State institutions, against any acts of racial discrimination which violate his human rights and fundamental freedoms contrary to this Convention, as well as the right to seek from such tribunals just and adequate reparation or satisfaction for any damage suffered as a result of such discrimination.

9   Forbes, I. and Mead, G. (1992) *Measure for Measure,* Department of the Employment Research Series No 1.

10   Evrigenis, D. (1985) *Evrigenis Report,* European Parliament, p.77. cf. Forbes.

11   Committee for the Elimination of Discrimination was established in 1988 to monitor and receive reports by the EC.

12   Forbes, I. and Mead, G. (1993) *Measure for Measure.* Department of Employment, p.10 (op. cit.).

13   Ibid.

14   This is the CRE's view. 2nd Review of the Act 1992

111

15 Community law of aliens. See Meehan (op. cit.)

16 This is a matter of politics. The feminist lobby in Northern European countries, together with the return of women to the labour market and the demographic fear of shortage of skilled workers, have all contributed to regulative change initiated by Barbara Castle, when she was a Minister.

17 This also permeates the literature on law. For a general debate see Lloyd, C. (1991) 'Concepts, models and antiracist strategies in Britain and France', *New Community,* vol. 18, October.

18 For an overview, see Wilpert, C. (1991) 'Migration and ethnicity in non-immigration countries', *New Community*, October, p. 49.

19 Scoritno, G. (1991) 'Immigration into Europe and public policy. Do stops really work?', *New Community*, vol. 18, October.

20 The requirement to be citizens adds to the exclusion of ethnic minorities as does the pre-condition to abandon one citizenship to gain the other.

21 Rath, J., Kees, G. et al (1991) 'The recognition and institutionalisation of Islam in Belgium, Great Britain and the Netherlands', *New Community*, vol. 18, October.

22 Forbes (op.cit.), p.22

23 Forbes (op.cit.), p.28

24 Banton, M. (1991) 'The effectiveness of legal remedies', *New Community*, October, pp.157-66.

25 Forbes (op.cit.), p.28.

26 Ibid..

27 Most European countries (except GB) adhere to a minimum wage under the Social Chapter adopted in 1991.

28 For debate on the subject, see Rath, J. and Kees, G. et al. (op. cit.).

29 The CRE is a quango staffed with civil servants it has powers to investigate employers and to support individual litigation.

30 In so doing they were advised by the Saudis, who created the structure to retain their own influence. Rath et al (op.cit.).

31 Head Imam has historically had the ear of the state in Belgium. See Rath et. al. (op.cit.).

32 One view is that this is segregationist multiculturalism. See Professor Amy Gutman's paper on multicultural education presented at Education and Democracy Conference in Jerusalem in 1992.

33 This is often evident in conferences in Europe. Also see Lloyd, C. (op. cit.).

34 This has caused considerable controversy over the famous head scarf issue in France. The French state education is historically wedded to secular ideals since the last century, and symbols of religion are not allowed in schools. The French interpret their secularism in terms of non alignment with religion and allegiance to national philosophy.

35 Forbes (op.cit.), p.36.

36   Dholakhia, paper presented at IWA Conference, 1989, Dominion Center, Southall, Middlesex.

37   Forbes (op.cit.), p.162. See *Searchlight* issues.

38   Forbes (op.cit.), p.36.

39   Forbes(op.cit.), p.36.

40   Forbes (op.cit.), p.36.

41   L122-4J. Ibid..

42   L133-105

43   In fact the French have criminalised marriage between 'aliens' and settlers causing considerable distress to people who fall in love.

44   M. Hannoun also tried to establish basic cultural rights by publishing a lot of actions the government need to follow.

45   *The Guardian*, 4 May 1990.

46   Forbes (op,cit.), p.36.

47   MG - GR (88) cf. Forbes (op.cit.), p.7.

48   M. Coll. (90) cf. Forbes (op.cit.), p.12.

49   Aounit, M. (1990) *Situation du Racism Strategies et Action dans MRAP*, MRAP International Report, January.

50   *Le Monde*, 21 March 1997.

51   Immigrant Policy, The Hague 1990, Council for Scientific Policy for Government.

52   Banton (op.cit.), p.164.

53   MG - CR (90) 2.P.2.J. Cf. Forbes (op.cit.), p.57.

54   Asscher-Vonk, L. (1983) *The Netherlands Bulletin of Comparative Labour Relations.*

55   Hessler, p44.)

56   It has 20 local offices like the British RECs and is legally aided. Forbes notes strategic case selection by the LBR (p58.) For relative success of the system see Bocker, A. (1991) 'A pyramid of complaints about racial discrimination in The Netherlands', *New Community*, vol. 17, July.

57   Immigrant Policy (1990) 36th Report Netherlands Scientific Council for Government Policy.

58   Ibid.

59   Ibid.

60   Dholakhia (op.cit.)

61   This is a group made of 8 ministers from eight countries similar to the Terevi group (in members) which deals with drugs, crime and immigration.

62   Dholakhia (op.cit)

63   Dholakhia. (Op.Cit)

64   Forbes (op.cit.).

65   Forbes (op.cit.), p.52.

66   Treu, T. (1985) 'Italy', *Bulletin of Comparative Labour Relations*, p.145.

67   Forbes (op.cit), p.52.
68   Treu (op.cit.), p.157.
69   Treu is referring to discrimination in general, but it is applicable to race.
70   EPC (1990) report on Italy. Cf. Banton.
71   Birmingham Report 1992, .
72   Wilpert (op.cit.), p.52.
73   Ethnic Germans were allowed in from USSR on the basis that their ancestors
      were German.
74   Wilpert (op.cit.), p.52.
75   EPC (1990)
76   Forbes (op. cit.).
77   Lynch, J. (1983) *Multicultural Education in a Global Society,* Falmer Press,
      Brighton.
78   Wilpert (op.cit.).
79   Gasrew (1991). Cf. Wilpert (op.cit.).
80   Forbes (op.cit.).
81   Forbes (op.cit.).
82   Dholakhia (op.cit.).
83   Dholakhia (op. cit.).
84   Forbes (op. cit.).
85   Forbes (op. cit.).
86   Law 1264 /1282 apply to all EU members and enables foreign workers to
      belong to trade unions
87   DeJong, D. and Zwanboom, M. (1991) *Equal Treatment and Discrimination
      in Europe Final Report: International Alert*, Netherlands Institute of Human
      Rights.
88   Greece (1993), Runnymede Trust.
89   Dholakhia (op.cit.).
90   Ibid.
91   Forbes (op. cit.).
92   PE 139.214. p4. Cf Forbes (op.cit.) and Mead (op.cit.), p.68.
93   DeJong et al. (op.cit.).
94   Wilkie, M. (1990) 'Victims of neutrality; race discrimination in Denmark',
      Nordic Journal of International Law. Pakistanis and Vietnamese are more
      likely to seek citizenship; cf. Jepperson (1990) 'Young second generation
      immigrants in Denmark', Social Forsking Inst. Booklet no 32, Copenhagen
      pp 35.
95   Ibid, p11.
96   Ibid, p12.
97   Forbes (op.cit.).
98   Forbes (op.cit.).
99   Scientific Council for Government Policy.

100 Forbes (op.cit.).
101 Forbes (op.cit.).
102 Forbes (op.cit.).
103 Forbes (op.cit.).
104 Dholakhia (op.cit).
105 Marshal, ECJ., *Equal Opportunities Review*, September/October 1995, No.57
106 Joint Declaration before the Council in 1986. Maastricht Declaration (1991).
107 CRE Review (1993)
108 European Parliament Combating Racism in Europe - Churches Commission for Migrants in Europe.
109 Deferenne v. *Sabena* 149/177 (1978) ECR 1365.
110 CRE Review 1993.
111 CRE Review 1993.
112 Cited from CRE Review 1993.
113 Experts report CRE courtesy of Dev Sharma, established in 1994 in Corfu.
114 Council Directive 75/117/EEC.
115 Briefing on Europe, CRE Aug 1995.
116 Ibid.
117 CRE Review (op.cit.).
118 CRE Report (op.cit.).
119 CRE Review (op. cit.).
120 See list of resolutions in Combating Racism in Europe, Strasbourg 1993, p. 23, 1994, Churches Commission for Migrants in Europe.
121 Forbes (Oo.cit.).
122 Forbes (op. cit.), pp 70-76.
123 See Fekete, N. and Webber, F. (1994) *Inside Racist Europe,* IRR.
124 Cf. Forbes (op.cit.), p124.
125 *Bulletin of Comparative Labour Relations* (1985). Cf. Forbes (op. cit.).

3 The use of British race law by individual complainants

An overview of developments and factors which shape the use of the Race Relations Act

British law offers protection against discrimination to individuals on the grounds of race, gender and to a lesser extent against disability. It offers little protection against racism per se and even less assurance in relation to diversity[1]. In this chapter, key developments over the last decade in relation to the Race Relations Act 1976 are charted, in addition we delineate the social and psychological and systemic factors which make it difficult for the aggrieved party to turn their disputes into claims.

The Race Relations Act

The year 1995 marks the completion of three decades since the British parliament took its first step to make statutory civil provision to counter racial discrimination by enacting the first Race Relations Act (1965). This was followed by a revised and broader, but mainly conciliatory Race Relations Act (1968) which established the Race Relations Board to which complainants could go together with the Community Relations Commission whose brief was to promote good community relations. A 1976 Act based on the US Civil Rights Act (1964) allowed direct access to tribunals for employment cases and to county courts for other complaints. It expanded the meaning of indirect discrimination, and interposed a power on the newly formed Commission for Racial Equality (CRE) which combined the Board's duties on law enforcement with the promotional and strategic responsibilities of the Community Relations Commission[2]. The Act like its predecessors retained the strong privacy exceptions. Parliament proposed stringent measures related to the rights of the respondent insofar as CRE rights *vis à vis* investigation of other organisations were concerned.

The lead for enforcement over the last decade has remained with the CRE assisted by the Community Relations Councils (funded by the CRE now known as Racial Equality Councils), as well as the voluntary sector agencies such as the Citizens' Advice Bureaux[3] and Law Centres which took on a supportive role as they flourished during the early eighties[4].

The Act appears to have enjoyed considerable support with 43% of the British population supporting toughening up the Act and 50% agreeing with enforcement in 1983[5]. From the debate on equality and the European Union it was becoming palpably clear that, despite the deficiencies of the British Act and its rather varied impact, British provision and experience in this sphere is likely to be a source of guidance to other European nations - the majority of which have not attempted to develop a specific enforcement framework to deal with discrimination.

Indeed, there are real concerns that, unless steps are taken at European level to develop progressive legislation, the limited development of support structures and gains made in the interpretation of British law could easily be lost or undermined in the European Union[6]. As the campaign for anti-discrimination legislation develops in Europe, it is important to reflect and analyse origins, enactment and the subsequent transformation of British anti-discrimination law in a wider social, political and economic context. Yet another reason for an evaluation of the Race Relations Act is to analyse critically the position taken by the British government in the Thatcher era to racial discrimination and to the proposals to make it more effective. As we show later the prevailing state view of the period has been that the anti-discrimination law is essentially a supportive extension of the voluntary eradication of discrimination by employers and service providers rather than conversely[7].

This view encompassed the assertion that legal sanctions to counter discrimination were not necessary in Britain; in any case they do not work[8]. This view gained momentum as Britain increasingly interfaced with the free market culture and was accompanied by the severe undermining of legal services hitherto supported by the local authorities and charities for the benefits of disadvantaged groups. This occurred because of a considerable reduction in local government expenditure by central government in the late eighties[9]. And this was accompanied by the emerging notion that voluntarism should mean no input by paid professionals[10]. Nevertheless, it would seem that many voluntary agencies (such as Community Relations Councils, Law Centres and Citizens' Advice Bureaux) which took on the role of supporting the Act over the last two decades have managed to survive, albeit curtailed in numbers and suffering severe financial constraints[11]. In such a climate, to enable the law to work effectively it is essential that debate on the effectiveness of the 1976 Race Relations Act is extended beyond technocratic analysis to include an assessment of the capacity of the legal support system, a theme pursued in this chapter.

The use of the Act

The legal establishment reluctantly acknowledges that the 1976 Act has been under-utilised and it has failed to make a significant impact in countering discrimination. Indeed, in the Kapila Lecture in 1986, the vice-chancellor of the Senate, Browne Wilkenson, pointed out the poor utilisation of the Race Relations Act in Great Britain in contrast to similar legislation in the USA.

I could not think of a single case in this country which achieved a major shift towards equal opportunities for a substantial body of blacks. There has been no organisation of black civil rights lawyers who persistently and with moderation have pursued remedies under the Act. White lawyers (apart from a handful of socially committed barristers and solicitors) have been absent from race cases, except in those few where legal aid or CRE funding is available. The limited funding available to the CRE prevents it from supporting many cases which it would like to support. There is no way in which heavy cases, involving elaborate discovery, statistical evidence and difficult points of law, can be brought in the High Court: all cases must be brought in the County Court or Industrial Tribunal which, with the best will in the world, cannot handle such litigation. The damages do not provide any spur to large organisations to change their policies[12].

This pessimistic view was not shared by the departing Director of the CRE in 1992 who took a generous view of the past decade in *The Times*:

In recent years, test cases have been brought in the higher courts. The purpose has been to establish ethnic-monitoring data in proving discrimination; to increase the level of compensation for injured feelings; to reduce circumstances where indirect discrimination is justifiable; to reduce the scope of statutory immunity from racial discrimination law; and to establish Sikhs and Gypsies as protected ethnic groups [13].

A cursory reading of the legal activity generated by the Act in terms of filings in courts and applications in tribunals presents a very depressing picture. Over the first ten years there were 23.5 cases filed every year in county courts[14]. The figure has not changed significantly since 1985. The other alternative route (mostly taken for employment cases not supported by legal aid and relatively safe from payment of costs risk for the appellant) suggests that there are around 1,100-1,200 filings per year. The average number of cases disposed of per year over the first ten year period is around 400 which is a tip of the iceberg given the estimated 10,000 acts of discrimination in employment alone[15].

Of the total, the majority 81.5% of the cases were employment cases, 14% segregation, and the rest were victimisation 2.6% or indirect discrimination 1.9%, thus indicating the difficulties of proving both indirect discrimination and victimisation due to the stringent tests applied by the courts. As shown in Table1.8, selective cases which go to the Employment Appeal Tribunal (EAT) have three times as great a success rate as that observed at first IT level. Increasingly this system of dispute processing has been criticised for its growing formalisation and professionalisation[16].

Of the total cases heard, only 4.2% of tribunal cases between 1977 and 1986 were upheld, 37.1% were dismissed and the rest were withdrawn, mostly at a higher rate than average, either at pre-hearing or hearing stage. The success rate figure has improved since then to around 6-7% (Table 3.1). The rest were conciliated or withdrawn under circumstances that are not entirely clear. Both CRE-assisted cases as well as cases assisted by advocates did better, with CRE doing better than average as shown in the table below. This could be due to a high degree of selection by the CRE, or the possibility that more difficult cases are passed on to barristers, a matter we return to later on[17].

In addition to the evidence that discrimination persists without significant shift, it is worth noting that the proportion of cases has not decreased, and the spectrum of litigants is well distributed in terms of class (53% manual, 18% professional, with 50% of the cases concentrated in manufacturing[18]). Recent data suggests over-representation of cases in clerical, professional and technical areas although not in management[19]. This is partly indicative of the disparate impact of the last recession on ethnic minorities and the

Table 3.1 Outcome profile and characteristics of applicants

Outcome Profile	Settled %	Withdrawn %	Upheld %	Dismissed %
All Cases (PSI) 1991	25	36.5	8	28
Ditto Tremlett (1992)	32	37	6	25
PSI (1986-88)	41	27	10	24
Non-assisted (PSI) 1991	24	37	7	29
Non-CRE assisted (Kumar 1984-86)	-	-	6	-
CRE assisted (PSI)	48	11	34	3
Ditto Dhavan (1976-1988)	36.1	-	24.1	39.6
EAT cases (1976-1986) Dhavan	22.7	7.6	15.6	53.8
Characteristics of Applicants (1992)				
Asian	22	33	8	31
Afro-Caribbean	22	47	4	24
Private	28	31	10	27
Public	13	55	5	25
Voluntary	35	35	4	22
Employed	16	53	4	24
Non-employed	26	35	7	24

Sources: McCrudden et al (1991), Dhavan et al (1988), Tremelett (1992), *Survey of Industrial Tribunals*, Research Series 22 DE, Dhavan and Luthra et al (1980) unpublished report for the CRE.

121

broader shift in the economy. The success rates against the private sector appears to be higher than average while withdrawal rates are somewhat higher than average for the public sector, indicating the established experience of the public sector.

The Act in a wider comparative context

Recent data (Table 3.2) confirms earlier findings and suggests the following features of the Act in comparison with other tribunal cases. Firstly the race discrimination applicants tend to be younger, more likely to be multiracial-unionised, and more likely to be professional white-collar workers with less than average or median length of service. Secondly around 80% of the responding employers analysed by Tremlett et al were first time respondents. Yet the overall dismissal and pre-hearing withdrawal rates are higher as are indeed the rates of conciliation as compared to the averages for other areas. The conciliation rates are poor as the Policy Study Institute implied, partly because of the stigma attached to them and the fact that employers see this as unprincipled compromise or caving in.

Most disturbingly, the success rates are much lower in the case of race discrimination than in other areas of litigation including the Sex Discrimination Act, suggesting that a much harsher test is applied. Race discrimination applicants in the case of respondents were more likely to bypass the internal organisation procedures and go to the tribunal which suggests a lack of faith in the internal systems.

As shown in Table 3.2 the cost of defending a race discrimination case is higher than average of all cases, yet it does not appear to push up conciliation rates. The median figures for compensation are lower than in other areas including those for sex discrimination. The impact of the Act on changing the policies of organisations seems minimal (Table 3.2). This raises an issue about the use of the Act as tool for management of change in organisations, or indeed the issue of follow up of the Act.

Under-utilisation of the Act has produced a range of predictable responses. Sceptics, who often take a non-interventionist stance

Table 3.2 Features of employers and IT applicants by type of case categories

Features	Unfair dismissal (%)	Redundancy payment (%)	Wages Act (%)	Sex Discrim. Act (%)	Race Relations Act (%)
Median Age	39	48	31	28	32
Length of Service	3.9	5.3	1.0	1.5	1.6
Prof./Tech	8	7	6	12	25
Clerical	13	10	10	34	23
Union Member	32	35	20	25	35
Median Size	42	19	19	30	25
1st Case (employer)	64	74	85	90	77
No Change in Procedure	40	39	57	53	60
Outcomes					
Settled	46	46	47	53	32
Withdrawn	20	22	25	21	37
Upheld	14	22	19	11	6
Dismissed	20	11	9	15	25
Conciliation	21	29	38	21	21
Pre-hearing Leading to Withdrawal	19	30	23	24	46
Economic					
Median Compensation	£1923 £2773	£688	£265	£1425 £2595	£1185 £3495
Employer Costs	£1845	£781	£293	£1500	£2300
Representation Costs	£44	£29	£27	£35	£42
Costs Requested by by Employer	£6	£5	£7	£8	£13

Source: Luthra M. (1995) constructed from Tremlett et al (1992). The 1992 *Survey of Industrial Tribunals*, Department of Employment.

reiterate their doubts that discrimination is not a suitable subject for enforcement-oriented legislation[20]. Such scepticism also finds an entirely different voice in analysis that the systemic claims to the political economy have reconstituted the struggle against discrimination in ways that have perceptibly and imperceptibly altered its focus and possibilities[21]. The symbolic importance of the Act as a moral code or as a cohesive force which captures a sense of community has been highlighted by researchers[22]. While these debates persist, more practical reflections have been cast on the evidentiary and procedural aspects of the legislation[23].

Less attention has been paid to the overall observation as to why within the overall pool for litigants, black and ethnic minorities are more likely to take their cases to tribunal and then more likely to lose them than those in other categories, i.e. even the limited engagement is ridden with higher than average risk and a very limited benefit of the intermediate steps such as conciliation.

Rule-making, evidence and statutory changes

Emboldened by a chorus of criticism, the CRE undertook a review of the Act in 1984 and 1986 and unsuccessfully canvassed changes in both the procedure and evidence by which discrimination is proven, and suggested modified institutional changes in aspects of the tribunal and court structures through which, and in the shadow of which, outcomes are determined[24]. Although politically less problematic, this approach misunderstands the framework within which the legislation operates and makes over-simplified assumptions about how statutory and other legal norms are appropriated for use by society. Indubitably the Act has a great deal to answer for, and led at least one discerning observer to question the political integrity behind this legislative initiative in that:

Greater importance has been accorded to being seen to be doing something than actually doing it[25].

But we need to look more closely at both the intended design impediments inherent in the legislation as well as how its provisions have been received and transformed.

This is not to suggest that the CRE did not concern itself with important questions of procedure and substance. It had itself confronted some hard-nosed due process, natural justice problems, in the use of its own investigative powers, particularly in the context of investigating central government departments. Through its individual assistance to complaints, it had also encountered problems concerning the burden of proof, inadequate replies to Section 65 questionnaires (sent by the applicant to elicit information from the respondent), the insufficiency of damages and, *inter alia*, problems of discovery of documents[26]. But on the whole its approach in the eighties remained rule-centred, concerned with the normative structure and language of the rule in the belief that if rules were correctly formulated they would be appropriated for rigorous use by the ethnic minorities and the legal community. To some extent this approach survived in the second set of proposals for change. The CRE did make some gains mainly in the arena of case law but there were also some losses.

There was no new race discrimination legislation as such following the 1986 review so the chance of wider change never presented itself*. Equally it did not prove possible to get a Private Member's Bill adopted. On the whole, government responses to CRE reviews could only be described as 'lost opportunities'. Nevertheless some gains have been made through the CRE reviews. For instance the code-making power in Section 47[27] has been extended to permitting the making of codes of practice in the area of housing. Planning control has been brought within the scope of the Race Relations Act (Section 19A)[28]. Prior to this CRE had to rely on piggyback legislation[29]. On the employment side, the government made small administrative concessions in relation to positive action. Section 13 of the Act has been revamped so that the protection for work-experience trainees has been improved[30]. Similarly Section 37 has been changed so that positive action training for non-employees does

---

* One exception to this is the recent Race Relations Act (1996) which extends the scope of the Act to Northen Ireland.

125

not now require ministerial designation of training bodies[31]. The government responses are shown in Chart 3.1, some of which were critical of the CRE presentation.

As the chart suggests, the government here is taking a minimalist and voluntaristic position with preference for codes of conduct and gradual integration of anti-discrimination law on a piecemeal basis rather than making other law subservient. While statutory changes have been limited in scope, there have been more significant changes interpretation as a result of case law. For instance, the level of compensation for injury to feelings has been increased (*Alexander* and *Noone*, both in the Court of Appeal) which is likely to contribute to higher awards[32].

The circumstances under which indirect discrimination may be justifiable have been restricted somewhat as the Court of Appeal in *Hampson* restated the law[33].

In addition to this, the scope of statutory immunity from racial discrimination law has been reduced (the House of Lords in *Hampson* narrowly construed Section 41). The *Amin* decision[34] still effectively stops the Commission or anyone else from using the 1976 Act to deal with governmental activity. Some, but not all, of the difficulties in the law on victimisation have been ironed out by the Court of Appeal in *Aziz*[35].

On the systemic side the idea of a discrimination division in the industrial tribunals has not been followed up in Great Britain, though such a course was virtually what was taken in Northern Ireland. The government refused to extend legal aid to cover racial discrimination cases in industrial tribunals on the grounds that such provision could not solely be made for discrimination cases.

The Commission's powers to bring law enforcement proceedings are still limited in scope to assisting individuals, dealing with discriminatory advertisements, instructions and pressure to discriminate, persistent discrimination, enforcement of non-discrimination notices and the bringing of judicial reviews. There is no general right to take law enforcement actions or to bring class actions, and the limitation imposed by the *Prestige* decision[36] on the

126

Chart 3.1 Government responses to selective suggestions - 1992 CRE Review

CRE request	Government Response
Make the Act not subservient to other legislation	This applies to many other statutes. The goverment will integrate anti-discrimination law if relevant in new legislation.
Legal aid	Will have to be across the board for other areas of tribunal: no costings provided.
Compulsory ethnic monitoring	Cost implications. No evidence that voluntary codes do not work.
Contract compliance	Neither local government nor central government are enforcement agencies
Racial violence should be criminalised	Not needed: enough law on books.
Anti-religious discrimination statute	No serious case or evidence to justify it.

Source: Michael Howard, the Home Secretary's letter to Herman Housley, Chief Executive of the CRE July 1994.

Commission's power to carry out formal investigations still remains. No power has been given to the Commission to accept binding undertakings to carry out good practice. The Fair Employment Commission in Northern Ireland, on the other hand, has wider powers than the CRE.

The remedies to deal with discrimination are still limited in the industrial tribunals to those concerned with the individual not the discriminatory situation. After 81 days of hearing, and having given the respondents ample time to look at systems, the tribunal in the major police case of *Singh* v. *Nottinghamshire Police* could only make *suggestions* for change. It had no statutory power even to make formal recommendations, let alone to order change[37]. Even as they apply to an individual, the remedies available do little about putting that person in the position they would have occupied but for the discrimination.

There is still an artificially low limit on compensation in industrial tribunals - currently £10,000 - which is imposed by government and affects the level of compensation for injury to feelings. In Northern Ireland the limit in the Fair Employment Tribunal is £30,000. The case of Marshall, heard in the European Court of Justice, albeit based on sex discrimination, is likely to expand further the scope for damages which have also been going up under employment law[38].

Even in the area of voluntarism, the code-making power, although extended to housing, has not been widened to other areas. Ethnic monitoring, though recommended by codes and approved for use in proving racial discrimination by *West Midlands Passenger Transport Executive* v. *Singh*, has still not been given a statutory basis[39]. Indeed, the approved questions under the local government legislation on contract compliance stopped local authorities from asking for such data from proposed contractors. The problem caused by the Court of Appeal decisions in *Perera* and *Meer* in the definition of indirect discrimination remains[40].

Legal support and victimhood

There is a great deal of general evidence to suggest that many laws give rights to people who do not use these laws to further claims to which they are, at least, legally entitled. I endorse the view that in order to understand this phenomenon a few logical steps back need to be taken to the shadowy beginnings of a dispute when it is still a grievance in the mind of a claimant. A lot of claimants simply clump it; others make a claim and then lump it[41].

There are innumerable reasons as to why this happens. People do not have enough information about their rights. When the actual incident complained of occurs, they do not have the support and expertise to take them through their problem. There are many instances where there has been grievous invasion of rights, but the victim of this transgression is not really aware of the exact contours of the problem except to feel a muted irritation. There may be limited access to help. And even where help is available, it may be too expensive for the victim[42].

Although median costs are low for applicants (see Table 3.1), the figures are many times higher for cases that have professional representation. In addition to the financial costs, the exercise of going through the motions may be too humiliating or too onerous as there is a prospect of victimisation or of being a second class citizen[43]. There are numerous problems in getting evidence and enormous pressures to settle. The ultimate amount in damages may affect the cost-effectiveness of the exercise. There may be a lack of faith in the system as a whole particularly, as in this case, the tribunal system is led by lawyers who may deem the case to be vexatious.

Poor representation of ethnic minorities in the legal and the judiciary system further undermines this confidence[44]. There are only four judges, nine Queen's Counsels and 4% of the tribunal members are from ethnic minorities[45], mostly confined to 'employees' side and major cities (see Table 3.3).

Currently appointments of IT members are made once every three years. A much higher number is needed if there is to be a permeation of understanding of discrimination. A bold step may be necessary in terms of having ethnically mixed panels. Cases of racial discrimination in employment matters are heard by industrial tribunals which sit at eleven different venues in England and Wales and at four venues in Scotland.

In the independent/voluntary sector - for instance in the law centres, CABs and trade unions - such representation tends to be better. Yet their role in advocacy and support remains a marginal one. The most disappointing aspect of this group has been the trade unions which pick up only a small percentage of cases, offer little support and were inclined to pass the case on to Racial Equality Councils[46].

Since law in Britain is primarily practised as part of a private market economy, lawyers may not feel that it is worth their while to take on discrimination cases. The cases may be too complex, requiring far more work than the short- or long-term dividends which may flow from winning or losing. Bearing all these pressures in mind, it is not surprising that a large number of people simply lump or clump their grievances and claims; however, some settle, and a

Table 3.3 Breakdown of ethnic minority IT lay members by region

Location	Employee Panel	Employer Panel	Total
Birmingham	9	2	11
Bristol	3	0	3
Bury St Edmunds	1	1	2
Cardiff	0	1	1
Leeds	9	0	9
London - North	15	6	21
London - South	7	3	10
Manchester	4	0	4
Newcastle	4	0	4
Nottingham	7	0	7
Southampton	4	3	7
Total	**63**	**16**	**79**

Source: Luthra M., compiled from CRE (1994).

few fight to the bitter end, exhausted by the experience of attempting to vindicate a grievance.

It is the American anthropologist Gallanter (1976) who has made a crucial and substantial contribution towards theoretical development in this sphere by illustrating how the operation of rule formation often depends upon the strategic interplay among actors in the system, the significance of indigenous or embedded systems of normative ordering that pervasively emerge in the shadow of the formal legal system, and the relationship between the law as a system of symbols and a system of bargaining endowments.

He challenged the conventional view that the law is indeterminate and malleable in nature and wedded to some notion of fairness and that each post-autocratic expression may yield some benefit[47] by arguing that law is what one makes of it. All one needs is the right kind of institutional skills to use it. Advantaged and powerful groups in society are better placed to do so than others, the latter category including individual unsupported complainants[48].

Gallanter drew upon a spectrum of evidence concerning the role of law in social life, including data on the number and organisations of lawyers, the evidence of awareness of law among the population, media coverage of legal institutions and events. His approach has been multidisciplinary, applying both sociological and anthro-pological techniques of data gathering and interpretation. Recently he has extended this approach to applying a social-psychological approach in an analysis of victims of discrimination to explore how and why victims fail to turn their grievances into formal complaints. He concluded that victims are bound by a social psychology of victimhood: exclusion, distortion and even sacrifice[49].

Such empirical work on the social psychology of victims is lacking in the UK, although in a local survey of ethnic minorities in Hounslow we found 85% of the ethnic minority people had encountered some form of multiple discrimination while they have been in the UK. Of these very few people (10%) converted these into grievances because of two main reasons: they felt it to be too much bother (60%), or too expensive (55%). Given the resources needed to prepare a case and the complexity of preparation recognised by the Royal Commission and the length of hearings, these fears are well founded[50].

It is the anger and sense of injustice rather than the compensation which is the driving force behind a complaint in the beginning. McCrudden's (1988) analysis suggest that in CRE-supported cases the drop-out or withdrawal rates are three times less (see Table 3.4) as compared to other supported cases, partly due to the moral support element[51].

Yet in our analyses of cases between 1977 and 1986, the CRE supported less than 10% of the requests for complainants' aid in employment and less than .07% of the non-employment cases. Such sifting acts as a powerfully discouraging factor to newcomers and contributes to the poor use of the Race Relations Act. As the number of applications has gone up the number of cases in which representation is given has improved but representation percentages are still around 14 to 15% as shown in Table 3.5. The average number of cases won has declined in the nineties as compared to the figure for the eighties as suggested by CRE's Annual Report 1994, although conciliations and settlements are up.

Key players and political economy of law

In terms of the total number of cases which are heard in tribunals, the CRE still remains a major player (24% direct representation) supporting the private market economy of lawyering with some interesting economic features (12% of the cases in 1992 had a CRE-supported lawyer). Firstly the lawyering community did not respond very strongly to the use of the Act up until the recession hit the lawyers in the nineties and many young black lawyers were looking for work. This pattern has been in contrast to immigration law which has had a historical support from private lawyers assisted by the fact that rewards such as reuniting the family are clear cut in contrast to discrimination, and the success rate is much higher[52]. Fighting discrimination cases is a difficult and often humiliating experience for the complainant, particularly when employers improve their chances of winning multifold[53] by using specialist employment lawyers and the complainant is not legal-aided. This scenario has led to the development of an employers' lawyers market, whose services

132

Table 3.4 Outcome of full hearings and evidence and witness score by representation at the hearing

Outcome (a)	CRE Staff	CRE Barrister	Other Barrister	Solicitor	Other (b)	None
Settled	-	12	-	6	4	3
Withdrawn	-	4	21	19	13	8
Dismissed	46	61	61	61	71	82
Upheld	54	23	18	25	11	7
Evidence of Witnesses						
Hearing Mean Score	1.90	1.60	1.25	1.50	1.52	0.95
Base Unweighted	32	46	25	14	18	18
Weighted	50	99	56	33	45	77

[a] Column percentages. [b] Includes law centre, trade union, and others. The base is full hearings of cases brought by individuals.
Source: McCruddenn et al (1991) *Justice at Work,* PSI.

are often beyond the reach of the complainant.

For progressive lawyers it has not been cost-effective to enter into the market unless there was an expectation of continuity of clients, unless they had a wider interest in some overlapping field (e.g. employment law, which itself is not a very profitable activity unless you represent employers). In any case there are very few black and ethnic minority barristers who specialise in civil law; thus such work is often passed to young, budding barristers who may take it on to acquire some experience[54].

Table 3.5 Complainant aid by the CRE: number of applications for assistance and legal committee decisions

Year	Total number	Total committee decisions	No assistance	Advice and assistance	Withdrawn	Representation (%)
1990	1381	1341	228	792	133	188 (14.0)
1991	1655	1454	146	782	138	388 (23.4)
1992	1557	1544	104	907	138	353 (22.7)
1993	1630	1709	128	1175	156	250 (15.3)
1994	1937	1957	116	1394	219	228+112* (17.6)

* where representation arranged through others
Source: CRE Annual Report 1995.

Our analysis in 1988 showed that lawyers on the fringe of this market felt that the price of continuing their interest in such work was too high, and litigants found fighting race discrimination cases too expensive. Accepting that an identifiable sector of race discrimination lawyers exists, some took the view that the pressing interest of a few lawyers was sufficient. The third significant feature of such lawyering was that it was caught within the conventional mould of case-by-case lawyering. Our own research showed that when lawyers talked about law reform it was done with a kind of legal ethnocentricity of practising lawyers, even when they were otherwise committed to the cause of the community and developing anti-racist strategies[55]. This leads to an inability to understand fully how grievances develop into disputes and eventually into cases. The emerging notion of public interest law or community law in the UK displays an ambivalence towards developing the kind of institutional lawyering and support arrangements which strengthen the foundations on which this development rests. Meanwhile most cases (including combating race-discrimination) have remained uncomfortably in the domain of conventional lawyering.

This obviously presents a serious problem for complainants whose outrage, energy and anger in the initial phases needs to be supported. Although compensation tends not to be at the forefront of the minds of applicants, the level of it, together with costs, is likely to push employers towards settlements[56] which, as PSI study pointed out, are particularly non-conciliatory in race discrimination cases[57]. This is despite the observation by Tremlett (1992) that the overall median cost to the employer is quite significant as compared to the applicant (see Table 3.2). This is likely to be less of a factor in the corporate and public sector bodies which have full-time lawyers. Currently data on damages is not fully adjusted for inflation, hence comparison is not available; but the impression is that the damages - and in particular compensation through settlements - has gone up well beyond the tribunal limits. There is also evidence that compensations for injury to feelings and aggravation have increased at a higher than average rate in race discrimination cases[58].

Voluntary strategic-aided support work

It is important to make a distinction between routine legal aid, concerned with servicing the individual case, and strategic legal aid which seeks to enable a greater use of law and the legal system across the board. Several social action groups in areas such as immigration, mental health, consumerism, employment, housing and social security law have grasped the future possibilities for such wide ranging use. They have developed case strategy, created effective lobbies in parliament and engendered greater rights-consciousness in ordinary people assisted by para lawyers who have expertise in clearly defined areas. Hitherto these developments appeared to be somewhat absent from the field of race discrimination law.

To some extent, both the Law Centres and the trade unions have tried to make some serious initiatives about race discrimination. Dhavan and Luthra's evidence from a study in 1988 also highlighted the limited capacity of law courts to take on 'routine' and strategic case work, which has been weakened further since the research was conducted. Most Law Centres, although well endowed in terms of training, tended to off-load their problems on to the CRE or RECs[59]. The analysis suggests that the head offices of the unions were quite responsive, and interested in corporate policy development but less confident about the support that they gave to the field as a whole[60]. But an appropriate estimate of trade union support can only be made after a more detailed analysis of what happens at shop floor level and the actual 'back up' available. From the current available evidence, trade union branches are reluctant to risk resources and tend to pass the buck on to other institutions.

Part of the problem has been that unions tend to see individual cases as less important issues than those which affect large numbers, and they tend to seek preliminary advice from very cautious legal departments who are not prepared to examine cases from an innovative angle. As shown above on the whole, current organisational arrangements tend to push case work in the direction of the CRE, which sees itself as a strategic safe player leading to a lot of sifting of cases. The TUCs recent initiative to establish a national Law Centre is a move in the right direction.

Dhavan and Luthra's analysis of Citizens' Advice Bureaux (CABs) also showed that of the 111 CABs who responded to the survey * most received 1.52 cases in the period 1986-1987; only one CAB had taken a case to the tribunal, and only three had any experience of litigation work. Here part of the problem was that the CABx see themselves mainly as referral agencies, mostly referring to CRE/REC or the Law Centres. In the case of the CRCs (Community Relations Councils), only 11% of the staff worked full-time on casework and 20% devoted more than half their time to it. This historical shift away from casework was partly CRE-led, who pushed CRCs towards policy work[61] causing considerable damage to the movement. Race discrimination enquiries constituted 26% of the

* With the exception of six CABs whose figures were very high and so were taken out to work out averages. (M. Luthra unpublished paper).

total enquiries dealt with by Racial Equality Councils, of which one third were employment-related, yet Community Relations Officers (CROs) were not trained in law. The CRE tried to train them in 1987 and more recently revived its attempt, but it could not boost the participation of CROs (now called Race Equality Officers) in advocacy work[62].The ethnic minority organisations were even more poorly equipped to assist the CRE in its use of the Act. Most, like Race Equality Councils, could not even provide a case collation service let alone an advocacy service as their personnel had little experience of or training in such work. And in most cases they were never recruited to combat discrimination in a legal arena.

Chart 3.2 Pathways of casework

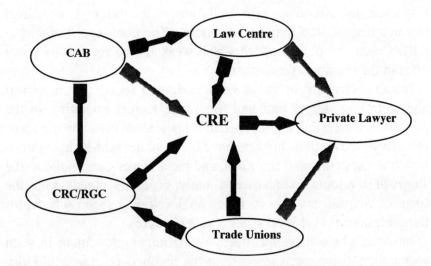

Source: Luthra, M. (1988) *Survey of Organisations and Players.*

Our quest for the institutional basis for a strategic use of race discrimination law led to discussions about the need for a national back-up centre which would provide support for those giving advice and strategise the use of law. Obvious parallels were drawn with similar developments in immigration law, specific reference being made to the Joint Council for the Welfare of Immigrants and UK Immigrant Advisory Service (UKIAS). The CRE was seen as being in a crucial position to do more in terms of information, training and its own support. But the CRE was generally resisted by respondents as the appropriate location for an independent 'back-up' centre. Black Rights established in 1986 was discussed by a few as a viable alternative, along with the Law Centres Federation. But even those sympathetic to these organisations felt that an Anti-Discrimination Centre should be explored as an independent initiative. Subsequent to this, the CRE did establish an Independent Legal Defence Centre in 1994, which could not get off the ground for a variety of reasons. The CRE, if serious about training Race Equality Officers in litigation work, needs to examine whether the current post holders are suitable for advocacy work, or whether this role should be restricted to effective case collation. In the end a radical restructuring of staff may be necessary. The poor legal training of CRE's own complaints officers also weakens the support they can offer in the pre-appearance phase.

Overall, as shown in Table 3.6, a variety of social, psychological and technical factors pull and hindrance factors operating in the process of converting a grievance to litigation. In my view the focus of analysis and actions hitherto have been on the right-hand columns which are systemic and technical, and these stages correspond to the stages of development of a case. Clearly, given the impediments, the focus of analysis has to be as much on developing social support for the complainant as it is on seeking rule change.

One area where there has been significant improvement in such social support has been increase in the numbers of ethnic minority members on IT panels, improved damages by virtue of Marshall and improved figures for injury and feelings as well as exemplary damages are also encouraging. As evident from the experience of the Fair Employment Commission (Northern Ireland) for 1933, the tribunal awards per case averaged £9,486, whilst the figure for CRE was only £3,115. The figures for settlements were £16,364 and £3,955 per case respectively. This suggests that the fact that the remit of the Race Relations Act is being extended to Northern Ireland, together with the outcome in Marshall, are likely to push up the level of damages even further.

Yet the increasing use of lawyers by respondents and complexity of the system can easily wear down and discourage a complainant. The current proposal by the Lord Chancellor to provide legal aid for tribunals would go a long way towards resolving some of these issues. It is also evident from research (Table 3.2) that during the post-litigation period there is little by way of organisational change, even when there is multiple litigation over a period. This is partly due to the fact that when people pay other people's money (rate payers or shareholders) and utilise public resources to defend, there is little incentive to settle. The CRE has recently used Section 62 in county court after industrial tribunals upheld nine complaints of discrimination against one local authority (Bradford) to implement an action plan on equal opportunities.

Only in a handful of industrial tribunal cases are there any interim measures or reappointments of applicants, very few pre-hearing settlements, despite the fact many organisations see the fall-out from such litigation to be damaging in terms of public relations, the time spent to be excessive, and the cost incurred to be substantial. This is leading to a trend of no-fault-settlements in the USA, a pattern which is likely to develop in the UK as damages escalate and the number of Crown bodies exempted from the Act diminishes. 1994 has seen the highest number of cases brought to the tribunals - 2,355, up 26% from 1993. Over one-third were settled by ACAS - a figure which is likely to increase if the Lord Chancellor's proposals for legal aid for tribunals is accepted.

Table 3.6 Typology of pull and barrier factors affecting counter-discrimination cases

Factors	Social Pschyological	Economic	Systematic	Technical
Pull Factors	• Anger • Rage • Trade union membership	• Compensation: good if one wins; including compensation for injury. • Costs rarely awarded against complainant	• Case rarely struck down at pre-hearing	• Agency support or legal support
Hind-rance Factors	• High risk of loss • Shame of losing • Fatigue • Fear of victimisation • Sustaining energy levels	• No legal aid • Expensive if not supported by CRE • Could pay damages (although very rare)	• Increasing pre-hearings • Detached client culture • Poorly trained lawyers • Poor representation of ethnic minorities in judicial system	• Burden of proof on complainant • Little chance of re-appointment • Discovery problems • Managing RR65 • Witness victimisation and reluctance

Source: Luthra M. (1995) Based on interviews with applicants and literature survey.

Conclusions, issues and challenges

Clearly the British government over the last decade has taken a minimalist stance based on a reactive incrementalist view of the role anti-discrimination law, leaving advancing the scope of law mainly to the local and recently to European courts to refine it, with a continuous emphasis on voluntarism despite all the evidence of its failure. Government over the past decade has failed to seize the opportunities to revise the Race Relations Act, although both European case law and some UK-based case law has *de facto* revised it.Given the psychological pressures the experience of discrimination creates for the victim, there is a need to create a collective arbitration service for the public and voluntary sector in which complainants could choose to go (on a no-fault basis) and bypass the more tortuous and risky route of litigation. Some local authorities have used this route successfully by asking independent arbitrators to intervene and also to break the entrenched position taken by personnel officers.

The anti-discrimination law remains primarily in the voluntary domain or at best at the margins of private lawyering with the employers increasingly using private sector lawyers. Some sections of the public sector, particularly local authorities have become rather good at defending their position. Furthermore there is no reason why both solicitors and barristers could not be released from ethical restrictions to be able to represent aggrieved parties in tribunal on a solo basis instead of having two advocates.

Another route would be to support such cases with legal aid, a proposal which has been attacked by the Chair of the Law Society, on the basis that it will accelerate the process of hijacking of the tribunals by the anti-discrimination lobby. What he failed to mention was that race discrimination cases constitute a tiny fraction (less than 2%) of all the cases appearing in front of tribunals. As I have emphasised in this chapter, converting grievances through the processes of naming, blaming and claiming requires considerable support all the way by the case collator and/or advocate. The RECs have a crucial role in this process. A careful selection of competent REOs may be necessary on a regional basis to support such work. It is also quite ridiculous that the RECs, although part of the CRE network, are not allowed to refer cases directly to the barristers. The TUC proposal to set up a national law centre warrants discussion in terms of the possibility of linking it with a national law centre aimed at discrimination. In the event of legal aid becoming available for

141

tribunal work, it is important that only credible and competent solicitors with expertise on employment law are allowed to practise in the field. Again, given the recent *Which* magazine report, about poor service given by solicitors, some accreditation by the CRE or Department of Employment could help.

At the legal level, there is an obvious need for an agency or a unit which will utilise the law with more conviction and understanding and will be prepared to take more risks than the CRE does to develop a radical dimension to law. This agency should develop expertise in the area and have a defence fund. There are some models with different degrees of government control on agencies such as the CRE and the United Kingdom Advisory Service (UKAS).

Two issues need addressing. First, the initial energy of the victim could be sustained by rapid risk assessment provision, i.e. a kind of a phone line supported by regular appearances on the radio. Second, the REO could be trained to collate the evidence, seek further particulars, and negotiate on behalf of the client. In addition, CRE could improve the skills of its own complaints officers or ensure that only people who have a good grasp of employment or anti-discrimination law are appointed.

Recent changes in the law following Marshall have lead to the passing of the Race Relations Act (1994) which lifted the ceiling on damages. As the experience of the Fair Employment Law 1964 in Northern Ireland suggests, damages have been three times higher than those deserved under the Race Relation Act (1976) - hence employer response has been very positive. This suggests that the Race Relations Act is in for an interesting period, particularly if legal aid becomes available for tribunal representation.

References

1   The Disabled Persons Act has been extremely poor in making an impact as sanctions are lacking for lack of enforcement of the Disabled Persons Act 1944 and 1958. For a wider analysis of the Act see the parliamentary

debates on the subject aimed at passing the Civil Rights Act. See Harry Barnes, 'Battle of the Bills', *Morning Star,* 23rd January 1995.

2   The litigation and promotional work facilities were split between the Race Relations Board and Community Relations Commission until 1976.

3   The CABs are advice institutions in Britain rooted in the old consumer advice tradition, while the first law centre was established in 1974 in Kensington. Both of these received a boost in number in the early eighties particularly under municipal socialists.

4   Brown, C. (1982) *Black and White Britain,* PSI.

5   For the dialogue of the deaf between the French and the English see Lloyd, C. 'Concepts, models and antiracist strategies in Britain and France', *New Community, v*ol. 18, October 1991.

6   These fears were expressed at many conferences in the early nineties.

7   This is evident from the government position on contract compliance as shown later. The government has been willing to produce codes of practice despite their ineffectiveness. A Local Government Management Survey of the top 100 companies in October 1993 showed that while 80% collected data, only 1 in 10 had set any targets in respect of race. *Equal Opportunities Review* (October 1993). A more recent survey by CRE (Business supports tougher standards *The Times* 18th January 1991). suggested that while 88% of major employers had equal opportunity policies, only 45% were doing something and 47% acknowledged the need to widen their pool of employees: 45% accepted the benefits of such a policy as providing skilled and good staff.

8   Ibid.

9   Local government has been subjected to severe financial constraints over the last decade. See Union reports over cuts over the last four years.

10   In Ealing the conservative Chair of Community Affairs Committee, Ms Yerolomon, demolished the whole budget in 1993 on the grounds that volunteers did not need professional support and volunteers were meant to be unaided.

11   The number of law centres and CABx has been reduced significantly. In the case of law centres by one third since 1988, and staff has been cut. Federation of Law Centres.

12   Wilkenson, B., Kapila Lecture, 26th November 1986.

13   Whitlaw, J., 'Race law takes a step forward', *The Times,* 9th October 1990.

14   Dhavan, R. and Luthra, M. (1988) *The Use and Non Use of Law,* CRE 1988, unpublished report.

15   Ibid.

16   Increasing professionalisation is debated in various IPM journal articles.

17   Mccrudden, C. et al (1991) *Justice at Work,* PSI. Difficult cases are passed on to experienced lawyers as CRE staff lack such experience.

18   Dhavan and Luthra (op. cit.).

19   Ibid.

20   McCrudden et al (op.cit.) have shown poor conciliation rates for race cases: people take entrenched positions as it is regarded as a matter of principle.

21   Analysis of the House of Lords parliamentary debates showed this: see Dhavan et al (op.cit.) Chapter 3, and it surfaces time and again.

22   House of Lords debate summarised in Dhavan et al (op. cit.).

23   See CRE Reviews 1986, 1994.

24   The term 'in the shadow of law' has been borrowed from Gallanter (op.cit.).

25   Dhavan et al (op.cit.) cited from the Chapter on House of Lords debates.

26   First review of the Race Relations Act 1986 CRE.

27   Section 47, RRA of the Act. Previously restricted code formulation to emplyment

28   Section 28, RRA. Complements in direct discrimination provision. The provision makes it unlawful for benefit agencies to embody conditions which are indirectly discriminatory, one exception being ministerial circulars.

29   Here I use the term to define enactments where CRE slipped in elements to do with equality on the back of major statutes. One example is the Local Government and Planning Act 1988.

30   Section 13, RRA 1976. In general, training bodies are not allowed to discriminate in training recruitment unless they use section 37.

31   Section 37, RRA. Section (3) allowed designated bodies to engage in positive discrimination in training subjects to certain conditions.

32   *Alexander* v. *Noone* (Court of Appeal 1988). Reaffirmed later on. It was held that injury to feeling awards should not be nominal.

33   *Hampson* v. *DES* (Court of Appeal 1988). Restricted the definition of indirect discrimination to exclude restrictions which may flow from statutory instruments.

34   Amin, K. and Richardson, R. (1992) *Politics for All,* Runnymede Trust.

35   *Aziz* v. *Trinity Street Taxis Ltd* (Court of Appeal 1988). In the case of victimisation, the complainant had to prove that the victimisation was done under or with reference to the Race Relations Act.

36   *Prestige Group plc* - v. - *CRE* (1984) IRLR 166 HL. A tenuous belief on the part of the CRE is necessary to embark upon an investigation under section 49 of the Race Relations Act.

37   *Singh* v. *Nottinghamshire Police Constabulary* (1992) EAT. Cost £150,000 to the CRE.

38   Since Marshal (August 1995 ECJ) No 2. Since then, various tribunals have exceeded the £12,000 limit several times- in latest case the total award was £2800. (See EOR No 57 September, October 1995). Ceiling on exemplary damages continues, although changes proposed in a Law Commission paper

(News EOR 53).

39   *West Midlands Passenger Transport Executive* v. *Singh*   (Court of Appeal 1988).

40   *Meer* v. *London Borough of Tower Hamlets*, confirmed *Perera* v. *Civil Service Commission* (Court of Appeal 1988) requirement in selection requires a barrier (not a preference) to qualify indirect discrimination.

41   Lump and Clump it. This term has been borrowed from Gallenter which followed on from Felstone, W.L.F. and Abel, R.C. (1981) 'Emergence and transformation of disputes. Naming, blaming and claiming', *Law and Society Review,* 15, pp 633-52.

42   A number of studies have indicated that geographical access, networks, opening hours, etc., all affect the uptake of services. For an overview, see Luthra, M. (1988) unpublished mimeograph, Brunel University.

43   US Programme: Bumillar, K. (1984-86) 'Anti-discrimination law and the enslavement of the victim. The denial of self respect by victims without a case', working papers of Dispute Processing Research Programme, Michigan University, USA.

44   Gallenter, M. (1973) 'Why the have-nots have come ahead. Speculation on the limits of legal change', *Law and Society Review*.

45   Goulbourne, S. (1985) 'Minority entry into legal professions', Policy Paper in Ethnic Relations, Warwick University, November.   The Royal Commission on Legal Services (1979) (Cmnd. 7648) expressed concern in relation to this matter.   See also 'Racial discrimination in the legal profession' (1990) *New Law Journal*, August. The CABx passed on the cases to Law Centre who in turn passed it on to the Councils for Racial Equality accordingly. Our qualitative research of trade unions showed that although there are paper policies, they were very reluctant to take on cases. See Kumar (1986) *Industrial Tribunals under the Race Relations Act,* CRE. For a generous view, see chapter by F. Dubois in Dhavan et al (1988) *Suffering Discrimination Silently,* CRE, Brunel University.

46   Gallanter, M. (1973) 'Why the haves come out ahead. Speculations on the limits of legal change', *Law and Society Review*.

47   Ibid.

48   Ibid.

49   Gallenter (op.cit.).

50   Dhavan et al (op.cit.).

51   McCrudden (op.cit.) p.146.

52   Immigration law has been supported by state funded UKIAS (now known as the Immigrant Advisory Service) providing a free service. Despite this a private lawyer's market flourishes.

53   McCrudden et al. (op.cit.).

54   Young ethnic minority graduates have problems getting articles or pupilages

to build up experience. In a project we evolved at the Ealing Race Equality Council we were inundated with young people wanting to volunteer.

55 Dhavan et al (op.cit.).
56 Jones et al. (op.cit.).
57 This is because such cases are seen as issues of principle if in the case of public sector or shareholding organisations. Other people pay for defending. McCrudden (op.cit.).
58 See McCrudden on damages. See also *Equal Opportunity Review* Nos. 53 and 57.
59 Dhavan et al (op.cit.). See also Newton et al (1992) *Struggle and Strife* pp 25-27, Wellingborough REC, who also made the same point two years later.
60 Dhavan et al (op.cit.).
62 In a paper called *The Yellow Peril* (Sharma et al, 1984) this point was made. Despite training 60 REOs, only two engaged in anti-discrimination work. Newton (op.cit.), p.43.

146

4 Contemporary legal issues and the state

Case studies of legal responses to racial violence, cultural diversity and the law on contract compliance

Having surveyed the Race Relations Act in Chapter 3, this chapter analyses state responses to three major issues which have emerged during the past decade. The issue of diversity which came to the fore in the wake of the Rushdie affair, as well as some of the race and culture debates in education (see Chapter 5) instigated by the McGolderick affair in Brent[1], publication of the *Murder in the Playground* inquiry in Manchester, and a Cleveland court's decision to enable a white pupil to move out of a predominantly Asian school, has been contentious[2]. Wider diversity issues about halal meat, the opening of shops on Sundays, religious holidays and prayers at work, have all been brought to the courts for adjudication[3].

Racial harassment was first raised as an issue in the early eighties, highlighted by the 1981 Home Office report, *Racial Attacks*. At that time it was perceived to be confined to council estates, and hence was treated as a housing issue. This attitude changed with the publication of the CRE report *Learning in Terror* (1988) which connected with the debates about bullying in schools (see Chapter 5) and surfaced several times as a major issue in the late eighties. In contrast, the demise of the contract has been less of a public affair although of no less importance in terms of its capacity to reduce the impact of discrimination in employment. We begin with the case study of government responses to racial violence.

Racial violence, harassment and the law

The Race Relations Act offers no protection from racial violence unless it takes place in an employment context. Racial harassment and violence has been the subject of many police and central government reports over the past decade. Although the debate has moved on from acknowledging the existence of harassment in 1981[4] to a prescriptive stage in the nineties, there is little evidence that the problem is becoming contained. Indeed the evidence appears to indicate that in recent years ethnic minorities are increasingly vulnerable to such violence, particularly Asians. Awareness of this problem has not necessarily translated into concerted action. Indeed, the Select Committee Report (1990) noted that of the 43 police authorities in 1988 only four had adopted a policy of giving priority to racial attacks despite the recommendation to do so by the same committee in 1986[5].

The nature of racial harassment and violence

Experience and a variety of studies[6] indicate that racial harassment is substantially, if not exclusively, a public-sector housing phenomenon, usually concentrated in identifiable areas, mostly on council-owned estates. The British Crimes Surveys of 1988 and 1992 suggested that Asians increasingly continue to be victims of crime in disproportionate numbers (an increase from 56% to 66% in 1992). While the level of racially-motivated crimes may have tapered off in the case of Caribbeans (from 34% to 24%), there is evidence of a sevenfold increase in attacks on the Jewish community from the HAC[7]. No region or sector of Britain is immune from the problem, including Scotland and Wales which up until recently were thought to be relatively free of this menace[8]. In fact the recorded

148

number of offences has gone up in the provinces at a higher rate than for London.

The overall number of attacks is difficult to establish due to considerable under-reporting. According to HAC only 1 in 16 acts of racial violence or harassment is reported. Nevertheless in 1984 the Metropolitan Police recorded 1,389 incidences, while the figure for 1988 was 2,214 incidents, 2,908 in 1990 and 3,889 in 1992, an almost doubling of the figure over a decade. Overall nationally the reporting figures on racial harassment have been going up over the last decade as shown in Chart 4.1. To what extent this is due to increased reporting or to an actual increase in racism is difficult to establish, although the British Crime Surveys 1988-1992 suggest only a small increase. This is contradicted by[9] other studies which suggest that recorded figures are a tip of the iceberg. Of the recorded crimes, according to the Home Office, 30% were 'cleared up' leading to 279 arrests in 1988[10]. Since then the clear-up rate has fluctuated. It declined to 13% in 1989, and was noted to be 15% in 1994[11].

Chart 4.1 Racial incidents reported to the police in England and Wales 1988-1993

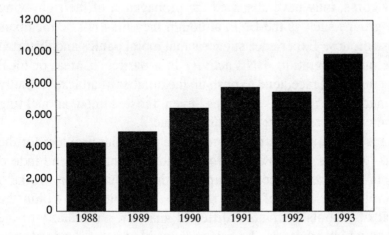

Source: Police records 1988-1993.

149

Attacks are frequent and vary from verbal abuse, spitting (which is often loosely defined as racial harassment) and assault, to property damage and arson. In many cases, a sense of siege is created, making the lives of individuals and families intolerable. Little is known about the psychological implications of what, in some cases, is tantamount to prolonged torture. Over the past decade it is estimated that some fifty people [12] have died of racial attacks, and many black and ethnic minority people have been jailed for defending themselves whilst the figures for prosecutions under the public order for racial incitement is a mere nine for 1987-1991 [13].

Victims and perpetrators

Victims are principally Asian, and to a lesser extent Caribbeans; although evidence of victimisation of other groups such as the Vietnamese and mixed families is beginning to surface, along with recent arrivals such as Somalis [14]. Women, often housebound, suffer most. Attacks and bullying generate a sense of fear which inhibits victims from coming forward and actually making complaints about harassment and violence. Research indicates that the perpetrators, usually white working-class teenagers who are frequently known to their victims, may have absorbed the propaganda of the right-wing fringe groups such as the BNP, although they may not be members of these groups. Experience suggests that moral panics and distorted debate on immigration, BNP activity in a particular area, or local arguments about race, tend to push up the number of attacks[15]. Badly explained race relations policies, even those aimed at tackling harassment, can also have a negative impact[16].

The age group of perpetrators presents a particular problem for the law, as juveniles are protected from custodial sentences and indeed there is little evidence to suggest that punishment works[17]. Furthermore the issue of racial harassment or violence within the context of schools warrants a different analysis, particularly to the extent to which adults can be held responsible for the deeds of their children[18].

The limits of law and government responses

Like other crime prevention or social policy issues this has its own constraints and dilemmas. The one most often cited by police, and in many cases housing authorities, is the lack of evidence in order to be able to prosecute, although in a significant number of cases the perpetrators are known to the victims. Critics of the police argue that police response tends to be slow; their action lacks vigour, making arrests difficult[19]. The fact that a large proportion of perpetrators are teenagers is claimed to complicate the issue in terms of liability. Lack of codified law on racial violence is cited as another problem leading to a situation where expertise in these areas does not develop and lawyers cannot focus on the issue. Others argue that motivation would be difficult to prove and such a law would primarily have symbolic importance. The proponents of this school argue that current legal provision has not been utilised seriously, partly as the due process of law tends to be subservient to political expediency. One example would be the situation in which some local authorities find themselves where their action could lead to the eviction of white families which could have adverse implications for politicians' vote banks[20]. Similarly, traditional organisational ranking of offences militates against the 'bobby' on the beat taking such offences seriously despite Home Office directives to do so[21].

The Home Affairs Committee in 1988 and 1994 has recognised the problem of both racist police officers and the under-representation of black and Asian officers in the force undermining the confidence of the ethnic minority communities in the police[22]. The fact that hitherto only two officers have been charged in all of the 73 cases of complaints against the police does not inspire confidence[23].

The government has, since 1988, established an interdepartmental Racial Attacks Group (RAG) to co-ordinate cross-department developments. It has published various guidelines in addition to the DoE's *Good Practice Guide.* The government decided not to establish special squads, similar to rape squads, to deal with the issue, although the option of developing a specialist intelligence unit within the CID to deal with organised racist gangs remains open[24]. Nevertheless some 12 racial-incidents units exist within the Met and some other services, for instance in Kent[25]. To what extent this approach is successful remains to be evaluated. Increased police patrolling in certain areas appears to reduce the rate of attacks, but this option presents a problem in sensitive areas and may even create or add to tensions.

Many black lawyers feel that lawyers in local authorities and the Crown Prosecution Service (CPS), which serves on behalf of the police, lack commitment and vigour in follow-up, a situation repeated in the courtroom by the prosecution. This is a point which was emphasised in a recent interdepartmental Racial Attacks Group (RAG) report in relation to the CPS[26]. Furthermore, both the CPS and the courts appear to be reluctant to give significant weight to the 'aggravated' element of race in legal proceedings[27]. The CPS was rebuked by HAC in 1994 for taking three years to act on two recommendations, including the one on monitoring, which was acknowledged to be flawed and not dovetailed with police monitoring systems[28].

According to the CPS there have been 140 cases from April 1993 to April 1994[29] of which 79% were proceeded with, whilst 18% were dropped due to lack of evidence. Both the CPS and the other prosecutors will have to take note of the Crown Prosecution Code which instructs them that:

A clear racial motivation will be regarded as aggravating when assessing whether prosecution is required in the public interest[30].

In addition the victim charter, according to HAC, needs to be borne in mind, as whatever applies to domestic violence should apply to racial violence insofar as the quality of provision of information and support to victims is concerned. Where local-council responses are concerned the progress varies, with some boroughs such as Leicester, Newham, and Greenwich having relatively advanced models, and others lagging behind.

On the litigation side, the extent to which hard-pressed councils' legal departments, saddled by the government's legislative reforms, have had the time to build expertise for effective litigation is questionable. Although local authorities have wide-ranging scope, in terms of legal action[31], on tackling street attacks or attacks on owner-occupiers, their record in terms of legal action in respect of their own tenants is hardly inspiring. To date there have been no more than 40 attempts to evict tenants[32], an area which warrants research. Attempts to establish a free representation service by black and ethnic minority lawyers to compensate for the lack of zeal on the part of the CPS have not borne fruit as yet. This is partly due to the difficulty of raising funds to pay legal costs in the event of abortive legal action, and partly due to the organisational development. The Law Centre movement, another option, has been severely weakened by government cuts and historically never developed prosecution expertise due to its ideological position[33].

The recent legal debate and developments

Sporadically, racial murders put racial violence and harassment on the agenda for a while. Three courses of action have been marshalled. In its review of the Race Relations Act the Royal Commission expressed support for an offence of racially motivated violence supported by the CRE as an alternative count to usual assault[34]. The government argued that it burdened the police with the difficult task of making such distinctions and gathering evidence[35]. They rather favoured influencing the sentencing policy which can be discounted on the grounds of the Newton hearing [36].

On the issue of racial harassment the proposal was put forward on the basis of the poor provision in Section 5 of the Public Order Act which requires proof as to the intention of the perpetrator rather than the objective reasonably foreseeable test. Secondly, it did not take into account the compound effect of various small actions which collectively create terror. Thirdly, only a repetition of the offence made it subject to arrest in addition to the constraint that the fine was only up to £1,000. The government argued that these measures would push criminal law boundaries into civil law (trespassing, nuisance), and could create tensions between neighbours[37]. Nevertheless a House of Lords amendment to the Criminal Justice Bill led to the introduction of an intentional harassment clause which was criticised for having a similarly adverse effect on ethnic minorities as was the case with 'sus law' in the seventies.

The third debate has been about Part III of the Public Order Act under which the CPS accepted only 18 cases hitherto, of which 13 were prosecuted with the permission of the Attorney General who was (according to the police) not responding to well-prepared cases. The police felt that they could not arrest or fingerprint people who distributed racially indictable material, and the intentionality (to incite) clause was very problematic. The government rejected these arguments but added Section 125 to the Criminal Justice Act and the Public Order Bill to make distribution of it an arrestable offence[38].

Clearly there are no simple solutions to the problem of effectively tackling this hideous crime. While the current victim-centred approach is essential, the emphasis needs to shift towards prevention and community education of perpetrators, giving hope to communities to prevent the generation of a violent youth culture. As a starting point there are some structural issues the government needs to address which may facilitate the emergence of more effective responses by councils. The key one is obviously lack of good housing in the case of some councils where black and Asian tenants can be housed without being at risk - a matter the DoE could well address. The DoE could consider developing a building programme aimed at reducing the pressure on selected estates. This has to be coupled with a rigorous and serious estates and community development programme at a highly localised level using high calibre multiracial teams in partnership with local councils' estates with the assistance of local authorities, and targeting these in terms of developing recreation facilities, crime prevention measures, improvement of layout and design, lighting, and improving the quality of accommodation.

Traditional community work approaches have been aimed at pressure group and single ethnic group politics with little experience of dealing with conflict within multiracial communities. There is some preliminary evidence that this approach may pay some dividends[39]. French experience indicates that for a multiracial-agency approach to work in terms of crime prevention, initiatives have to involve local people and should be programme-based rather than project-based and framed in a wider social policy context, i.e. resources should be set aside for long-term, well-established projects with a coherent overarching youth and crime prevention policy, rather than providing meagre resources for short-term projects lacking visible impact. Such an approach has to be combined with a developmental approach in terms of estate improvements.

The police for their part may want to explore the ideas of developing specialism among some colleagues in relation to racial harassment. One option to explore would be to develop a tier of police which has no arresting powers, on lines similar to some US forces within police sensitive areas. My experience of training police officers led me to believe that more substantial training measures, coupled with integration of racial and cultural sensitivity into promotion criteria, and explicit enforcement of disciplinary measures are required to make the service competent in dealing with multiracial communities equitably. Finally, no reasonable person could deny the importance of a serious government-led, community education programme to counter racism.

The government cannot plead shortage of resources nor is it possible to argue for a market solution to this. The black and ethnic communities, in particular the lawyers, may wish to explore the possibility of establishing an independent organisation supported partly by the government or totally on a multiracial-funding basis similar to JCWI[40] which will seek to carry out selective legal work and develop campaigns around legal action in addition to acting as a back-up centre to the local councils and various monitoring groups.

The division between those who propose that a new law is needed to establish the offence of racial harassment, and those who feel that there are enough 'generic' laws on the statute book which cover various aspects of this crime, and they only need to be utilised, is an artificial one. The fact of the matter is that both are needed. There are well-established precedents of established statute which target a vulnerable group for high penalty protection from violence in both the US and India[41].

An offence of racial harassment and racially-motivated violence, both as a civil and criminal remedy, would bring together a plethora of semi-effective and confusing sector-related remedies to focus the mind of both the local government and CPS lawyers. The civil aspect could make local authorities and police liable for damages, adding to community pressures.

As to the issue of proving motivation[42], we can draw upon both the US experience as well as the lessons from sexual assault and rape cases. In any case the charges will be brought under two counts, if one count with racial motivation failed then a second count will still stand. These measures have to be supported by a training programme aimed at the judiciary[43]. There is a lot to be said for training people who gather evidence in the police force as well as in the CPS[44], local government, and indeed even the voluntary sector. The CPS needs to focus its mind in terms of recruiting highly experienced and committed staff for such work. The local authorities would do well to appoint lawyers who are able to utilise legislation with commitment.

Contract compliance

Contract compliance has been operational in the US since 1965 for federal contracts and for local government contracts. Contractors were expected to provide data to establish good faith effort in meeting their targets established by the Office of Federal Contract Compliance (OFCCP) involving 6,000-7,000 reviews of firms employing some 3 million employees per year. This was established to co-ordinate all contract compliance for federal contracts. Larger contractors were expected to publish affirmative action plans taking local labour market factors into account. There is a system of appeals provided by the Department of Employment.

Local authorities such as Washington DC and New York employ a sizeable inspectorial force to ensure compliance on technical and social aspects. Both OFCCP and the district councils have developed a persuasive approach over the years, but since 1968 when there was the first debarment there has been a number of debarments. The provision is further aided by 'set aside' arrangements for both small and minority businesses in terms of the allocation of contracts. Contracts under this arrangement are often split up or modified to ensure that small businesses and minority businesses get a fair share of business[45]. Despite challenges from the right and some adverse decisions in courts, the compliance system has survived the Reagan and Bush administrations[46].

Most of the evidence on contract compliance suggests that it has increased employment integration of minorities as well as supported minority businesses' development[47]. Although its impact in some industries which are highly casualised such as construction industries is less notable, nevertheless overall upward mobility of black and ethnic minority workers and benefits such as training provision, mobility and job security, were found to be better in complying firms[48]. Furthermore there is strong evidence that despite early corporate resistance by employers in subsequent years, they prefer compliance to be able to show their customers that they have a socially responsible business [49]. In a recent article in the *Economist*, the performance of companies on the stockmarket who pursue policies on diversity was found to be better.

In the UK the issue of contract compliance was raised first in 1973 in relation to government comments, but was not followed up[50]. Historically, contract compliance has not raised any new principles of public policy for the UK. Government contracts have been used to support employment policies since the 19th century. The House of Commons passed its first fair wages resolution in 1891. The economics historian, Ellen Leopold, uncovered a fair wages resolution passed by the London County Council in 1889 which reads as follows:

> That the Council shall require from any person or firm tendering for any contract with the Council a declaration that they pay such rates of wages and observe such hours of labour as they are generally accepted as fair in their trade, their tender should not be accepted[51].

In the post-war period, the notion of contract compliance, although it was not called that, was mooted in the White Paper on Racial Discrimination. In paragraph 19 it was noticed that:

> Since 1969 all Government contracts have contained a standard clause requiring contractors in the UK to conform to the provisions of the Race Relations Act, 1968, relating to discrimination in employees and subcontractors do the same[52].

The government considered it its duty to take an active role in eliminating racial discrimination but concluded:

> It would be an unacceptable burden to require all contractors to supply as a matter of form full particulars of their employment policies[53].

And it lay there until 1982 when the GLC experimented seriously with the idea of compliance[54], using the Local Government Act (1978), and established a contract compliance unit followed by some other urban local authorities[55]. These units varied in terms of size and commitment and many were funded by the Section 11 resources but most sought to ask questions from firms for contracts above £56,000. The GLC's own analysis showed that only a small proportion were in compliance[56]. The compliance eventually gained the support of the IPM (Institute of Personnel Management)[57] and even that of some Tory ministers in the wake of the Scarman Report (in the context of giving priority to local labour).

By 1986, 53 authorities had established contract compliance for goods and services and 72 used it for construction. Of the total, 19 had contract compliance units (AMA 1986). Yet enforcement of equal opportunities was not a matter of serious consideration.

The free market philosophy of the new right in the Conservative government led it to take an exception to contract compliance. The government used the expanding list of issues with which the contractors had to comply, in seeking government contracts as an excuse to undermine the provision. This together with the argument that such compliance was no business of local government[58], led the government to curtail the powers of local councils in relation to such compliance. Some lobbying by the CRE led to retention of the right to seek some information by a local authority as part of the 'reasonable' information it needed to have, albeit restricted to six questions[59]. In response to the CRE's request to re-install a contract compliance provision, the government took the view that the remit of law enforcement should be restricted to the CRE and other agencies should not intervene or assist. In any case, the government argued that codes of practice issued for employers were sufficient and the CRE had failed to show that they do not work[60]. In fact, there is considerable evidence of the failure of such codes including the CRE's own code of practice[61].

In parliament, although doubts were raised about such voluntarism, and the reliability of responses to the six questions, the government took the view that, being honourable, contractors were likely to give correct information. The government also used the impending European Union legislation as a reason for curtailing compliance activities[62]. In reality the demise of the local government contract compliance units followed, accelerated by the rate-capping legislation which starved local government of cash. Furthermore, Section 11 funding was withdrawn for purposes of funding staff to carry out contract compliance[63]. Paradoxically at the same time the government took its first steps to push local government into adopting a contract culture.

Evaluations of both contract compliance experience in the UK and in Northern Ireland [64] show benefits. IPM research in 1987 showed that contract compliance not only enhanced good and fair personnel practice, it also improved health and safety, coherence of terms and conditions of employment, and enhanced training opportunities[65]. The idea of restricting contract compliance to counter religious discrimination and limiting it to Northern Ireland is intellectually untenable, and appears to be hypocritical on the part of the government. The government did not address such questions when it came to the establishment of the fair employment agency in Northern Ireland, partly due to the influence exercised by the Irish community in the US[66].

The introduction of the EU directives on contracts created another difficulty for the very rudimentary remaining provision. The secretary of state is likely to issue a new set of guidelines to check with the issue of lack of the EOP element in the EU procurement directives. The government is likely to dilute the provisions further by restricting these to employers who have been found to be discriminating[67]. This is despite the fact that litigation on procurement has established the principle of social conditions for contracts, provided they are referred in the contract notice and are *not* used to give preference to one potential contractor over another[68]. The latter conditionality obviously presents a difficulty. Recent concessions about EU rules which forbid giving preference to firms which offer jobs to the disabled has left a door ajar in terms of making a case for race equality on similar lines[69].

Paradoxically the rise of contract culture necessitates the need for contract compliance and a 'set aside' facility for both small and ethnic minority businesses. As more and more local government and health services are put out to tender to be run by independent contractors, there is a strong argument for some sort of basic compliance to aid establishment of 'capacity' within the black and ethnic minority communities. One proposed strategy has been to establish an Equal Opportunities Accreditation which purchasers could adopt as a requirement for providers/contractors across the board in government institutions[70].

Culture, constitution and the law

Britain, to all intents and purposes, constitutionally remains a Christian state, although in practice it could be regarded as a *de facto* secular state[71]. The emergence of the new right in the eighties together with the Rushdie affair led to considerable debate about issues surrounding tolerance and religious discrimination. Historically, British law has had to deal with issues related to invisible minorities since the last century.

During the post-war period the major conflict was over the wearing of crash helmets led by Sikhs, followed by *Mandela* v. *Dowell Lee*[72] where the House of Lords ruled that a school was discriminating racially when it excluded a Sikh boy for wearing a turban. In the absence of law against religious discrimination, the law lords applied a five-point test to establish what constituted an ethnic group. The line of cases which followed this led to the declaration of Jews and Gypsies (not travellers), followed by Scots (but not Muslims)[73], to be deemed as an ethnic group. This has led to intensive lobbying by Muslims. However, it has been held that discrimination against Muslims would amount to indirect discrimination if the complainant were a member of a racial group in which Islam was a dominant faith (*CRE* v. *Precision Manufacturing Ltd*)[74]. Indirect discrimination, however, is difficult to establish, and some element of 'intention' to discriminate has to be established.

Education and religious education

The government in its zeal to restrict multifaithism to ethnic minority enclaves, introduced a local groups Standing Advisory Committee on Religious Education (SACRE)[75] to take decisions about curricula in such areas where they could seek exemption from the legal requirement that the religious education teaching content should be primarily Christian[76]. In theory, those parents who are not satisfied with their locally-agreed syllabus can request separate religious education for their children; in practice, very few bother. Certainly there is no provision enabling withdrawal from secular lessons (for instance Biology). Some take the view that this is a breach of the European Convention on Human Rights, Article 2 (first protocol), although DES does not agree[77].

The issue of segregation became intertwined with the teaching of multiracial culturalism where the House of Lords in *Cleveland v The Secretary of State for Education* allowed a white parent to withdraw a child on the grounds that freedom to choose the school, albeit on the grounds of race, took precedence over other considerations including LEA decisions. Here the Education Act superseded the Race Relations Act and overturned Lord Justice Balcombe's analysis in *Hampson* that prevention of racial discrimination might be regarded as a fundamental constitutional norm[78]. Although there are no studies of the impact of this ruling on racial segregation between schools in the context of the local management of schools, given the evidence of a sustained desire on the part of the white population for segregation,[79] it is not unlikely that such a pattern will emerge eventually.

The argument for religiously (not racially) separate schools has been led by Muslims mainly on the grounds that the state aids Catholic, Anglican and other denominational (mainly Jewish) schools, therefore Muslim schools should be given similar aid. Currently there are 14 non-state-aided Muslim voluntary schools which perform on a par with the average for the areas in which they are located. The Secretary of State has generally refused permission for state aid on the grounds that there is ample existing provision, a position which contradicts the much cherished Conservative notion of choice.

The Education Reform Act (1988) attempts to accommodate the needs of non-Christian pupils and their parents in a variety of ways[80]. Although all schools in the state sector must provide for daily acts of collective worship and for classes in religious education, any parent who is apprehensive about Christian indoctrination may request that his or her child be withdrawn from either or both of these activities. In LEA schools the collective worship has to be *wholly or mainly of a broadly Christian character* when judged over a school term, but schools may obtain exemption from this provision if the local SACRE decides that it would be inappropriate, for example, where there is a sizeable number of pupils of non-Christian faiths. The principal religious traditions of the local area have to be reflected in one of the four groups entitled to be represented on each SACRE[81].

In LEA schools, classes in RE have to follow an agreed syllabus and must not be given in the form of doctrines that are distinctive of any particular denomination. Many of the existing syllabuses are multi-faith and any new syllabus adopted after 29 September 1988 must:

Reflect the fact that the religious traditions in Great Britain are in the main Christian, while taking account of the teaching and practices of the other principal religions represented in Great Britain[82].

This position has been reaffirmed in the Department for Education circular (1/94) on religious education despite many problems, leading the Church of England to signal that such worship should be abandoned as it made little sense in inner city areas.

Parents who are not satisfied with their local agreed syllabus can request separate religious education for their children in accordance with their faith, and the LEA must normally arrange this so long as the cost of such tuition does not fall upon the authority. No pupils can lawfully be refused admission to a school or be sent home for a breach of the school rules about uniform simply because he or she is complying with cultural rules about dress. Hence Sikh boys may wear turbans at school, and Asian girls may wear *shalwar* (trousers).

Family law

Paradoxically there has been less conflict in this area. The basic law governing the solemnisation of marriage in England is set out in the Marriage Acts 1949-86. These Acts stipulate detailed rules concerning the location and time where and when a marriage may take place, and who should conduct the ceremony. However, two religious denominations are exempt from all these regulations concerning the formalities of marriage, namely Quakers and 'persons professing the Jewish religion'. Sikh, Hindu and Muslim marriages can be registered in temples and mosques.

English domestic law makes no concessions, however, to other laws or customs in relation to the question of capacity to marry. A marriage in which either party is under 16 years of age, or is within the prohibited degrees of relationship as defined in the Marriage Acts 1949-86, or is already married to someone else will automatically be void. Although there has been no decided case on the subject, it is certain too that English law would disregard any prohibition falling outside its own rules, for example, the Islamic ban on marriages between Muslim women and non-Muslim men, and the Jewish prohibition forbidding Jews from marrying Gentiles.

Facilitated marriages are treated as valid in themselves, although the immigration rules make it unnecessarily hard in practice for parties to such marriages to gain entry to the UK for purposes of settlement[83]. However, if an arranged marriage taking place in England is pushed to the point of compulsion so that it amounts to a forced marriage entered into under duress, the marriage is voidable.

The only way of obtaining a divorce in England is through a decree granted by a court. Hence, neither a Muslim divorce by *talaq* nor a Jewish divorce obtained by a *get* from the Beth-din nor a purely consensual divorce arranged in accordance with Hindu, Chinese or African custom will be accepted as valid if it occurs within the British Isles[84].

The sole grounds for divorce in English proceedings is that the marriage has irretrievably broken down, and there are five alternative[85] ways in which evidence of such breakdown can be established. One of the factual situations evidencing breakdown is that the parties to the marriage have lived apart for a continuous period of at least five years immediately preceding the presentation of the petition[86]. However, a respondent may successfully defend a petition brought on the grounds that a divorce would result in grave financial or other hardship and that in all the circumstances it would be wrong to dissolve the marriage.

In a number of cases Hindu wives, resident in India, have attempted to resist divorce in England by utilising this defence, pleading that social and religious attitudes and conventions in their communities would result in their being shunned and degraded. In no case has such a defence yet succeeded because the facts of each case have revealed a level of hardship which, in the view of the English courts, has been insufficient to qualify as grave. According to Poultar, the possibility of this defence succeeding in circumstances of hardship has at least been clearly acknowledged[87].

The English courts have used a wide discretion, within certain statutory guidelines, to decide whether to make orders for financial provision upon separation and divorce and if so, how large an amount should be specified. In *Brett* v *Brett* (1985) the wife, an orthodox Jewish woman, had obtained a decree of divorce from the English courts on the grounds of cruelty under the old law[88]. Another example of indirect accommodation of a religious obligation into a financial provision order is furnished by *Khan* v *Khan*[89]. In this case a deserted wife sought to buttress her claim for maintenance by arguing that no account should be taken of her own earning capacity since it was not Muslim practice for a married woman to go out to work to earn an income. The High Court declined to take judicial notice of such a practice and pointed out the need for evidence to support it. Had she been able to provide such evidence, there is no reason to think that this would have been disregarded by the court. In two cases the English courts have been prepared to enforce contracts for the payment of deferred downer *(maher)* by Muslim husbands upon divorce[90].

165

Religious observances

Members of religious minorities are legally entitled to freedom of worship; to construct, own, manage and register their religious buildings, and to be able to swear their own distinctive oaths in judicial proceedings in different capacities. They appear, however, not to be protected by the blasphemy laws against having their faiths reviled and ridiculed in a scurrilous or contemptuous fashion. The precedents suggest that the law as it stands only safeguards Christianity and the particular rituals and doctrines of the Church of England. In 1979, in *Whitehouse* v *Lemon* (the *Gay News* trial), the only modern case on the subject (itself based on a private prosecution), Lord Scarman declared:

> The offence belongs to a group of offences designed to safeguard the internal tranquillity of the Kingdom. In an increasingly plural society such as that of modern Britain, it is necessary not only to respect the differing religious beliefs, feeling and practices of all but to protect them from scurrility, vilification, ridicule and contempt[91].

He emphasised that his criticism of the common law offence of blasphemy:

> Is not that it exists but that it is not sufficiently comprehensive. It is shackled by the chains of history[92].

After the decision in *Whitehouse* v *Lemon,* the question of possible reform of the law was referred to the English Law Commission, which published a working paper[93] in 1981 and a final report in 1985[94]. The three Commissioners disagreed with Scarman's view and recommended that the blasphemy law should be abolished altogether.

Parliament failed either to abolish the offence or to extend its ambit to other faiths, taking the view that such legislation would create more difficulties, and that in any case there were not enough cases to warrant legislation. This infuriated British Muslims, who felt powerless victims of religious discrimination when they were informed that no steps could be taken to prosecute Salman Rushdie or Viking Penguin for blasphemy. In Poultar's view, had the law been extended to take full account of the multiracial-cultural nature of British society, many UK Muslims might well have been satisfied with a prosecution for blasphemy rather than being prepared to endorse the more draconian measures advocated by Khomeini[95].

Employment

The Race Relations Act 1976 in outlawing indirect discrimination, is able to offer protection to certain ethnic group's cultural practices and religious norms in circumstances unavailable to members of the majority community. For instance, in appropriate circumstances (and these are defined according to the circumstances), Asian women have been given a concession to wear trousers at work when white women would not be, and Sikh men cannot be denied jobs simply because they insist on wearing turbans or as in the case of Rastafarians because of dreadlocks, rather than the company's prescribed headwear. In most cases employers can show material fact in resisting the above concessions to ethnic minorities[96]. Sometimes indirect discrimination can be evoked as a substitute for religious discrimination, but as larger sections of some communities become secularised the disparate impact argument is likely to weaken*. Indirect discrimination is difficult to prove and historically no damages have been awarded although exceptions are beginning to emerge.

Criminal law

The approach here has been of conformity. Culture has not been allowed to be used as an excuse for kidnapping in family feuds, limb sacrifices, overzealous punishment to children and non-attendance at

*This has happened in some cases already

school. Some customs, such as female circumcisions, have been specifically outlawed. Poultar (1990) identifies three exceptions sanctioned by parliament. These include the Shops Act 1950 allowing Jews to open on Sunday (now irrelevant), the Slaughter and Poultry Act 1967 to allow ritual slaughter for Jews and Muslims; and finally the Helmet Act 1976 which gave exemptions to Sikhs from wearing helmets when riding motorbikes and more recent legislation allows them to do so on construction sites.

At one level one could argue that courts are more willing to take cultural aspects into account as mitigating circumstances when sentencing. Yet at the same time the insensitivity of the courts in many areas continues. For instance, cases continue to come to light where interpreters are not used despite considerable progress in this area[97], sometimes leading to drastic consequences. In the famous case of *Kemarinski* (1989), ECHR held that a person charged with a criminal offence has the right of free interpreting assistance. In the UK, the Police and Criminal Evidence Act (1984) prohibits the interviewing of anyone who has difficulties in speaking English in the absence of a capable interpreter.

Lack of appropriate provisions for oath-taking and poor knowledge of ethnic minority customs persists[98]. Finally there has been much debate about the law on blasphemy as well as on the incitement of religious hatred (similar to the incitement of racial hatred according to the Public Order Act).

Recent debates and developments

Apart from the issue of blasphemy, another argument being put forward has focused on protection from religious discrimination. Firstly, the proponents argue that there are contradictions and anomalies in state provision. Having legislation to counter religious discrimination in Northern Ireland, but not in the rest of the UK, is an unjustifiable anomaly. The same applies to the offer of full protection to some groups (e.g. Sikhs, Gypsies and Jews), in tandem with a more limited offer of protection to multiracial-racial and multiracial-national groups such as the Muslims or (perhaps Hindus), though the indirect discrimination route has several pitfalls and drawbacks. They argue that protecting racial groups under incitement law but not religious groups (except Christians through blasphemy) is inequitable. The government view is that injecting law into religion would create more strife which would therefore outweigh the benefits.

Two documents are frequently invoked by campaigners seeking change: the Universal Declaration on Human Rights and International Government on Civil and Political Rights, in addition to Article 9(1) of the European Convention on Human Rights[99]. The moral and political arguments include the observation (although no evidence) that the level of discrimination against some religious groups is higher than others (Muslim campaigners in particular claim this). Ironically it is the disadvantage argument which is more frequently cited as evidence[100]. However the assertion that discrimination against Muslims has increased recently is not supported with evidence as yet. The British state has however acknowledged the presence of religious discrimination in Northern Ireland in the context of differential treatment of Catholics and has taken rigorous statutory and affirmative action style steps to counter it, pressed by the US Irish lobby.

At the heart of the matter appears to lie a number of basic questions: What is the nature of British secularism? Why does the British state remain allied to Christianity? Should the state, or even the local state, be in the business of funding the promulgation of religion at all, and if so then should it not support all faiths? Is it appropriate that the ambit of anti-discrimination law is extended by way of defining various religious groups as ethnic groups?..

The second major issue is the extent to which religious segments within the ethnic minorities communities are likely and able to resist increasing secularisation. Do they really want to confront secular and rational thought, for instance by withdrawing children from Biology lessons on the grounds of such lessons leading to unwarranted sexual awareness or fear of secularisation which flows from learning Darwinian theories? While the first argument carries considerable weight, the force of secularisation is likely to very difficult to resist. In any case, an anti-scientific and too rigid a stance is likely to be detrimental to the intellectual integration of ethnic minority children even in a *de facto* British secular society.

The crux of the matter lies in defining the separation between the personal and the public domain in terms of the right of the state to intervene in the latter, for instance for the protection of weaker and or disadvantaged groups such as children and women, or to be able to offer education on common albeit negotiated values including human rights and multicultural values.

Conclusions, issues and challenges

The debate about whether or not to have a specific piece of legislation aimed at racial harassment and violence has on the whole come down in favour of those who support such legislation. The state has been very reluctant to accept the argument that creating an explicit crime of racial harassment and/or violence would help establish case law and assist in effectively countering racial harassment. However, recently the government has accepted the notion of harassment in law under which racial harassment can be dealt, although not specifically as racially-motivated harassment. This reluctance to address racism explicitly can be put down to callous disregard for the experience of ethnic minority groups, partly based on parliamentarians own lack of direct experience and limited exposure to such issues.

The arguments deployed in the previous chapter show that the legal instruments are only one element in converting grievances into a claim or dispute. This applies even more so to racial harassment. Independent community support is necessary to assist clients in borderline cases. In this regard the most notable failure recently on the part of the ethnic minority legal community was their inability to establish an independent prosecution centre. The aim was to develop and build prosecution expertise to deal with racial harassment. The major obstacle in establishing the centre and the reason for its non-start was that of cost, including the costs awarded against the complainant in civil action.

In the case of contract compliance the intervention of the state has been malign and at odds with its measures taken in Northern Ireland making its position intellectually untenable. It has relied on voluntarism and fear of EU legislation to cloak the fact that its stance is driven by an ideological dilemma of non-intervention in the labour market, despite having had difficulties in cases where during regeneration in the late-eighties many developers never employed the local workforce. The dismantling of the contract compliance units in local government means that there is hardly any staff to check and cajole suppliers and contractors to adhere to an equal opportunity policy at a time when contract culture has disproportionately hit ethnic minorities and is likely to exclude them from the benefits which may flow from it.

Bodies such as the TECs now have a key negotiating role in relation to local business but are highly compromised in making a case on behalf of the black and ethnic minority people, as employers are also suppliers of training opportunities and the TECs do not wish to upset them as they help the TECs to meet their government set training targets. The partnership approach also compromises local government which is increasingly having to team up with local business to attract monies into their areas, often turning a blind eye to breaches or absence of equal opportunities.

It is apparent from the foregoing survey that unlike its American counterpart the British experiment with a softer version of social contract compliance was local-government-led and poorly funded with little enforcement provisions, i.e. it was more symbolic than effective. The new contract culture which has emerged in housing, health, and social services is likely to short-change ethnic minorities whose economic base has been underdeveloped by virtue of the government's malign action. In the context of urban policy, failure to develop a statutory response in the form of a minimum gesture of employing local populations in major partially or fully state-funded projects has been a regrettably missed opportunity during the period of economic expansion.

Although the US experience suggests that in some cases contract compliance can ghettoise black business by small-scale procurement or create surrogate white business, it must not be forgotten that, as Galbraith pointed out, the development of big business has historically required state sponsorship, through procurement, particularly in the initial phases of development. Although Edwards (1995) has argued that philosophically the notion of enhancing diversity (and the performance pattern of careers) is at odds with the notion of statistical parity in each sector, like many other contradictory ideas, these two notions have been appropriated and supported with confident enthusiasm by the American corporate sector. So much so that US firms which win Department of Labour awards for successful affirmative actions have had their share price boosted after the declaration. It would appear that the notion of diversity in terms of representation to reflect the labour market or consumer profile sits quite happily with targets and modern corporate marketing philosophy.

On the question of response to cultural diversity the British judiciary has been essentially pragmatic and incremental about making allowances to accommodate different cultural needs, as long as they do not strike at the fundamental principles of British law or clash with basic human rights. In the absence of a universal notion of human rights (some people regard the right to have their children taught in a particular way as a human right) and a well-defined British constitution, this debate is likely to continue. One way forward has been explored in recent essays by both Sir John Laws and Brown J. Wilkinson[101] who have argued that British common law recognises some fundamental rights as desirability of values about which there is no serious argument in the community of developed nations. Whilst it would be relatively easier to argue that state-supported apartheid or segregation or even discrimination in employment are unacceptable British norms, some issues, such as equality of welfare provision, diversity in curriculum and issues related to religious diversity, are riddled with deep philosophical disagreements. These are, perhaps in the first instance not best dealt with by judges. Platforms for arbitration on such issues are needed for reconciliation and dispute resolution between groups on matters of religious or cultural conflict. Above all, some broad agreement on the nature of British secularism and its implications for family, education and criminal law needs to be hammered out between committees. A bill of rights could instigate such a debate and can go a long way toward rectifying the current muddled position.

References

1   McGoldrick Affair in Brent in London involved the sacking of a white teacher who was well supported by local Asian parents on grounds of heresy by heavy-handed antiracist bureaucrats.
2   Macdonald et al. (1989) *Murder in the Playground*, Longsight Press, London.
3   See Section III
4   The first official acknowledgement was in 1981 in a report by the Home Office, 'Racial Attacks'. Since then a variety of government reports have been produced.
5   Home Affairs Select Committee Report, (1990) HMSO.
6   Austin, R., Luthra, M., Fitzgerald, M. and Oakley, R. (1988) 'Study on racial violence: summarised', unpublished studies in six areas for local authorities. For a summary see Luthra, M., 'Kept in the dark', *The Guardian*, 7th September 1988.
7   Mang et al. Home Office Research and Planning Unit paper 82, British Crime Surveys 1988 and 1992. Home Office Research study 132. Home Office. BCS 1992 found that 8% attacks were antisemitic.
8   See Scottish Figures from Strathclyde Region, Strathclyde Regional Council.
9   See Virdee, S. (1985) *Racial Harrassment and Violence*, PSI.
10 Met Reports have a problem with the way clear up rates are defined, as the definition includes cases terminated due to lack of evidence.
11 Met Report (1994).
12 See *Searchlight* reports 1982-88.
13 One of these cases is that of Satapal Ram. For others see Gordon, P. (1990)

Racial Violence and Harassment, Runnymede Trust.

14 Austin, R. Fitzgerald, M., Luthra, M. and Oakley, R. (1988) *Racial Violence; A Good Practice Guide for the Local Authorities,* DoE.

15 Both GACARA in Greenwich and Newham Monitoring Group claim this.

16 DoE Study (op.cit.).

17 Young people are overrepresented amongst perpetrators, Austin et.al. (op.cit.). There is considerable amount of literature on the limitations of punishment for penal reform.

18 Juveniles are over-represented amongst perpetrators as we found in our study of six local authorities. (Austin et al (op.cit.).)

19 Critics of police include Home Affairs Committee, see also various annual reports, by victim Support Groups such as GACARA in London Borough of Greenwich, Newham Monitoring Group and Southall Monitoring Group.

20 In 1988 LBG deferred a case as an evocation so as not to affect voting

21 Murder, assaults, rape, rank high on police priorities in terms of involvement. Personal experience of working with Police.

22 Home Affairs Committee reports 1988 and 1994. HMSO

23 Ibid.

24 I proposed this in LBG in my capacity as the Head of Race Equality - difficult to establish if such surveillance takes place.

25 Home Affairs Committee(HAC), 28 May 1994.(26) RAG cf. HAC. (op.cit.)

26 For the first time there is an ackowledgement the CPS may be failing on this issue.

27 This is certainly the view held by black lawyers.

28 HAC 106.

29 HAC p.107.

30 Ibid.

31 Forbes, D. (1988) *Action on Racial Harassment,* LAG and London Housing Unit, May.

32 This is an estimate. The total number of evictions is around 40-50.

33 Most lawyers who work for volunteer organisations, for Law Centres, have only defence expertise.

34 Royal Commission cf. Home Affairs Committee (1994) (op.cit.).

35 Ibid. p.xxviii.

36 Newton (1982) 4 Cr. Appeal R (s) 388 ruled that the judge should resolve any dispute in the facts between parties when passing a sentence. Archibald, Pleading Evidence and Practice (1993) pp 1669-1671.

37 HAC. Ibid.

38 HAC para. 93-97 for debate HAC 1994.

39 See Buckingham, G. and Martin, M. (1988) 'Community development, harassment and racism', unpublished paper on Camden experience.

40 Martin, I. in Dhavan and Copper, J. (eds)(1986) *Public Interest Litigation,*

Oxford.

41 See *State* v. *Beabe* (1984), *People* v. *Gorpe* (1988) and *State* v. *Smith*. All established the principle of compounded offence if racial violence takes place. Cf. Parekh, B. (1990) 'Racial violence - a separate offence', a discussion paper. All-party Parliamentary Group on Race and Community Relations refers to the principle of compounded offence in the US where there has been violence .

42 Similar arguments were marshalled when the Sexual Offences Acts were passed.

43 There is considerable resistance to such training, despite recommendations by the senior judges.

44 Currently CPS has 6.4% employees who are of black and ethnic minority origin.

45 I discovered this during my secondment with the Washington DC council in 1985.

46 Regan appointed judges who tried to undo some of the progressive gains made under the civil rights movement.

47 See Leonard, A. (1984) 'A review of the effect of the executive order 11246 on employment'.

48 Leonard, ibid.

49 In the US, 80 per cent of all jobs in manufacturing and 83 per cent of all jobs in transport, public utilities and communications, are covered by contract compliance; yet employers were very positive about it. Standing Committee, A Local Government Bill, 17 Nov. 1987. For a wider debate see US Commission Civil Rights Selection Affirmative Action Topics USCCR. Vol. 1 and 2 Washington DC USCCR

50 *Annual Report* (1973), Race Relations Board. Complained that government was not monitoring its own contracts.

51 Fair Wages Resolution 1889, LCC.

52 White Paper on Discrimination (1968) Cmnd 6234, para 19-20. HMSO.

53 Government response to White Paper, para 20. (54).

54 They were inspired by the American experience in which contract compliance has played a major role. See Edwards, J. (1995) *When Race Counts*, RP, London, N.Y., Chapter 5.

55 See Local Government Act 1978.

56 GLC report 1982 28.10 and IEC 816 -243 .83 para 3.1.

57 Contract Compliance (1988) Data Monitoring, undated.

58 House of Commons debate on the M Howard p 793 17 Nov. 1983, and the IPM report indicating ideologisation of the concept.

59 Some borough solicitors took the view that councils can go beyond the point of simply asking the question and can also ensure that there is racial discrimination in the personnel process. Memo of the solicitor to the council

to Peter Howis 198 CCU Lewisham.

60 Howard, M. (1987) in Local Government Bill, Parliamentary Commons Debates, 17th Nov. Standing Committee A P 794.

61 Ibid.

62 Large contracts have to advertise in the European Community, and minimalist compliance is indirect through the social chapter on the continent

63 Home Office Circular 1988 followed by The Scrutiny Report, July (1989), HMSO.

64 See Candry, A., 'Contract compliance go ahead in Ulster', *New Society,* 24th July 1987. The author mooted that the British government moved due to the fear of withdrawal of American social funds.

65 (1987) *Contract Compliance. The UK Experience*, IPM.

66 The government argued that it had taken on board the role of enforcement given the special circumstances of the region and had not delegated it to local authorities (PD op.cit.).

67 I am indebted to Dev. Sharma for letting me have a look at an advance copy.

68 Ibid.

69 See Parliamentary debates. ref 1 previous Chapter

70 (1994) 'Contract compliance - A new proposal', CRE internal paper.

71 I use the term here to explain that on the whole in the civic life and polity of Britain religion does not play a large role as explicitly.

72 *Mandala* v. *Lee* HL (1983) AC. 848.

73 These are based on the test established in *Mandala* v. *Lee* in the House of Lords which included a common language, shared history and geography over a period.

74 *CRE* v. *Precision Manufacturing*.

75 SACRE Standing Advisory Committees were criticised by OFSTED, the education watchdog, for producing too varied results.

76 The variation in the content up and down the country caused much dismay, and then the proportion of Christian content was fixed.

77 For a wider debate see Chapter 5.

78 The Government also refused to acknowledge the supremacy of the Act over other acts in its response to the CRE, 1994 Review.

79 Loveland, I., *Journal of Law and Society*, vol. 20, no. 3, August 1993. Harris Poll; 40% of white parents in the home counties would prefer their children to attend a single (white) race school, *TES,* 11th December 1987.

80 ERA Act 1988, Section 8.3 expects that teaching must reflect the fact that the principal religion of Britain is Christianity, whilst taking into account the teaching and practices of other religions.

81 The Church is fed up with the rather muddled position taken on the matter.

82 ERA Act (1988), Section 8.3.

83 Poultar, S. (1990) 'Britain as a plural society', report of a seminar discussion

        paper, no. 3, CRE.
84   Ibid, pp.12-29.
85   Ibid.
86   Ibid.
87   Ibid.
88   *Brett* v. *Brett*. Cf. Poultar (op.cit.).
89   *Khan* v. *Khan*. Cf. Poultar (op.cit.).
90   Poultar (op.cit.).
91   Scarman cf. *Whitehouse* v. *Lemon* (1979) AC 617, Law, p. 12. Cf. Poultar.
92   Ibid, p.13.
93   English Law Commission cf. Poultar.
94   Ibid.
95   Poultar, p18.
96   See Employment Law Casebook.
97   Female Circumcision Act (1988).
98   Access to Justice (Feb. 1993), Nuffield Foundation, 28 Bedford Square, London, presents considerable evidence of steps undertaken to improve access. See Wilkenson, B.J., Kapila Lecture, 1993. Satpal Ram is one such case. For other cases see *Search Light* issues over the last four years.
99   For a detailed discussion, see *Muslims and the Law in Multiracial Britain* (1993), UK Action Committee.
100   For evidence of this, see magazines such as *Islamic Education* and *Islamia* 1992-1994.
101   Wilkinson, B.J. cited from Loveland, I. (1993) *Journal of Law and Society*, vol. 20, no. 3, autumn.

177

Conclusion to section II and the way forward

As shown in Section II of this book, Britain has a relatively advanced system of counter-discrimination apparatus and statute mainly in the civil domain with concept, such as indirect discrimination and positive action which are well-developed in comparison with other countries, although the Netherlands and Belgium are catching up quite fast. It is quite likely that the British system is somewhat weaker in the criminal domain and in particular in the area of incitement. Currently the British CRE's powers will exceed other similar bodies on the continent. The main strategy for change and development in law is likely to be to argue for a European directive on race law legislation. Insofar as third country nationals are concerned the notion of graded citizenship likely to be a favoured outcome.

Chapter 2 evaluated the arrangements and analysis hitherto with a focus on the use of the Race Relations Act by the individual complainant. The complaints have been going up steadily. However there are a large number of barriers including victim psychology and the incentives and disincentives are not exactly loaded in favour of the complainant. The political economy of lawyering including the very cautionary stance of the CRE in the dispute processing framework do not enthuse the complainant either. Although it would seem that the old Conservative Party supported the Act through its passage, the new right element sees the Act more as an interference

178

in the marketplace.

At a much wider level it appears that both private sector lawyering as well as public-sector lawyering are victims of inertia and a culture of disengagement in relation to legal issues such as those related to racial violence/harassment and race discrimination law. In the case of private lawyers it flows from the inadequacy of the market to enthuse lawyers in an area where the complexity of the cases and lack of guaranteed income does not encourage action. In the case of public sector lawyers, bureaucratic and political strait-jacketing limits their capacity to help. In both cases the detached solo lawyer model fails the complainant.

Present government's attempts to deal with the tribunal system as proposed in the Green Paper are aimed at giving far too much power to the chairs of tribunals in terms of pre-hearing or stopping a case midstream, are all likely to be discouraging factors, particularly as there is considerable under-representation of ethnic minorities amongst chairs of tribunals and there are no conditions attached to becoming a chair in terms of having received training on race equality issues[1].

Chapter 3 charted developments in three areas, i.e. racial harassment and violence, contract compliance and the issue of cultural diversity and the law. As we have shown, the case for legislation against racial violence has been made convincingly but the state failed to grasp the fact that having clear legislation instead of a large number of statutes focuses the minds of lawyers in terms of application of law as well as building expertise. It also focuses the mind of the judiciary insofar as penal policy is concerned. Systemic issues such as the reluctance of the CPS, problems related to gathering evidence and the failure of the legal community to develop private prosecution facility are all major agenda items.

Caution is needed in relation to excessive reliance on multi-agency approaches and the need to have the support of trained lawyers at an early stage of case collation and evidence-gathering could not be more emphasised. Independent victim support is essential notwithstanding the good practice models developed by many local

179

authorities, as indeed is social action to tackle antagonism between communities, particularly young people.

State intervention in relation to contract compliance has been malign and intellectually untenable given the fact that in Northern Ireland the government has taken radical measures to tackle religious discrimination using the US model, highly motivated by the troubles and the Irish lobby in the US. The red herring in European legislation stopping such action is borne out by both the enforcement in Ireland as well as the EU support for such measures for the disabled. The notion that employers would voluntarily endeavour to assimilate a minority workforce is fanciful given the fact employers have failed to support national training schemes for which they do not see immediate benefit. As the US experience shows, employers have to be coaxed to act so as the learn the benefits of such schemes in the long run. The notion that countering discrimination is the CRE's (as opposed to government's) responsibility is to argue that the improving health of the nation is the responsibility of the local health inspectors. There is scope for the minimalist contract compliance, including the right to ask questions, which could be published backed up by a AMA/ALA database and regional inspection teams (rather than those based on individual authorities) aided by accreditation systems in which the purchaser could flex their muscles in relation to the supplier. The government's view that law enforcement is the role of the CRE is also quite contrary to the emphasis placed on community law enforcement ideology. The lack of a brief on the part of the TECs to challenge discrimination appears to be intellectually untenable. It seems strange that whilst they are supposed to train young people, they are required to do little, or have few powers, to take issue with the local employers. To this end a joint action between the TECs and the CRE may be necessary.

Insofar as systemic development is concerned, there are a number of areas where development is necessary such as establishing independent back-up centres specialising in anti-discrimination and racial harassment/violence. Within state structures here is a need to argue for a special division in the tribunal structure as well as the

CPS, and the specialist divisions in the police need piloting and evaluation.

Thought needs to be given to setting up a multiracial-faith/multicultural commission whose main function should be to educate and arbitrate on cultural and religious conflict issues. A cohesive and integrated system of community and civil rights advice is needed to replace the fragmented system in operation at the moment. The current reliance on the increasingly marketised legal service is highly inappropriate for anti-discrimination law in the absence of legal aid. In this sense the two options of franchising legal aid and/or establishing a state-supported complainant aid needs to incorporate the psychological needs of the victims of discrimination who increasingly face professionally supported opposition. Focused arrangements with targets linked to performance pay may be necessary to ensure full benefit for the complainant from the recent changes.

Despite improvement in the levels of compensation and exemplary damages, the individuals who engage in discriminatory practices are rarely punished and the cases of reinstatement are exceptions to the rule[2]. It is the shareholders in the case of the private sector or the taxpayer who foots the bill for discriminatory action. Some time ago I suggested that once the case is settled, the Institute of Personnel Management should be automatically informed for the personnel officer involved to be taken off the list. Employers need to be persuaded to check the extent to which discrimination may have flourished under the leadership of a particular personnel officer prior to recruiting such staff.

The CRE also needs to present a case to the government which is better costed and better empirically supported that the ones made hitherto. The case of Marshal has shown there are major implications in sex discrimination cases for race law; therefore alliance between the EOC and the CRE in a strategic framework is necessary. This may become institutionally easier in the light of the Labour Party's proposal to establish a Human Rights Commission with appropriate divisions on race, gender and disability. To what extent Labour will honour their agreement to implement all the proposals outlined in the second review remains an open question. However, one thing is clear: ECHR is likely to play an increasing role in shaping the British anti-discrimination law in the near future.

References

1   Gailbraith, J. (1974) *Economics and the Public Purse.*
2   Edwards, J. (1995) *Where Race Counts*, RRP, Chapter 5.
3   *The Economist,* 11th March 1995.

SECTION III

Social Policy

5 Race, diversity and educational attainment

Education and training developments over the last decade

The spectrum of education debate has changed considerably over the past decade with the distinction between education and training increasingly coming under criticism, even eroding further in some areas and with increasing emphasis on more involvement of the private sector[1]. This has partly been driven by the increasing realisation of the inegalitarian and exclusive nature of the British education system which continues to fail a large number of young people compared with other European countries, manifested in relatively poor but improving staying-on rates[2]. This concern, together with the increasing realisation amongst employers that the education system is not providing them with competent school-leavers[3] coupled with their reluctance to contribute financially to training, has led to a number of important developments[4] outlined below.

Firstly, the government has increased the contribution of the employers' perspective to the curriculum through state funded programmes such as CPVE, TVEI with greater emphasis on the world of work, as, for instance, through education business partnerships and the enterprise programme for universities. Secondly, the government has sought to develop a decentralised training programme in the form of Training and Enterprise Councils (TECs) with the hope that employers will contribute voluntarily to training, in accordance with its antipathy towards a training levy[5]. It has chosen the marketplace through contract mechanisms to increase the involvement of the private and independent sectors to contribute to vocational training with a greater focus on getting youth to come off the unemployment register[6] and recently has attempted to lure the so-called underclass with training vouchers[7]. In so doing, it has argued that a targeted and regional approach to training, guided by local employers and with funding by results would lead to improved employment prospects, based upon training, than those delivered in the past[8].

As part of this development, government initiatives have also expanded higher education provision over the last decade, leading to the removal of distinctions between the polytechnics and universities. In addition, through the establishment of NVQs, a system has been introduced for awarding agreed vocational competencies approved by various trade associations of employers followed by the introduction of broader generic qualifications such as the GNVQs to act as an alternative to the elitist A levels[9]. The new universities, most of which are inner city based, have embraced these changes at a time when members of black ethnic minority communities were increasingly seeking access to education. Over the last decade student numbers in higher education have doubled, although staff provision has increased by only 6%[10] and the duplicate introduction of both quality assurance and management systems models, without sufficient consideration of the needs of an academic culture, has particularly affected the new universities with poor teacher to support staff ratios[11]. Thus the very communities and groups who need a well-supported education receive poor provision when compared with that offered by the more established older universities.

The state school system has also been subject to radical change with

186

the introduction of the National Curriculum and decentralisation in organisational terms through LMS, which have been broadly welcomed by parents[12]. This has set schools free to manage their own budgets and increase their powers in relation to staff recruitment and school admissions policies. These changes have been accepted by most teachers, however reluctantly, although one view is that headteachers and governors now exercise too much power which had previously been kept in check by the LEAs.[13]. Furthermore, LMS has undermined the capacity of the LEA to collect data on ethnicity and to be able to coax schools into implementing equal opportunities policies[14]. So whilst local authorities remain responsible for many actions taken by schools, their capacity to intervene in school policies and the curriculum has been greatly reduced[15]. The government has also contracted out the inspection facilities and capped education budgets, leading to a loss of, or reduction, in the school advisory provision for racial equality and multiculturalism.

On the testing and outcome side, poorly managed, overly ambitious and ill thought through reforms, particularly the introduction and subsequent modifications of SATs, has led to considerable stress and reform fatigue amongst teachers. Furthermore, the introduction of league tables aimed at measuring outcome with little regard to intake has created a collective sense of demoralisation within the teaching profession about the loss of deeply-held values. There is considerable doubt about the application of 'Darwinian' principles (the bad schools will die and that the good ones will become beacons of light) and the capacity of the social market to deliver pupil mobility as guaranteed by law[16]. Both concepts are hampered by many factors such as housing, employment, education and literacy of parents, i.e. all the factors which black and ethnic minorities are more likely to have to contend with as compared with the indigenous population[17].

The removal of the further education sector from LEA control, and the reduction in the funding for FE courses, has increased the emphasis on fee paying in this sector having adverse impact on the provision of courses for adults, particularly in the inner cities[18], although to some extent, this has been contained by the rise of tertiary colleges. Incorporation of FE colleges on the one hand has created a closed competitive culture, while on the other they are expected to collaborate in partnership mode in accordance with the wisdom imparted in the last two government papers[19]. The emasculation of local authorities, the privatisation and incorporation of FE and the Careers Service, has led to a situation which may be described as education pluralism going dysfunctional with no focal point for local strategic planning which has been detrimental to the development of equal opportunities.

Urban education and the race dimension

The training crises in the inner cities were apparent from a variety of studies, including that by Gray et al (1987)[20] which showed that inner city youth were less likely to have higher grades, were less likely to follow the A level route or less likely to be employed full-time if they sought employment than their counterparts in the suburbs, but were instead four times more likely to be on YTS training programmes. The government had already acknowledged, in the early eighties, that a significant proportion of pupils were being let down by their schools. In response LAAP was launched by the DES in 1982 aimed at 13 local authorities. HMI evaluation of the scheme at the end of the eighties suggested that the programme was separatist and failed to improve attendance but nevertheless it enhanced the social and personal education of the pupils[21].

The problem of poor attainment in the inner city continued as described in a report from the Office of HM Chief Inspector of Schools, *Access and Achievement in Urban Education* (OFSTED, 1993) which was based on a survey in seven urban areas of England with high levels of social and economic disadvantage[22]. Residents, according to the report, were poorly served by the education system and this weakness in provision within individual schools was further exacerbated by poor links between schools. Good pre-school provision, according to the report, increased the chances of young children benefiting from later educational experiences. Yet access to pre-school education, however, was not assured in all areas, despite the fact that under-achievement by pupils was apparent at an early stage in primary schools. Many pupils did not recover from early failures in acquiring the basic skills. Teaching communication skills, particularly oral and written, required more skilled teachers in both primary and secondary schools.

The report also highlighted the fact that support arrangements were poor for pupils with particular learning needs. Curricular planning did not directly address the needs of children from disadvantaged backgrounds with the view to raising their levels of achievement. Much teaching was found to be superficial and lacked pace, neither challenging pupils nor securing their participation. School managers rarely set standards for institution-wide practices in planning, teaching and assessment. Monitoring and evaluation of pupils' learning and of teaching outcomes was frequently weak. The report blamed poor 'staying-on opportunities' for those who perfomed poorly at GCSE level on providers for not co-ordinating with others in the provision of a range of courses. It may also be noted that many providers gave no priority to programmes for low achievers at age 16. Youth and adult education, according to the report, varied markedly in adequacy, range and quality. Youth services were inadequately staffed.

The quality and standards of much of the work revealed by the survey were found to be inadequate and disturbing. Long-term planning, improved dissemination of effective practice, carefully focused interventions and concerted efforts between services were all required to bring about improvement. In the light of this report, the House of Commons Select Committee on Education is to examine the quality of education provided for children in urban areas. All of these obviously impinge disproportionately on ethnic minorities as they reside in disproportionate numbers in an urban setting.

Class and disadvantage

Evaluation of the Standard Assessment Task (SAT) results for seven-year-olds in 1991 and 1992 indicated that social class appeared to be the single most important influence on educational achievement[23]. The London Research Centre analysis of 1991 SATs suggested that about 37% of variation in educational performance may be explained by social status[24]. The rest, according to Nuttel's assertion, could be attributed to home circumstances and parental encouragement[25]. This view is backed by considerable evidence of factors such as homework, religiosity and family life contributing to higher than average achievement[26].

The optimism of policy-makers was dwindling as indicated by Barber[27] in *Raising Standards in Deprived Urban Areas*, who asserted that current national education policy by itself was unlikely to alleviate the huge educational difficulties facing deprived urban areas. This, it observed, was due to the fact that markets shifted resources from the weaker to the stronger, and urban schools were getting less support than they needed. In the absence of an urban policy on education the ability of LEAs to solve the problems was constrained by expenditure restrictions, and in some cases, their own poor efficiency and the lack of co-ordination within their own organisation and between themselves and other relevant service organisations. A range of possible solutions was recommended by the authors, which included:

- real growth in spending at small but predictable annual increments over a long timescale, with resources distributed towards areas of greatest need and linked to reform targets;
- a local organisation to co-ordinate child-centred services, to support schools, to promote innovation and experiment, and to co-ordinate business, education and community involvement, intervening where a school consistently fails according to recognised criteria;

- community-oriented strategic school development plans, and recognition and development of the potential of teachers, ancillary staff and other adults in the community;
- universally available child care and nursery education, primary schools concentrating on basic skills, a range of strategies to improve pupil motivation in secondary schools, a wider range of after-school educational opportunities, and encouragement of specialisation of schools (but without a return to selection by overall academic ability);
- and a continuation of the improved participation by students in post-compulsory education.

The independent National Commission on Education (1993)[28] recommended establishing locally-elected education boards supported by an Education and Training Department to plan provision, reduce primary class sizes, raise literacy and develop nursery provision and offer a diploma to replace A levels, GCSEs and vocational qualifications, have all been ignored by government. In fact the class sizes have been rising and the reading recovery programme has been axed.

The only positive response has been the launching of the modern apprentice scheme for 16-17-year-olds and government has required TECs to collaborate with local FE institutions in its White Paper on competitiveness[29]. Little has emerged by way of policy insofar as urban education is concerned during the period in which child poverty has increased, much of it concentrated in inner cities. Child Poverty Action Group also documented the disparate impact on ethnic minority groups[30]. The TECs for their part have failed to make an impact on enhancing young ethnic minority people's access to employment[31].

Another key development over the last decade has been the introduction of the compulsory teaching of a modern language at the secondary stage, in addition to the introduction of a European dimension in the curriculum. As we argue later, it is very likely that inner city schools remain quite deficient in terms of preparing their students for benefiting from the opportunities in the European Union[32].

Race and education: developments in the eighties

The publication of *Education for All* (1985)[33] gave credence to the concepts of multicultural and anti-racist education, assisted by the emerging new left and anti-racist movements within education[34]. These encouraged most self-respecting urban education authorities to adopt explicit policies concerning such issues[35]. By the late eighties, many authorities such as Berkshire, Haringey and Birmingham had adopted such policies.

With ILEA leading, many local education authorities spent considerable time developing paper policies. Some of these were implemented using Section 11 funding for the posts of advisers. Prevailing notions claimed that these often obfuscating and overstating policies relied on a 'trickle down' effect assisted by executive thrust for their fullest results. This approach had its limitations and it did not work very well in ILEA, and only marginally better in other LEAs[36], being at odds with the reflective and personal development culture in education. A cumulative model of disadvantage embracing, race, class and gender was put forward of which race and gender were slightly more successfully promoted[37]. These models invariably came to be supported by various educational actvist groups such as ALTARF, NAME and CARE as well as those within the NUT and other similar organisations.

Much of the academic energy amongst those concerned with racism in the eighties went into debating distinctions between 'multicultural' and 'anti-racist' education, almost as if they were mutually exclusive concepts. Both 'MCE' and 'ARE' in some quarters were thought to be antidotes to under-achievement; the presumption being that a curriculum more relevant to ethnic minority young would lead to improved self-esteem which in turn would

192

enhance educational performance. This was partly based on Milner's (1981) research using dolls and distracted attention from the analysis of factors relating to the prevailing racism of teachers and the issues around disadvantage, including disadvantage at home[38]. The considerable research emphasis was on comparative under-achievement using a white group as control, as opposed to relative progression, to some extent created a victimology of its own thus catalysing the culture of failure within the same groups.

Community languages and supplementary provision

Many committed educationalists worked hard to improve an acquisition of the English language and to introduce mother-tongue teaching in the wake of ministerial statements that community languages should have a status similar to EU languages[39]. Section 11 funding was used to develop good ESL models and mother-tongue teaching in some schools. The National Council for Mother-Tongue Teaching was established in 1980 and renamed in 1985. Despite this, as a recent study of four multi-ethnic schools by Tomlinson (1992) showed, in the late eighties just under half the students were learning community languages outside school, although 60%-80% of the children of different ethnic groups used their mother-tongue when interacting with their parents[40].

The DES (now DfE), had supported the development of the Bradford Bilingual Project (1979-1980) the evaluation of which showed that, while bilingual teaching enhanced learning for native speakers, its impact on speeding up the learning of English[41] was neutral. The Bedford Study, the Linguistic Minorities Project (1978-1982), concluded that the cost of primary mother-tongue teaching was prohibitive, in contrast to Bradford, which kept costs lower by employing bilingual teachers. These findings partially countered the disadvantage model prevailing at the time that mother-tongue teaching can be damaging to the learning of English.

Yet over the decade, despite support from EEC (now EU) documents (Directive 77) backed up by liberal interpretation by the ministers[42] at the time, community bilingualism remained a small affair, mainly as the education system monopolised the continuity of home and school language. Unlike many other European education systems, the British system rarely required students to be competent in two languages up until recently. There has been considerable support for mother-tongue teaching amongst parents[43], although it rarely extended to the teaching of all subjects in the mother tongue. This is partly because of the realisation that English is a transnational, elite language, and one suited to a mobile lifestyle[44]. Similarly, recent studies suggest that although pupils see religion as a matter located in the private domain, language is perceived to be the responsibility of the school[45].

Awareness, supported by evidence in reports by committee of inquiry (Rampton, 1981 and Swann, 1985)[46] that the school culture and ethos probably interacted with other factors to fail their children academically in the case of Caribbean communities and culturally in the case of Asian communities (Swann deemed that mother tongue was a home affair), gave rise to the supplementary schools movement. In the case of Asians such schemes were restricted initially to temples and mosques and only permeated into schools during the late eighties, mainly with the assistance of Section 11 funding.

It is in this movement that some of the early seeds of separatism were to be nurtured by Caribbeans on the grounds that their children were being educationally short-changed[47] as well as Asians on the basis that their language and religion were being eroded. These never really developed into separate schools in the case of Hindus or Sikhs, but in the case of Muslims there are now some 13 independent secondary schools which perform on a par with the average British school. One view is that the demand for such schools may be an expression of a demand for single-sex schools[48], a view which has been contradicted by the position taken by the Muslim Education Trust, the Muslim Education Council and the Muslim Parliament.

By the end of the eighties, through the Education Reform Act the government had decreed that learning of a modern European language was compulsory after age 11. A concession was granted to 19 community languages which could be taught, albeit subject to availability of resources and numbers of pupils in schools. Only south eastern Asian languages such as Chinese were initially granted the opportunity to have added resources for teaching, acknowledging the difficulties in learning their different alphabets, scripts and grammatical structures. At the same time, changes in Section 11 rules restricted mother-tongue teaching to its use only as a bridge to the learning of English[49]. As shown in Table 5.1, the popularity of a language is a function of either its economic utility or the extent to which it is supported by resources, coupled with the enthusiasm for those languages in a particular community. Thus European languages and languages such as Chinese and Japanese have bitter currency in the new world order.

Some languages, i.e. Urdu, are well supported by teaching provision in a large number of mosques and considerable financial support from Iranian and Saudi sources. Learning Urdu is also part of the process of Ashrafisation on part of what is a Kashmiri and Punjabi Muslim population (see Chapter 1). Given the poor uptake of some languages, i.e. Hindi, the DfE has raised the issue of efficiency in regard to holding examinations in these languages on the basis that only small numbers appear in such exams. The net effect is that in areas like London, the figures for using a second language at home range between 1-5% *

Multifaithism

The notion of multifaith education was developed by a coalition of liberal whites and moderate community leaders, but it never really struck a chord with some ethnic minority groups. It did, however, permeate into some urban schools, at least if not by choice then by virtue of the faith held by a large number of pupils. Unlike the multicultural versus the anti-racist education debate, one does not find the issue of the secularism versus religious separatism debate argued with the same passion[50]. The former ILEA approved the first

*LRC (1995) *Education the Key Facts.*

195

Table 5.1 Languages taken at both GCSE and A level

LANGUAGE	'A' LEVEL	GCSE
French	28,903	307,010
German	11,229	115,014
Italian	874	5,153
Arabic	0	638
Bengali	134	1,951
Chinese	800	1,823
Gujarati	0	1,302
Hindi	30	295
Japanese	301	452
Punjabi	159	1,444
Turkish	132	666
Urdu	789	6,190

Source: DfE (1994).

Muslim school in the early eighties, but the promulgation of multifaithism was only accepted pragmatically as being better than nothing by parents rather than being whole-heartedly embraced in principle, as shown by GLC researchers' interviews with Bengali mothers at the time[51]. Further unhappiness of a significant number of ethnic minority parents with religious education was observed by Tomlinson during the late eighties. She noted in her study of multifaith schools that Hindu, Muslim and Sikh parents, along with Christian Pentecostal parents, were less happy with their children's religious education than their Protestant, Catholic or Jewish counterparts[52].

The agenda of supplementary schools, (although I suspect there has been a decline in their number), remains the same as identified by Tomlinson[53] a decade ago, i.e. cultural identity for Asians at large, Islamic identity for Muslims and improved educational performance for the Caribbeans.

The Mandela case forced the British judiciary to deal with the issue of religious discrimination in the context of dress in schools by classifying Sikhs as an ethnic group[54] and relying on the principle of indirect discrimination. The issue of appropriate food to cater for religious needs in schools came to the fore, as indeed did the issue of sportswear[55], and these were mostly dealt with by schools on a commonsense basis. Yet little emerged in terms of a statute which would ensure that schools offered a balanced multi-ethnic curriculum, if not on a nation-wide level, then at least in the inner city districts with substantial ethnic minority populations.

Access and disadvantage in the eighties

The research agenda never really addressed the issues of primary disadvantage, the home and gender factors and their implications for educational attainment (despite some indications that girls, particularly of Caribbean origin, did better than boys). For political reasons these were never properly dealt with by the Swann Report [56]. A related debate centred around the issue of the disproportionate exclusion from school of Caribbean boys[57] and the disproportionate labelling of both Asians and Caribbean pupils as ESN (educationally subnormal) thus implicating the Education Psychological Service and its attitudes towards these ethnic minorities. There was emerging evidence that some of these patterns of disadvantage were being replicated at both further and higher education levels.

In the case of training, as early as 1983 evidence was emerging that the ethnic minority young were primarily being offered places by the public sector with limited access to the private sector[58], a situation which did not change a great deal with various programmes run by the MSC, then followed by TED (Training and Enterprise

197

Department).

Despite the good image of Asian youth as being studious and compliant, it was apparent (see Table 5.2) that they were being treated even worse than their Caribbean counterparts insofar as training opportunities were concerned. Only in London was there some degree of parity. The evidence of channelling ethnic minority students into sectors of education or employment based upon stereotyping was also emerging[59].

Table 5.2 Submission to placement ratio for ET (percentages) of 16-19 age group by ethnicity (percentages)

	White	Afro-Caribbean	Asian
South East	12.1	19.1	25.1
London	8.1	13.1	16.1
West Midlands	13.1	34.1	32.1
East Midlands	14.1	31.1	24.
Yorkshire and Humberside	19.1	21.1	24.1
North West	15.1	20.1	29.1
All	13.1	16.1	21.1

Source: MSC Ethnic Minorities and Job Centres, Feb. 1987, Table 4.9.

The improvement in staying-on rates for pupils of Caribbean origin remains minimal compared to that observed for pupils of Asian origin. Recently, the passing-on of the training role to the TECs has not made a great deal of difference to the position of these groups. Although the situation in relation to access to training may have improved, access to employment for qualified ethnic minority groups remains an issue of some concern.

In the further education sector there is much resentment amongst parents that NVQs are being aggressively marketed to the inner city residents, and in particular to black and ethnic minority youth when,

Table 5.3 Staying-on rates for 16-19 age group (percentages)

	1982		1988/1990	
	Men	**Women**	**Men**	**Women**
White	25	24	36	38
Afro-Caribbean	26	37	39	48
Asian	58	51	60	51

Source: Brown, C (1982) *Black and White Britain,* PSI, and Labour Force Surveys (1988-1990).

in their parent's opinion, they should be doing A levels.

Two features are evident from Table 5.3 in the nineties. First, the staying-on rate has improved, with particular improvement amongst Caribbean women who have also caught up with their Asian counterparts. Second, the Labour Force Survey data suggests that these changes are independent of class variables in the case of ethnic minorities. There remains, however, large variation insofar as the educational opportunities for ethnic minority women are concerned, with Chinese and African women grasping educational opportunities at a rate much higher than that for other groups. Generally speaking, the staying-on rate reflects the level of education of the previous generation of parents[60].

Conflict in schools and other institutions

Swann (1985) had raised the issue of racist name-calling[61] which was subsequently picked up by the CRE report *Learning in Terror* (1988)[62], and followed up by Kelly's (1990) analysis of around 1000 pupils in a large urban LEA. These last two reports together illustrated the offensive, alienating and pervasive nature of the phenomenon of bullying at school[63]. As shown below, much of this behaviour translates into overt racial harassment.

Table 5.4 Bullying and racial harassment

	Bullying		Racial Harassment	
	London Borough of Newham (%)	London Borough of Ealing(%)	London Borough of Newham (%)	London Borough of Ealing (%)
Asian	43	34	16	19
Carribean	35	53	16	27
White	34	58	8	7

Source: Batra, S. (1988) *In the Interest of our Children*, London Borough of Ealing; *Boosting Educational Achievement* (1988), a report of enquiry, London Borough of Newham.

Conflict in schools emerged as a major issue in the late[64] eighties, in terms of tensions in the playground in the wake of the *Murder in the Playground* (1988) inquiry in Manchester. Two other strands contributed to this debate. First, the government's emphasis on crime prevention[65] in the nineties and second, the much wider debate about bullying[66]. Murders with racial overtones and involving young people in Thamesmead and more recently Camden[67] also raised concerns around this issue. Hewitt (1992) recorded the notion of a story under each tree in Thamesmead to symbolise how the young not only thwarted the impact of anti-racist education but they also appropriated it for their own use[68]. The emergence of mixed gangs in terms of gender and race is also a new phenomenon[69], as indeed was the development of racist materials on video and through the Internet[70], where blacks could be 'zapped' as aliens. The increasing use of terminology from the language of aliens as applied to the ecology debate is also of major concern[71]. The reports cited above for the table also raise two issues: first, that pupils of Caribbean origin find school more disciplinarian than white or Asian groups and second, that parents of Caribbean origin do want more discipline at school. Currently we know very little about how the perception of discipline and its associated discipline strategies may differ between parents and teachers.

Some new ground is however being broken; Cohen's research[72] focused on playground conflict stressing the need to train dinner and caretaking staff. There are many good working models for mixed and 'all white' schools, including primary schools. Hitherto, the Piagetian notion of the incapacity of a child to grasp abstract ideas, and the notion of protecting children from the realities of life, has been an obstacle to the development of a pedagogy related to multi-culturalism and counter-racism despite the research that racism and racial bullying begins at very young age[73].

Black and ethnic minority teachers

By the end of 1988 the evidence for the under-representation of black and ethnic minority teachers in schools was well established, with only 2.6% of the total being of such a background, despite the fact that the government had specifically targeted teachers for A-type vouchers[74]. Within the ethnic spectrum Indian and Caribbean teachers were well represented although not in overall terms; other findings suggested under-representation in special needs and disproportionate representation in the lower scales with 76% found to be on salary scales 1 and 2 (see Table 5.5). Even controlling for qualifications, the rejection rate in applications was almost double for ethnic minorities, and they were half as likely to be invited or encouraged to apply[75]. A very few were in senior positions.

Considerable evidence of black and ethnic teachers' marginalisation has emerged, in particular in relation to Section 11-funded teachers[76] in addition to the evidence of the under-representation of ethnic minority students within teacher training, and the poor affinity of Asian graduates for the teaching profession*[77].

The Hackney experiment aimed at recruiting black staff from the Caribbean in the absence of suitable staff in post, yielded some interesting lessons[78]. The search for more black teachers is a laudable project, but the educational attainment of African pupils without a

* This is probably due to very traumatic experiences of first generation teachers in the UK

Table 5.5   Black and ethnic minority teachers by country of origin, sex and age-range taught (percentages)

Group	Male	Female	Primary	Secondary
Asian	10	16	12	14.2
Caribbean	17	23	20	20.4
Pakistani	9	5	5.3	7.9
Bangladeshi	n/a	n/a	n/a	n/a
Indian	54	46	51.6	47.5
Other	10	10	n/a	9.5
Ethnic Minorities	2.5	2.6	1.8	2.18
White	96	96	n/a	n/a
Senior EM	10 (24)	4 (11)	n/a	n/a
Sc 1 - 2	70 all	84 all	n/a	n/a

Source: Ranger, C. (1987), *Ethnic Minority Teachers*, CRE.

Table 5.6 Representation of ethnic minority groups in teacher training

Qualification	New-Caribbean (%)	Asian (%)	White (%)
PGCE	0.8	1.8	97.4
BED - Final	1.3	1.3	97.4
DEGREES (other)	1.5	1.1	97.4
ALL	1.0	1.6	97.4

Source: Ranger, C. (1988), *Ethnic Minority Teachers*, CRE.

noticeable presence of African teachers casts doubt upon the correlation between the presence of black teachers and the performance of black pupils, unless the issue is located in a wider context[79].

Quality assurance

In contrast to the general focus on the process of education and curriculum development, little analysis exists concerning quality assurance. OFSTED was established to complement HMI and to take over the work of the diminishing number of local authority advisers. In most cases the work is being undertaken by companies who had little interest in equal opportunities, although there is an equal opportunities audit as part of the OFSTED inspections for which the inspectors are trained. OFSTED has an Equal Opportunity Unit but little exists by way of an annual report based on the inspection. Recently it has debated as to whether equal opportunities should be part of reports or be the regular panel section in the report. Furthermore, ESL provision is excluded from such inspections. Given the power of senior inspectors who head companies and who tend to be white males,[80] the recruitment of black and ethnic minority inspectors has become marginalised. The inspection organisations for further and higher education suffer from similar representation problems.

Higher education: the sacred cow

Higher education is traditionally deemed above discrimination, so much so that neither the Swann Report nor the Rampton Report addressed this sector. It emerged on the agenda with the St George Medical School Report[81]. Searle and Stibbs (1989) showed that the proportion of post-graduate students in teaching remained lower than required, and Caribbean entrance and success rates were both lower than other groups - in the case of Caribbeans, replicating their performance profile at school level[82].

203

The over-representation of some ethnic groups in the new universities is a two-edged sword. Although good as access, nevertheless qualifications from these institutions still remain second choice for employers[83]. As we have argued elsewhere, there is little clear evidence of discrimination in terms of access to higher education, although there are problems in relation to certain sectors such as teaching[84] and social work[85] and, in particular, law and medicine[86].

Insofar as admissions to universities is concerned, multivariate analysis showed that black Caribbeans and Pakistani groups standardised for grades were slightly less, while Chinese and other Asian groups were more likely to be admitted to older universities. Although causal factors are unknown, the data largely reflects achievement of students at 'A' levels. The four older English universities still have a long way to go in terms of having adequate representation of ethnic minority students amongst their students and staff.

Such wide variations suggests that availability of academic institutions and even their proximity to ethnic concentration could lure reluctant groups such as the Bangladeshi women into higher education. One explanation is simply the lack of knowledge about education amongst some groups, particularly African-Caribbeans[87], although it still does not explain how Caribbean women manage to obtain such opportunities[88]. The issue of the higher than expected access of certain groups to higher education can also be put down partly to staying-on rates, but also to persistence, perhaps rooted in the culture of their countries of origin. This, however, is only applicable to approximately one-third of the ethnic minority applicants who resit their exams, slightly more than their white counterparts. The data does not make a distinction between resits to improve results and resits because of failures. The Asian resits rates could be partly attributed to their orientation towards medicine, dentistry, law and accountancy which have high entry qualifications and partly to parental and peer pressures to access such professions. The gender imbalance in the higher education of ethnic minorities is

Table 5.7 Chances of ethnic minority candidates entering university in comparison with that for white students (=1), standardised by academic performance

Ethnic Group	Old Universities	New Universities
Caribbean	0.66 (0.73)	1.62 (1.44)
Asian	n/s (n/s)	1.28 (n/s)
Black (other)	0.75 (a/s)	1.23 (n/s)
Indian	n/s (a/s)	1.27 (1.19)
Pakistani	0.87 (0.86)	1.22 (0.73)
Bangladeshi	1.26 (a/s)	n/s (0.86)
Chinese (other)	1.37 (1.31)	0.87 (0.81)

( ) adjusted for academic performance and socioeconomic variables.
n/s = p> 0.08. a/s = p>0.08 but >0.05: Data based on the exponential of the beta co-efficient.
Source: Madood, T. et al.(1994) *Ethnic Minorities in the Higher Education,* (PSI in collaboration with UCAS)

evident from Table 5.8 which shows that it cannot be justified on the grounds of male/female sex ratios or on the grounds of academic achievement at A level.

Clearly although the participation rates of women as compared to men in their own ethnic group entering higher education, are quite high for Caribbean women, the overall Caribbean participation rate, i.e. ratio of admissions to representation in the 18-24 age group in terms of the proportion of total admissions, is around one-third that of students of Indian origin and matches that of the Bangladeshis. The profile of these participants in terms of background warrants further analysis.

The universities on their part have been slow to respond to such issues in terms of gathering meaningful data. A 1990 survey for the Committee of Vice-Chancellors and Principals showed that only

Table 5.8 Proportion of women applicants and admissions for university by ethnic group by results of applicants and A level qualifications

Group	Female applicants as percent of males	Females accepted as percent of males	Total male / female percent accepted in higher education and in their respective proportion in 18-24 age group (in brackets)
Bangladeshi	66.8	61.8	0.45 (0.41)
Chinese	102.8	95.6	0.78 (0.40)
Indian	93.5	91.4	3.48 (1.82)
Pakistani	66.1	64.17	1.70 (1.20)
Black African	81.7	82.17	1.30 (0.42)
Black Carib.	165.9	157.44	1.00 (1.06)
White	106	99.9	84.6 (93.07)

Source: Luthra, M. (unpublished paper).

66% of universities monitor applicants' ethnic origin, while 52% monitor the ethnic background of their current staff. although in most cases the databases are often quite poor for meaningful analysis. CVCP has also issued guidelines to universities outlining best practice on the employment of people from ethnic minorities, in the wake of universities being increasingly dragged through tribunals for discrimination*. The Higher Educational Statistical Authority has asked all universities to collect data on ethnicity and a staff survey is also pending.

* In 1995 Glasgow, Manchester, London Guildhall, Kingsway College and Leeds University.

The new right, teacher training and multiculturalism

During the late eighties both government criticisms and national events were to reshape the scene on equality and diversity. Multicultural education, and in particular anti-racist education, increasingly were presented as dysfunctional and divisive by the new right (Flew 1988) and were argued to be aimed at the past rather than the future[89]. This demonisation of multicultural education was aided by the press presenting distorted perspectives on anti-racist education, such as the McGoldrick affair, which led to considerable distortions of the Bent programmes subsequently vindicated by the Lane Report[90]. In some cases, anti-racist policies were badly implemented even by the left as shown by the Manchester inquiry[91] and were possibly a distraction from the business of improving attainment[92]. The school effect was added as a further dimension in the explanation of the poor performance of some groups within education[93]. This point was further criticised for not taking school policies and teacher attitudes into account. The problem did not lie with the teacher, it was the anti-racist zealots who were creating the problem - a viewpoint which became incorporated into the 'political correctness' debate in reaction to the academic work of people such as Bernal who challenged the Eurocentric view of the development of European civilisation[94].

Government intervention in the admissions process through ERA in theory allowing schools to recruit students irrespective of location, was soon forced by the Greenwich ruling, to mean, in practice, that the means of transport, housing location, as well as the capability to fill application forms[95] were the determining factors in providing access to quality schools. Grant-maintained schools were already creaming off good pupils although the evidence of enhanced educational value is absent, yet even the good state schools are offering places on a selective basis to retain their position in the new education social market[96].

The attack from the new right (O'Hears 1988; Flew 1988), focused upon teacher training, castigating academic educators for their obsession with various 'isms' while others, such as the Hillgate group, accused them of undermining British heritage[97]. In response to this, and partly to erode the reflective element in teacher training, the government passed on the responsibility for initial teacher training to schools as well as making provision for non-graduate, non-teachers to be accepted as licensed teachers after two years of training. Similarly for Key Stage 1 teachers, the government is allowing pupils without A levels but with one year of training to become nursery teachers[98]. This vocationalisation of teacher training, together with increasing state control over the content of the National Curriculum, and the absence of any reference to race equality, means that the scope for multicultural or counter-racist teaching is much diminished and may require use of cross-curricular themes for its inclusion within a balanced, meaningful and relevant curriculum.

Curriculum battles

Insofar as the curriculum is concerned, the battle shifted to two areas, both related to the notions of national identity. ERA (1988) outlined the curriculum which, in terms of history and English, was to be defined by returning to a British imperial perspective[99] with DES abandoning its earlier position in the eighties that post-imperialist Britain needs a different kind of curriculum. Also, the reform overload during the next several years squeezed out multicultural or anti-racist education by tightly defining new subject requirements. However, in an attempt to develop a coherent curriculum the DES also promulgated the notion of cross-curricular themes like citizenship which can be appropriated by teachers to offer some scope for curriculum integration. Although the Schools Curriculum Council promulgated the notion of an equal opportunities dimension to the curriculum it was never accepted by the DES.

ERA also created the monster of 'nativism' where parents belonging to an ethnic or ideological group could obtain control of a school (for instance Stratford GMS case Southall Villiers school) and thwart progressive education. The relatively diminished role of the LEA combined with the loss of race advisers due to changes in Section 11 rules, has meant that headteachers could run their schools in most cases by the rubber stamping of decisions by parents. Social justice in most cases is not at the top of the agenda of governors, and consequently black representation has remained poor and governor training on equality lines has been lacking[100].

A part of the new right's agenda has been concerned with dominant Christian values in the curriculum. Multifaithism under ERA was restricted to the inner cities with the emphasis on Christian values and subject to the availability and uptake of resources. The schools' commitment was determined also by whether or not the newly recognised New Commonwealth community languages were to be taught as part of the National Curriculum, albeit as part of Section 11-funded access to curriculum programmes for community languages[101]. The exclusion of multiculturalism from mainstream education has strengthened the hand of the new ethnic right in the growing number of temples and mosques, who are inclined through supplementary schools to spread a narrow nationalist and particularistic ideology(see Chapter 1).

European multiculturalism emerged as a competitor to internationalist multiculturalism but at the same time could also be seen as an ally. On the one hand it legitimised the notion of diversity, while at the same time it restricted the notion of such diversity to Europe. Bilingualism in schools, in a New Commonwealth context, has been somewhat eclipsed by the emerging emphasis on learning a European language supported by a variety of measures and resources. Given the economic and cultural currency of European languages, together with a redefinition of the use of Section 11 restricting its use for mother-tongue projects only for purposes of access to English, the system has become loaded in favour of European languages.

This marginalisation of mother-tongue provision in the absence of a national language policy has coincided with two types of debates. Tosi (1989) has pointed out that the debate surrounding bilingualism has divided between two camps: those who feel that in order to enhance the status of community languages, the dichotomy between foreign languages and community languages (elitist bilingualism and minority bilingualism) needs to be resolved, and those who are interested in the role of such language teaching in terms of developing linguistic competencies[102].

Urban policy and race: government responses and their evaluation

Despite Mrs Thatcher's rhetoric about paying attention to the inner cities in 1988, little emerged as a focused policy on inner city education. The National Commission on Education report *Learning to Succeed* (1993)[103] criticised the government for its lack of such focus in allocation of resources and asked for an Urban Disadvantage Unit to be set up, which has failed to materialise up to the present. The government, through the DfE, has provided some programmes over the last decade, most of which remain unevaluated in terms of their implications for racial equality . This is somewhat surprising as the government, over the last decade, has used the phrase 'inner city' as an alternative to 'race'.

Some of these, such as the reading recovery programme, have been hailed as successful[104] but have been curtailed and a large portion subsumed into other schemes such as the Single Regeneration Budget. Lately some measures, such as the city technology colleges, have been found to be too expensive and have failed to unlock private sector resources, as has been the case with the TECs and the EBPs, all of which rely significantly on employer volunteerism to provide an interface between training and work experience. This model does not rely on the training levy (a percentage of the turnover) approach which the French have adopted to provide training to their young people. Consequently, a large number of employers prefer to poach rather than to train people.

Table 5.9 Mainstream urban education programmes

Programme	Objective	Target	Evaluation
GEST LEA receives 60% monies £8m budget in 1994/5	Improve curricular delivery, home/school links via teacher in training. Inner city schools: quarter of LEA benefit	Inner city schools: (one fourth of LEA) benefit	Not carried out
£9m aimed at truancy	To reduce truancy	School truants	
Inner City Adult Literacy and Numeracy Open Centres	To tackle literacy and numeracy among adults	10 centres mostly in inner city areas	Unavailable
ALBASU £1.1m 1988-1991	To tackle adult literacy		English literacy rates vary from 25% amongst Hindi-speaking adults to 49% amongst Urdu-speaking. Evaluation and report in pipeline
Reading Recovery Scheme			Well respected. Evaluated positively - but discontinued
City Technology Colleges	To develop good practice, high class models of technology-orientated institutions	Mostly in the inner cities, aimed at 11-18 age group, focus on GMC schools	Positively evaluated but failed to unlock private sector monies
The Technology Colleges: Sept 1993	To take forward the developments of the above		Currently number 15

Source: Luthra, M. (1995), literature survey.

Not only do the universities face the challenge of accommodating, supporting and sustaining the confidence of a more diverse student population. They also face the issue of targeting the least privileged, people with families and people learning English as their second (or more) language - all present a challenge at a time when education is being marketised and being subjected to contract culture. A recent MORI survey showed a 60% drop in the number of older people taking training mainly caused by increasing government restrictions on study hours when on benefit[105].

Table 5.10 Economic awareness programmes

Programme	Objective	Target	Evaluation
Establish Education Business Partnerships	To forge partnerships and develop a focal point for many initiatives unleashed over the last decade	National	Some 111 EBP exist UK-wide. Only 16% had any explicit element related to race in their policy
Compacts	Early target: inner cities	Extended to other areas	Evidence on improving attainment not convincing
TVEI and TVEE	To introduce the young to the world of work	16-18 age group of young people	Evaluations generally positive
City Schools Programme	To provide support to young people with behaviour difficulties	Many inner city areas	Evaluation awaited

Source: Luthra, M. (1995), literature survey.

Table 5.11 Minority specific programmes

Programme	Objective	Target	Evaluation
Section 11	Early emphasis on multiculturalism, bilingualism - some funding for equalities changed in the 1990s towards integration	NCWP groups in the early period, latterly included all minorities	Only a security report but not an independent evaluation. Generally well-supported by the profession
Ethnic Minorities Grant 1989-1994	Economically orientated training	NCWP and other ethnic minority groups	Terminated in 1994 and absorbed in SRB

Source: Luthra, M. (1995), literature survey.

Given the poor literacy rates in both mother-tongue and English amongst ethnic minorities, many older workers in particular or those who were excluded, pulled out of the market for a variety of reasons. Both the success of Workers Educational Institutes and that of courses provided by some large companies suggests that older people's appetite for education[106] remains intact and is in fact increasing.

Some pending issues

Attainment, the home and primary disadvantage

Whilst the issue of students of West Indian origin not making progress in a secondary educational environment has been subject to intense examination in some quarters, pupils of Bangladeshi and Turkish origin compared with their Asian peers came late to the notice of those concerned with such matters. The late Professor Nuttel has shown that class on its own could not account for the better performance of Indian children[107]. Nor could it explain the

213

relative lack of progression of the Caribbean child. This is particularly so when compared to the Bangladeshi and African children taking all the socioeconomic factors into account. As shown below in a study of GCSE performance in all subjects and in English and maths, almost all ethnic groups did as well or better in English than the white pupils suggesting that bilingualism may be a key factor in enhancing the learning of another language, although this does not explain their progress in maths. The impact of learning English language on GCSE results is now well established.The evidence from cohort studies on assessment from junior to secondary school suggests that although the differential patterns of achievement are established during early years of schooling, some groups slide back whilst others groups are able to exceed at secondary level. The research also noted the relative better performance of girls of Caribbean origin supporting earlier work [108].

Clearly the issue of disadvantage for at least three groups, Bangladeshis, Turks and Caribbeans, needs to be investigated in a wider context. Both home and school environments need to be analysed. The observation concerning a 'staying-on culture' amongst some groups to catch up with qualifications could be rooted in the educational tradition of the country of origin and restricted to pupils who have been partially educated in their home country. Therefore, such students are making their own progress anyway. In any case there is no reason why students who try and try again should have their success regarded as less of an attainment than that of others; in fact it should be the other way around, given the observation that ethnic minority young are quite keen to learn English. The debate about contribution of social and parental support factors (Verma et al 1987), multiculturalism and racism in school (Stone 1981), and more recently the school effect (Smith and Tomlinson 1989) to attainment still remains unresolved.

A religious dimension to the debate on disadvantage emerged in the wake of the Honeyford and Rushdie affairs. This was used to add weight to the demands for Muslim voluntary schools to be publicly funded on parity with Church of England, Roman Catholic and

Jewish schools. As argued above (and in Chapter 1), at least at national level the evidence of poor performance of the Muslim children is lacking and the support for segregated schools at best is marginal - hence the case cannot be made for such schools on educational grounds.

In terms of policy development, there are issues about assisting these ethnic groups, in particular to stay on at school. There is some evidence that offering school / student compacts may enhance staying-on rates, although they may not influence achievement and

Table 5.12 Differences in GCSE performance in total, English and mathematics scores across three years, 1990-1992

Group	English			Mathematics			Total score		
	1990 *	1991	1992 **	1990 *	1991	1992 **	1990 *	1991	1992 **
Black African	0.3	0.4	0.5	(-0.1)	0.2	0.3	3.4	4.0	4.6
Black Caribbean	(0.1)	0.2	(0.0)	-0.5	-0.2	-0.3	(-0.9)	(-0.3)	(-0.6)
Black (Other)	N/A	(-0.1)	(0.1)	N/A	-0.3	(-0.1)	N/A	(-0.8)	(0.3)
Indian	0.5	0.6	0.7	0.8	0.8	0.8	7.9	6.9	8.2
Pakistani	0.3	0.6	0.6	0.5	0.8	0.7	6.3	7.2	7.2
Bangladeshi	0.3	0.4	0.3	(0.3)	0.8	0.6	4.7	6.1	6.3
Chinese	N/A	0.7	0.7	N/A	1.4	1.4	N/A	10.6	10.7

All vs 'white' figure in brackets are not significantly different from zero.
* Slightly different ethnic categories were employed in 1990; additional categories not shown include: other black; Greek; Turkish; other European; other white.
** In 1992 non-examination pupils were included in the multilevel sample for the first time.
N/A Data is not available.
Note: 1990 sample   n = 4633 (42 schools)
      1991 sample   n = 11334 (116 schools)
      1992 sample   n = 9379 (87 schools)
Source: Thomas, S., Pan, H. and Goldstein, H. (June 1994); *Report on Analysis of 1992 Examination Results.*

215

progression is less conclusive. Nevertheless, some higher education institutions are trying out adult compacts[109] with the results of any assessment of their effects upon ethnic minority students yet to be published.

The evidence of the impact of nursery education on performance in subsequent years is well documented[110]. Athey (1990) has pioneered an enrichment programme which claims to bridge the gap[111]. Both Labour and Conservative parties have repeatedly promised to offer nursery places for all 3- and 4-year-old children, although given the cost no party has established a date when this may be on offer. A publicly funded programme managed by LEAs was initially restricted to urban areas and directed to the poorest families and unemployed parents in the form of a nursery voucher offered by the DSS and/or the Inland Revenue. The government has instead come up with a £1,000 voucher scheme which falls short of the £3,000 per child cost and requires matching funding. Further targeting could be through any of the available disadvantage indexes[112]. Significantly the debate about the role of homework in accelerating academic development has been minimal, despite some evidence[113] to this end.

There has been some attempt to set up local authority homework centres in addition to some voluntary efforts that are well utilised by pupils. Such provision is an extension of the supplementary schools movement in the UK and there is probably a lot of volunteer energy which could usefully be tapped. Accelerated education schools which focus on instructional strategies with extra homework, a longer day and considerable peer tutoring, represent another form of this concept.

Access, segregation and attainment

Regressive forces are also at play when one examines the poor access to education amongst Pakistani and Bangladeshi women. One possible reason for these barriers is the absence of major single sex institutions. In this matter, there is likely to be an agreement in terms of prescription, if not analysis, between feminists who believe that women do better in single sex schools and whose belief is supported by evidence, and those who feel that mixed schools are a bad moral influence on their daughters. Western and secular education is seen as threatening to a cohesive value system, leading to possible conflict[114] particularly in the case of groups where religion and politics are intertwined and there is less of a left wing tradition[115].

In my view, at least at the level of 14-18-year-olds, there may be a need to develop single sex educational institutions for ethnic minority women which will encourage access to further and higher education. This could play an important role in channelling minority women into male-dominated areas of education and training as well as giving access to post-sixteen education to women who are restricted on the grounds that they do not wish to attend mixed gender schools.

In a wider context a debate about the nature of British secularism is needed. Such a debate would consider the issue of whether we would want to promulgate the notion of state support for schools which may create intellectual ghettos and stop pupils learning about each others' culture and sharing educational experiences together. To cite the example of the success of Catholic and Jewish schools is problematic, partly due to the resources they have had and partly due to the fact that dialogue between British Christians and British Jews has been established for a longer period in the West than is the case between Christians and other New Commonwealth faiths.

In any case, the price Catholics have paid for going to a Catholic school in terms of discrimination has been heavy as they were identified by their school name by employers. In similar fashion, the idea of recruiting a Muslim educated at a Muslim school or a Sikh at a Khalsa school is likely to be used as an additional screening device by employers. Furthermore, such schools are likely to be mono-religious in terms of teachers and other staff - very different from a mixed, or predominantly white school. The Jewish and Catholic communities both have had a large enough economic sector of their own in which to accommodate their school leavers in terms of jobs, in addition to the extra advantage of being able to 'blend in' with the majority community. The experiences of India and Ireland (Northern Ireland has only ten integrated schools) in terms of setting up separate schools could not be regarded as positive as it prevents students from gaining experience of other people's lives.

In the struggle to capture the moral and economic domain the majority exclusionists and minority exclusionists, i.e. the white right and the ethnic right, have colluded at times. For instance, Baroness Cox introduced a Bill in 1991 backed by the Christian Schools Campaign, Muslim leaders and the Chief Rabbi to set up evangelical schools at a time when the proportion of religious education teachers was falling. A halfway house could be to argue for multifaith schools which are built on strong and proper internationalist principles, with a strong emphasis on religious education and understanding of all the faiths relevant to the students in the school. Such schools could have the same degree of emphasis on ennoblement as they do on enablement.

Equal access to training is an issue which is unlikely to go away irrespective of the administration in power. Labour's proposal for a national levy to fund training might expand the number of places but discrimination by the private sector to ethnic minority youth, despite their acquisition of qualifications, is unlikely to disappear[116]. One option would be to route the admissions through the local authorities thus undermining the scope for discrimination. The TECs for their part need to evolve a 'kite mark' exemplifying good practice, as they are able to do business with employers who have an effective equal opportunities policy. Unfortunately, the current secrecy of TECs allows them to get away with matters being hidden from the public gaze[117].

The new universities, mostly located in the inner cities, endeavoured to recruit inner city students during the phase of expansion while the teaching resources remained the same. This has often meant that a lot of students from the inner cities are not getting adequate support to raise their standards.

Erosion of the level of student grants is causing great hardship to students at university as reported in the NUS 1995 survey, particularly to ethnic minority students*, yet the budget needs to be apportioned in a much more intelligent manner, supported by a graduate tax and incorporating part-time students within a wider strategic framework.

Disruption and exclusions

Education has returned to the heart of the debate in the nineties[118] in terms of its role in tackling what is perceived as anti-social behaviour. This issue has been a main concern for the Caribbean community over the last two decades. The fact that neither Caribbean girls nor African boys are excluded to the same extent as African-Caribbean boys, suggests that it could not simply be reduced to a 'colour' issue. The recent Canterbury survey suggested that the ERA (Education Reform Act), and other reforms such as LMS (Local Management of Schools), may have raised exclusion rates by three times over the last three years. I could not help noticing the similarities with observation on figures in relation to conflict with parents amongst the Caribbean homeless males. This, together with their interactions with police officers points towards the way authority figures at large may perceive Caribbean males and vice versa in an educational context. There are issues about the relationship between the parents and pupils as there are between the teacher and the pupil which need further exploration[119]. Ghaill (1989) in her analysis has shown how young people of different groups express their dissent to school culture[120].

The issue about the dynamics between teacher expectation of some ethnic minority groups and young people from these groups who may be using their own stereotypes to act out their dissidence warrants further analysis, as does the issue of different punishments being imposed upon pupils of different ethnic origins [121].

Whatever the causal analysis, the process of exclusion is academically and socially damaging, and it makes the young prone to juvenile crime or, as Sivanandan puts it, *one exclusion leads to the*

* They are less likely to come from privileged backgrounds.

219

other exclusion[122]. In my view it also leads to some negative inclusions in society - i.e. one can become part of the alternative economy and culture of crime.

Some Racial Equality Councils, such as Lewisham and Hammersmith, have made successful interventions in terms of providing support for Caribbean youth to see them through their difficult years, by creating a role of combined youth worker/mentor/advocate. The Commission for Racial Equality needs to continue to assist the development of such specialisms and needs to encourage other RECs to adopt a similar approach to their work in this field.

The schools for their part need to evolve conciliation programmes involving parents, educational psychologists and other suitable agents - a kind of school ACAS managed by the LEA which should swing into action before the decision to exclude any student is taken. Such a provision could also embrace the development of a programme aimed at both pupils and teachers on conflict management.

The open school movement, now embracing some 100,000 schools[123] was developed in the USA and had its roots in the urban unrest in the 1960s. Some of the programmes have been well evaluated[124] and lead me to the cautious conclusion that at least in most cases they do not damage the life chances of their pupils, and that there is certainly a positive attitude towards schooling amongst pupils. The schools are often run on democratic lines and do not have conventional subjects or curriculum boundaries. Most of the activities are in the form of learning contracts in an environment in which pupils have substantial influence in the running of their schools, although there are paradoxical limitations to empowerment[125]. There has been little debate about the relevance of open schools to black pupils within the black communities, partly because most of the first generation ethnic minority parents have received a conventional disciplinarian education.

The UK-based variation of the concept has been the community school movement in Britain developed in the seventies. Although inspired by the above ideas such schools are symbolic of, rather than variants of, open schools. The movement has offered an alternative to 'sin bins' for difficult pupils who chose to go to such schools when mainstream schools have failed them. In Britain this notion has inspired the 'city in schools' project where disruptive students are given special teaching with targeted, generous resources but within school boundaries. The Home Office is also evaluating a similar programme based on a Michigan programme funded in 1993.

The British equivalent of the US magnet school is the City Technology College which appears to have been relatively inclusionist[126]. There are now 17 of these colleges, located mostly in new buildings and well-equipped in terms of new technology. They are well-provided financially, supported almost wholly by government as private sector funding has not materialised, contrary to government expectations. Some LEA schools have been allowed to become CTCs if they have managed to obtain private sponsorship.

Dwindling bilingualism and ESL teaching

Two major issues face ethnic minority bilingual students. First, there is the attraction of learning their mother tongue which had quite often not been mastered earlier. Second, there are barriers, including the fact that teaching is only available in the local religious institution, where the clergy use it for their own purposes associating their language teaching with narrow nationalism. Or it is taught in odd places by people who have little experience of teaching.

Ideally, language should be taught either in schools in the conventional way, using bilingual teachers. An alternative option is possible use of interactive learning packages in schools or at home via a distance learning model with parents as co-teachers. Using inspection and language terms the teaching of community languages needs to be incorporated within the curriculum in organisational terms. From the stand-point of pedagogical attitudes, this is an important point, but given the political economy and the historical experience that minority languages rarely survive on a large scale, the logic of creating a European and community languages organisational domain has considerable merit, as ethnic languages will come to be seen as valid in their own right. Distance learning at a very young age involving mothers is a method of mother-tongue learning and retention and needs further attention to its possible advantages and demerits, as do projects with embassies and religious establishments which are open to scrutiny and inspection by the LEA. As with mainstream language teaching, there is a shortage of qualified teachers in this field, particularly in the inner cities and there are hardly any community languages inspectors.

With the removal of Section 11 funding for bilingual teaching and the recent rationalisation of various exam boards, provision for New Commonwealth languages has been undermined. The state vandalism incurred by drastic cuts in relation to Section 11 funding is not only going to destroy the pool of expertise in this area it is also likely to slow down the improvement in attainment of some ethnic groups. OFSTED (1993)[128] in their analysis of 96 LEAs in 1991/93, concluded that there was a need for the Section 11 funding to continue, especially for newly arrived refugees and younger children from settled ethnic minority families. It urged LEAs and schools to improve and maintain the level of and quality of support for ethnic minority pupils by building on the success generated by Section 11 projects. The report emphasised the contribution made by Section 11 staff to enhancing 'confidence and progress of the pupils' and to 'support and guidance' in relation to disadvantaged groups. It also acknowledged the contribution of bilingual assistants and teachers in raising the standard of achievement of pupils. Yet at the same time the government was cutting down the size of Section 11 funding. The issue of ESL is not restricted to young people. In a recent ALBASU survey it was suggested that only 30% of ethnic minority adults including refugees reached a basic survival competency with one-third having zero competency.

Clearly as shown in Table 5.13 there is considerable public support for ESL teaching amongst the public which needs to re-emphasised.

222

Table 5.13 Positive responses to multculturalism (%)

	1983	1987	1989
Special classes in English	82	80	79
Mother-tongue teaching	17	17	19
Teaching minority group pupils history of their country of origin	43	40	41
Teach such history to all children	78	73	75
Allow traditional dress in school	46	44	43
Send children to own-religion school	-	-	15
Separate classes in religion by parental request	34	36	40

Note: the figures for 'don't know' or NA did not exceed 6% in any year.

Source: M. Luthra constructed from *British Social Attitude Surveys* (1983, 1987, 1989), SCPR Gower.

Although the support for mother-tongue teaching is low, given the support for teaching the history of their country of origin. There is scope for expanding support. Beside these figures are pre-European development in education. Given the emerging evidence of enhancement of English* competency through awareness of community language, a case needs to be made for retention of mother-tongue teaching. Furthermore, mother-tongue communication is an important tool of social control and discipline, and can be essential for conflict management within the family.

European multiculturalism versus internationalist multiculturalism

The 1983 EC (now EU) Resolution required member states to set out their policies for incorporation of the European dimension in

---

* In 1995 examinations, Asian school-leavers performed better than white peers in English.

education and invited them to implement a number of measures. The UK government prepared its policy statement with clearly stated objectives (DES 1991), including helping students to acquire a view of Europe as a multicultural, multilingual community. It is an unusual definition of multiculturalism, that, according to Tomlinson, is an attempt at removing the element of race from it. Europe is seen as having histories, geographies and cultures, based on the nation states and a common core civilisation. Young people are to be prepared to participate in the economic and social development of Europe, with all the opportunities the European Union presents. Knowledge about political, economic and social developments, past, present and future, including knowledge about the origins, workings and role of the EU are seen as important, and a sense of European identity is to be promoted through first-hand experiences, where appropriate. An understanding of the EU's interdependence with the rest of Europe, and with the world is also an explicit policy, although the latter is somewhat underplayed.

The EU as an identifiable political and economic entity is the major focus, not as a vibrant and diverse multicultural community.The government sees the Centre for Information on Language Teaching (CILT), the Central Bureau for Educational Visits and Exchanges and the UK Centre for European Education (UKCEE) within it, the Education Policy Information Centre (EPIC Europe), and especially all of its curriculum-development agencies, including NCC and SEAC, as being concerned with implementing the European cross-curricula dimension.

The programmes of study, here defined as 'matters, skills and processes' and the Attainment Targets in history, geography and modern foreign languages are means to reflect Britain's place in Europe. The advantage that flows from this remit is that these concepts could be applied equally to a wider international context and the under pinning values cannot be confined to the European dimension [129]. A similar argument could be extended to knowledge, skills and attitudes. The ten knowledge goals include 'to examine political and economic trends and policies for their present and future effects upon European society'. The five skill goals include 'to develop social skills in support of linguistic skills as a means of effective communication'. The five attitudes and values include 'To make pupils aware of and help them respect the rich cultural heritage they share with other young Europeans'. Overall, as it stands the National Curriculum is explicit on a coherent European dimension, not integration.

European education now involves teaching and learning *about* Europe within a global perspective, preparing students for life, work and citizenship *in* Europe by enriching students' personal and social education *through* direct experience of interaction and contact with Europeans. This is further underpinned by a strong Eurocentric assumption about the historical, intellectual and institutional values and developments shared and developed (in isolation) by all Europeans.

A number of organisations including ESHA are encouraging schools to develop a European dimension.The Council of Europe promotes human values in Europe and publishes many attractive and informative documents. The European Union through its local agencies provides opportunities to learn about Europe in a workplace setting and funds teacher and student exchange schemes, curriculum link programmes, joint conference and work experience and placements plans. Most of the programmes focusing on the over 16 age group occasionally provide preparation resources for an exchange and generally tend to require transnational partnerships which are expensive to build and administer. Teacher exchanges run into the problem of cover and support during preparation or during the exchange itself[130]. Many projects require matching funding either by parents or by the local authorities.

There is little by way of an urban focus in European educational policies. Often, resources generated through the ESF fund aimed at training have been very difficult to match with local funding. Until very recently the definition of the word 'migrant' which excluded third country nationals, disqualified British ethnic minorities from benefiting. Given the emphasis on matching funding and the need for subsidies by parents to support European multiculturalism, it is likely that the ethnic minorities young would be debarred from the process by virtue of their low income and high unemployment rates Nevertheless, given the historical interactions between European and other civilisations, the contribution of these cultures to European development, the mutual dependence between Europe and other parts of the world, there is an opportunity to subvert the British government's agenda and appropriate it for wider purposes. Furthermore, Europe offers a unique opportunity for exploring international perspectives on modern circumstances.

Even in its present form, European multiculturalism is a powerful tool for widening the debate on the nature of the subject and for embracing internationalism.

From anti-racism and liberal multiculturalism to counter - racism and critical multiculturalism

Many forces, including reform fatigue, budgetary cuts, restructuring of Section 11 funding, the new right's consolidation of the anti- 'politically correct' discourse, as well as the climate of anxiety which emanated from the enforcement of a contract culture upon education have all led to a situation where anti-racist and multicultural education have been severely curtailed. Often, these matters are left to black and ethnic minority teachers and academics who themselves are vulnerable and marginalised in the educational institutions where they work.

This has, however, failed to dent the academic and pedagogical discourse on multiculturalism, diversity and environmentalism; all have emerged as major narratives linked with the ongoing debate about post-modernism and identity (see Chapter 1). The impact of these narratives hitherto has been confined to sophisticated quarters of social science education. The marketisation, vocationalisation and what could only be described as de-intellectualisation of education including that of teacher training has been acting as a wall against the permeation of such discourses, via training, to the professionals. While academic institutions resist responding to diversity, educationalists are coming under increasing pressure to maintain their credibility in having to cater for diverse student populations, particularly those attending inner city institutions.

Table 5.14 Anti-racism and counter-racism

	Anti-racism	Counter-racism
Focus	Person-based organisations, mainly academics and teachers attitudes	Behaviour and attitude of whole organisations and communities including parents, caretakers and movements
Modality	Educational development Rights, fairness	Wider personal development. Active alliance with the person against his/her racism
Emphasis	Race and racism	Citizenship. Democracy. Human rights
Relies on ...	Explicit anti-racism	Explicit and implicit, through plays, the hidden curriculum, art, drama and cross-curricular themes
Principal arguments	Past and current, moral and legal arguments	Plus future, plus sound business,Educational attainment and professional arguments
Segregation on religious grounds	Ambiguous position	Non-segregationist - but taking competeing equalities into account
Segregation on gender grounds	As above	As above
Parental rights	Ambiguous	Balanced against professionals. Some values non-negotiable

Source: M. Luthra (forthcoming).

Table 5.15 Liberal and critical multiculturalism

	Liberal multiculturalism	Critical multiculturalism
Group analysis	White people treated as homogenous culture	Assumption challenged and ethnicity acknowledged
Identities	Identities are obvious and so are diversities	Hybridity, diversity not obvious constructed historically
Common culture	Work towards common culture conceived as consensual	Full of tensions which flow from power abuse by dominant groups
Difference	Emphasis on difference	Hybridity, diversity as a challenge to internationalist Macdonalisation
Otherness	The idea of otherness leading to nation-centred discourses	Can be a beginning of the liberation from prison of ethnocentric paradigms
Equality	Traditions of other nations counter-egalitarian hence regressive	Traditions also resist McDonaldisation*
Values	No absolute values (relavist) or universalistic	There can be some shared values, i.e. generalism
Segregated education	Concession to particularistic education	Only on grounds of enhancing access to attainment
Underpinning analysis	Rationalist and secular	Internationalist, Humanist and multifaith

Source: M. Luthra (forthcoming).
*I have used the term here as used in the literature on post-modernism to indicate the domination of American culture in the global youth culture.

Many of the criticisms of liberal multiculturalism are directed towards its focus on ethnic minority students, which leaves white parents out of the debate in the case of schools. Furthermore, the

Islamic critique of its obsession with rationalism and the critique from the left that it panders to fundamentalism all need to be dealt with. The emphasis on 'the other' can lead to the development of narrow nationalist perspectives. Similarly the confrontational person- centred approach of anti-racism needs to be modified to locate it in a wider context of doing things, such as developing a practical means of tackling racial bullying, and forming alliances with like-minded and influential people in institutions.

As shown in Table 5.13 there is considerable support amongst the white population for some measures, which needs to be widened by relying on the educational attainment and economic arguments.

Young people inclined towards racism also tend to be poor achievers - a point that needs to be driven home to parents that counter-racism education can open educational windows in the modern world. Much of the good work of Verma et al, Troyna et al focusing on all-white schools, the Runnymede Trust work on cross-curricular themes, Young's work on science and racism, all need to be disseminated to schools through an inexpensive medium.

The public attitude towards multiculturalism is not wholly negative when it is not cast in a separatist or segregationist light in a climate of moral panics, whipped up by the British tabloids as shown in Table 5.13. The challenge lies in taking them along through a process of critical multiculturalism and counter-racism, using notions of citizenship and human rights.

Given the evidence of hyphenated and composite identities at primary level and exclusionary tendencies observed amongst young white children at a very young age, the challenge lies ahead in producing curricula and pedagogical approaches which enable the young to grasp the idea of multiple identities with equal emphasis on similarity and differences.

Conclusions, issues and challenges

Clearly, given the differential achievement and progress of different ethnic minority groups, a causal analysis relying on systemic exclusions or discrimination as the only factors in causal analysis is insufficient. The debate and research has to shift from comparisons to relative progression amongst different groups and at obstacles which impede this progress. Areas such as homework, incentives and rewards systems utilised by different ethnic minority groups and the extent to which parents regard education of their childeren as a joint project in terms of allocating resources support and time as well rewards are all issues which warrants further analysis.

In this respect a clear distinction betweeen disadvantage and discrimination is necessary as there is the need to make a distinction between primary disadvantage, i.e. literacy rates of parents born in developing countries, to secondary disadvantage, i.e. the child may have poor competency in English because of poor parental competency or by virtue of the fact of living in an inner city environment which as we have shown can contribute a lot to poor attainment of groups which are located in such environment, in particular and increasingly if this overlaps with locations of poorly performing schools.

Clearly most of this attainment when translated into examination results is replicated in higher education, which relies on traditional entry requirements. As the evidence suggests, although some universities have been found to be discriminating, there are question marks against some institutional practices leading to higher failure rates in some areas amongst ethnic minorities students. The overall evidence in relation to higher education admissions and applications rates suggests these differences to be marginal and explainable by other factors. In terms of staff, universities including new universities still fail to reflect the population they serve and the old universities such as Cambridge and Oxford still have an under-representation of ethnic minorities students and staff.

This then brings us back to school education trapped in an imperialist and elitist mode with too early specialisation favouring early developers and those who come from middle class white backgrounds. This is then further amplified by the differential

230

availability of pre-nursery education and replicates itself in higher education.

Generally speaking, the ideological differences between the two main parties are organisational rather than philosophical. Labour is more likely to return schools to LEA supervision, although LMS is likely to be retained in a modified form with the increased influence of parents. This is likely to create a 'parentocracy' influencing schools with their own prejudices and pandering to a notional nostalgia for the 'good old days' of their childhood. The National Curriculum, however, is likely to remain for the foreseeable future, albeit with some flexibility allowing for specific situational and contextual adaptability. Labour will continue to publish information on schools and is likely to abolish A levels which will probably be replaced by a baccalaureate scheme for the provision of educational and training qualifications in a much more attractive, coherent and streamlined format. Education is likely to remain in the grip of parentocracy, hence narrow nationalism.

The challenge here is how to present counter-racism in a positive light, without alienating the white working class male youth who feel beleaguered[126] and uncertain about their indigenous identity and their parents who remain somewhat hostile to internationalist education. The pre-nursery education in its current form is unlikely to stay, as it will not assist the people it is aimed at, and the extent to which it is utilised by the ethnic minorities communities would warrant monitoring.

Clearly educational attainment has ceased to be a major issue with almost all ethnic minority groups achieving better results than their white counterparts and in all cases making a major improvement which have been translated into good representation at university level. The outcomes are however differential and it remains a matter of concern that young people of Caribbean origin are not progressing well when compared to the newly arrived Bangladeshis and Chinese school pupils who historically tend to be at a disadvantage in competency of the English language. Furthermore it is difficult to deduce from the foregoing evidence that it is a simple matter of colour given the better progression of African pupils and the very disadvantaged Bangladeshi pupils.

To what extent this progression of Asian pupils could be attributed to the support given by the ESL progrmmes such as Section 11 or to multicultural education remains a moot point. As to the issue of poor performance of Caribbean pupils, studies are needed matching single parenthood and class to see if these factors are influential. In either case and without being complacent it would appear that despite reform fatigue and damage to race equality and multicultural education over the last decade the educationists appear to have stemmed the tide of disadvantage.

Nevertheless a number of changes warrant attention. First, the Secretary of State should insist that responsibility for monitoring and evaluating all ESL work should rest with the DfE and OFSTED. Second, central funds should be transferred from all the other departments and managed by the DfE as a single specifically targeted fund. Third, it should be allocated to LEAs, grant maintained schools and colleges not on the basis of competitive bids, but on the basis of proven need, and for as long as the need was proven. Fourth, the SCAA should develop both policy and advice in this area of work (it could, for instance, publish definitions of fluency levels which tie the assessment of language learning into the national curriculum). Fifth, OFSTED should require registered inspectors to include appropriate experts on their teams and to inspect the ESL work in schools with a substantial proportion of second language speakers. Finally, the Teacher Training Agency should give urgent consideration to the establishment of adequate initial and in-service courses so that all Section 11 teachers working in the field could have access to accredited training.

Returning to the issue of attainment, a word of caution is also necessary here in drawing inference from grossed up data on attainment in which better performing pupils make up for the disadvantaged inner city schools. Studies are needed to deal with some very severe areas of disadvantage such as Tower Hamlets. The impact of local economies in sustaining morale and providing role models to the newcomers should not be underestimated.

This picture of progression and disadvantage at school level appears to be replicated by different ethnic groups at university level admissions although a lot more, mostly women, appear to be contributing to the 1% Caribbean figure which is only a slight under-representation in the sense that the Caribbeans have made considerable progress. Little is known about the routes being taken by students and the extent to which these students enter classical universities and their failure or drop out rate.

In either case the issue of under-education of women of Bangladeshi and Pakistani origin remains an unaddressed issue. Although according to OPCS, in the age band of 18-29, their economic activity now matches that of Indian girls, their educational activity at higher education level lags behind. This is partly attributed to the need for employment and partly to the suspicion with which Muslim parents continue to see the higher education system. Although the separate school argument cannot be advanced on the grounds of under-achievement of Muslim young people, there is an argument for having single sex women's colleges on the grounds that Muslim communities need a transitional period of adjustment. Instead of pumping resources into separate religious schools of any kind, separate women's colleges or universities could be funded to assure Muslim parents about the moral climate in educational institutions and to improve young women's access to education.

Normally religious educational institutions are well endowed with funding. The rather muddled and undefined position of the British state and its selective funding of some denominational schools of any sort defies the logic as to why tax-payers should promulgate religion when such provision should be funded by the congregation. As the experience of many societies shows, tax-subsidised religious segregation is no more intellectually defensible than racial segregation.

Multicultural education needs to be taken out of the 'ethnic ghetto' and widened with a critical element acknowledging the diversity of white groups. Counter-racism has to be professed in a human rights and citizenship framework with a view to working with the individual against his or her racism. Schools need to broach the issue with parents and serious public relations drives aimed at parents, including parent governors are needed.

In the area of conflict in schools three issues remain to be dealt with. First it needs to be emphasised that racial harrassment is probably hindering the full utilisation of ethnic minority pupils' potential. Second the main area of conflict which needs examination is the dynamics between largely female white teachers and boys of Caribbean origin. Research is also needed on exclusion rates in relation to boys who are taught by black teachers and those where the head or the deputy head are of Caribbean origin. Data needs to be separated for African pupils to enhance meaningful analysis. On the practical side and in terms of the community agenda, programmes such as open schools need to be explored with multiracial staff for such pupils. The City in Schools programme needs to be evaluated.

Although most schools set homework, the role of collaborative and individual homework needs further analysis. Although the educationalists are divided on homework the evidence seems to support the fact that it plays a key role but can be exhausting for teachers. Here there is desperate need to establish homework centres supported by the army of retired teachers and other professionals.

On the issue of critical multiculturalism and counter-racism, studies are needed as to the form in which a package would be acceptable to both pupils and parents alike belonging to ethnic all groups. The findings could then be incorporated in an Education Charter for parents which all schools need to persuade parents to sign. A similar charter could be developed for students and teachers in higher education.

Despite its limitations European multi-culturalism presents an opportunity to open the debate on ethnicity and multiple identities within Europe with the scope for widening it. Some concerted effort is necessary, to ensure that inner city pupils do not miss out learning European languages or having exposure to European culture. To this end some European exchange centres need be evolved with a partnership between the DES, the trade unions (who have such centres for young people) and local educational institutions and possibly the travel agent sector. This will remove the reliance on personal resources on part of inner city parents.

Much of the academic literature does not filter through to schools and universities although many educational magazines do a good job in the process of permeation. A broadsheet on multicultural education through the internet could be an invaluable tool for teachers. The CRE could team up with the Open University and OFSTED to produce sector and key stage-based economical packages for consumption by schools.

On the issue of quality assurance, OFSTED and its equivalent in higher education needs to produce an annual summary report on equal opportunities including its analysis of the results every year. A good practice guide by OFSTED on equal opportunity and diversity would be helpful. The University Grants Commission on its part should seek a report on equal opprtunities every year prior to deciding funding allocations. In the case of training, standards in equality are needed which are checked by an independent TEC inspectorate. Generally as elsewhere there is a need to integrate quality and equality assurance systems. The current Dering review of the 16-19 age group does not take the issues of inner city education including the role of TECs into account.

As Sniderman and Piazza (1993) have shown in their overview of American educational responses to racism, education can enhance racial tolerance amongst the majority community. In Britain it remains an under-utilised tool in tackling racial prejudice. The challenge lies in using the educational tool in such a way as to take the majority community along as well as in tackling racism along with emerging sectarianism (see chapter 1).

References

1   For a wider view of commercialisation, see Dale (1985) *Educational*

Training and Employment: Towards New Vocationalism, Pergamon Press. For a literature survey of career steering and ethnic minority training see Cross, M., Wrench, J. and Barnet (1990) 'Ethnic minorities and the sareer service - An investigation into processes of assessment and placements', DE research paper no.73.

2   See Finegold, R et.al (1991), *The British Baccalaureate,* IPPR Education and Training Paper, no.1.

3   See Atkinson and Spilbury (1993), IMS Study for ALBSU, which suggested that in reading and basic mathematical skills, one third of British workers were less than competent. See also the report of NEDO and the Training Commission - *Young People and the Labour Market: A challenge for the 1990s,* (1988) National Economic Development Office.

4   For a history of the CPVE and TVEI see Dale (op.cit.).

5   One argument against this, apart from the hope that the employers are willing to contribute, is that it will lead to earmarked taxation. Recent surveys suggest considerable support amongst employers for such a levy in Britain.

6   Much of the earlier scandals around companies defrauding TECs were associated with this kind of zeal.

7   Training Vouchers were introduced with the knowledge that for young people YTS training had become discredited (see Dale).

8   For a criticism of this kind of pocket / patch approach see Chapter 7.

9   GNVQ were introduced in 1992 as an alternative to A levels. The Deering Review has proposed technical 'A' levels to be established.

10   I am thankful to the AUT for this information.

11   I am grateful to Professor Wendy Couchman (Head of School, Education and health studies, South Bank University) for these observations.

12   DES (1989) *Parental Awareness of School Education: Interpretive Report.* Public Attitude Survey Company on behalf of the DES. The survey found little difference of opinion between various ethnic groups.

13   This point was repeatedly made in conferences on the ERA and the Equal opportunities

14   Data collection has been made voluntary.

15   LEAs retain only 10% of the budget, and now have very few inspectors and advisors to influence the curriculum. They are expected to provide cover for instance for cases of discrimination although they only have one vote on the governing board.

16   *Greenwich* v. *Secretary of State for Education* 1988. The Court of Appeal decided that Greenwich could not give preference to pupils in its own boundaries on the grounds that the GLEA was spending more money on education per capita to support Greenwich pupils.

17   Often, the observation that almost every child obtained its first choice of

school is cited as evidence, but they did so before LMS. The question here is whether working class parents are able to utilise the much vaunted choice or is it merely a choice for schools to justify themselves on behalf of 'good' pupils from middle class families. (See also unpublished DFE report on choice).

18   This has had an impact upon courses in language teaching, many of which have disappeared.

19   Government White Paper, 1993 (HMSO).

20   Gray, J. et al (1987), 'Education and training opportunities in the inner city', *Youth Cohort Study England & Wales*, Youth Cohort Series, No.7, Training Agency (PE).

21   Stradling and Saunders (1991), cf. Mitler.

22   OFSTED (1993) *Access and Achievement in Urban Education.*

23   Report of the ENCA Project, SEAC, Leeds University 1992, and Assessment Testing of 6 and 7 year olds, Leeds University, NUT 1992.

24   McCallum, I. (1991) *Pupil Attainments and Social Status*, LRC.

25   Nuttall, D. (1986) *Educational Opportunities For All?*, Research Studies RS 1040 / 86 ILEA Research and Statistics Branch.

26   Doria, P. (1990) *Escape from Disadvantage*, Falmer Press, Brighton.

27   Barber,M. (1993) *Raising Standards for Deprived Areas*, NCE Briefing Paper, 16 July.

28   Report of the National Commission on Education (1993) *Learning to Succeed.*

29   (1994) *Helping Business to Win*, HMSO. (1994) *Forging Ahead*, HMSO.

30   Bradshaw, J. (1992) *Child Poverty and Ethnic Deprivation*, National Children's Bureau for UNICEF.

31   Jones, T. (1994) *Ethnic Minorities in Britain*, PSI.

32   Inner city schools had poor European policies due to a lack of appropriate resources including modern languages teachers. See Bright, M., 'Children of Europe Unite', *The Guardian*, 4th July 1995.

33   The Swann Report (1988) *Education For All*, HMSO.

34   Boddy, M. and Fudge, P. (1992) (eds) *Local Socialism*. See also Ousley, H. on local authorities' initiatives. See also Bal,l W. and Solomos, J. (1991) *Race and Local Politics*, Macmillan, Basingstoke.

35   Ibid.

36   I am grateful to Neil McLelland, the Director of Education, London Borough of Greenwich, for this comment as he was Division 6 Senior Officer in ILEA in the 1980's. In his view, anti-racist education did not permeate down to the Education Divisions.

37   Ibid.

38   Milner, D. (1975) *Children and Race*, Penguin. Swann also avoided discussion of the home factors.

237

39   For early account see 'Pressure from the Caribbean community'. See Parekh, B. (1992) 'The hermaneutics of the Swann Report', in Gill et al. (ed.) *Racism and Education.*

40   Tomlinson, S. and Smith, J. (1992) *The School Effect,* PSI.

41   For an account of the Bradford Bilingual Project 1979-80 and Linguistic Minorities Project, Bedfordshire, see Fitzpatrick, P. (1987) 'The open door', *Multilingual Matters,* Clevedon.

42   EC Directive 77.486/EEC

43   See ILEA report on Bangladeshi mothers view of schooling in Tower Hamlets Research Studies, RS 1029/86.

44   In India, for instance, people do not see English as the possession of the English. Instead it is perceived as a transnational language of the clever and the mobile.

45   See Chapter 1.

46   For a critique of Rampton and Swann from a left perspective, see Mullard, C. (1992) 'Rampton, Swann and after', Working Paper 3, Centre for Multicultural Education, Institute of Education,

47   Tomlinson, S., 'The black education movement' in Arnot, M. (1987) *Race and Gender Equal Opportunities in Education,* Open University.

48   Anwar, M. (1994) *Muslim Youth in Britain,* Islamic Council.

49   Home Office Scrutiny Report, July 1988.

50   There is a lot of debate about multifaith teaching versus separate subject or one religion teaching. A large section of Muslim parents in particular resist multifaith teaching.

51   See ref. 43 above.

52   Tomlinson, p.86.

53   Tomlinson, cf. Arnott.

54   *Mandela* v. *Lee.* See Chapter 1.

55   Most of these cases appeared in the north of England and were resolved by withdrawal or by a change in dress rules.

56   See Parekh, B. in Gill et al. (ed.), (op.cit.).

57   Early evidence of exclusion and ESN is articulated by Tomlinson and Arnot in *Race and Gender...* (1985), Open University. Recent data by Cooper et al., *(Children and special needs)* suggest the West Indians are still twice as likely to be put in special needs schools.

58   For an overview see Wrench, J. (1994) 'New vocationalism, old racism and the career service', *New Community,* vol. 16, no.3.

59   Brooks, D. and Singh, K. (1982) 'Aspirations of Asian school leavers', Warwick Univerity with Leicester.

60   Luthra, M., an analysis of educational outcomes , OPCS and other data (forthcoming).

61   The Swann Report (1985) *Education for All,* HMSO.

62   CRE (1988) *Learning in Terror.*
63   Kelly, E., 'Use and abuse of racial language in secondary schools', in Dumphries and Vernon (eds) (1990) *Race Relations in Urban Education*, Falmer Press, Brighton.
64   The McDonald Enquiry, (1988) *Murder in the Playground*, The Burnage Enquiry, London Longsight.
65   See conference papers on Role of Education in Crime Prevention.
66   See Kelly, E. (op.cit.).
67   The murder of Steven Lawrence in the London Borough of Greenwich led to research by Hewitt cited below.
68   Hewitt, R. (1992) *Sagaland*, London Borough of Greenwich.
69   Hewitt,R. (1992) *Sagaland,* LBG. See Luthra, M., 'Kept in the dark', *The Guardian*, 17th September 1987.
70   Cohen, P., (1993) lecture given at CMMR, Institute of Education. 'Young boy network', *New Stateman*, 5th May 1995.
71   I am thankful to Crispin Jones of the Institute of Education,showing me an un-named author's notes trawling literature on ecology, and littered with phrases such as 'aliens', 'foreigners' when making references to plants. 'Plants and prejudice: barriers to an understanding of the multicultural city ecosystem', unpublished paper.
72   Cohen (op.cit.).
73   Cohen (op.cit.).
74   A type vouchers were used for selection of professionals as part of the immigration policy and were restricted only to New Commonwealth immigrants.
75   Ranger, (op.cit.), pp. 66-7.
76   Home Office Scrutiny Report (1990), Section 11 of the Local Government Act 1966. See Dorn, A. and Hibert, P. (1987) 'A comedy of errors' in Troyna, B. (ed) *Racial Equality in Education,* Tavistock, pp 59-70.
77   UCCA (1992-3) 'Ethnic origin background to the commentary', unpublished summary paper, supplement to 31st Report. The figures for teaching applications were merely 2% for Asians, 3.3% for black African/ Caribbeans and 72% for white applicants.
78   I am thankful to the Director of Education for Greenwich, formerly head of Division 6 of ILEA, who shared this view with me.
79   Schools were not prepared for the arrival of teachers from the Caribbean. Unpublished paper by the Director of Education for the London Borough of Hackney for Institute of Education.
80   OFSTED system requires independant inspectors to set up teams to bid for inspection contracts..
81   CRE (1988) *Medical School Admissions*, Report of Formal Investigation at St George's Hospital.

82   Searle, P. and Stibbs, A., 'The under-representation of ethnic minority students in post graduate training', *New Community*, January 1989.
83   This is less true of technical courses related to engineering or electronics.
84   Ranger, C. (op.cit.).
85   See Chapter 6.
86   Jocelyn Barrow Report (1994), CRE. See also St. George's Hospital investigation by the CRE (op.cit.).
87   Stradling and Saunders, cf. Mitler.
88   See Table 5.9.
89   Flew, A. (1990) *Power to the People*, Sherwood.
90   The Lane Report, Brent's Programme for Racial Equality in Schools, HMSO, April 1988.
91   See full title *Murder in the Playground: The McDonald Enquiry, The Burnage Inquiry*, London Longsight.
92   Stone, M. (1981) *The Education of the Black Child*, Fontana.
93   Smith, D.J. and Tomlinson, S. (1989) *The School Effect*, PSI.
94   Bernal, M. (1993) *Black, Athena*, Free Association Press.
95   CRE (1992) Secondary School Admissions, The Watford Enquiry, investigation by CRE.
96   See full title. In fact the evidence is to the contrary as evident from a DFE (1990) study not published at the time of writing.
97   O'Hears, A. (1988) *Who teaches the teachers*, Social Affairs Unit.
98   DES (1992) *Reform of Initial Teacher Training*.
99   Runnymede Trust (1992) *Equality Assurance.*
100   'Social justice and social division; Governor training in a school', in Gill, D., Mayor and Blair (1994) *Racism and Education*, Sage Publications with Open University.
101   New Commonwealth languages were recognised as community languages. Many LEAs had bilingual teaching assistants to aid young pupils' access to English. See OFSTED (1993) op.cit.
102   Tosi, A. 'Neither a deficit nor an asset; children's bilingualism in education', *New Community,* vol.15, no. 4, July 1989.
103   NCE (1993) *Learning to Succeed*, Report of the National Commission on Education, Paul Hamlyn Foundation.
104   Ibid.
105   Tuckell, A. and Birch, 'Learning For a Life Time', *The Guardian*, May 1995.
106   Kinsha, P., 'People power', *The Guardian*, 16th May 1995.
107   For a summary of Nuttel, D. et al's work see Report on the Analysis of 1990-92 Examinations Results, publ. AMA in conjunction with Institute of Education.
108   Sammons, P. (1994) *Gender, Ethnic and Socioeconomic Differences in*

Attainment and Progress - a longitudinal analysis, Curriculum Studies Department, Institute of Education.

109 One such COMPACT has been in operation in London Borough of Greenwich and University of Greenwich.

110 Sylva, K. (1990) 'Does early intervention work?', *Archives of Disease in Childhood,* vol.64, pp.1103-1104. Clay, M. (1985) *Early Detection of Reading Difficulties,* Heinemann, London.

111 Athey, C. (1990) *Extending Thought in Young Children,* Chapman Hall, London.

112 Vouchers have not been taken up by local authorities. The actual cost per child is around £3000. Likely to help working, rather than non-working, mothers.

113 Luthra, M. and Carr-Hill, R. (1996) 'Ethnicity and homework', unpublished mimeograph, Institute of Education.

114 Most tecs admit this. LFS:1985-1995. Suggest high unemployment rates amongst well qualified ethnic minorities

115 Tecs are often afraid to tackle equal opportunities issues with large employers as they might upset them. They do not publish data and tend to be unaccountable.

116 The same sector which is growing rapidly is a particular culprit

117 Ghailil, M. (1988) *Young Gifted and Black,* Open University, Milton Keynes.

118 See Gilbourne, D. (1991) *Race, Ethnicity and Education,* Unwin Hyman.

119 Sivanandan (1995) unpublished lecture.

120 Barr, R. D. and Colsten, B. et al (1975) 'An analysis of six evaluations. The effectiveness of alternative public schools', *Viewpoints,* vol. 53, no. 4, pp1-30.

121 For a succinct overview of these see Trickett, et al. (1985) 'Natural experiments in an education context', *Am Jrnl Community Psychology,* vol. 13, no. 6.

122 Gruber, A. J. and Trickett, E. J. (1987) 'Can we empower others and the paradox of empowerment in the governing of an alternative school?', *Am. Jrnl. of Community Psychology,* vol. 15, no. 3.

123 OFSTED (1993) *Education Support for Minority Ethnic Communities.*

124 Shennan, M. (1993) *Teaching about Europe,* Council of Europe, Strasbourg.

125 Sniderman, P.and Piazza, T. (1993) *The Scene of Race,* The Bellkop Press, Cambridge Mass.

126 The black Director of Education in Hackney, Gus John, has made this point several times

6 Race, health and social services

Before embarking upon this chapter it is important to reiterate that the impact of two recessions over the last decade on members of black ethnic minority communities has been severe in terms of unemployment and poverty[1]. Both of these affect physical and mental well being. That, in the case of many ethnic minority groups, has followed a period of feeling just about settled and secure after the trauma of immigration and consequent difficulties which flow from dislocation, and uncertainty of social and legal status. There is evidence that restructuring of the economy with corresponding organisational changes have hit ethnic minorities disproportionately[2].

Like education and training, there has been a significant government attempt to create convergence and collaboration between health and social services professions, partly driven by statute, and partly by the ideal of the notion of care in the community. This has given a greater role to social services, and local government has handled the transition quite well and in some cases even saved money. There has even been flotation of the notion that, given the very successful reform undertaken by local councils under very difficult circumstances, the local authorities could act as purchasers on behalf of their residents, if not manage the whole of the health service.

Both health and social services have been subjected to internal market forces with increasing their interaction with the private sector. The health service reforms in terms of marketisation have been established to a more advanced stage as compared with the social services[3] enabling the latter to pace itself. The government has also offered social services exemptions from market testing on the child care element and supporting the change with a ring-fenced fund provided under the Community Care Act (1990). One exception to this has been the rather rapid de-institutionalisation of mental health and relocation of such clients in the community creating many interactional issues with other areas of provision such housing[4] and follow-up support. In addition the issues around the establishment of clients' needs which often leads to variations in the contribution clients are expected to make, remain unresolved.

Like the health service, social services reforms were aimed at increasing welfare pluralism and choice. As is the case with health the extent to which this has happened, leading to an improved choice and wider spectrum of providers, remains questionable[5]. At least during the period of 1989-1993 a significant proportion of the community care budget was directed towards restructuring arrangements[6]. Now that this process is almost complete it would be interesting to see if the system can engage with disengaged groups including members of ethnic minorities groups, given an increased element of discretion, means testing and charges levied upon clients.

Despite these changes the shortage of social workers in the inner city areas continues[7]. Both consumerism[8] and the new managerialism have undermined the public service spirit and morale of social workers, yet at the same time there is a lively debate about the use of resources and the role of other sectors in making care provision. Most social service departments still find themselves in a position where they can only carry out emergency and reactive child protection work, encouraged by the Children Act (1989), and act as arm's length managers in relation to day care and residential provision[9].

Whilst social services in recent history have had decentralised operations, such a decentralisation process in the health service has been taken almost to the individual hospital trust level coupled with considerable delayering of the regional and district health authorities. This undermined many of the corporate developments in health including early developments in race equality in the eighties. The quality assurance drive has not as yet produced a central health service quality assurance management mechanism, unlike those established in social services, the SSI, which has a brief for ensuring equal opportunities.

Health and social services: institutional responses

Historically there has been no duty enshrined in the Race Relations Act to enhance community relations in the health service, unlike Section 71 of the RRA which bestows such a duty upon the local councils. Furthermore, there has been little central government-funded provision for the health service equivalent of Section 11 funding, historically made available to social services. The latter were also part of the municipal anti-racist movement. Consequently, up until 1988 there has been erratic and patchy policy development on race equality in the health area with the exception of projects, such as anti-ricket campaigns or sickle-cell assistance, aimed at specific conditions. However, social services departments in urban areas were well on their way to developing organisational structures and had appointed race equality advisers by the mid-eighties.

In 1988 the CRE published its second report on social services which marked a decade since the ADSS/CRE report[10], and indicated that a number of developments had taken place. Inspired or supported by its newly formed black perspective committee, CCETSW (the professional social work training body) was beginning to address the issue of social work training during the late eighties. Race units established in the early eighties survived well in social services departments[11] leading to significant policy development in some authorities. In contrast, an analysis of developments in district health authorities by Hicks (1988) showed that only a handful of authorities had gone as far as to produce

244

policies[12]. The good practice initiatives demonstrated by some authorities were not being replicated, according to a National Association of Health Authorities survey[13]. Lack of a credible database could have serious implications for the enforcement of quality standards in health[14] and indeed in social services and the same could be said of race equality issues.

Even in the case of social services progress has been patchy and uneven. In a recent audit Butt et al (1992)[15] have shown that although some 92% of social work departments monitored service by ethnicity, only one third took the trouble to analyse it. Only one fifth of social services departments had utilised the positive action facility to recruit and train minority social workers[16]. Inspired by CCETSW guidelines, some of the innercity academic institutions also have attempted to integrate race equality issues into their courses, although over the last decade there has been a battle over the retention of an anti-racist perspective in social work training the curriculum of which is controlled by CCETSW as the government has made rightwing appointments[17] leading to the rolling back of earlier developments in the eighties[18]. Several training models were developed[19]. In particular, Katzian models of anti-racist training were taken on board because of their Rogerian[20] origin with an emphasis on the personal and self at the expense of organisational and community development. The concept of 'curing' white people of racism through therapy was attacked by the rightwing of the political spectrum for its disabling nature and by the left for being distraction from dealing with institutional racism in British society[21].

As shown in Table 6.1 from the roughly equated data from two surveys, two years apart, only a quarter to one third of social services departments who had paper policies had gone as far as to develop action programmes and they were even less likely to be documented, although the figure was likely to be much better for urban authorities. Most of the development appeared to have been confined to three major areas, i.e. child care and day care related services (Table 6.2). Many (20%) social services departments were still planning some development and there had been some progress

Table 6.1 Equal opportunities survey

	CRE Survey 1988 (%)	Butt et al 1990 (%)
Equal opportunities policy	61	64
Statements	34	63
Action programmes	24	32
Action programme documents	9	15
No	70	92

Source: Developed by M. Luthra from CRE (1988) and Butt et al (1992)

Table 6.2 Council social services responses

	Projects funded (%)	Intended projects (%)
Child care and related services	26	53
Welfare advice	16	-
Day care and related services for the elderly	29	3
Women's refuges	6	-
Disability	6	-
Mental health	3	13
Anti-racist training	-	13
Translation services	-	13
Recruitment of EMG workers	-	13
Sheltered accommodation	-	3
Total	35	38

Source: Constructed by M. Luthra from CRE Survey, 1988, *Racial Equality in Social Services*

246

over the two years (1988-1990) including the progress in doubling the number who were using the ERKM system to monitor, although as Butt et al point out most authorities did not do much with the data gathered.

Table 6.3 Rough indication of progress amongst social services departments (1988-1990)

	CRE 1988	Butt et al 1990
EM foster and adoptive parents	23	59
Same-race policy	18	58
Translation	49	51
EM home helps	-	36
Recruit EM workers	-	56
Race unit / adviser	23	27

Source as in Table 6.2. EM = ethnic minority

Some of the above aspirations, particularly in controversial areas such as same-race adoption/fostering policy leading to a campaign to recruit more black and ethnic minority adoption and foster parents, has progressed along with the recruitment of ethnic minority workers (Table 6.3). The key preconditional variables enhancing the likelihood of these initiatives were if the department had given priority at planning stage to ethnic minority groups and if it had an equal opportunity policy, followed by a clear implementation strategy and someone responsible for implementing it.

By the beginning of the nineties it was evident that some health authorities with significant ethnic minority concentration had appointed advisers, mainly at very junior level, with a considerable lack of understanding in relation to the experience and skills needed to manage change[22]. This was made worse by the lack of support from management for policy entrepreneurs and advisers to do their job properly[23]. To add to this, there had been a dramatic drop in the number of ethnic minority members on health boards between 1989 and 1992 in direct contradiction to government intentions[24] with the result that the number of paid executive members at the last count was extremely low[25].

Table 6.4 Ethnic minority representation by District Health Authority and Regional Health Authority (percentages)

Ethnic Group	Regional Authorities		District Authorities	
	1989	1992	1989	1992
White	97	99	97	98
African	0.5	0.7	0.2	0.1
Caribbean	0.9	0	0.8	0.1
Asian	1.4	0.7	0.3	0.4
Other	0.5	0	0.3	0.4
Total	221	141	3155	1562

Source: Jewson, N.I. et al, King's Fund Survey, University of Leicester, *BMJ*, 1993, 307: 604-5.

As shown in Chart 6.1, the Department of Health has taken some steps over the last decade following the appointment of an adviser. The extent to which the government and the DHSS has been well served, in terms of development of intellectually rigorous research and funding strategy, remains a moot point.

The last five years has seen a growth in the number of DoH funded voluntary sector organisations[26], mostly short-term projects[27], in the arena of mental health[28]. A brief analysis of nation-wide health projects revealed that the majority were on a short-term and neighbourhood basis, lacking the capability for long-term survival and were rarely evaluated[29]. Such short-termism has created false hopes, increased staff turnover, and has hindered development of

Chart 6.1 Developments over the last decade

Year	Event	Development
1989	Health Adviser on Ethnicity	Department of Health appointed an adviser on ethnic minority health and established a £500,000 fund for project development on the health of minority ethnic populations.
1990	Department of Health / King's Fund Grants	Dept of Health funded three projects of the King's Fund Centre to examine dimensions in mental health, career issues and purchasing. The King's Fund awarded DHAs with grants to examine equity and diversity issues in purchasing.
	Departmental Working Group	Established in the Dept of Health to examine health and ethnicity issues.
1991	Patients' Charter SHARE	Introduced to make NHS more 'user sensitive'. Dept of Health funded King's Fund Centre to develop an information exchange on health and race issues.
	Primary Care Code of Practice	Secretary of State for Health launched voluntary code drawn up by Commission on Racial Equality who has also published a guide to contracting for health authorities.
1992	Chief Medical Officer's Report	Devoted a chapter to minority ethnic health issues whilst *Health of the Nation* identified minority ethnic populations as a 'special group'.
	Guidelines on patients' spiritual needs	NHS Management Executive issued guidelines on religious needs of patients from different faiths.
1993	King's Fund Grants	Grants provided to four statutory/voluntary partnerships to improve access to health care for people from minority ethnic populations. King's Fund Centre also produced a professional checklist for managers on improving services for minority ethnic populations.
	Ethnicity and Health Unit	Established for a period of three years by the Dept of Health to encourage and support various agencies in improving access to health services for minority ethnic populations. Dept of Health published a guide for the NHS as part of its *Health of the Nation.*
	Department guide	
1994	Equality across the board and ethnic minority staff in the NHS	NAHAT/King's Fund Centre published Dept of Health funds report announcing recommendations on increasing minority ethnic non-executive NHS memberships. Secretary of State for Health launched 8-point action plan to achieve equitable representation for minority ethnic groups at all levels in the NHS.
1995		Demise of the Ethnic Health Unit. Discussions about an Equal Opportunities Unit.

expertise. Similarly poor research strategy has led to ad hoc, empirically unreliable, and often duplicating research, concentrating on a few ethnic minority groups and unamenable to wider generalisations.

Two areas, however, show clear progress: first, the appointment of some front line bilingual workers; and second, the development of translation units, in many cases in the form of joint ventures between social services and health. The early development of the appointment of race equality advisers in the late eighties and early nineties was undermined by restructurings in the nineties subsuming many of the equal opportunity advisers into new posts.

Disadvantage and discrimination in health: indicators, patterns and issues

Research on race and health has been primarily located in the epidemiological paradigm with both 'sociology' and 'political economy' perspectives marginalised[30]. Furthermore, such research has been criticised for using rigid, often too broad, ethnic or race categories such as Asians or blacks and thus often confusing the two. In many cases, the data was not standardised by socio-economic background or class, or split by UK/non-UK born categories.

Ethno-epidemiologists, unlike social scientists, feel less comfortable with socially constructed notions of race and ethnicity and have difficulty reconciling it with the relatively objective status of genetics.

There is a major problem of treating ethnicity and race as proxy for 'pure' and fixed gene pools, particularly when no attention is paid to stratifications within ethnic minority communities or their medical social histories. Critics[31] have, however, failed to come up with a proposition as to what should be used as a substitute in place of race and ethnicity to represent or identify a group of people who at any particular time may share a fairly homogeneous pool of genes. There

250

is however agreement about smaller group studies taking race, class and gender into account which will thus help refine the data obtained. OPCS in 1991 has attempted to broaden its ethnic categories but the number of groups still remains small and the census does not incorporate an adequate number of variables on health.

Table 6.5 Mortality rates per 1000 by condition and place of birth (males only)

	Ireland	Indian Sub-continent	Carib. Continent	African Continent
All circulatory disease	117	133	77	127
Coronary heart dis.	114	136	45	113
Cerebrovascular dis.	123	153	176	163
All respiritory disease	157	88	61	105
Bronchitis	150	74	48	73
Pneumonia	171	107	82	145
Tuberculosis	330	400	175	516
All extenuating causes	190	85	105	99
Accidental poisoning	272	128	157	130
Fire/burns	410	121	248	98
Homicide	366	261	242	105

Source: Constructed by M. Luthra, compiled from Balrajan, R. and Bulsu, L. (1990), 'Mortality amongst immigrants in England and Wales 1979-1983' in Britten, M. (ed.) (1990), *Mortality and Geography: A review in the mid-nineteen eighties,* OPCS Series D8 No. 9, London.

251

Despite these limitations, research has repeatedly thrown up patterns which cannot simply be dismissed as art effects, although observations need to be further refined. In terms of mortality, clearly different male populations are at risk from different diseases. For instance, the Irish-born followed by Caribbean-born are at high risk from external causes whilst African-born followed by the Asians are at high risk from tuberculosis. Respiratory disorders leading to high mortality are high for the Irish-born followed by the African-born. Whilst the Indian-born are at particularly high risk from coronary heart disease, the Caribbean-born are at high risk from cerebrovascular disease.

Table 6.6 Mortality rates per 1000 by condition and place of birth (female only)

	Ireland	Indian Sub-continent	Carib. Continent	African Continent
All circulatory disease	118	136	141	136
Coronary heart dis.	120	146	76	97
Cerebrovascular dis.	117	125	210	139
All respiritory disease	140	104	101	106
Bronchitis	149	88	99	94
Pneumonia	122	115	116	118
Tuberculosis	164	1009	112	557
Accidental poisoning	303	79	160	132
Fire/burns	188	214	191	313
Homicide	215	279	511	185

Source: Constructed by M. Luthra, compiled from Balrajan, R. and Bulsu, L. (1990), 'Mortality amongst immigrants in England and Wales 1979-1983' in Britten, M. (ed.) (1990), *Mortality and Geography: A review in the mid-nineteen eighties,* OPCS Series D8 No. 9, London.

The SMR* patterns are very similar for women in each group except that in some cases the figures for women are not lower than males, contrary to expectations, as is the case of Indian-born women for coronary heart disease and fire burns. The major difficulty with this data is that it relies on place of birth as a substitute for ethnicity, and that although the data is standardised by class (assuming a set of health risk factors in Britain correlate with class in the developed world), this may not apply very well to people who may have spent half or two-thirds of their lives in the developing world.

Chart 6.2 Long-term illness by ethnicity

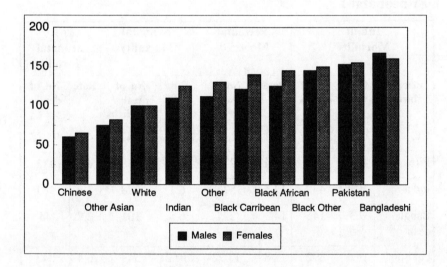

Source: OPCS 1991.

Generally, mortality rates over the last two decades amongst ethnic minority groups of New Commonwealth origin have been higher than those of the indigenous population but have been declining over the last decade[32]. The data from OPCS suggest that overall sickness rates of ethnic minorities vary from one group to another. As shown in Chart 6.2, with the exception of other Asians and Chinese, all ethnic minority groups are likely to suffer disproportionately from

* standard mortality rates.

chronic illness as compared to their white counterparts. Another noticable feature of Chart 6.2 is the extent to which the communities which have high economic activity amongst women have a lower rate of female illness (one worrying exception to this being the black other category which is predominantly made up of young black people of Caribbean origin who tend to have a high rate of illness). As yet little is known about the relationship between long-term illnesss and class, economic activity and occupational clustering amongst ethnic minorities.

Table 6.7 Infant mortalities (perinatal, neonatal and post-neonatal)

Place of birth	Infant Mortality		Perinatal Mortality		Neonatal Mortality		Post-neonatal Mortality	
	Rate	No. of deaths	Rate	No. of deaths/ stillbirths	Rate	No. of deaths/ stillbirths	Rate	No. of deaths
UK	9.7	21,515	10.1	22,503	5.6	12,438	4.1	9,077
Eire	10.1	269	10.4	279	5.9	158	4.1	111
India	10.1	459	12.5	576	6.1	278	3.9	181
Bangla-desh	9.3	145	14.3	225	6.5	101	2.8	44
Pakistan	16.6	892	18.8	1,022	10.2	549	6.4	343
Caribbean	12.9	274	13.4	288	8.4	179	4.5	95
East Africa	9.3	255	12.8	351	6.3	172	3.0	83
West Africa	11.0	128	12.7	149	8.0	93	3.0	35

Source: Balarajan, V. and Raleigh, S.(1990), 'Variations in perinatal, neonatal and post-neonatal and infant mortality by mother's country of birth 1982-85', in Britten, M. (ed.)(1990),*Mortality and Geography: A review in the mid-nineteen eighties*, OPCS Series D8 No. 9, London.

Whilst overall adult mortalities differ slightly for different ethnic groups, both pre-natal and post-natal infant mortalities amongst women in some ethnic groups tend to be higher than average. These appear to have been declining albeit at differential rates, with children of Pakistani-born mothers being at most risk[33] followed by infants of African and Caribbean-born mothers. The risk for Pakistani-born mothers increases very significantly in perinatal situations.

Thus in the case of explaining high coronary heart disease and high non-insulin diabetes among Asians, the epidemiologist has relied on the existence of a 'poverty gene' evolved to preserve energy[34] in conditions of scarcity of food which would be detrimental to health in an affluent setting. The difficulty with this argument is that given the highly stratified nature of Indian society and strong traditions of endogamy, upper caste (by inference upper class) people should be relatively protected from a high level of coronary heart disease risk, a position which is not supported by any evidence. As yet, there is little evidence to show that living in a relatively affluent area offers better protection to Panjabis who have lived in the bread basket of India for a few hundred years. In any case, it is very difficult to support the hypothesis that poverty levels endured by the masses in Europe and in India were very different some 400 years ago.

The underlying presumptions about the purity of a gene pool also presents a problem. For instance, in the case of Punjabis it would be difficult to argue that they have had a homogeneous, static gene pool. Recently Barker has come up with a more plausible theory which, relying on the low weight versus heavy weight data on babies born in 1980, standardised by class, shows that low weight babies tend to be at higher risk from diabetes[35] and coronary heart disease in comparison with plump babies. This observation, although claimed to hold true in India, does not explain the difference in risk levels between rural and city people in India and the theory still has to accommodate the low coronary heart disease amongst Mediterranians.

Furthermore, genetic studies including DNA research[36] show that variation between ethnic or national groups (6-10%) is far less than the variation of 84% between members of a defined group. Correlations between morphological factors, and skin colour and disease patterns, at best are tenuous and the idea that the information flow is oneway, i.e. from the DNA to the phenotype itself, is also under scrutiny[37]. Given the limitations of this explanation, some epidemiologists rely on cultural factors while others prefer systemic selection for explanatory factors. The latter implies that members of a group are sifted by virtue of immigration, either through immigration rules or through the process of self-selection.

Custom and lifestyle can also be crucial variables, although one should be careful about falling victim to exoticism in research. For instance, the practice of marrying first cousins could, in theory, increase genetic defects. Little is known about the extent of this behaviour in some communities, such as the Pakistani community, and there is little hard data on the extent of its correlation with congenital deformaties in the UK setting, although some evidence in Pakistan does exist[38.]

Similarly, there is some qualitative evidence that exercise or body-shaping forms less of a component of self-worth amongst Asians than, for example, it does amongst the Caribbeans[39], although a more rigorous analysis of first and second generations is needed. Likewise as we show later, surveys suggest significant differences in sexual behaviour (see Table 6.9), drinking and smoking habits depending upon the taboos in different communities, creating considerable difficulties for clear-cut correlations. Matched and reliable data for the group being studied is often lacking and therefore creates difficulties with eliminating or confirming the causal contribution of genetic factors.

Similar problems exist in relation to associating the elements to be evaluated with social background, as class in Britain does not equate well in terms of class in the subcontinent or in an immigrant setting. This is particularly so within the context of links between class and patterns of disease. For instance, the dietary habits of the British working class are unlikely to match those of the ethnic minority

Chart 6.3 Disease patterns with genetic factors as likely major variables

Disease	Groups at risk	Comments
Coronary heart disease	Asians. SMR highest amongst ages 20-39 for Asians and 30-39 for Africans.	Vegetarianism made no difference. Some relationship with diabetes, it decreased between early seventies and eighties, except for Indian and African born.
Diabetes	Asians, particularly males Mortality rate highest amongst Caribbean women.	Possible relationship with central obesity. Differences between rural and city population in developing countries of origin. Risk factor of renal disease.
Stroke (CVD)	Caribbean females in particular, followed by the Africans. Decline over the seventies.	Relationship with hypertension which is thought to be higher amongst Caribbeans.
Hypertension	Caribbean and in particular females.	Salt intake implicated.
Sickle cell Thalassemia G6PD	Caribbeans, Africans. Asians (Pakistanis). Cypriots.	Could be linked to congenital deformaties.
Infant congenital deformaties	Pakistani infants.	Consanguinous marriage patterns could be a casual factor

Source: M. Luthra, literature survey .

population and their disproportionate presence in the secondary labour market is unlikely to be accounted for by standardisation. Those who rely on socioeconomic models would find that the influence of any particular background might not be as large as expected. Self-selection or selection by virtue of immigration rules could be positive or negative in terms of socioeconomic groups, although hardly any studies have examined the health implications of such selection hitherto. Taking these factors into account we have summarised the position on the basis of a literature survey in Charts 6.3 and 6.4. Let us now turn to some specific conditions in detail.

AIDS

AIDS in the late eighties and its association with the black communities from Africa became a controversial issue[40]. Many observers enforced the notion of association between AIDS and African immigrants despite the fact that it is now a global issue and considerable amount of transmission of infection takes place from mother to child through breast milk and vaginal deliveries[41]. Duh et al (1994) point out that US studies suggest that there is a link between the socioeconomic position, and being at risk from AIDS as well as making the observation that the proportion of children who are suffering from AIDS adds to the overall figure considerably[42].

Table 6.8: Ethnic groups of reported AIDS cases per 1000 over age sixteen

Group	Homo-sexual intercourse	Hetero-sexual intercourse	Drug use injection	Blood	Mother to infant	Other	Total
Asian	0.048	0.028	-	0.0073	0.0007	0.0026	0.0799
Black	0.178	0.515	0.0127	0.0207	.0.062	0.0207	0.8296
White	0.111	0.0058	0.0006	0.0054	0.0005	0.0004	0.1321

Source: Adapted from Balrajan, R. (1993), *Ethnicity and Health, A Guide for the NHS*, Department of Health.

258

Chart 6.4 Disease patterns: likely ecological, cultural and systemic factors

Observations	Susceptible Groups	Comments
AIDS	Caribbeans and Africans and increasingly other groups	Main transmission through heterosexual contact. Some being passed through deliveries and breast milk
Psychosis	Caribbeans and Africans UK born are equally at risk	Debates between protagonists on contribution of systemic, cultural and genetic factors. Hospital admission rates higher in the UK than Jamaica
Suicide rates	Asians at large; women age 16-34 in particular. Only group where women live shorter period than men	More likely to live with partner's family. Stress and isolation
Infant deaths	Asians and in particular Pakistanis, followed by Caribbeans and Africans	Life style not established as a casual factor, and lack of immunisation as a child, congenital deformaties or sickle cell disorders all contributory
Cervical cancer	Caribbeans - empirically, Asian women due to poor access to screening	Poor marketing of screening to Asian women adds to risk. Some relationship with type of birth control method used
Tuberculosis	Asians, Africans, Chinese,Vietnamese and Irish homeless	Recent arrivals from developing world particularly ay risk. Poor housing, poor nourishment and overcrowding could be key factors
Sexually transmitted diseases	Caribbeans, Africans, Asian men and increasingly other groups	Evidence impressionistic only

Source: M. Luthra (1995), literature survey.

259

Table 6.9 Sexual encounter and number of partners (%)

Description	White		African-Caribbean		Asian	
	Male (%)	Female (%)	Male (%)	Female (%)	Male (%)	Female (%)
1st heterosexual intercourse <18%	58.1	51.3	63.2	44.4	71.8	31.6
Total heterosexual partners*	6.3	4.3	7.2	3.2	5.3	1.6
Pregnancy termination	-	15.9	-	31.8	-	11.5
Sexually transmitted diseases	5.6	4.5	15.1	11.9	4.2	1.9
Homosexual relationship	7.4	-	3.8	-	7.8	-
Sex workers contact*	6.4	-	7.3	-	18.2	-
Total	854	769	58	49	129	57

Source: Knox, E.G, MacArthur, Simons, K.J. (1994) *Sexual Behaviour and AIDS in Britain*, HMSO, London. *Excludes 16 cases initiated with a male only.

In Britain, as shown in Table 6.8, black people of African and Caribbean origin are eight times more at risk from AIDS than are members of other ethnic groups, and in most cases there are people who have been in contact with infected Africans. Whilst transmission is restricted to homosexuals in the case of Asians and white people, other means of transmission are now more prevalent amongst the black population. In particular, it appears that the virus is now being passed down through the maternal nexus and is well-lodged in the heterosexual community. The prevalence of AIDS if attributed to the simplistic and highly contestable explanation of its origin in Africa does not explain its prevalence amongst British Caribbeans who have been increasingly forming partnerships with indigenous white partners[43] rather than with Africans.

On the whole, little information exists by way of both class and age group analysis in the UK. More careful collection of data is needed identifying links between AIDS, particularly young people's lifestyles and sexual behaviour than has been the case hitherto[44]. Similarly to develop a risk assessment, a better profile of substance abuse amongst various ethnic groups, particularly amongst the young, is needed. Some research shows slightly differential patterns of use and extent of knowledge of risks. Similarly analysis of different ethnic minority groups in terms of use of contraceptive methods, including anal intercourse and rhythm methods, is needed to assess levels of risk. Table 6.8 outlines some research which relies on small samples and therefore can only be indicative of the significant differences which may exist.

Mental health

The over-representation of black people as detained patients in the psychiatric system has been attributed to either genetically determined high illness rates, self-selection by immigration, the reactions of black people to racism or some cultural dissonance that exists between black patient and white practitioner, particularly in relation to mild psychosis and to drug-related psychosis[45]. The underlying assumption that there is vulnerability of some ethnic groups to mental illness and this can be separated from the quality of the professional services that are on offer or the institutional processes of psychiatry, has been challenged as well as the notion that psychiatric judgements can be free of ethnocentric elements. Consequently some writers[46] have broken outside this mould, questioning the validity of current methods of diagnosis and the validity of research data emphasising the need to examine social models of 'mental illness', and highlighting the role played by racism in the interaction between the psychiatric system itself and black people. We have summarised the debate below as it stands.

Chart 6.5 Mental health and the black community: traditional paradigm challenged

Issue	Argument Against	Argument For
Conceptual	• Assumption that it is not culture bound • Diagnosis located in a western paradigm of illness	• Black psychiatrists do not make any difference
Definitional	• Case definition not standardised, hence culture bound	• Standardisation produces similar results
Systemic	• Differential referral patterns including too many compulsory admissions via Section 136	• Systemic selection through immigration not helpful as evidence suggests that 2nd generation appears to be at risk too
Research	• Class and locality data lacking, relies on hospital admission data • 2nd generation data limited • No split data between African and Caribbean	• Unlikely to make a lot of difference • 2nd generation data limited
Treatment	• Overuse of medication at the expense of therapy	• Need for more therapy, meditation combining Eastern and Western tradition

Source: Developed by M, Luthra from Sashidharan, Fernanado, Littlewood and Lipsedge.

 A further set of contributory factors often put forward or an explanation include environment factors in which ethnic minorities may find themselves. Drug-related psychosis in the case of mental illness amongst Caribbeans, and the 'poverty gene' in the case of diabetes amongst Asians interacting with modern affluence amongst the rich are two examples. Within this context the impact of racism, for instance, in the case of schizophrenia remains unexplored by virtue of the expense involved in utilising complex methodologies and means of data collection. Another example is where little cognisance has been taken of the fact that all ethnic minority communities, in their immigration phase, including the Jewish and the Irish in their earlier periods of settlement, were disproportionately represented amongst the 'mentally ill'[47].

Table 6.10 Age-standardised rates of admission to mental hospitals by selected place of birth, age 16+, 1981

	Standardised admission rate for all diagnoses per 100,000 population*			Standardised admission rate for schizophrenia and paranoia per 100,00 population**	
Place of Birth	Male	Female	All	Male	Female
England	418	583	504	81	74
N.Ireland	793	880	838	-	-
Eire	1054	1102	1080	-	-
All Ireland	-	-	-	191	162
Caribbean	565	532	548	278	181
India	317	326	321	77	82
Pakistan/ Bangladesh +	259	233	245	105	31

* Refers to admissions in England and Wales
** Refers to admissions in England
+ All diagnoses figures refer to Pakistanis only
Source: Cochrane and Bal (1989; 1987)

Table 6.10 displays age-standardised rates for psychiatric hospital admission in 1981 by place of birth based on the work of Cochrane and Bal (1989; 1987)[48]. Psychiatric admission rates are commonly used as an indicator of the underlying prevalence of psychiatric morbidity, although as it is argued below, the assumption is not always a sound one. Cochrane and Bal were specifically concerned with the mental health of migrants, but for present purposes it is worth noting once again the deficiency of place of birth as a proxy variable for ethnicity.

Table 6.11 Mortality from suicide by selected place of birth, England and Wales, 1979-1983

Place of Birth	Age 20-49*		Age 20-69		Age 15-24	
	Male	Female	Male	Female	Male	Female
All Ireland	143	165	126	331	130	197
Indian Subcontinent	74	121	71	149	103	84
Caribbean	80	67	80	84	59	30
African	125	132	122	94	126	32

* Number of deaths not available

Source: Raleigh, V. and Balarajan, R. (1990) 'Suicide and Self Burning Amongst Immigrants from the Indian Sub-continent', *British Journal of Psychology*, pp.46-50.

In addition to the Irish and the Caribbean-born, the rate of admissions are quite high for 'all diagnosis' for Indian born although not as high as the figures for the Irish-born and people born in Eire. Suicide and parasuicide among young South Asian women have been a particular focus of attention. Table 6.11 indicates that suicide in women aged 20-49 born in the Indian subcontinent is 21 per cent higher than the general female population; in the 15-24 age group there is nearly a threefold difference (Balarajan and Raleigh 1993). A study by Merrill (1989)[49] found that the incidence of self-poisoning by South Asian-born men aged 16-34 was up to three times less than that for English-born men; corresponding figures for women showed about a 10 per cent excess for the South Asian born.

The relative low figures observed for the Caribbeans and very high figures for women of Irish origin present an interesting contrast in terms of copabality of different groups in a dislocational setting. As yet recent and second generation data are lacking for a meaningful analysis.

Overall figures for Asians do not appear to be consistent with rates in the subcontinent. Merrill presents two common scenarios among young Asian women,one of 'culture conflict' around the issue of traditional or western-style marriage, and second marital problems among women who have recently come to Britain to join their husbands. Merrill suggests that parasuicide - which must be distinguished aetiologically from suicide - is a Western 'culture-bound syndrome' which young Asian women have appropriated from their European counterparts, and which constitutes a form of ritual whereby non-dominant members of a social group are able to resolve inevitable intergenerational conflicts. Further empirical research is needed to clarify the issue as to why the whole of the Asian population is at higher risk.

Yet another issue which has not been paid attention is the issue of traumatised refugees. The implications of such a trauma are evident from disproportionate admissions of refugees in mental hospitals in areas such as Ealing.

Young people at risk

Although the research is somewhat impressionistic with regard to lifestyle of different ethnic minority groups some assessment could be made as to the risk in light of the evidence we have. Generally young people drank less in volume than their parents[50]and Muslim young were less likely to drink than other Asian youths. The black youth of African Caribbean origin were only at slightly higher risk than Asians in terms of regular drinking (Table 6.12).

265

Table 6.12: Drinking, smoking and sexual habits of 9-15 and 16-19 age groups (percentages)

Ethnic group	Drank last week*	Average units/week*	Regular drinkers	Smoked last week	Had sex last week	Sexually active
African/ Caribbean	22	3	29	32	53	66
White	33	5	55	28	51	62
Asian	4	2	13	10	24	37

*9-15 years
Source: constructed by M. Luthra (1995) from HEA (1992), *Today's Young Adults* (16-19 year olds), and HEA (1992), *Tomorrow's Young Adults* (9-15).

These results have been confirmed by the HEA survey (1992) which suggests the patterns of behaviour differ somewhat with African Caribbean young behaving more like the white youth whilst Asian youth showing signs of moving towards this youth culture albeit still being reluctant joiners. The survey also found that whilst the knowledge base with regard to drugs and sexual protection was very similar in three groups, African-Caribbeans males were more likely to expect women to carry condoms[51]. Informed resources also suggests that in areas which are socioeconomically deprived, the Asian young are at far higher risk from drug abuse than the national surveys will have us believe.

In comparison to the US, very little research on drug use and ethnicity has been carried out. In the past few years, however, a small number of studies have investigated issues of substance mis-use among minority ethnic groups in Britain with a view to making drug services accessible to people from minority ethnic groups. Even in areas with high rates of HIV infection among drug users of the various ethnic minority groups very little research has been carried out in the UK. One study on drug injectors carried out by the

Centre for Research on Drugs and Health Behaviour[52] found that from a sample of 534 injectors, the rate of HIV infection is higher among 'non white' people (17%) than 'white people' (13%).

Chart 6.6 Impressions of risk factors by ethnic group

	White	Irish	Asian	Caribbean	African	Chinese	Cypriots
Coronary heart disease	***	**	***	*	***	-	-
Diabetes	*	*	***	***	*	-	-
Hypertension & stroke	**	**	*	****	*	*	*
Tuberculosis	*	**	****	**	***	***	-
Other respiritory	*	*	*	*	**	-	-
Cancer	**	*	*	*	**	-	-
Cervix cancer	**	***	**	***	*	-	-
Liver cancer	-	*	**	***	***	-	-
Thalessima	-	-	*	*	*	*	***
Sickle cell	-	-	-	***	****	-	*
AIDS	**	-	**	***	****	-	**

Source: Literature survey, Luthra, M.(1995).

267

A study based on the analysis of North West Thames Regional Health Authority (NWTRHA) Drugs Misuse Database has shown that drug users from black and minority ethnic groups are not under-represented in the uptake of services, although this may be true of smaller groups[53]. However, these results should be treated with caution as data are based on first, rather than sustained contacts, and because the study provides no assessment of the crucial question of whether the needs of individuals from minority ethnic groups are met[54].

Moreover, local and agency-based research show that there is little evidence that existing drug service provision is attracting and adequately meeting the needs of black and minority ethnic drug users[55]. A study carried out in Lewisham confirms earlier observations that black drug users are under-represented at drugs agencies[56]. Research carried out in Bradford and Haringey also indicate that black and ethnic minority people are less likely to use services, and that there is a lack of representation of minority ethnic clients and staff[57]. Furthermore, a study on black women substance users has also shown that black women were less likely to approach their doctor with personal problems and anxieties at an early pre-crisis stage[58].

Need of risk assesment

Given the forgoing account of lack of reliable data, it is obvious that it will be very difficult to develop an overall risk or need assessment of different ethnic groups[59]. Nevertheless relying on the SMR data as well as hospital admissions an impressionistic picture shown in Chart 6.6 emerges.

Social services: discrimination, disadvantage and other key issues

As stated earlier on, over the last five years there has been an increasing tendency for social services to charge for day centres, meals on wheels as well as to ration[60] the service, expecting clients to contribute despite savings made by many social service departments. The emphasis in child care has shifted from prevention to crisis management, creating professional dilemmas for social workers[61]. These factors can militate against communities which are disengaged and deprived.

The doubts about the purchaser/provider split remain as commissioning roles appear not to be well established in social services[62]. Authorities lag behind in developing profiles of assessment needs and have failed to link them to their budgets and rational allocation processes[63]. Furthermore, the fear that the introduction of competition would fragment the service persists and the much cherished notion of enhanced user participation does not appear to have been put into practice according to the Social Services Inspectorate. These areas present a particular challenge within the context of ethnic minority users and the independent sector.

On the specific of equal opportunities the SSI has devised an equal opportunity assessment methodology although overall the record in terms of publishing collective reports on equal opportunities in regions and local authorities remains poor, and the Chief Inspector's report on partnership (1994) had little to say on equal opportunities and lacked any data on the subject[64].

There is also a danger that the ethnic minorities voluntary sector would be subjected to competition, and given its precarious position it is unlikely to be able to compete with large white independent or voluntary organisations. Second, as regards the ethnic independent sector, little exists at present, apart from a few nursing homes and some domiciliary care agencies. The development of such a sector would have to be included as part of the economic development process, aided by the local authorities or the TECs, if plurality of provision is going to become a reality.

Child care: fostering, adoption and child abuse

Historically, with the exception of community social work, social services remain reactive, rather than proactive, in promoting social and political change. Earlier writers (Fitzherbert 1967) located social problems in the family and argued for social services to employ 'tough casework' in their dealings with African-Caribbean families, who mistakenly put their children into care as it was thought to help integration and was seen as just a child care service[65].

Policy practice and provision in social services is said to be directed to meet the interests of the child. Child protection under the Children Act (1989) remains a major priority of social services departments. Given the somewhat differing traditions of child care and discipline between ethnic minority and white groups, this is likely to be a minefield in the context of diagnosis in a multicultural society. Some of the old problems of under-access and over-access of other groups to different services continues to be identified in different studies we have reviewed in this chapter. For instance, over-representation of Caribbean young in local authority care continues, while Asian young are under-represented. Studies controlled by class and family type are lacking, although the high occurrence of single parenthood, a mixed race background, council tenancy and the diagnosis of mental health amongst the mothers appear to be common denominators[66]. The socioeconomic disadvantage element is not decisive and in a Barnes (1993) sample, black children of skilled manual fathers were represented at a level which is twice that of the equivalent white group. The gender element does not appear to make any difference, and like school exclusions, it remains an unexplained phenomenon.

Furthermore, there are no national statistics on the number of black children in care. We know very little about the circumstances under

270

which families come to the attention of the personal social services and their subsequent treatment by these agencies. In short, although much has been written about the care careers of white children, the understanding of black children's care experiences has been largely impressionistic and anecdotal, filled to some extent by Tizzard et al (1992)[67].

One view is that agencies such as health visitors, schools, and the police all tend to over select black families and young people, although Barnes in her study found no support for this view. She did however note that the centralised power structure of many social work departments meant that social workers had little or no say in the formulation of policies concerning ethnic matching and resented the lack of flexibility in relation to such policies.

Another study by Row et al (1989) with a large sample across four authorities suggested that black young people were admitted for longer periods than white children. Often more voluntary and temporary admissions of ethnic children were made, frequently at pre-school and primary-level age groups. Ethnicity was relevant to outcome of placements for such children. Mixed parentage young were as much at risk as those from a homogeneous parental background. Significantly, when both parents were black they were more likely to remain in contact with their foster children[68].

Not all of these findings were confirmed in the Barnes study. She was however able to illustrate how it is possible, with rigorous efforts from local authorities, to redress some of these imbalances in relation to a black ethnic group - albeit at the cost of neglecting other ethnic groups such as the Chinese. The poor socioeconomic situation of black parents played an important part in social worker decisions to rehabilitate and discharge children. Barnes (1993) noted that black children were not only likely to be admitted into care more quickly than white children in cases of socioeconomic and family difficulties but were also less likely to be treated with an open mind than similar 'white' cases. She asserts that social workers' negative views about black families led them to be unnecessarily cautious, and they tended to adopt a 'rescue mentality' and as a consequence

271

over-reacted in these situations, sometimes leading to misdiagnosis.

In terms of rehabilitation and discharge from care ABSWAP, in their evidence to the House of Commons (1983), described a sample of 100 children (50 black, 50 white) in one London borough who all came into care within the same period. After six months there were clear differences in the patterns of rehabilitation of these children. In the white group, the proportion of children remaining in institutions was likely to be reduced by 60%. However, with the black group, the proportion was likely to be reduced by only 20%. Thus, the chances of black children being rehabilitated into their natural families or substitute families were greatly reduced[70].

One view is that state social work tends to perpetuate oppressive social relations in its portrayal of the 'acceptable' family as having two parents who are white, middle class, heterosexual and able-bodied, which pathologised the Caribbean family[71]. Consequently, the competence of black families, particularly as they are more likely to be one-parent, to rear children was questioned, viewing them very much within the assimilation/integration framework.

This theory argues that referrals from such families invariably result in an examination of family structure, and how it may be jeopardising the welfare of the child. In these situations, state care through the local authorities is sometimes seen as a better alternative, and the 'rescue mentality' of the social services is particularly noticeable. This tendency has been heightened in the wake of two cases where black children had been killed at the hands of their parents and guardians (Jasmine Beckford in 1985and Tyra Henry in 1987). It has been asserted that following these tragedies, social services have become extremely cautious[72]. Given the very strict and long procedure laid down it is understandable. The extent to which the increase in the number of both single parents (a large proportion of social workers themselves are single parents) and the presence of black and ethnic minority social workers has made a difference, warrants further analysis.

Recent debates and evidence about child abuse has implicated the family, particularly the modern extended family with stepchildren.

Social workers probably do not see the family as the sanctuary it once was for children and the pool of families which falls in the classic middle-class range with stable marriage and a job category is fast disappearing. Ethnic religious matching invariably shrinks this pool further. Indeed some councils have reversed their policies on ethnic matching in some cases assisted by law[73], partly because of press hounding and partly because of the continuing shortage of ethnically-matched foster parents and adopters.

The evidence on the premise that matched ethnicity leads to better established sense of self-identity or better social mobility and adjustment is lacking[74]. Many campaigns have been launched to find ethnically-matched fosterers and adopting parents. There is now a register of such matching. The problem of adoption between relations continues to be intractable. Overall there is little evidence of maladjustment amongst young people who have been fostered or adopted by people of a different ethnic origin although Barnes' data suggested that black parents were more likely to keep in touch with thier foster children and there is some evidence of reduced contact with members of one's own group if adopted transracially.

Nevertheless the Children Act (1989) does enshrine the notion of taking religious and cultural needs of children into account when applying the Act, although a national organisation is lacking which can continously recruit foster and adoptive parents on behalf of the ethnic minorities. Johnson argues that the models developed to cope with child abuse are culturally insensitive[75]. The stereotype of the colluding Asian mother and ideas related to community surveillance leading to little abuse have to be challenged[76]. In fact the whole area of child abuse requires further research in an ethnic context.

Process issues

As stated earlier, much of social work in a current context relies on personal interaction with the client and/or his/her network to intervene. Much has been written about this area essentially focusing on the role ethnocentric assumptions can play, either leading to an inferior service delivery or an enhanced element of social control. I have reframed some of the responses against a typological construct of various approaches to social work outlined by Coulshed (1992)[77], as shown in Table 6.13

Table 6.13 Social work interventions race equality issues

Crisis intervention	• Rescue mentality can come into operation (Barnes 1992)
Working with families	• Failure to take into account reality of racism (Ahmed 1990) • Background clash creates limitations for good social work intervention (Liverpool 1991)
Interviewing assesment recording	• Accurate, relevant, and must address culture in a constructive way when reporting (Ahmed 1990) • Self-assessment a possibility • Poor data base (Butt et al 1994) • Who does the assessment?- an important issue (Butt 1990)
Counselling	• Notions such as therapeutic relationship, self-disclosure, individualisation and self-awareness may be antipathetic for some ethnic minority groups (Dominelli 1988).
Networking and mobilising resources	• Networking methods vary from one ethnic group to another
Task-centred practice	• Rewards and incentives may be different for different groups
Behavioural approach	• Mentoring and role models important particularly for the young (Morgan 1986) • Rewards and incentives may be different for different groups
Psycho-social approach	• Self-identity needs enforcing and accepting (Maxime 1986) • It has been cast in a western model (Feranado 1994)

Source: Literature survey (1995) M. Luthra.

Common issues between health and social services

Now we turn to some of the issues which are common to both health and social services.

Knowledge, access and use of services

The issue of ethnic minorities and service accessibility remains on the activist agenda for both health and social services. The knowledge of service provision and registration rates for GPs are high or on a par with the white population amongst both Asians and Caribbeans, although the Asians' higher consultation rates with GPs could partly be a function of the presence of Asian doctors, (although only one-fifth preferred an Asian doctor), probably because of their minority language competence[8], and partly as a displacement activity for poor contact with mental health services. Studies in Newcastle suggested consultation with patients was perceived to be a trivial issue by many GPs[79].

Ethnicity took precedence over gender[80] in terms of contact with GPs, and there was little follow-up by appointment[81]. Knowledge of primary care services was poor in many areas, such as midwifery, followed often by poor link provision[82]. Researchers noted that personal contact and video contacts were more effective than posters and letters. Other studies show poor uptake of pre- and postnatal services[83]. Similar problems of knowledge and use were found in relation to cervical and breast screening[84]. Although use of health and family planning are poor, the use of sheaths was noted to be similar amongst women.

Recent standardised studies by the HEA (Health Education Authority) suggest that registration rates are similar for all groups with a higher rate of registration with Asian GPs for both men and women, although some older people complain[85] that Asian GPs are too westernised. According to an HEA study, African-Caribbean men are half as likely to visit GPs while Bangladeshis visit twice as much. In the case of the latter it probably added to their waiting time. Gillam et al showed second follow-up appointments were less likely for ethnic minorities and that there were poor referral rates of people with disabilities to district nurses.

Whilst African-Caribbeans were least happy with the explanation given of their conditions, the Bangladeshis were most happy, according to the HEA study. The converse was true in relation to the time given to them. Screening rates were low for Asian women. This could be due to the large number of male GPs involved and there is substantial evidence that Asian women wish to be examined by female doctors for gynaecological examination. Concerning the provision of mental health, as we have shown before, whilst some communities such as Caribbeans are over-represented others such as Bangladeshis are under-represented[86].

The last report on the health of the nation (1986) was released in 1992, and gave HEA data and SHARE examples of successful projects such as breast and cancer screening as well as examples of departmental efforts to research psychosis and AIDS[87]. The paper does not deal with the implementation of issues related to racial diversity and equality. Instead, it simply leaves it to the local health authorities to arrive at decisions about actions and targets to take account of ethnic minority needs and cultural sensitivities[88].

The debate about non-use of services is not a new one[89]. Studies suggest that there is a significant difference in knowledge levels between Asians and Caribbeans[90] with Asians far less likely to know about such provision than Caribbeans, particularly amongst older people, although both tend to be less knowledgeable than their white counterparts.

Lack of knowledge on the part of ethnic minority groups[91] regarding services such as meals on wheels and luncheon clubs[92] as being available to all who would gain by their use, is not uncommon. Attendance at day centres - unless they are specifically designed - is poor, with considerable anxiety about being on their own, the provision of the right sort of food and being able to speak their own language together with a lack of confidence in using English[93].

Table 6.14 Service delivery and ethnicity selective studies

Service	Studies	Key Findings
Home help Meals on wheels	Roony (1987) Atkin et al (1989)	• Under-usage by Asians who had poorer knowledge than whites and African Caribbean people
Luncheon clubs Respite care	Farah (1986) Fielding (1990)	• Provision ethnocentric • Need twice as high for Asian families
Community Psychiatric Services	McCalman (1990) Farah (1986)	• Poor knowledge of rehabilitation facilities • One-fifth of over-55 Caribbeans responsible for care of others
Chiropody	Donaldson & Odell (1986)	• Older ethnic minority people did not know of services
Midwifery	Bowler et al (1994)	• Female presence at delivery objected to • Ethnocentric arrangements • Lack of English assumed to indicate stupidity
Nursing	Acute Services (1995)	• Low threshold of pain asssumed • Food issues • Visiting relatives objected to

Source: Luthra, M. (1995) literature survey.

Respite care use is also deterred by a lack of knowledge, as well as a feeling of guilt about leaving disabled relatives or children with strangers. There is some concern shown regarding the linguistic and cultural capabilities of the staff involved with such matters[94]. Within this developing provision there is a gender dimension, i.e. day centres tend to cater for men and there is little single-sex provision[95]. On the whole, the evidence suggests that once services are sensitised and established they work well.

An ageing population

The British ethnic minority population having completed the settlement phase is ageing with various consequences. Nationally the proportion of people in the 45-64 age group varies between 14% of people of Chinese origin to 25% of people of Caribbean origin (white 22%) and from area to area. It is estimated that by the year 2005 there would be some 260,000* elderly people from ethnic minorities.

The current provision offfered by day centres, unless in the heart of the home district with link workers, are rarely utilised by the minority elderly. There are some highly successful local authority-funded projects, such as Milap Day Centre in Southall, although the problem of small numbers and difficulties of communication between elderly from different religious backgrounds presents a real challenge to the local authorities. Increasing numbers of ethnic minority elderly feel that they have lost their children to western cultural and educational influences. Their status tends to be lower than the white elderly[95] and they tend to get poor service from state provision. Some try to settle back in their country of origin but find that their former country is much changed, and many have difficulties with accessing their benefits if they return to their country of origin[96].

Current data suggests that the figures for Asian elderly who live alone is around 4%-5% whilst the figure for African-Caribbean elderly is 30%, and that for the white elderly is 44%. One in six African-Caribbean elderly lose contact with the family[97,] whilst in

* Assuming that one third of those born outside the UK would return to their homeland to retire

278

the case of Asians the need to live independently, but near by, has not been explored. A lot of Asian elderly find communication with their westernised children problematic and their dependent relationship oppressive and depressing.

Disability

As shown in Chart 6.3, the level of chronic illness which in most cases leads to disability is very high amongst all ethnic groups except in the case of the Chinese and other Asians. This is also supported by the emerging evidence from the recent HEA (1994) survey[98], which suggested that diabetes, heart disease, rheumatism and stomach problems accounted for excess disability in Asians, whilst diabetes, high blood pressure, stroke and sickle cell were implicated in African-Caribbeans. We have also shown that the SMR for accident rates is very much higher than average amongst most ethnic minority groups (see Tables 6.5 and 6.6). Research from Europe suggests that the concentration of ethnic minorities in some occupations puts them at risk from accidents although the accidents do decline over the period of settlement[99]. Studies are conflicting on the level of disability[100] amongst ethnic minorities, although Martin et al's standardised data by age showed no major difference.

Common stereotypes such as that Asian families reject their handicapped children and ethnic minorities parents show little interest in toys for child development, continue to interfere with the issue of access. Similarly the invisibility of carers of persons with disability and the stress they endure is enhanced, but ethnocentric assumptions about family support continue to get in the way of making equitable provision.

Human resource and equal opportunity

Apart from the human resource debate, there is the issue of the use of tissue donation. One area that presents a particular problem is that of blood donation, bone marrow transplants and eggs for invitro-fertilisation[101], as shortages of these resources are disparately felt by the minority population. Here concerted action is needed in terms of encouraging ethnic minorities not to fear donating directly or through donor cards. There needs to be a national policy on inherited disorders. In addition, a research centre is needed along with a register of work being carried out to ensure that there is no duplication of effort.

Nationally, the ineffectiveness of a dwindling number of equal opportunities advisers is evident from the fact that trusts are not targeting ethnic minorities for employment purposes, although a majority had set targets for women[102]. There is some evidence that some trusts and health authorities are setting equality targets and linking it to performance pay.

An NHS regional complaints system needs to be established to deal with discrimination to avoid further trauma. Currently, given the present hierarchical culture of the NHS, from personal experience too many people fail to differentiate their claims and their advisers, being relatively low status, are thus not able to make structural changes.

Undergraduate training courses for both health and social services need to move closer together, in addition to sharing knowledge about equality and diversity. A regulatory rather than advisory model of implementation is needed, coupled with some well-developed means of implementation such as guides for purchasers with advice on establishing systems of institutional change. The present government checklist is not very helpful, as it does not take the notion of institutional resistance into account.

The long-held understanding that health education was free from racial discrimination was challenged by the CRE publication of the St George's Hospital Medical School Report[103], and the recruitment and admissions procedures for nurses in South Manchester[104] followed by other studies. This was additional to the CRE report on overseas doctors published in 1987 which could not establish discrimination but found a failure on the part of the NHS to deal with the specific training needs of such doctors. Subsequent testing and analysis[105] shows ghettoisation of black doctors in unpopular sectors of medicine. As early as 1987, GLARE (Greater London Action on Race Equality)[106] found that employment policies were in a critical condition and only five local authorities were following the CRE code of practice. The punishment for challenging the system was evident from the arrest made of two doctors who exposed discrimination in the recruitment and appointment of ethnic minority doctors[107] and the situation of Dr Memon who was turned down 126 times for promotion after having won a case of discrimination[108]. The situation has been worsened by increasing loss of corporate control in what are now decentralised personnel services.

Table 6.15 Current percentage of workers in social care sector and those in training

Group	Current percentage	Amongst trainees	Source
Social workers	5% (recently qualified)		CCETSW
Doctors	28% (1985) - NHS only	Asians 12.3% Black 5.4% White 5.9%	UCCA (1993)
Nurses and health allied	Asian - 4% African-Caribbean - 13%	Nurses less than 5% in inner city areas	Baxter, C. and Cole, A. (1987/8)

Sources: UCCA (1992) CCETSW (1988) *Labour Force Survey 1988-1990*; Anwar, M. et al (1988), *Overseas Doctors*, CRE.

The changes in health services and the scramble for new jobs has led to an increased activity in the number of discrimination cases against the health authorities. Such cases are rarely found in social services which has sought to recruit ethnic minority social workers, partly some would argue to offload the problems of the inner cities onto them. It is very likely that most of the ethnic minority social workers and GPs are concentrated in the inner city areas. Although the last decade has witnessed an increase in the employment of black and ethnic minority social workers, an emphasis on racism awareness training and the promotion and introduction of equal opportunities, the overall picture is one of little change and many of the black social work managers are leaving the profession[109]. In a recent study, one-third of ethnic minority social workers felt that they had suffered discrimination[110] and the stress levels amongst them were twice those of their white counterparts[111].

Black nurses[112] have been ghettoised in the cinderella services often found on lower grades, excluded from promotion opportunities, discouraging other nurses not to join[113]. There is even a view that further immigration may be needed as the indigenous population requires more carers and as many of the British carers leave for the US and Canada.

The voluntary and independent sector

In the voluntary sector, the situation has not been very different. A study by NCVO found that while more than 90% of the users were black, the staff profile was the reverse. It[114] showed little difference since the 1984 survey by NCVO. The externalisation of local authority social services means that increasingly the very weakened ethnic minority sector finds it very difficult to compete with the well-established white voluntary sector[115] for provision of such services. In two reports published by the NCVO, it was noted that 97% of trustees in charities are white[116].

Conclusions, issues and challenges

Clearly there has been some progress in relation to adoption of race equality measures over the last decade, both in the areas of health and social services with health attempting to catch up with social services. Considering that social services identified the issues much earlier the progress still remains erratic and patchy and the agenda still looks quite substantial. Nevertheless the preconditions Butt et al have identified in relation to development in social services could be be benificial for making progress in the health service. It would appear that race equality advisers have survived in some urban social services departments despite a split in local authorities' functions in the commissioning and purchasing, whilst corporate development in health service has been undermined as the role of many advisers has been redefined during restructurings. Others continue to under-perform in the health service, essentially doing small-scale short-term projects and not being able to address infrastructural issues.

Some developments have been negative and regressive, particularly insofar as training is concerned. Blatant political interventions, including the dismantling of the Black Perspective Committee in social work training, have been a major issue not encountered in the health service as the health service has not begun to address the issue of training of medical or paramedical staff. A recent report by the BMA, however, has urged for introduction of a multicultural perspective in the humanities part of the curriculum. On the whole the medical model of training and to a lesser extent research remains relatively untouched by the debate about the issue of racism and when it is invoked it tends to be relatively preoccupied with ethnicity and diversity.

On the training side, the notion of simply relying on a political analysis (to replace what was called the tourist guide multi-culturalism based on broad categories) needs to be accompanied by the development of ethnic competencies. Social workers, including those who belong to minority ethnic groups themselves, need to be provided with detailed knowledge and competency of at least one culture aided further by working in multi-ethnic teams. Such a detailed picture does not have to present a static picture of culture or fall victim to a stereotypical view. The evidence of fluid, changing and increasingly mixed identities (see Chapter 1), and the relative westernisation of the first generation ethnic minorities, presents social workers with some difficult challenges. For instance, should the ethnic matching policy apply to an increasing number of young people of 'mixed origin', who will define their identity in multiple terms.

Chart 6.7 Model of disengagement

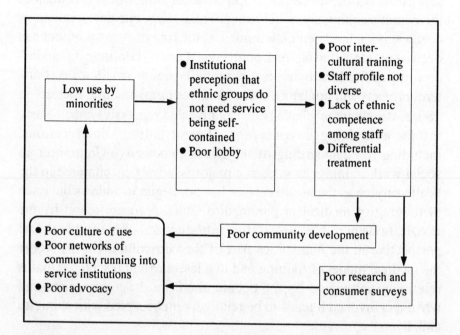

Over the last decade there has been considerable research in health with focus on ethnicity and national origins which appears to throw up some patterns which cannot be dismissed, I suspect because of the correlation between ethnicity, national origin and ethnic pool being quite good in most cases and within the context of first generation ethnic minorities. This needs to be improved first by examining small groups such as Punjabis and Gujeratis; second gene markers may be necessary to conduct meaningful research in the future. Hitherto the impact of research (which has been mostly in the form of local studies and is often unamenable to generalisations) on the improvement of ethnic minorities health over the last decade, remains questionable. And here it would seem that there has been a major failure in constructing a meaningful research strategy and dovetailing it with policy development. Research on ecological factors comparing different groups living in different environments appears to be minimal. Similarly the research on interaction between the client and various health professionals in hospital and other settings has been lacking. It is very likely that insofar as single gene disorders are concerned, research would show diversity in genetic variations with different groups disadvantaged in terms of their susceptibility to different disorders. The role of social policy and research is to be in a state of readiness for an effective response to such disadvantages. Carhill (1995) in his recent analysis has argued that western definitions of class are likely to be less useful than previously thought when analysing data on ethnic minorities. This poses an interesting challenge for research methodologists in relation to standardisation techniques.

As in the area of social services, there has been considerable research on uptake of services which has been useful in initiating policy adjustment. There remains, however, a need to carry out research focusing on approaches in specific areas such as crisis management work, child abuse, counselling and so on. In this sense the rhetoric of anti-racism needs to be replaced by counter-racism (see Chapter 5) and reformed by ethnographic insights and advice in each area.

Research in both health and social services in an ethnic context has lacked an evaluative dimension to test what works better and comparative surveys of users in some major areas are lacking, including surveys of the extent to which the presence of ethnically matched social workers are making a difference, for instance in the number of black young being taken into care. As to the issue of disengagement we have produced a cycle of disengagement as shown in Chart 6.7.

On the issue of organisational development, three issues emerge. One, the issue of a dwindling number of advisers in the district health authorities and the absence of a budget often marginalises the adviser. There are a number of poorly defined short-term, part-time which are not located in a strategic framework. Senior posts concentrating on race equality in quality assurance sections would help, but need also to address the employment issues. It would appear that government advisers have failed to anticipate the change in the NHS and its implications for equal opportunities.

In the social services arena the purchaser-provider split has created some opportunities for community development, which given the absence of an economic development policy to develop the ethnic care sector and demise of the ethnic minority voluntary sector, they are unlikely to be a major winner. Here the failure has been an absence of economic development policy which should have preceded community care. The TECs charged with economic regeneration are unlikely to be sympathetic to such ventures. A kick start fund based on partnership between the social services department, the TECs and the local banks, together with a coherent strategy, is needed.

It would appear that quality assurance structures entrusted with auditing and maintaining equal opportunities aspects, themselves need to be audited. In health there is no equivalent of the SSI although some ethnic minorities officers are located in the quality assurance departments. Their emphasis also appears to be dealing mainly with the efficiency and clinical audit type of work. The SSI has failed to publish annual reports on equal opportunities which are an overview of their inspections during the period and little has emerged in terms of what should happen to a number of very junior ethnic minority workers located often at the margins of a trust or health authority. Clearly at every level of commissioning some monitoring has to be carried out and response made to the local diversity of the population. The other central point of intervention is quality assurance which should be redubbed as quality and equality assurance to strengthen the regulatory mode.

The issue of carrying the burden of your own community needs revisiting. Workers who are given the caseload of, or have a brief pertaining to, ethnic groups need to be given other opportunities so as to ensure that they do not become victims of their own competency in terms of career development.

References

1 Amin, K. and Oppenhiem (1992) *Poverty in Black and White Britain*, CPAG and Runnymede Trust, London.

2 Escott, K. and Whitfield, C. (1994) *The Gender Impact of CCT in Local Government,* Equal Opportunities Commission, London.

3 The internal market ethos has not been injected into DSS to the same extent. The timetable for externalising services has been more liberal in relation to social services than other sectors in bad government.

4 This is evident from large number of emerging joint commissioning agencies as well as development of inter-professional studies in many universities, e.g. Southbank University.

5 Studies suggest that most of the purchasers are locked into buying from a limited range of established providers

6 During the period 1989-1992 a large number of new jobs, particularly care manager jobs, were created in social services departments.

7 Even in 1993 the turnover rate was 9.4%, vacancy rates were 8.1%. (Equivalent figures for 1994 were 9.5% and 7.7% respectively, *Community Care*, 27th April 1995.)

8 Rochern (1988). Cf. Johnson, M. (1989) *New Community,* vol. 15, no.2, pp269-74.

9 Associations of Directors of Social Sciences Response/CRE report (1978) surveyed 70 social service departments, *Multiracial Britain; The Social Service Response*, ADSS/CRE.

10 CCESTW, informed by black perspectives groups, took a considerable number of steps in developing antiracist perspectives.

11 Butt, J. (1991) *Equally Fair. A Report on Social Services Departments,* NISW (race unit).

12 Hicks, C. (1988) 'NMS colour blindness', *The Health Service Journal,* 98, 5102, 590-91.

13 Series of studies include: Macnaught, A. (1988) *Race and Health Policy,* Croom Helm, Beckenham; Macquasten, S. (1986) *All Things Being Equal,* Southern Derbyshire Health Authority, Derby; NAHA *Action Not Words: A Strategy to Improve Health Service for Black and Ethnic Groups*, London.

14 Fulop, N. and Jewks, R., 'Background information', *Health Services Journal,* 5th March 1992, pp28-9.

15 Butt et al, (op.cit.).

16 Stubbs, P. (1985) 'The employment of black social workers: from "ethnic sensitivity" to anti-racism', *Critical Social Policy*, 4, b, pp6-77.

17 The appointment of the new head of CCETSW in 1989 has led to an undermining of race equality training. Southbank University has endeavoured to develop a strong anti-racist perspective in their course.

18 The work of Mickletu group led to a black perspective working group in turn leading to introduction of Paper 30 of Diploma in Social Work which is being diluted, *Community Care*, 23rd February-March 1995.

19 Luthra, M. and Oakley, R. (1988) *Approaches to Race Equality Training*, ERU, Warwick University.

20 Rogers, C. (1942) *Counselling and Psychotherapy: Newer Concepts in Practice*, Houghton Mifflin, 1942.

21 See Sivanandan (1985) 'RAT - The degradation of struggle against racism', *Race and Class*, xxvi, 4, pp1-33. Luthra, M. and Oakley, R. (1988) *Approaches to Race Equality Training*, ERU, Warwick University.

22 I had the opportunity to carry out training for a group of such advisors. A large proportion of them have been absorbed into the mainstream.

23 Hughes, R. and Bhaduri, R. (1987) *Race and Culture in Social Services Delivery. A study of 3 SSDs by Manchester SSI*, DHS.

24 Jewson, N. et al. (1993) 'Changes in ethnic minority membership of health authorities', *BMJ*, 307, pp604-605.

25 Macnaught, A. (op.cit.).

26 SHARE documentation suggested this (Kings Fund).

27 In a random survey of projects we found only a handful which had been evaluated properly.

28 SHARE. (King's Fund)

29 The shortage of evaluation. Some of the exceptions are listed in the Good Practice list provided by SHARE, most of which remain empirically unevaluated.

30 See Bhopal in Ahmed (1992) *The Politics of Race and Health*, RR Unit, University of Bradford and B. and I.C. College.

31 Critics (of ref. 26) failing to offer alternative definitions. Raleigh, V.S. (1992) *Ethnic Monitoring: The Need for Consistent Classification*, SHARE 3, 7-8.

32 See also Balarajan, R. and Soni Raleigh, V. (1993) *Ethnicity and Health: A Guide for NHS,* Roys P. Bhat et al. (ed.)(1988) *Britain's Black Population*, Gower, Aldershot.

33 Ibid.

34   Poverty gene theory is outlined in McKeigue, P.(1990) 'Coronary heart disease in South Asians overseas', *Journal of Clinical Epidemiology*, vol. 42, no. 7, pp 597-609.

35   Barker, M., *The Independent*, 20th May 1995, reported a study of death records of babies born in Britain during the interwar years .

36   Jones, J., 'How different are the human genes', *Nature*, 1981, vol. 293, pp188-190.

37   See the programme called *Killer Proteins,* BBC, 1995.

38   Consanguinous marriages - are accepted as a reason for genetic disorder,but senior professionals admit that no one wants to launch a campaign against it as such marriages are appproved in the Koran.

39   Mori (1994) an unpublished qualitative study.

40   Duh, S.V. (1991) *Blacks and Aids: Causes and Origins*, Race and Ethnic Relations Series, vol. 3, Sage, London. Bhatt, C. (1992) *AIDS and Black Communities*, London Black HIV/AIDS Network.

41   WHO (1994).

42   Duh, S.V. (op.cit.).

43   One third of the Caribbeans in a 16-34 age group have white partners, OPCS (1991).

44   Rahim, A. (1994) *Drug Abuse and Ethnic Minorities Survey,* for HEA (16 to 25 year olds).

45   For a literature survey, see Shashi Dharan, 'Afro-Caribbeans and schizophrenia in the U.K.', 'The legacy of race science', 'The ethnic health dimension', the Health and Ethnicity NE and NW Regional Authorities, 21st June 1993, national conference. Cochrane, R. and Bal, G.Y. (1987) 'Migration and schizophrenia', *Social Psychiatry*, vol. 22, pp181-91.

46   Littlewood, R. and Lipsedge, M. (1988) *Aliens and the Alienists*, Unwin Hyman. Fernando, S. (1988) *Mental Health, Race and Culture*, Macmillan and MIND.

47   White, G (1980) *Rothschild's Building,* History workshop series, RKP.

48   Cochrane, R. and Bal S., 'Mental hospital admission rates of immigrants to England: a comparison on 1971 and 1981', *Social Psychiatry and Psychiatric Epidemiology*, 1989.

49   Merril, J. and Owens, J. (1986) 'Ethnic differences in self-poisoning: a comparison of Asian and white groups', *British Journal of Psychiatry,* 1986: 148, pp708-12. Raleigh, V., Bulusu, L and Balrajan R, 'Suicides amongst immigrants from the Indian sub-continent', *British Journal of Psychology,* 1990, pp46-50.

50   Cochrane, R. and Bal, S., 'The drinking patterns of Sikh, Hindu, Muslim and white men: West Midlands', *British Journal of Addiction,* 1990, vol. 85, pp75-64.

289

51   HEA (1992) *Tomorrow's Young Adults*.

52   Ettore, E., Stimson, G. and Crosier, A. (1991) *Trends in HIV Infection Among Drug Injectors in London*, The Centre for Research on Drugs and Health Behaviour, Executive Summary, no. 5.

53   Northwest and Thames Regional Health Authority

54   Daniel, T. (1991) *Drug Agencies, Ethnic Minorities and Problem Drug Use*, The Centre for Research on Drugs and Health Behaviour, Executive Summary.

55   Perera, J., Power, R. and Gibson, N. (1993) *Accessing the Needs of Black Drug Users in North Westminster,* The Centre for Research on Drugs and Health Behaviour with the Hungerford Drug Project.

56   Mirza, H., Pearson, G. et al (1991) 'Drugs, people and services in Lewisham', London University Monograph: Goldsmith College.

57   Awaiah, J., Butt, S. and Dorn, N. (1992) 'Race, gender and drug services', London: ISDD Monograph.

58   Dawn (1991) 'Drugs, alcohol and women now', *Black Women and Dependency: A Report on Drug and Alcohol Use*, London.

59   See Balarajan and Luthra (forthcoming).

60   I am thankful to many senior colleagues in social services who have confirmed this observation.

61   Social services have been reluctant to proceed with spliting their functions in many cases.

62   BBC Radio 4 Survey, *Unwritten Rules,* 21st April 1994.

63   'A-C talking care progress reports', *Community Care,* December 1993.

64   The Chief Inspector (1995) *Partners in Caring*, the Fourth Annual Report of the Chief Inspector, SSI.

65   Barnes, R. (1993) *Black Children in the Public Care System*, Batsford, London.

66   Tizzard, B. and Phoenix, A. (1993) *Black, White, or Mixed Race*, RKP.

67   Rowe, J., Hundleby, M. and Garnett, L. (1989) *Child Care Now*, BAFF, Research Series 6.

68   ABSWAP (1983), House of Commons.

69   Fitzherbert (1967), Cf. Atkins (op.cit.).

70   Carby, B., 'Theory and practice in long-term social work', *British Journal of Social Work*, 1982.

71   Hildrew (1986), Cf. Atkins (op.cit.).

72   I am thankful to M. Johnson (Warwick University) for this comment some time ago.

73   Phillips, M., 'Abuse of power', *Social Work Today*, 31st March 1992, pp16-17.

75 Tizzard, B. and Phoenix, A. (op.cit.).

76 Coulshed, V. (1988) *Social Work Practice: An Introduction,* Macmillan, Basingstoke.

77 Wright, C. (1983) 'Language and communication problems in an Asian community', *Journal of Royal College of General Practitioners*, vol. 33, pp101-4.

78 Gillam, S.J., Jarman, B., White, P. and Law, R. (1989) 'Ethnic differences in consultation rates in urban general practice', *British Medical Journal*, vol. 299, pp953-7.

79 Ibid.

80 Hicks, C. and Hays, L. (1991) 'Linkworkers in antenatal care: facilitators of equal opportunities in health provision or salves for the management conscience?', *Health Services Management Research*, vol. 4, no. 2, pp89-93.

81 Pershad (1990). Cf. Atkinson (op.cit.).

82 McAvoy, B.R. and Raza, R. (1988) 'Asian women: (I) contraceptive knowledge, attitudes and usage, (ii) contraceptive services and cervical cytology', *Health Trends*, vol. 20, pp11-17. McAvoy, B.R. and Raza, R. (1991) 'Can health education increase uptake of cervical smear testing among Asian women?', *British Medical Journal*, vol. 302, pp833-6.

83 Ibid.

84 Gillam et al (op.cit.).

85 Roudat, K. (1994) *Black and Ethnic Minorities Health and Life-style Survey,* HEA, MORI and NHS, Ethnic Health Unit.

86 Ibid .

87 Cmnd. 1986 (1992) *The Health of the Nation*, HMSO, London.

88 Norman, A. (1985) *Triple Jeopardy: Growing Old in a Second Homeland*, Policy Studies in Ageing No. 3, Centre for Policy on Ageing, London. Patel, N. (1990) *A Race Against Time, Social Services Provision to Black Elders*, Runnymede Trust, London. Atkin, K., Cameron, E., Badger, F., and Evers, E. (1989) 'Asian elders' knowledge and future use of community social and health services', *New Community*, vol. 15, no. 2, pp439-46. McCalman, J.A. (1990) *The Forgotten People*, King's Fund Centre, London. Holland, B. and Lewando-Hundt, G. (1987) *Coventry Ethnic Minorities Elderly Survey, Method and Data and Applied Action*, City of Coventry Ethnic Development Unit, Coventry. Bhalla, A. and Blakemore, K. (1981) *Elders of Minority Ethnic Groups*, AFFOR, Birmingham.

89 Donaldson, L.J. and Odell, A. (1986) 'Aspects of the health and social service needs of elderly Asians in Leicester: a community survey, *British Medical Journal*, vol. 293, pp1079-82.

90 Roony, B. (1987), *Racism and Resistance to Change: A Study of the Black*

291

Social Workers Project in Liverpool SSD, Liverpool University.

91   Atkin, K., Cameron, E., Badger, F. and Evers, E. (op.cit.).

92   Roony, B. (op.cit.).

93   Aitkin, K. et al.

94   Poonia, K. and Ward, L. 'Fair share of (the) care?', *Community Care*, 1990, vol. 796, pp16-18.

95   Holland, B. and Leonardo, H. (1987) *Coventry Ethnic Minorities Elderly Survey*, City of Coventry Ethnic Development Unit, Coventry.

96   Bolderson, H. (1991) *Disability benefits while living abroad*, CRE.

97   Norman, A. (1985) *Triple Jeopardy: Growing Old in a Second Homeland*, Policy Studies in Ageing No. 3, Centre for Policy on Ageing, London.

98   HEA Survey (|1994) *The Health and Life-style of Black and Ethnic Minority Groups in England*.

99   Bresson, J.R., Neulat, G. and Palaise, J. (1974) 'La pathologie des migrant en medecine du travail; Archieves des maladies', *Professionelle Medecine*, vol. 35, p9925. Baker, C. (1987) 'Ethnic differences in accidents at work', *BMJ*, vol. 44, pp206-211.

100 Martin, J., Meltzer, H. and Elliot, D. (1988) *OPCS Survey of Disability in Great Britain: The Prevalence of Disability Among Adults*, HMSO, London. Moledina, S. (1988), *Great Expectations: A Review of Services for Asian Elders in Brent*, Age Concern, Brent. See also Farrah, M. (1986) *Black Elders in Leicester: An Action Research Report on the Needs of Black Elderly People of African Descent from the Caribbean*, Social Services Research, 1, pp47-9.

101 Rickford, F., 'Culture shades', *Social Work Today*, 25th June 1992, p10.

102 *Morning Star*, 12th January 1994, Equal Opportunities Review.

103 CRE (1988) *Medical School Admissions*, CRE, London.

104 Cf. CRE, *Annual Report*, para. 161:35, CRE, London.

105 Smith, D.J (1987) *Overseas Doctors*, CRE, London.

106 Glare (1987) *In Critical Condition*, Greater London Action for Race Equality, London.

107 Esmail, A. and Everington, S. (1993) 'Racial discrimination against doctors from ethnic minorities', *BMJ*, vol. 306, pp691-2. McKeigue, P.M., Richards, J.D.M. and Richards, P. (1990) 'Effects of discrimination by sex and race on the early careers of British medical graduates during 1981-7', *BMJ*, vol. 301, pp961-4.

108 Dr Memon story was outlined in *The Independent* on 2nd July 1994.

109 *Community Care*, 29th September 1991, pp32-3.

110 La Valle, F., Lyons, K. and Grimwood, C. 'My brilliant career', *Social Work*

Today, 10th September 1992, pp14-15.   For a recent study suggesting a high level of stress and discrimination experienced by black social workers, see NISW and LGMB Survey in *Community Care*, 27th April 1995.

111   Wilkson, R. and Wilson, G., 'Pressure points', *Social Work Today*, 11th June 1992, pp16-17.

112   UNISON report cf. Audre, A, *The Voice*, 4th April 1995.

113   Baxter, C. (1988) *The Black Nurse - An Endangered Species*, National Extension College, Cambridge, Training in Health and Race. Cole, A. 'Limited access', *Nursing Times*, 17th June 1987, vol. 83, no.24, p20, surveyed 22 schools of nursing to find under-representation of ethnic minority nurses.

114   NCVO (1985) *Black on Board*, Building on Trust and Networking in Europe, NCVO.

115   Ahmed, A. (1989) 'Contracting out of equal opportunities', *Social Work Today,* 21, 8, 26. Ahmed, A. (1990), *Practice with Care*, Race Equality Unit, London.

116   NCVO (op.cit.).

Conclusion to section III and the way forward

Clearly in all four areas of social policy we have looked at there have been some gains and losses. For instance in education there has been a marginalisation of anti-racist and multicultural policies whilst at the same time there appears to have been gains in terms of improved performances at school level as well as fairly good representation in the universities.

The disproportionate representation of ethnic minorities in the urban space means that a large proportion of students are not reaching their full potential at school or after school and there is little evidence that the TECs are able to counter both the urban effect and the race discrimination in terms of getting ethnic minority young people into jobs. Here the Caribbean male appears to have been particularly disadavantaged in terms of making gains and there is still scope for pushing attainment levels of pupils of Bangladeshi and Pakistani orgin The undermining of the Section 11 programme which was well supported by OFSTED, professionals and parents alike, has particularly eroded the expertise base developed over the years and has affected the loss of ethnic minority teachers.

Social services, like education, has suffered set-backs in the training area although the gains in terms of increased number of black and ethnic minority social workers have not been reversed. In health there has been some government attempt to lay the foundation of some sort of policy, albeit without a strategic framework in terms posts aimed at many activities related to ethnicity specific provision which are not located in a strategic framework. Senior posts of research or funding policy leading to considerable waste and duplication. Training and curriculum development remains extremely underdevloped particularly in nursing, midwifery and medical courses all of which need to take the issue of race and ethnicity on board.

It is sad that quality assurance structures entrusted with auditing and maintaining equal opportunities aspects need to be audited themselves. In the process of writing this chapter I was deeply disappointed to see poor databases, lack of annual reports, little by way of audits so that the information and even published reports were so difficult to acquire on equal opportunities. In health there is no equivalent of the SSI and OFSTED although some ethnic minorities officers are located in the quality assurance departments. Their emphasis also appears to be concerned mainly with the efficiency and clinical audit type of work.

Contract culture has created opportunities for some specialist ethnic minorities workers particularly in health, but at the same time it has undermined early innovations as is the case in the health service and to some extent in the education service. The absence of a Section 11 facility for the health service has delayed many-much needed developments. Overall it would appear that policy development has shifted to the policy enterprise model from the institutional framework model, often requiring funding from somewhere else. It is even more difficult to enshrine the race equality dimension in the new configurations which have emerged in a nineties contract culture framework.

In a contract culture setting the issue of diversity versus efficiency surfaces in a variety of forms, and is utilised as an excuse for non-action. For instance, to appoint several bilingual workers is seen as very expensive, notwithstanding the fact that such speakers may be competent in two or even three languages. In any case, if language competency is needed, then you are gaining a social worker with an extra competency which should be recognised and rewarded.

Instead, such competencies tend to ghettoise workers who feel that when promotion is considered, the white establishment will view their experiences with minority clients as marginal and use that to deny them promotion. The same issue has emerged within the context of Section 11 funded teachers and equal opportunity / race advisors. An additional dimension to this issue is that many workers find that as they have to confront the system to bring about change, this confrontation in turn could lead to systemic exclusion, outcasting and denial of promotion.

This is not to say that diversity does not present difficulties and dilemmas for organisations used to recruiting on conventional lines from the labour market. Flexible recruitment and jobsharing can obviously add to the process of widening the spectrum of ethnic competencies. The wider issue of using black workers to deal with black clients without recognition of 'ethnic competence' remains on the agenda as indeed does the issue of limiting their experience. One way out would be to evolve the notion of core ethnic competencies which must be acquired by all social workers, with some workers then specialising in one or two cultures. This must not be restricted to black and ethnic minority workers. The payment for such a competency would be helpful and its accreditation could take place via appropriate courses and secondments under experienced black workers who themselves have to be formally trained. A word of caution is necessary here: I have noticed over the years an appalling stereotypical knowledge amongst some black and ethnic minority workers about their own cultural and ethnic groups, partly because they were taken on board without any scrutiny of their knowledge base and analysis of their ethnic competence. The notion of catering for a large number of group languages is perceived to be too expensive in the new efficiency culture yet successful peripatetic schemes do exist and partnership with other agencies could help.

The issue of ethnic matching of clients with staff, i.e. pupils and teachers, clients and social workers, patients and doctors, particularly in primary health care, appears in the literature as a measure aimed at improving uptake of service by communities who may be disengaged, as well as improving the quality of those services for those who use such services.

Whilst the evidence of uptake and improvement in services by the use of bilingual workers is well established, particularly in the case of communities which may not have a large number of people who are non-English speakers, the situation is more complex in relation to ethnic matching. The evidence of ethnic matching leading to better results in some areas, for instance, adoptions, fostering and teaching, remains doubtful and weak. Secondly, while in some areas ethnicity transcends gender as, for instance, in the use of Asian GPs by Asian women, the reverse is likely to be true in the case of areas where the need is looked down upon. The issue of confidentiality complicates the matter in the eyes of the client, as, for example, in mental health or domestic violence. In this context then black and ethnic minority workers have to build a client group over a longer period (e.g. Southall Black Sisters, for domestic violence) and may be aided by ethnically mixed teams. I have argued elsewhere that mixed teams could be very effective in managing change and conflict in neighbourhoods with hostile and disgruntled white people. Such appointments are excellent substitutes for the use of a lot of translated materials which are poorly utilised due to rather poor literacy rates amongst ethnic minorities.

The other argument centres around the issue of role models within services, inspiring new comers and potential ethnic minorities recruits. Institutions in the business of care often expect all black workers to be internal change agents. But many black workers do not take on this role as their personal circumstances do not allow it, or they feel that they do not want to carry the burden of change on their backs on behalf of their communities. Nevertheless the emergence of equal opportunities which time and again are increasingly seen as gender related, at least in employment terms, has meant that race equality has been sidelined by the white, female-dominated human resource profession.

Historically, a cumulative or triple jeopardy model of discrimination in disadvantage has been applied to target social provision as well being used as a tool of analysis. This model has considerable limitations within the context of the services discussed. First of all, within employment, women are over-represented in some areas, such as midwifery, so that men could feel isolated. Similarly, in recent years, some of the professions have become working class domains leading to an inverse snobbery about class. Thirdly there is some evidence that within ethnic minorities men have suffered to a higher extent from unemloyment than women who have been able to rely on the growing service sector.

The class element has been least supported or discussed in social policy in terms of identity, mentoring and positive action. Too often, poorly explained policies and the feeling amongst the white working youth class that there is no one to champion their cause have created a backlash. Paradoxically, the cumulative disadvantage model also creates a state-sanctioned static victimology, which in turn could damage the capacity of the individual to pull out of adverse circumstances. In this sense, an analysis of the social and economic mobility and progression of these groups, in terms of periodic and intergenerational changes is likely to produce a better picture than the cumulative topping up of disadvantage indicators. Current OPCS data frameworks do not allow for such analysis.

Under the heading of the 'Back to Basics' programme, the government has invoked a debate about family values which sometimes has been seen as a cloaked attack on the Caribbean family, in particular, within the context of dysfunctionality. Broadly speaking, studies of the majority population suggest that the life chances of children born in a single-parent setting are damaged if controlled for class and socioeconomic background. The experience of the black family and in particular that of the Caribbean family in the US is at odds with this observation. Despite the relative success of the Asian family as a counter-disadvantage force and the support it still enjoys amongst young people, it has been pathologised as isolationist and controlling and penalised for attempting to take care of its own members, by the society at large.

Currently an urban policy dimension to social policy is lacking in

298

this field, making it very difficult to develop national strategies. The lack of experience and knowledge of Home Office officials concerning the educational requirements of minority groups has been a problem when considering Section 11 applications. The emergence of the Single Regeneration Budget (SRB), which is supposed to lead to the establishment of regional offices, must take this factor into account.

The role played by referral agencies such as the police at the enforcement end to the health and social services at the caring end of the spectrum of services needs analysis. The police were much more likely to refer black youngsters for reasons of delinquency and the schools are more likely to exclude them and they are likely to get differential punishment. There is much evidence that black youngsters were less likely to be cautioned than white youngsters and much more likely to receive custodial sentences. To what extent it is question of colour (i.e. are the African young equally selected for such treatment) or a question of the representatives of the establishment interacting with the dissentful behaviour of Caribbean males, remains to be settled. The evidence of racist attitudes amongst teachers, social workers and police officers has been gradually building over the years. Further analysis of health service professionals is needed. The evidence is quite good on differential patterns of recruitment in nursing and medical education.

In conclusion, it would be pertinent to stress that I feel it is possible to construct a partial theory or explanation concerning the nature of interaction between black and ethnic minority people and the system. It seems that the system excludes in some areas while it cumulatively includes young black people in the oppressive areas such as law and order sectors. In all areas of social policy there remains an issue of over-inclusion of the Caribbean groups in the social control domain.

Unscheduled inclusion

The passage into an institution could be by means of an institutionally prescribed passage, e.g. a police referral to mental health hospital or frequent exclusion could lead to a juvenile crime record, or even voluntary (i.e. some people put their children into care because they mistakenly think it benevolent).

Transitional inclusion

Whether or not the person's passage through an institution has in any way been altered, by the actions of staff within the institution, or the policies and procedures which are actively pursued by the institution, i.e. school policies, policies of a hospital in terms of therapy being given to patients, can all amplify the the scope of entrapment and brutalising of an individual. It is very difficult for a person to make an exit out of this cycle without having to re-enter (i.e. regimental socialisation) and having a negative track record often makes reintegrating into mainstream society very difficult.

Repeated inclusion

In analysing the role of social policy in tackling disadvantage the relationship between these stages and their routeways from one stage to another needs to be borne in mind.

In fact the model in Chart 6.8 could be applied to both the health and social services. The relationship between exclusions in education, adolescent crime and institutional interventions can be established, although variables such as single parenthood, mixed marriage or combinations there of may be manifestations of class rather than ethnicity. Actually the model applies as much in a class context, particularly on council estates, as it does to race .

Race is likely to have a multiplier and amplifying effect on the disadvantage suffered by those groups who are disproportionately located in a proletarian setting and are culturally and phenotypically integrated amongst the poor working class. More imaginative interventions are needed, such as programmes aimed at reducing school exclusions and offering help to parents with managing conflict with their offspring. Whole family support systems and young people's support mechanisms are needed.

Chart 6.8 Model of repeated inclusion

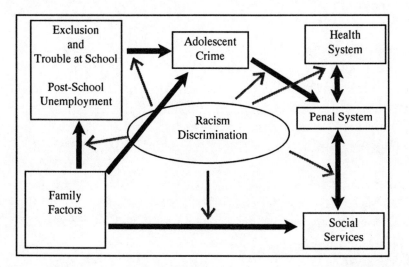

On the institutional response side, one measure which could help is to extend Section 71 of the Race Relations Act* to all institutions. There is no reason why Section 71 responsibility to enhance good community realtions should be restricted to local government. It should be extended to all health authorities, trusts and all educational institutions. Both the SRB and the remaining Section 11 provision need to be linked to the elimination of discrimination and disadvantage, forming a new emphasis towards programmes which embrace the key issue of removing barriers for ethnic minorities.

* This bestows a responsibility on the local authority to enhance good local community relations.

SECTION IV

Housing, Enterprise and Urban Policy

7 Housing, equity, ethnicity and the state

An overview of housing developments in the past decade

The analysis of race and housing development in terms of the role of the state, the changing market and ethos of post-war housing, in a social policy context first and foremost, has to be related to different phases in the settlement and development of black and ethnic minority communities. Second, it has to be located in the wider context of the interaction of the settler with the economic and social markets and the two layers of state, local and central wherever relevant. As shown in the first edition of *Britain's Black Population* (1988), ethnic minority settlers underwent the following stages, each with its own debates, narratives and consequences. These were:

1   A 'laissez-faire' period (1950-67): individual economic migrants and their settlement in slum housing.
2   Settlement and relocation of families, the local state and early ownership in the inner cities (1968-75).
3   Access to public sector housing, state intervention and the new violent slums (1975-80).
4   Tenure and quality debate, community action and the local state (1980-1988).

5   Credit economy, ownership and welfare pluralism in housing (1980-93).
6   Emergence of the black voluntary sector and the new regulatory model (1985-95) of race equality.

All of these stages include significant elements of the previous stages which continue to operate in parallel with the dominant trends of the period. In each of these stages the intrusion of politics can flow in either or both directions. That is from the state (mostly local) or from individuals.

Other factors which impinge upon the relative progress of the different ethnic communities include initial developments such as time of arrival of a group, their initial employment and tenure orientations and the composition and purpose of arrival and the policies pursued by the local and central state at the time. These determine tenure which in turn can have a large impact on the level and type of amenities enjoyed at different stages. Amongst the post war groups only the East African Asians were given new housing as part of the dispersal policy; other immigrants had to compete for older housing in a different sector. Unlike their predecessors, post-war settlers had wider options, yet some of the barriers and prejudices they encountered in the context of housing, and public health particularly, were no different from those encountered by the invisible pre-war immigrants. Yet at the same time the complexity of the post-war systems also obstructed their access and created opportunities for gatekeepers to discriminate.

As shown elsewhere[1] by the late-seventies both local, and to a lesser extent central, government have colluded with racism frequently due to political opportunism or in response to nativism. The debate in the public sector on race and housing had moved from public health access, to quality of access in the pre-seventies era to 'entrapment' in high rise and often violent new slums. Such accommodation was high density and poorly designed housing in which a large proportion of powerless Caribbean and to some extent poor Asian families were channelled by urban gatekeepers as the less deserving[2] into poor quality housing. This was accelerated by the pressure on

306

council housing management to reduce the cost of intermediate bed and breakfast accommodation and their own preference for inner city locations - all of which contributed to channelling ethnic minorities into the sink estates along with the other 'non-deserving' of society. As these estates became concentrated with ethnic minorities they were less acceptable to white tenants and became targets for managers to further channel ethnic minorities into such estates[3]. Many of these estates had already become prone to racial harassment - a process perpetuated by reduced mobility of tenants because of the sale of mostly better quality council housing and new financial regimes in the mid-eighties.

By the mid-eighties, the 'new municipal left' had fully captured and established a powerful base in urban local government. Black and ethnic minorities groups were beginning to flex their political muscle in some London boroughs through a number of newly elected black politicians as well as through their demographic strength. Most major Labour authorities had appointed race advisers in housing, a small number were in the process of instituting more 'objective' allocation systems based on need (e.g. Greenwich), and others had a system of creating mixed property pools for lettings, homeless categories, etc. All in all these *may* have been successful in stopping further differential allocation and improved representation of black and ethnic minority staff - but its impact on quality of housing was marginal[4]. Already such changes had led to a great deal of pressure being applied on the council by organised tenants' movements to roll back its needs-based point system which put many ethnic minority groups at the front of the queue.

Overt racism had moved from a local political plane to become part of the tenants' and residents' associations, with nativism as a firm element in such a philosophy at a time when racial violence was increasing[5]. A similar problem existed in relation to breaking the stronghold of Direct Labour Organisation *vis-à-vis* construction - still dominated by powerful white unions, who also supported local municipal socialism,[6] often excluding black workers. Nevertheless the publication of the Hackney investigation and the existence of these models encouraged many local authorities to monitor their allocations[7]. On the employment aspect the municipal left did improve the minority access into the housing establishment, including the developing black voluntary sector, in the mid-eighties.

Credit economy and welfare pluralism in the eighties

It is from 1980 onwards that the idea of welfare pluralism was promoted which combined the idea of the new left and new right. The new left critiqued the domination of bureaucrats and the failure of institutions to involve and be accountable to weaker sections of the community (blacks, single parents) while the new right highlighted the notion of voluntarism - both agreeing on decentralisation and plurality of provision for different reasons[8]. Ironically it was in the owner-occupied housing sector where a stronghold of discrimination was being broken. This came about due to a boom in lending facilities which gave many black and ethnic minority groups the opportunity to borrow money and buy a house on credit. Generally unemployment amongst black and ethnic minority people has remained ahead of white people particularly during the recession. There is evidence that a large proportion of black and ethnic minority people lived in the worst areas in terms of employment opportunities[9]. Consequently with the exception of Indians, Chinese and whites, other ethnic groups were barely able to sustain their level of owner occupation. Some groups such as the Bangladeshis suffered heavily and were unable to sustain their level of owner occupation. This probably contributed to the increase in racial harassment as owner occupation is the only sector which seems to offer some degree of protection from racial harassment, although this is limited[10].

A sizeable proportion of the black and ethnic minority population who acquired low quality properties were trapped[11] as house values declined in the late eighties particularly in the north of England and the Midlands. Furthermore, in such areas high unemployment and dependency ratios were making the maintenance of these properties

308

very difficult. The English north-south divide was to offer a choice between a job or a house, the latter usually only saleable for a loss of equity. This is, however, less of a substantial problem amongst Asians in Scotland where emphasis on self-employment, a gradually growing ethnic economy and the availability of cheap-end properties provided a cushion (Luthra forthcoming).

The ownership of such properties is likely to make an extremely poor inheritance but is nevertheless, a considerable leg up for a whole generation of Asians. Like self-employment, owner occupation offers status, autonomy and the possibility of various family members contributing to the property albeit at the expense of privacy. Nevertheless, a relatively poor share of good size, quality property owned by black and ethnic minorities in the housing market is likely to be a major contributing factor in the cycle of deprivation. Even such a limited stake in equity is sometimes resented by the white working classes. Some Labour councils were known for ideological reasons to be reluctant to improve the quality and size of black people's share of local equity by enhancing owner occupation for ideological reasons [12]. Generally, properties held by black and ethnic minority groups in the UK decline in value due to the over-representation of blacks. The areas decline since these groups find it difficult to repair property due to vulnerability to unemployment. In the case of Asians, having purchased their properties often without the benefit of tax relief they then find these properties just about sustaining or declining in value in areas of unemployment[13]. Nevertheless the distinctive pattern of Asian housing with high affinity for owner occupation including outright ownership irrespective of class and the region they live in can substantially be explained in cultural terms, i.e. historical fear of loans and capacity for collective action and mutual aid based on village and kin ties (Luthra forthcoming).

During 1984 and 1988, the government vigorously promoted the sale of council housing. Unlike many other working-class people able to buy their properties from the council on discount, the option to buy has only been open to black and ethnic minorities to a limited extent, particularly to communities at high risk from racial harassment and violence such as Bangladeshis. Indeed many of them who exercised their right to buy regret doing so, particularly on estates which have become increasingly prone to racial violence[14]. Even so over the period of the last two decades, as shown in Chart 7.1, the overall trend amongst most ethnic minority groups has been to increase ownership at the expense of the decline in representation in the local authority sector, with the exception of Bangladeshis who appear to have had difficulty in increasing owner occupancy.

Chart 7.1 Owner occupation by ethnic group

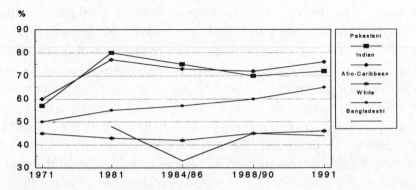

Black voluntary sector and the regulatory model of race equality

Many studies in the eighties including the PSI study (1982) showed that Caribbeans have pioneered entry into the voluntary sector. Conversely there has been poor representation of Asians in this sector, partly due to a larger household size (see Chart 7.1) and partly due to their under-representation in the public sector which historically have had 50% nomination rights*. The magnitude of the difference in proportions evident in the voluntary sector (2.5% Asians in contrast to 3% of white people[15]) still cannot be explained by factors such as location, particularly as the location of housing associations overlaps substantially with the spatial distribution of the black, and in particular the Asian, population.

* Local authorities historically could nominate 'suitable cases' for rehousing to local housing associations.

310

It has taken the Housing Corporation a good deal of time to acknowledge that housing associations could end up replicating many exclusionist policies of the public sector leading to under-representation of black groups in nominations, a longer wait, and disproportionately low access to houses. For instance in a study in Liverpool in 1983 Ferdifru found that a major local housing association in Liverpool catering for the elderly had blacks in single figures despite the fact that blacks had been living in Liverpool for many hundreds of years and constituted about a third of the population[16]. Similar observations, including the lack of equal opportunities policies, were to be later noted in the CRE's investigation of Collingwood Housing Association and in the work of Provan and Jesson on Birmingham associations[17].

Historically the voluntary sector in England has been substantially controlled by middle-class whites and highly geared towards catering for the subjectively assessed 'good tenant' sometimes creating little 'white islands' amidst inner city areas of high concentration of black and ethnic minorities. Their stock was developed through a system and in particular the notorious TIC (Total Indicative Cost) system which was introduced in 1982 and generally pushed housing associations towards a high level of conversion into smaller units[18]. The race implication of which was explored by Ealing Family Housing Association which approached the CRE in relation to such a trend being indirectly discriminatory. Its greatest failure until 1985 was in not being able to cater for vulnerable ethnic groups, single parents, ethnic elderly and large families although the situation appears to have changed significantly since 1985* when the government decided to shift the resources over to housing corporations.

As part of the changes, the Housing Corporation was able to launch a long-term programme with funding of £12 million in 1986/87 increasing to £52 million in 1989/90 and producing some initially impressive results[19]. Nevertheless the black voluntary sector is establishing itself visibly. A recent threat has however emerged as the Housing Corporation decided not to support further independent

* Rent evidence suggests that white-dominated housing associations are quite keen to provide for ethnic minorities.

311

housing association development and there is increased emphasis on borrowing from the private sector despite high interest rates. The housing association grant rate has been steadily falling and is down to 55% where it is likely to stay leading to net saving for the exchequer with increasing rents and private sector borrowing to balance the books. Small black housing associations find it difficult to attract private loans to finance their schemes, pushing them towards mergers or becoming satellites of larger associations[20]. There is considerable frustration amongst the black housing associations that the DoE is very unhelpful in responding to their needs, and changing financial rules are detrimental to their growth[21].

The 1988 Housing Act also strained relationships between local authorities and housing associations making transfers of local authorities difficult. Nevertheless in response to the code of practice, the Housing Corporation has established a monitoring regime with established race equality targets which on the last count, although four out of five had monitoring systems, only a quarter had targets. Given the marketisation of rents, reluctance of housing associations to accept nominations from homeless people, and the increasing fear of losing its privilege of a high staff-tenant ratio and to rank along with local authorities as providers for the poor, the housing associations need watching to ensure that they do not go the same way as local authorities did.

The increasing reliance of housing associations on private finance has linked the level of tenant's rents to the fluctuations in the money market, albeit somewhat tenuously. Recent government moves to link the level of rents that housing associations can charge with grants may ease the situation a little.

Differential progress in the eighties

The PSI study's conclusion in 1982 summarised the overall position at the time:

Blacks are more often found in flats, and those in flats are more

312

often at higher floor levels, and those with houses are less likely to have detached or semi-detached property; black families have smaller property on average, and, with larger households sizes, their density of occupation is much higher; black households more often share rooms or amenities with other households; the properties black families own or rent are older; and they are less likely to have a garden. These differences are not the product of the different ethnic tenure patterns: they remain when the comparison is restricted to council housing or to owner-occupied property [21]

Table 7.1 Tenure by ethnic group 1981 and 1991 (households %)

	Owner Occupier	Council	Private Rented
Bangladeshi	49 (44)	31 (37)	19.1 (9)
Caribbean	43 (48)	44 (35)	12 (6)
East African	69 (54)	14 (13)	16 (24)
Far Eastern	51 (62)	13 (13)	35 (17)
Indian	77 (81)	12 (7)	10 (6)
Pakistani	82 (76)	11 (10)	9 (9)
NCWP	60 (59)	24 (36)	14 (11)
All	58 (66)	29 (-)	13 (7)

Source: OPCS 1981 and 1991. ( ) = 1991
Note: all figures are rounded up so do not add up to 100%.

Earlier on in 1978 the NDHS data had shown that the Chinese and Bangladeshi communities were over-represented in highly overcrowded premises attached to the workplace[22].The picture with regard to the private rented sector has changed in the nineties. Ethnic

313

minorities are now over-represented in the private rented sector to a lesser extent than a decade ago (10.8% as compared to 7% of the general population in 1981) with Chinese (17.0%), black other (13.6%) and Africans (17.8) being highly over represented in this sector (Table 7.1). Another noticeable feature of Table 7.1 is the large decline in the proportion of council tenants with a small increase in owner occupation amongst Bangladeshis. The Chinese meanwhile, enjoyed a good decade, having fled from the private rented sector into owner occupancy partly due to their better employment prospects in the eighties (see Chapter 8).

Amenities

As is evident from Table 7.1 and Chart 7.2 there has been considerable improvement in providing amenities and reducing overcrowding particularly in the owner occupation sector - but the gap between black and white households in age, size and type of property persists. Pakistanis own the worst properties often without central heating (Table 7.2). Indians and in particular, Pakistanis and Bangladeshis, still remain very disadvantaged in terms of amenities as compared to other groups. This is mainly due to their concentration in the private rented sector. In Chart 7.1 we have also shown the relationship between overcrowding levels and large families and particular with high dependency ratios except in the case of the 'black' category which despite this high ratio does not suffer from over crowding or lack of amenities. This is partly due to over-representation of black Caribbeans in the public sector provision which is often better built in terms of modern amenities, partly because single-parent families tend to be smaller and to a lesser extent due to preferential policies pursued by some councils towards single parents in relation to the public sector housing.

The overall picture suggests that both the Chinese and Caribbeans experience relatively low level of disadvantage as compared to other groups in terms of access to amenities. The Chinese by virtue of spatial distribution and Caribbeans due to their disproportionate

314

Chart 7.2 Overcrowding, large households and dependency ratios

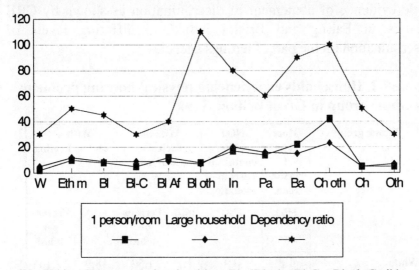

W = White Eth m = ethnic minorities Bl = Black Bl-C = Black-Caribbean
Bl oth = Black other In = Indian Pa = Pakastani Ba = Bangladeshi
Ch oth = Chinese other Ch = Chinese Oth = other

access to both public sector and housing association accommodation compared with other ethnic minorities groups. The more recent entrance of Bangladeshis and the Chinese into public sector housing (primarily due to overcrowding in tied accommodation which has historically been a priority for council housing departments) has helped them in terms of improving their enjoyment of amenities.

Despite these gains a large proportion of Asians still live in overcrowded terraced housing according to the English Housing Conditions Survey (DoE 1992)[23]. The same survey partly attributed overcrowding to a large number of concealed households. Nevertheless taking a long view of the history of housing they have done rather better in terms of amenities over the last 15 years than the earlier post-war immigrants. Even in overall terms figures for those ethnic minorities households with amenities has improved from 67% in 1971, 76% in 1977, 93% in 1981 to 97% in 1991 according to census data[24]. Yet the level of disadvantage suffered by ethnic minorities is extremely high in the private rented sector and there is little evidence of abatement of discrimination as shown by CRE studies in Ealing and Bristol indicating differing levels of discrimination on the part of lettings agencies [25].

Table 7.2 Households experiencing physical housing problems by ethnic group in Great Britain, 1991

Ethnic group	More than 1 person/ room	NOT self-contained accom-modation	Without exclusive use of bath or WC		Without central heating	
	(%)	(%)	(%)	Persons per h/hld	(%)	Persons per h/hld
White	1.8	0.9	1.2	1.50	18.9	2.16
Ethnic Minorities	13.1	2.4	2.1	2.09	17.8	3.33
Black-Caribbean	4.7	2.0	1.4	1.65	17.4	2.30
Black-African	15.1	6.51	5.1	1.73	15.8	2.46
Black-Other	5.6	3.2	2.4	1.67	20.2	2.27
Indian	12.8	1.0	1.1	2.65	12.4	3.59
Pakistani	29.7	1.2	1.7	3.31	34.2	4.94.
Bangladeshi	47.1	1.3	2.0	4.17	23.6	5.19
Chinese	10.6	3.5	3.2	1.95	16.0	2.82
Other Asian	11.0	3.7	3.0	1.79	12.1	2.86

Source: CRE (1991) Census Local Base Statistics.

On a relative scale as shown in Table 7.2 it is the Bangladeshis and Pakistanis who in particular lag behind the indigenous population and suffer from multiple disadvantage in terms of access to amenities, i.e. lack of exclusive use of amenities and central heating. These factors then appear to coincide with overcrowding in the case of Pakistanis and Bangladeshis. Notwithstanding the degree of sharing, the Chinese and the Africans have done quite well to catch up with the white group. The latter due to a relatively large middle class contingent and the former due to the expansion in the ethnic economy[26] and through dispersal.

Homelessness

Despite the owner occupation boom in the eighties there is a problem of homelessness amongst young blacks, particularly youth of Caribbean origin. This can be substantially attributed to high rates of unemployment amongst young blacks and also to some extent to the rising conflict in the Caribbean family[27]. A recent survey[28] however has found very few young homeless black people on the street; most were found to be living in hostels. Nevertheless, as indicative from the OPCS 'black category' data (which is mainly made up of young blacks), just over one third of second-generation blacks are now owner occupiers. The government has launched lodgers schemes to assist young people needing accommodation, but ethnic minorities have been under-represented in the schemes according to the LRC survey[29].

Bangladeshi homeless families, according to the Home Affairs Committee (1987), also live in dangerous and overcrowded accommodation for long periods, in areas such as Tower Hamlets for example[30]. As concealed households are very predominant amongst Asians it is difficult to assess the actual level of homelessness amongst young Asians. Given the high degree of cohabiting with in-laws, and considering the strain on Asian women, it is likely that concealed households are taking a toll on the mental health of Asian women.

Quality of accommodation and life

There is little data on quality of accommodation by ethnicity. Both the National Dwelling and Housing Survey (1978) and the PSI (1982) noted a concentration of black and ethnic minority groups in pre-1919 or post-1960 properties, often on higher floors and on undesirable estates in the case of the latter[31]. The disparity between types of properties allocated to blacks and whites grew between 1972 and 1982 according to the PSI study in 1982[32]. Over the last decade many local authorities, particularly urban local authorities, have made serious attempts to remove the non-need elements in their allocation systems improving access to the public sector and movement within it. Others, such as Tower Hamlets, continue to discriminate despite instructions from the court[33].

It is in this high rise public sub-sector in which one finds the most disadvantaged sections *within* black and ethnic minority communities, e.g. single parents (particularly Caribbean and African single parents) and large families, particularly Bangladeshi families. Relatively less established* communities such as Bangladeshis are taking the brunt of racial violence through a systemic and explicit process, mostly, if not wholly but substantially, by young white people[34]. The situation is forcing people to make a choice between living in relatively spacious accommodation in the public sector or moving to avoid racial harassment. In the eighties racial harassment in East London was to bring the Asian youth into confrontation with the police. Racial harassment, although it reactivated the debate about race and housing, has also acted as a sponge to suck in limited resources in the form of 'harassment' monitoring projects and anti-racist campaigns, so much so that many race units in housing departments intended for policy development, were being forced to do casework.

Many councils have introduced penalties including enshrining clauses into contracts to be able to move the perpetrators. Yet most councils back down from using the law to avoid backlash from majority white working-class tenants. This feared or actual backlash

* In our survey of six authorities we found that some communities such as the Carribeans felt better established in the public sector than others

318

has led some observers to argue that the law should not be utilised[35]. The courts have also been reluctant to take into account the aggravated 'racial' element in what is often described as common assault. Consequently, as shown by Love and Kirby (1994), there have been very few court cases[36] and even fewer exemplary sentences despite murders on some estates. The government on its own part has issued joint guidelines to the courts via the Lord Chancellor's Office on the issue of harassment by landlords, but this has yet to happen within the context of racial harassment[37]. The ring-fencing of housing resource budgets, restriction on use of housing capital receipts or their transfer to housing associations have all led to an increase in council rents, which are now pegged to private sector rents. In 1991, a couple with two children and a rent of £26 lost all entitlement to housing benefit when pre-tax earnings reached £110 per week. Given the average income of black and ethnic minorities workers is lower and their unemployment higher, than their white counterparts, these factors have had a disparate impact on black and ethnic minority tenants in addition to adding to the frustration of all tenants. This in turn adds to the racial tension in public sector housing[38].

Equity

Despite this, there are positive achievements based on self-help in terms of establishing equity amongst certain groups. The Indians and Pakistanis now have a well-established level of owner occupation. The Bangladeshi, Chinese and African communities have done well in terms of establishing owner occupation and entering the public sector, considering that they are relatively recent arrivals, for instance, as compared to the Caribbeans. As Table 7.3 shows there has been a decline in the outright ownership patterns as some groups such as the Indians and Pakistanis engaged with the credit economy to improve their quality of housing. The quality of this equity is however poor as evident from lack of central heating

(Table 7.4). The overall pattern in terms of outright ownership has not changed for most ethnic minority groups except in the case of the Chinese, who showed an increased tendency towards owner occupation over the past decade.

Table 7.3 Type of accommodation and outright ownership by ethnicity

Ethnic Group	Detached (%)	Semi-Detached (%)	Outright owned as % of Detached and Semi-Detached
White	21.5	31	16.1
Indian	13.6	27.9	5.5.
Pakistani	6.3	18.9	3.2
Bangladeshi	4.1	10.0	0.8
Caribbean	3.2	16.5	2.1
Chinese	15.5	20.5	5.5
African	3.6	10.4	1.0
All Ethnic Grp	20	24	-

Source: Luthra, M. constructed from OPCS (1991) = % of overall tenure profile.

There was also considerable improvement over the past decade in terms of entry into the semi-detached and detached type of properties often located in better areas (Table 7.3), particularly in the case of Chinese and Indian communities. Again the development of a housing elite is a function of initially high owner occupation amongst some communities. This has not changed the fact that even in the owner-occupied sector (according to the 1994 English Housing Conditions Survey), both black and Asian households are twice as likely (18% and 15.7%) to be in a worse category of dwellings as compared to white households (7.1%), partly due to their over-representation in terraced properties[39]. Furthermore, 47% of Pakistani and 38% of Bangladeshi outright-owned properties lacked central heating as compared to 18% for the general population

320

(Table 7.4). With the exception of Indians and the Chinese, the quality of equity owned in terms of detached and semi-detached property is substandard and often shared by many households. The number of concealed households hides considerable homelessness amongst Asians.

Overall outright ownership and council housing are only influenced to a small extent by regional variations. For instance, outright ownership varies between 8% (England) to 12% (Wales) for Caribbeans, and 11% (Wales) to 17% (England) for Indians, with Scottish figures falling in the middle. These variations could be accounted for by the extent to which various communities feel established and in the case of Asians where there is an inverse relationship with class and probably literacy which partly explains the high outright ownership amongst Pakistanis but not the low level among the Bangladeshis.

Table 7.4 Outright ownership by ethnicity by year and presence of central heating (in brackets)

Ethnic group	1978 (%)	1984 (%)	1991 (%)	1993 (%)
White	24	26	24.4 (16.1)	24
Caribbeans	4	5	8.2 (22.6)	6
African	5	-	3.3 (16.5)	-
Indian	18	24	16.5 (19.4)	15
Pakistani	17	24	19.4 (47.6)	18*
Bangladeshi	8	-	5.0 (38.0)	8
Chinese	9	9	13.9 (15.6)	-

Source: Luthra, M. constructed from NDHS (1978), Survey by Mori for Educational Health Authority (1993), GHS (1984-93), and OPCS (1991).
* Includes merged figures for Bangladeshis.

321

Table 7.5 Percentages in council accommodation by selected areas (Bangladeshis and Caribbeans)

Ethnic Group	Inner London (%)	Scotland (%)	Wales (%)	GB (%)
Caribbean	48	29	28	35
Bangladeshi	65	19.2	7.1	37

Source : Luthra, M. constructed from OPCS (1991).

Regional variations are also very important at city level. Some cities such as Glasgow have had an established tradition of outright owner occupation funded for instance by a combination of low value property and short-term and part-lend part-rent loans[40].

Similarly the high affinity for public sector accommodation in some cases can be substantially explained by the spatial concentration of Bangladeshis, and to a lesser extent Caribbeans, in London (Table 7.5). As shown above, once the London factor is removed then the Bangladeshi tenure profile moves much closer to the Asians at large. This holds less true for the Caribbeans.

Equity, tenure and social relations

Recently there has been considerable debate about single parents and access to housing. The government is considering legislation to remove priority given to single parents by many local authorities. Black women, particularly of Caribbean origin have felt that this policy is a veiled attack on them. Research by Peach et al (1993) based on the OPCS data suggests that if council housing data is standardised in terms of class and socioeconomic groups, Caribbean single-parent women are still over-represented in council accommodation. They are particularly over-represented in flat accommodation as compared to their white counterparts. To what extent it could be explained in terms of a function of living in the

Table 7.6 Tenure by ethnicity by country (%)

	England Caribbean	England Bangladeshi	GB Caribbean	GB Asian
Owner Outright	9.3	7.5	8.2	13.5
Buying	61.2	55.6	4.8	63.0
Council	28.6	17.2	37	13.0

Source: Luthra, M. constructed from, OPCS (1991).

inner city or the contributing factor of a UK-based housing tradition or for that matter a manifestation of data which has become skewed as many white tenants moved out, remains unresolved.

Overall, single young female parenthood[41] appears to be a key variable, together with priority policies of the urban councils and availability of the right size stock in explaining the over-representation of Caribbeans in public sector housing[42]. There are also some significant apparent differences in terms of quality of accommodation given to Caribbean single mothers in comparison with white mothers, although Peach et al have not standardised their data by size of family or the route taken by them, i.e. it is quite likely that a larger proportion of Caribbean single parent women were rapidly housed through the homeless category which historically received poor quality accommodation.

On the equity side it has been argued that white single parents are better placed in terms of equity than their Caribbean and African counterparts although Peach et al (1993) have also underplayed the inheritance aspect in enhancing outright ownership and the length of residence in enhancing access to transferability within the public sector, both of which are likely to be higher for the white communities.

Whatever the psychological or moral arguments about single parenthood, it would appear that at least in the current systemic framework it is not conducive to equity building. Peach's notion that

323

class, to some extent, explains the tenure profile does not account for how in the case of Asian tenure, class is irrelevant as an explanation of tenure and equity[43].

Equity and housing enterprise

There is also some evidence that some groups, particularly the Indians in England[44], and Pakistanis in Scotland have established a small landlord class which feels somewhat unsupported by the government. Government policy currently has an emphasis either on resident landlording or on generating large housing companies[45]. This emphasis runs contrary to the small business rhetoric of the government and is symptomatic of the poor small landlord lobby. It is this sector that has absorbed most of the new refugees. Given the small scale of this sector it is unlikely that it can compete for large public sector property management contracts being considered for contracting out and these are centring in large ethnic minority group large property companies.

Coopers & Lybrand research (1994) suggests that the returns on the housing investment are no more than 4% as compared to the gilts and stocks which yield 6%[46]. In addition, the risk of damage to property (often unsupported by insurance), and fluctuating interest rates have focused the debate on bridging this yield gap. As for tenants on housing benefit, the payment of the rent by the Housing Board creates a trap in terms of seeking employment. Once a person is employed housing benefit is discontinued, leaving very little incentive to seek employment. This creates a poverty cycle, particularly for single-parent women who risk losing benefit if they take even a low-paid job and when they do, this can create tensions with the inner city small landlords who may be struggling themselves.

Consequently some ethnic minority housing entrepreneurs are taking the route of moving into commercial property, hospitality and nursing homes[47]. Ethnic minority groups who have built up housing

324

collateral have used it to establish business as well as developing housing enterprise as a step to enter other areas of business. A by-product of this has been the development of financial services in some ethnic communities[48].

Recent developments and pending issues

The government's broad policy appears to be to let housing associations and local authorities get the overall service delivery right, then these groups with specialist interest will be dealt with automatically. This view has manifested in the removal of the ethnicity element as a salient factor in calculating allocation of grants to local authorities. The government needs to gather data as it does through the HIPs programmes on the level of racial harassment as well as on allocations by ethnicity, including indicators such as length of wait, on similar lines to what it has been doing recently in relation to homelessness. The government has also reduced Section 11 funding considerably, hitting many projects aimed at monitoring housing allocations and victim support for racial harassment.

Despite the recession the government does not appear to believe that inflating the housing economy will have a major effect and the economists are divided too. Although there is little direct evidence that ethnic minorities have suffered disproportionately from lack of new building, casework experience suggests that certain groups such as large families and traumatised families who experience racial violence or low level harassment, have suffered delay in being given safer and more appropriate accommodation. Recent evidence based on allocations suggests that ethnic minority groups have suffered disproportionately.

There appears to be little government concern for the people who were encouraged to take out mortgages and whose subsidy has withered away without any warning (*Panorama*, 22 May 1995). This has obviously hit the Asian community with their affinity towards owner occupation and may well have forced some family members to stay together despite conflict (hidden homelessness) and probably has hindered the entrance of young ethnic minorities into owner occupation.

The Housing Corporation is likely to be subjected to a major review with the likely split between its regulatory and administration funding. If the Tories stay in power some of the housing association monies may be awarded to the developers directly to build. This may have serious consequences for racial equality. The prevalent view of the Treasury is to intervene very little (through tax incentives) so as not to distort the market, although for various sectors this is at odds with considerable guarantees which have been offered. The issue of protection and survival of the small housing association remains untackled and sectorised specialist provision is likely to be necessary.

The government has been able to reduce the treasury bill on housing and shift financial support to housing associations partly by reducing the mortgage tax subsidy (which is unlikely to continue even at the current level) as well enabling councils to use surplus from increasing rents to subsidise housing benefits. Building societies along with banks have contributed to lending, although as they behave more and more like banks they are compromising their local social objectives. Smallwood (1992) has shown building societies' difficulties in providing stable, low-start funding for house purchase without being too cautious[49]. Their rules also make it very difficult for low-income single parents and large families to take out mortgages. Their mergers and the change in their role runs contrary to the government plank of welfare pluralism.

A related and pending issue is that of how to bring about stability in the housing market which requires delinking housing finance from the interest rate and currency fluctuations in the wider markets. The popularity of the fixed mortgage schemes suggests that a housing bank which invests in partnership with other agencies and lends at the best fixed rates possible for the residential property may be an appropriate way forward. There is no reason why such a housing bank could not provide facilities to disadvantaged groups through local councils or even housing associations who have pioneered successful schemes of building for sale either on a full or a half rental basis. These have been quite popular amongst ethnic minorities.

The present government and indeed the labour party are both exploring arms'-length companies with tenants holding shares along with councils. The possibility of this will enable the government to keep public borrowing at a minimum level and enable such companies to borrow from the private sector. Given the poverty of public sector tenants and their scepticism about ownership and the cost of transferring and upgrading such stock, it seems likely that such schemes will bypass the disadvantaged tenants increasingly making the council stock a sink stock.

Over the past decade public sector borrowing has been kept low by ring-fencing the housing revenue account and government resources redirected to the Housing Corporation. This expansion has been helpful for some ethnic minority groups in terms of being able to leave some of the sink estates. In particular the Caribbeans have been able to benefit from it in terms of leaving the worst public sector accommodation. They have unfortunately failed to play any significant role in Scotland. Indeed, three investigations by the CRE investigation of housing association and their funders revealed a very poor record on equal opportunities in Scotland[50]. There is emerging evidence of disparity of income of housing association tenants with almost three quarters more new tenants not having earned income at all. Currently the lack of an organisational link between housing associations, building societies, banks and local authorities to develop a local housing strategy is a formidable problem.

The issue of accommodation for asylum seekers has not only been a bone of contention for the indigenous population, established settlers are also raising the spectre of nativism, i.e. international obligations versus the needs of local taxpayers. The sting could be removed by offering such accommodation for a fixed period and then reviewing the situation. The government is in the process of further curtailing the access of refugees to welfare benefits[51]. Secondly the expenditure figures on asylum seekers' use of accommodation could be published, given the small number of asylum seekers, to reduce the possibility of exaggerated claims made by the press. Furthermore a settlement fund for asylum seekers should be created at EU level to deal with the local white backlash problem, to reduce public anxiety based on nativism as it would be seen to be funded by Brussels rather than locally. Refugees are at the cutting edge of having to deal with some very hostile tenants on council estates.

A lot of local authorities are dumping newly arrived refugees in areas of ethnic minority settlements (which already have high unemployment and some concentration of social problems), through allocations or through leasing schemes. This tends to add to the depleting skills base in such areas as the refugees will take a long time before they are able to engage with the local economy. As John Crawly has pointed out (*The Guardian*, 24 Dec. 1994), the current housing policy does little to deal with racial segregation which he argues has been on the increase.

Despite the limited impact of two CRE investigations (Liverpool and Tower Hamlets councils), the CRE in its wisdom has decided not to pursue housing work which also affects racial harassment work. It has, however, produced a guide on ethnic monitoring in housing. Despite this, Love and Kirby noted that only one in ten authorities in their survey had data on existing tenants while two-thirds kept records of future tenants[52].

Nevertheless the Love and Kirby report noted that on racial harassment various local authorities have taken initiatives, including keeping records of incidents and 44% had developed a policy after 1989. The report also noted that just over half the authorities had established multi-agency groups and in most cases it would fall into the following categories which involved senior officers, although grades were not given. Although many took pre-litigate action, very few took legal action. Only 28 cases of legal action were recorded and only 12 tenants were evicted[53]. Considering the overall number of attacks this is a very small number.

The current approach remains a victim-centred and reactive one with most authorities offering relocation to the victims. Little has been done to establish a source of independent advocacy to push the local authorities and engage in surveillance and gather evidence. Although some authorities have responded with technical responses such as video surveillance and button alarms. Some possible aspects of development, are neglected, these include community education including that of tenants' associations, and youth education and community development aimed at integrating communities through community safety programmes (see Chapter 4).

Table 7.7 Local authorities' approaches to tackling racial harassment and violence: impressions from survey

	Housing	Education	Crime Prevention
Council based	*******	***	*
Voluntary sector based	**		
Campaigning groups	**		**
Police based	*******		
Multi-agency	*********	**	**
Technical	********		
Legal action	***		*
Community education	*	*	
Tenants' associations			
Parents' associations		*	
Community development	**		*
Youth work	**		*

* = 2 positive responses
Source: Luthra, M. (1995) literature survey and personal experience during Brunel research on racial harassment in 1988 and telephone survey in 1989.

Estate-based conciliation services, integrated community development together with crime prevention measures with a counter-racism dimension are necessary tools in the battle against conflict on council estates that have a racial dimension. Perpetrator-centred and preventative approaches also require DES intervention using educational aids such as the Anne Frank exhibition and targeted youth work. In addition, focused educational programmes aimed at schools from which perpetrators are drawn need to be developed.

On the homeless front some local authorities such as Birmingham have successfully tried self-build projects which need to be replicated on a large scale for the young in inner city areas. In my 1988 study of the Ujema housing association I found that an overwhelming number of young blacks left their homes like their peers as they did not get on with their parents. Anderson[54] et al (1993) have shown that young black people, and particularly young black women, are over-represented in hostels or accommodation for single people and rarely found sleeping rough. The traditional halfway house, i.e. staying with an uncle or aunt is not available in all cases. Halfway house projects will continue to be needed. Specialist projects of this nature are less likely to be funded as earmarked funding for ethnic minority groups has disappeared in the Single Regeneration Budget (SRB).

A major pending issue is that of housing refugees which has been an area of contention. Currently there are only 12 associations catering for refugees with less than 1000 dwellings, nearly half of which are short life. The absence of independent housing and poor command of English puts the refugees in a poor bargaining position in the social market. The draft for the 1996 Housing Act suggests that the government would split public housing into purchaser-provider sections leading to radical changes in local authorities, undermining current policy structures on racial equality and racial harassment. It would be interesting to see if Section 71 of the Race Relations Act (1976) would enable local authorities to put a condition on the private sector competition to spend money on issues such as racial harassment.

The weakening of the Homeless Persons Act would mean that hidden homeless in some communities will continue to add to overcrowding, while those who appear on the council list will face shrinking provision. The Act will redirect housing association resources into the private sector to encourage it to develop social housing while encouraging housing association tenants to buy their own properties, further eroding the public sector base. The government legislation on anti-social behaviour including provision for probationary tenancies may prove beneficial in coping with racial harassment in terms of dealing with perpetrators.

Conclusions, issues and challenges

Overall, the current government has been preoccupied over the last decade with owner occupation from which some communities (Chinese and Asian) have benefited. At the same time, urban local authorities' policies with a shift in emphasis on need which included single parenthood has benefited the Caribbean and Asian families.

In a world of increasingly centralised building societies and banks, as well as building firms and the concentrated ownership of land, blacks and ethnic minorities are mainly consumers, savers and borrowers rather than controllers and power brokers. Historically these institutions have had a one-way and somewhat parasitic relationship with the innercities, in particular with the black and ethnic minority population injecting only enough resources to sustain the inner city human capital required by the economy. These institutions, including the council sector construction industry, offer little employment to blacks. They have now been replaced by Direct Service Organisations which generally tend to be free of councils' corporate equal opportunity policies, and hence are even more likely to discriminate in hiring and firing and are not subjected to contract compliance.

The banks and building societies still have very few black and ethnic minority staff in senior positions even in some areas of high ethnic minority concentration. The key people who influence allocation at all levels of the state are politicians and the above-mentioned gatekeepers. The equivalent for the latter in the private sector would be front-line line managers and staff which are called exchange professionals. Sowell[55] (1981) has argued that such professionals have little incentives not to discriminate, and it is competition and incentives which will drive out discrimination. Yet at the same time it is the non-profit sector which has taken a lead on the issue including the council lending sector. Admittedly the deregulation of the eighties did undermine discrimination in lending. The situation is often further complicated by the fact that racial discrimination by such urban gatekeepers is intertwined with discrimination on other grounds such as class and gender.

Urban local government has made some progress in tackling race equality in the eighties followed by some major strides by the housing association sector. Most of the change has not come from community action although there has been community action; it has come rather from persuasive empirical evidence, lobbying by housing professionals and legal action. The demise of Housing Aid Centres and Law Centres as independent watchdog bodies is highly regrettable and need revival using a variety of resources such as the lottery and SRB (Single Regeneration Budget).

Generally there appears to be little by way of a concerted action plan to assist well-focused ethnic minority areas to increase move-out rates from appalling estates, or to assist by offering low interest rate loans to blacks to acquire some stake in the inner cities or to tackle the amenities problem in areas such as Tower Hamlets, Bradford, etc. The Department of the Environment has to provide a lead on tackling race inequality in housing on a long-term basis incorporating access, quality, location, structural and equity issues. A similar failure has taken place in terms of developing measures to increase black and ethnic minority employment opportunities in the construction industry and housing establishment. The Department of the Environment or the Home Office have failed to develop and subsequently provide any serious level of resources to tackle the most pressing issue of racial attacks, mostly concentrated on estates, despite the evidence of the relative success of the Priority Estates Programmes type of approach[56].

While it is useful to monitor allocations and move towards more objective systems of allocation, the discrimination flowing from misuse of discretion will only abate as and when black and ethnic minorities people are well represented in organisations involved in housing. Some local authorities have developed 'targeting' systems to offer fair employment opportunities and ensure fair allocation of housing. Others are grouping their properties in different quality categories, with the higher quality property queue for any of these categories having the longest wait. This is then used to offer a choice to the tenant so s/he can either wait for a better property for a certain period or s/he can settle for what is available.

Research is necessary on comparative systems of this nature to assess the effectiveness of such systems. One thing is however clear: with little to allocate in the wake of no building policies, such measures are likely to have a marginal impact on mobility or enhance choice. These measures are unlikely to eradicate discrimination altogether as the 'negotiability' and knowledge of 'areas'of black and ethnic minorities will still put them at a disadvantage due to lack of political clout together with limited lobbying skills, poor political representation and multiple disadvantage factors. This is accentuated by the logical preference to stay near their own communities. Those with large families, recent arrivals such as refugees, and the young, etc. are likely to be channelled into the less desirable properties as a 'management achievement' by the urban gatekeepers and exchange professionals. Thomas Sowell has argued that exchange professionals and urban gatekeepers have no incentive *not* to discriminate[57]. In the absence of this incentive they succumb to the pressures of having to make a choice. Management incentives are needed for fair allocations including establishing targets on equality for managers[58].

There is considerable evidence that differential levels of

disadvantage of ethnic communities, particularly in relation to overcrowding, could be partly attributed to large households. These factors often interact with exclusion factors such as lack of large family dwellings to produce differential outcomes for different groups such as a higher than average rate of overcrowding. As shown earlier there are substantial differences in responses of Asian and Caribbean communities in terms of tenure from the outset for a variety of reasons, including type and size of families. Asian owner-occupation remains generally high with the exception of the Bangladeshis who arrived in the UK in the seventies when income to house price ratio was high. The entry of Bangladeshis into catering coupled with their spatial distribution and high unemployment rates in the eighties stunted their aspirations for owner occupation. The Chinese, however, have been able to establish a fairly good level of owner occupation along with other recent arrivals such as the Africans. Insofar as the Caribbeans are concerned, they have built up a significant level of owner occupation until the seventies, which then appears to have declined, partly due to demolition and partly due to the second generation wanting to, or being able to, set up their own home in other sectors. Now many first generation Caribbeans are cashing their equity to return to the Caribbean to avoid the trauma of being old, de-statused and alienated in Britain.

Outright owner occupation in Britain has been historically very high amongst Asians. Although there is little by way of analysis of domestic economies, such a large difference cannot solely be put down to ecological factors including the availability of cheap property. Both the fear of loans, their need for autonomy in a family sense, a collective notion of property as a symbol of being someone in a foreign country, coupled with some shrewd collective domestic management have all contributed to produce this outcome.

Over the past two decades the overall trend for most ethnic minority groups has been out of council housing and into owner occupation or housing associations. The latter is particularly the case for ethnic minorities communities such as the Caribbeans, Bangladeshis, and to a lesser extent Africans - all of whom have already established

334

themselves in the public sector. These communities generally have better access to amenities and a lower level of overcrowding than they did in the past, Bangladeshis being the exception to this rule.

From the evidence available, the quality and value of equity held by black and ethnic minorities in property is disproportionately low. It is also prone to devaluation, as it is held mainly in older properties and in poor and declining areas (except London) and it faces mounting bills from disrepair which is exacerbated by occupiers facing unemployment and a high dependency ratio. Such housing makes for a poor inheritance, and hence offers limited opportunity in terms of social mobility. Currently research on the impact of two recessions on ethnic minority housing in terms of market activity and repossession has been lacking.

Nevertheless taking their overall period of settlement into account, the Asians and Chinese, and in particular the Indian and Pakistani achievement in housing in terms of owner occupation, is significant if measured in terms of both reasonable quality outright owner occupation but still somewhat poor in amenities. This will provide some support for a substantial number of second generation Asians, despite a larger than average proportion of concealed households and extended family members who will have to share it.

It must also be noted that some ethnic minority people such as those of Indian origin have evolved a housing enterprise culture which is linked to, as well as used as, a stepping stone to other enterprises. To this end ownership has provided a useful collateral as well as having been a first step towards the formation of a housing elite. Within the spectrum of ethnic groups the quality of accommodation inhabited by people of Pakistani and Bangladeshi origin remain substantially disadvantaged in housing amenities terms, followed by the Chinese, as compared to their white and Indian counterparts. An analysis of British-born ethnic minority groups is needed to assess how the young people of different groups are performing.

It seems that while Asians have an affinity towards the private equity maximisation, low amenities model of housing, the Caribbeans tend to gravitate towards the public sector, high internal amenities and low equity model. The Chinese and the Bangladeshis fall in the middle of these two models gravitating towards the first model with a pool of people still consisting of single migrant men who work predominantly in catering. The Africans, by virtue of rapid family fragmentation, gravitate towards the latter model. Over a long period with matriarchalisation of the indigenous family and perhaps improved life chances for single parents, the two models may meet in the middle. Currently as the situation stands, family structure, in particular the higher than average level of single parenthood amongst Caribbean and African communities, is strongly associated with their over-representation in the public sector and low level of equity.

Nevertheless should the sands shift towards owner occupation, race and housing activists need to argue for sustaining and protecting the hard earned equity for owner occupiers as they do for other groups. Given the poor state of the inner city housing stock and the very high unemployment level together with low income of some ethnic groups, the revival of improvement and repair grants, albeit on a partnership basis and restricted to inner city areas, is desperately needed.

The black housing association movement seems better placed to assist ethnic minority groups than ever before but its scale is too small to deal with the wider issues. It has, however, increasingly had to rely on private sector loans in order to expand. Changing financial rules and the fact that it is not large enough still makes it quite vulnerable. Although at the moment only a small proportion of housing stock has been taken over by the housing associations, one view is that housing associations would be less sensitive to counter-racism campaigning than local authorities*.

Clearly over the three decades there have been considerable housing achievements for the majority of the black and ethnic minority population, both in terms of increased owner occupation and quality of housing, i.e. in terms of household amenities. Yet a proportion of the black and ethnic minority population is still entrapped in hostile and sometimes violence-ridden sectors where

* This is expressed in Mullins, D., 'From Local Politics to State Regulation', *New Community* 18 (3), 401-403.

households have limited opportunities for quiet enjoyment on a par with white citizens. A substantial proportion, particularly Asian subgroups, still suffer from severe levels of overcrowding by virtue of having concealed households, and also partly due to the view they hold of the council sector, with its violent conditions. Nevertheless the entry of people of Chinese, Caribbean, Bangladeshi and African origin into the council and housing association sector is significant. Their relative familiarity with council housing, the changes in council policies in the inner city areas together with the Homeless Persons Act (1976), and learning from the earlier communities, have all assisted in this process of integration into public sector housing.

Insofar as the impact of different fair housing models is concerned, clearly the free-market ideology has helped a little in the reduction of discrimination in the lending market, the bureaucratic/political model has paid some dividends in the public sector and the voluntary regulatory model is being experimented with in the voluntary sector. In a sense one could argue that each of these models have been assisted by measures relevant and appropriate for these sectors, i.e. voluntary for the voluntary sector, competitive for the financial sector, and anti-racist, political/bureaucratic model for the councils. Emergence of empirical evidence, lobbying by professionals and the community together with legal action have all contributed to these gains. Different groups have utilised opportunities created by these different circumstances including state provision of grants, public sector housing according to location preference, their view of public housing and their particular cultural attitudes to property, and knowledge and skills within the framework of opportunities presented to them.

Any effective government policy on race and housing has to take the spectrum of varied developments into account. The spatial concentration of ethnic minority households in poor housing mostly in the inner city areas presents an opportunity to target them. A well-defined urban policy is needed with a well-established race equality dimension.

Hitherto the government's broad policy appears to be to let housing

337

associations' and local authorities' need get the overall service delivery right, then the groups with specialist interests such as ethnic minority groups will be dealt with automatically. This notion is not borne out by the continuing evidence on differential outcomes and the evidence of discrimination. Increased competition for public sector housing and poor mobility within it has created a culture ridden with tribalism and conflict. Studies suggest that both Priority Estates Programmes dovetailed with community safety programmes can[59] make an impact on tackling racial violence. Such programmes have, however, been found to be too expensive. The demise of youth work has further exacerbated the problem of tribal conflict between the young living in worse housing. The government's inter-departmental group RAG has so far failed to develop an effective programme of action aimed at both victims and perpetrators, involving different departments and aimed at problem areas using a national database.

There is only one way to ease the pressure as well as enhance opportunities for equity building and improve the quality of accommodation as well as enhance mobility. This would require a well coordinated interventionist programme involving the three sectors and led by a partnership of private and public sector finance coordinated at local level. This could be supported by a housing bank nationally and with legislation to review the goals of the building societies.

The housing association movement, although very successful in maintaining the conditions of properties and in creating good regulatory models, cannot solve the overall housing problem, particularly those faced within the public sector housing. Although better resourced, it remains an unaccountable movement. Its dialogue with other regeneration agencies appears to be lacking and it tends not to use housing development as a tool for creating opportunities for local black and ethnic minority workers. The housing association movement needs to develop its own contract compliance system.

As for refugees and asylum seekers, a better co-ordinated national refugee policy which is implemented in partnership with the housing associations and local authorities, supported by an organisational framework and a national register, would not only assist the settlement process, but will also go a long way to deal with the public perception of abuse, as well as play a greater role in tackling segregation.

References

1   Luthra, M. 'Race, state and housing', in Bhat, A. (ed.)(1988) *Britain's Black Population*, Gower, Aldershot.
2   Karn, V. and Henderson, J. (1990) *Race, Class and Housing*, Gower, Aldershot. See also Luthra (op.cit.).
3   Ibid.
4   For an overview of literature of differential outcomes in quantitative terms see Luthra (op.cit.).
5   Luthra (op.cit.).
6   West Midlands County Council (1988) *A Different Reality*.
7   Mullins, D. (1991) *Colour of Money*, London Race and Housing Unit.
8   Lund, B. (1993) 'The agenda for welfare in housing', *Social Policy and Administration*, *v*ol. 27, no. 4.
9   Blacks were concentrated in the wrong areas. *New Society* (January 1992.)
10   It is not a coincidence that both crime and unemployment on council estates has gone up in the same period when racial violence and harassment has increased. Cooper, N. (national organiser of the Churches National Housing Coalition), *The Guardian*, 21st June 1995.
11   Ward (1987) 'Race and residence', monograph, Ethnic Relations Unit, Warwick University
12   London Borough of Greenwich certainly discouraged such purchases.
13   Ward (op.cit.).
14   This was evident in Thamesmead (Hewitt, R. (1992), LBG) in the wake of the murder in 1991 and also in our study of the six authorities. (See Austin, Luthra et al) National Dwelling and Housing Survey, 1978, DoE.
15   According to OPCS's the figure for Asians is 1.4% now.
16   Merseyside Improved Housing - Reports to the Housing Advisory Group, cf. Niner, P., 'Housing associations and ethnic minorities', *New Community*, spring 1984, vol. XI, no. 3.
17   Ibid. (12), Provan and Jesson cf.Niner, P., ibid.
18   'TIC's Special Report', *Voluntary Housing*, February 1984.

19   Black Housing VI (8), September 1990 pp.4-11.

20   Grant, C (1991) 'Raising the stakes', *Roof,* vol. 13, no. 6, pp30-33.

21   FBHO see Chandran, K., 'Develop or die; A discussion paper', *Black Housing,* November/December 1993, vol.193, pp22-23. The total revenue budget of black housing Associations has increased from £100,000 to £600,00 (87-92) and capitalisation from 12 million to 52 million for with the total number increasing from 18 to 60.

22   Brown, C. (1982), *Black and White Britain,* PSI.

23   NDHS (1978), DoE

24   OPCS 1971, 1981, and 1991.

25   CRE (1992), *Sorry It's Gone.*

26   See chapter 8

27   UJEMA, see unpublished report of analysis of black homelessness by M. Luthra (1989) for UJEMA.

28   Anderson et al. In 1989 a Birmingham Housing Aid Service Survey reported that 72% of single homeless were black and 44% homeless families were black.

29   LRC Survey (1994)

30   Home Affairs Committee (1987) HMSO

31   Brown, C. (1982) *Black and White Britain*, PSI.

32   Tower Hamlets has been fined £30,000 for not complying with the non-discrimination order

33   Austin, R., Fitzgerald, M., Luthra, M. and Oakley, R. (op.cit.).

34   Austin, R., Luthra, M. and Oakley, R. (1988), *Good Practice Guide*, DOE.

35   According to the CRE the total number of cases brought to court is 40, in 6 cases of which evictions have been secured. The notion of utilisation of law leading to alienation of white tenants was put forward by Fitzgerald, a senior researcher at Home Office Research Unit. See also *Municipal Journal* 14-20th September 1990.

36   Love, A.M. and Kirby, K. (1994) *Racial Incidents in Council Housing,* HMSO.

37   Guidelines for judges has been issued lately

38   Harrison, P. (1988) *Inside the Inner City,* Penguin.

39   DOE (1992) *English House Condition Survey*.

40   See Luthra (forthcoming).

41   Peach, C. et al., 'Caribbean tenants in council housing', *New Community,* April 1993 .

42   Much of this has been empirically established.

43   Smith, D. J. (1974) *Facts of Disadvantage,* PEP.

44   A recent survey of the landlords who were using the HAMS for letting their properties. DoE commissioned survey carried by the LRC found 50% of the applicants to be Asian and 10% to be Afro-Caribbean.

45 Off the record interview with a DoE official. Cited from internal DoE documents.

46 Coopers & Lybrand, cf. DOE documents.

47 A number of people in the health allied professions have opened nursing homes in West London.

48 In West london there are a number of ethnic minorities insurance brokers and financial consultants.

49 Small, J. in Birchall, J. (1990) *Housing Policy in the 1990s*, RKP.

50 CRE investigation of SHSA (1989).

51 Recent changes make it difficult to access some benefits.

52 Love and Kirby (op.cit.).

53 Ibid.

54 Anderson (op.cit.).

55 Sowell, T. (1981) *Ethnic America*, Basic Books.

56 Foster, J. (1992) *The Impact of Community Safety Programmes on Crime*, DoE.

57 Lipsky, L (1988), *The Street-Level Bureaucrats - Dilemma of Individuals in Public Service*, Sage, N.Y.

58 The first attempt to tackle housing estates with large proportion of ethnic minorities took place in London between 1970-1987 focussing on 10,000 units mostly instigated in the wake of riots. Power, A. (1987) *Property Before People*. cf. Mullins (op.cit.).

59 As reference 56.

341

8 Urban policy, race equality and the state

An overview of urban regeneration and its implication for ethnic minority enterprise and employment

This chapter considers urban policy developments. Most members of black and ethnic minority groups live in urban Britain, with many living in what is described as the inner city. There is little evidence that this has changed significantly during the past decade although this lack of change might substantially be attributed to growth in the ethnic minority population.

Much government-led policy in the past two decades has reluctantly or otherwise focused on such areas, particularly in enterprise generation and owner occupation in housing. (The latter was examined in the previous chapter.) This chapter explores the wider issue of urban policy and inner city generation including employment creation to evaluate its implications for race equality. The chapter is divided into two sections. The first part of this chapter focuses on broader issues related to race and urban policy whilst the second part focuses on the developments in relation to the 'enterprise culture' and its implications for ethnic minority groups.

Early Thatcherism, monetarism and black Britons

The victory of the Conservative Party in 1979 produced a government committed to non-interventionist policies - that included policies on race equality. However that government was responsible for a multiracial Britain, 4% of which consisted of black and ethnic minority Britons, almost half of whom were born in the UK and were also disproportionately concentrated in the urban areas which were experiencing a continuing decline[1]. The average income and level of employment among this group was lower than that of the white population.

An initial taste of the Conservative government's approach to the inner cities was provided by a speech given by Geoffrey Howe as shadow chancellor. He argued that the problems of the inner cities might be resolved by an accelerated application of market principles in the form of enterprise zones, where a range of government taxes and regulations, for example on employment protection and workers' health and safety, would be moderated in order to stimulate private investment. Howe's speech, combined with increased funding on law and order, represented what Stuart Hall describes as:

> The new laissez-faire doctrine, in which market values are to predominate, is not at all inconsistent with a strong disciplinary state. Indeed, if the state is to stop meddling in the fine-tuning of the economy in order to let social market values rip, while containing the inevitable fall-out, in terms of social conflict and class polarisation, then a strong disciplinary regime is a necessary corollary[2].

The government also consolidated central control on local government finance by passing the Local Government Planning and Land Act 1980, under which the Secretary of State for the Environment was given powers allowing him to dictate local authorities' capital spending programmes. The same act also established Urban Development Corporations, under which

343

responsibilities for housing, transport and land development in defined areas of the city could be taken from local authorities and handed over to specially-appointed corporations accountable only to the Secretary of State for the Environment. These developments coincided with the rise of the new municipal left (see Chapter 1) and the slightly increased influence of black and ethnic minority groups at urban, local government level.

The package included the concept of inner city partnerships* which were given a new economic emphasis, and Howe's proposals for enterprise zones came to fruition. The Department of the Environment issued guidelines in June 1981, to inner city partnerships, just weeks before the outbreak of the urban riots. These made clear the primary objective of the government's inner cities' policy:

Schemes should be so framed so as to produce as great a visual impact as possible: tangible physical improvement will help to attract private investment ...[3].

In short, the ostensible aim of the new policy was to seize imaginative projects that would raise the expectations of people living and investing, or wishing to invest, in inner city areas. The two major programmes, the Urban Programme, and Section 11 funding, both survived these financial cuts, but only until 1983, when they felt the financial constraints (see Charts 8.1 and 8.2). The government did, however, take note that minority ethnic communities did not participate fully in its partnership programmes and stressed the need to support projects designed to benefit such groups while at the same time increasing the local authorities' discretion.

The early eighties marked a new turn in government philosophy with emphasis. Lee Bridges at the time wrote:

It is important to avoid seeing monetarism as a monolith, or to imagine that its application can proceed in a simple, straight-

* Inner city partnerships were established in 1978 under which partnership authorities has access to DoE grants.

forward fashion. Britain is not Chile, and in a society where local government, the welfare state and trade union bureaucracies are well entrenched, there will be substantial institutional barriers in the way of implementing monetarist objective[4].

Monetarism, inspired by the American economist Friedman, was partly marketed by exploiting many working class fears and generating moral panics, about the abuse of welfare services, and about the swamping of British culture by immigrants. This ploy was helped by the jingoism which flowed from the Falklands war[5]. Bridges[6] argues that this new economic programme was aimed at creating a black entrepreneurial class in the inner cities to which the government could turn for support in its efforts to repress dissident elements in the community. In reality, however, there is little evidence that the government has been seriously interested in creating a sizeable black middle class on American lines. For instance, over the last 15 years the government has shown little interest in issues such as contract compliance and the establishment of US-style business development agencies[7] to develop a black business base. Historically the UK government showed little commitment to the small business sector up until the late eighties, examines the DoE data for 1988 on actual expenditure on business programme start-ups in urban areas, it constituted only 6.3% and 3.3% of the total grant[9] although it did improve later.

Despite this emphasis on economic projects emerging out of the Urban Programme, including those on housing, only 14-16% of projects in 1985 had an economic dimension. Government expenditure aimed specifically at counteracting disadvantage amongst ethnic minorities totalled only about £158 million in 1986 (DoE and the Home Office).

Although there was an eight-fold increase in Section 11 funding between 1976 and 1988, and a thirteen-fold increase in the urban programme, the government's actual input in real terms remained more or less static (see Charts 8.1 and 8.2). Furthermore, the Urban programme was seen as ill-defined, and vulnerable to political mani-

Chart 8.1 Urban Programme expenditure

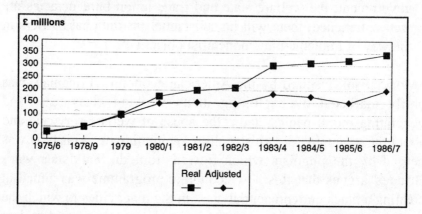

Chart 8.2 Expenditure under Section 11 since inception

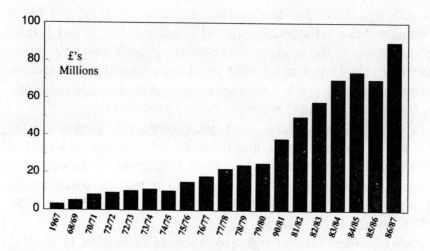

During financial years 67/68 and 68/69 grant was only payable at 50%.
Source: Home Office scrutiny report (1988). Note: The figure for 1994 was £130 million, cut down to around £4.6 million for 1995.

pulation, often short-changing ethnic minorities. It also failed in its objective of getting local authorities to spend more of their resources on areas of deprivation[10]. Similarly, the Section 11 programme, which was wound down in the early nineties (see Chart 8.2), was considerably misused by local authorities[11].

Chart 8.3 Distribution of Section 11 posts within service areas

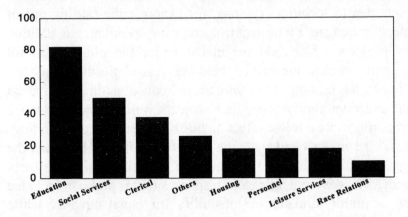

Source: Home Office scouting report (1988).

Chart 8.4 Distribution of Section 11 posts within education

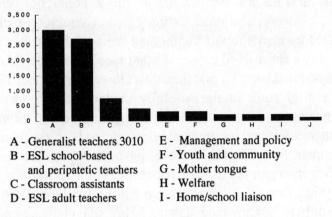

A - Generalist teachers 3010   E - Management and policy
B - ESL school-based   F - Youth and community
    and peripatetic teachers   G - Mother tongue
C - Classroom assistants   H - Welfare
D - ESL adult teachers   I - Home/school liaison

Source: As above.

347

A large proportion of Section 11 resources were spent on educational development, mostly on general teaching where the greatest misuse of funds also took place. Only a fraction of the funding was spent on the envisaged mother-tongue teaching or race advisory work (see Charts 8.3 and 8.4).

In 1988, the government took steps to monitor the achievements of its urban programme. Substantial cuts had already occurred in these projects due to technical reasons, for example the 'silting up' of partnership budgets[12] with recurring revenue spending. In addition many projects which had originated under the old Urban Aid programme reached the end of their five-year eligibility period for funding in the mid-eighties. Moreover, reductions in spending on social and community-orientated projects were already having a disproportionately adverse effect on black and ethnic communities.

One of the major challenges the monetarists had to face was the strong race dimension of the inner city disturbances in the early eighties. The government's early responses to this problem included giving a junior minister responsibility for racial equality while vociferously discrediting the disturbances as being led mainly by the 'loony left'[13] and denying the role of black unemployment as a contributory factor. Lord Scarman was charged with examining the inner cities' plight. His analysis did not recognise the existence of institutional racism, nor did he argue for a coherent, central government, interdepartmental strategy to counter racism. Nevertheless, Scarman's report highlighted the agenda for the inner cities and led to a short-lived consensus that race equality legislation did not always transform into practice. *The Observer* (October 1985) conducted a brief audit of the woefully inadequate responses to Scarman's recommendations, including the government's failure to set up an inner city interdepartmental corporate body to tackle inner city development (see Chart 8.5). There have, however, been some small post-Scarman gains at least on paper. In 1981 a declaration was issued accepting the notion of education for all, while in 1986 the Swann Committee[14] acknowledged that a failure to include a pluralist perspective in education constituted mis-education. The committee

Chart 8.5 Responses to the Scarman Report

Suggestions/ Recommendations	Responses to government 13th October 1985	January 1988
RACE RELATIONS ● Race questions should be included in the census question		Some moves being carried out
● Sustained campaign of positive discrimination to enforce race equality laws	None	None
● The Section 11 definition to extend beyond immigrants to include other disadvantaged groups (non-NCWP) but still to exclude voluntary bodies from applying for funding	Changes accepted although central control increased	PSI carried out a study
● Review of Community Relations Council's work	None	
● Set up inner city department	None	Yes, but no specific race discrimination measures
● Black people should be encouraged to set up own business	£20,000 spent by Home Office in Deptford, London & Handsworth	Ten enterprise agencies set up by BIC
EDUCATION ● Train teachers in the needs of ethnic minorities	Discussion paper on ethnic monitoring being produced	None Reliance on Section 11
● Develop programme to teach English	None	Overtaken by 1988 Education Reform Act
● Better Links between school and parents needed to be established	None	
HOUSING ● Major programme of rehabilit-ation based on community consultation	URHU* - non-specific to black and ethnic minorities	Local Government Housing and Planning Bill amended to give Section 71 (R.R. Act)
● Review of council housing to eliminate discrimination		No review

Source: Luthra, M. (1995) adapted and updated from 'Scarman, The Broken Promises', *The Observer* 13 October 1985. *Urban Renewal Housing Programme established. This programme was relatively small scale.

349

also highlighted the need to challenge racism. Yet from 1988 onwards, the same government which commissioned the report was attacking all efforts to challenge racism in education.

Two steps forward and one step back

Despite the Home Affairs Committee's criticism of the DES for its inability to play a leading role in race equality issues in education, few of the Committee's recommendations were directed at the DES. The DES reaffirmed its commitment to multicultural education and conducted a survey of local education authorities[15] which showed that, in principle at least, most LEAs were committed to changing the teaching and curricula to reflect the pluralistic nature of society.

Yet, according to Nixon[16], the DES's own response to the Home Affairs Committee report was very poor. As already described in Chapter 5, the DES's renewed interest in race equality issues was not to last very long as the government responded to the ideology of the new right in the late eighties and sought to control the curriculum, undermining many good race equality programmes at the same time[17]. Teacher training guidelines had not changed and were instead moving in the reverse direction by the end of the eighties, although government still relied on Section 11 to teach English. The evidence of underachievement in inner city schools continued to emerge[18].

On the housing front, about a dozen local authorities established housing race units in the early eighties[19] and began to monitor their progress. But the DoE did not issue a circular until 1983, when the councils were urged to monitor their allocations. Several urban local authorities took up this issue, albeit slowly and by 1985 almost forty authorities had taken steps to develop race units to manage organisational change. However, only a handful of these went much beyond offering platitudes[20].

Most, according to Young, were 'learners' rather than 'thruster' authorities and many were responding to the numerous housing studies and CRE investigations into housing departments[2] in the late seventies[1]. Urban Labour local authorities in the eighties have a better record of recruiting black staff, although this tends to be at the lower levels of the organisation, than central government departments such as the DHSS[22] and other areas of the civil service[23]. Yet the civil servants resisted keeping records on the ethnic backgrounds of civil service staff, although the DES and DoE were both urging councils to carry out ethnic monitoring[24].

This systemic resistance to the promotion of race equality was further aided by the emergence of the new right political philosophy. This movement confronted the egalitarianism of the municipal left and regarded anti-racism and multiculturalism as divisive, confusing and dysfunctional and a corrosive influence on the British value system[25]. The demise of the GLC in 1986 and the strait-jacketing of urban local government by the late eighties had weakened the support for the race equality movement, as these institutions were at the forefront of race equality experiments in an organisational context.

Atomisation, the new right and the new magistracy

The popularisation of the ideology of the new right can be traced back to 1982 when the Manhattan Institute sponsored and aggressively marketed Charles Murray's *Losing Ground.* This book, based on dubious data, popularised the notion that the US welfare system in the seventies had made it profitable for many poor black families to remain on welfare. Copies of this research were sent to British cabinet members in 1983[26]. The relationship between the US Heritage Foundation, a far-right organisation, and the British Conservative right in the UK has been well documented in the *New Statesman* and *Society*[27].

Proponents of the new right, including Seldon (1986), regard social needs as merely demands for which people do not want to pay[28]. They hold the controversial view that there has been uncontrolled growth in public expenditure over the past decade, and support libertarians such as Nozick[29] who argue that social welfare is not a right. They argue that welfare downgrades the principle of reciprocal responsibilities within the family and so undermines its value. The new right perceives the notion of social justice based on the principle of collective responsibility as detrimental to the rights of the individual[30]. In a racial context, these arguments are advanced by Sowell (1980) and Charles Murray both of whom argue that wage regulation and welfare provision discourages poor blacks from pulling themselves out of the ghetto and the underclass[31]. They also argue that total deregulation and a free market counter discrimination because discrimination is not in the market's interest. Not surprisingly, these views found their way into the UK government's think-tank[32]. As Parekh and others have shown[33], the new right believes in the cultural superiority of the Anglo-Saxon value system, and regards the institutional approach of race equality as racist itself.

Indeed, the government ferociously attacked the anti-racist stance of municipal socialism in the mid-late eighties[34]. It also attacked the Church's liberal left agenda produced in its report, *Faith in the City*, which argued for compassion and greater public expenditure. The government's response to such arguments was that injudicious public expenditure was often the cause of inner city problems rather than the solution[35]. Norman Tebbit, the then Conservative Party chairman, backed a conservative Rabbi's statement that there were many worse things than poverty[36]. The government's contempt for an anti-racist approach to social policy is reflected in early statements made by Keith Joseph (the then Education Secretary), who argued that there was precious little evidence of any racial prejudice amongst teachers; and in a statement from Tebbit accusing ILEA of driving pupils into truancy by feeding them anti-racist rubbish and called antiracist activism the new breed of anti-racist barbarians who wanted to subvert our fundamental values[37].

Collectively there is little that is new about the new right. The ideology is a revised version of 19th century social imperialism in its extreme form, with nationalism and neo-liberal economics woven in. Individually, these ideas of the new right have been rigorously challenged both in the past[38] and more recently[39], mainly on the basis that they assume the existence of perfect markets, and overrate the capacity of voluntarism to care for weaker individuals in society and regard culture to be static[40].

Centralisation and the continued ambiguity of central government

The new right, unlike neo-liberals and libertarians, argue for minimising the role of the state in welfare provision or the promotion of egalitarian ideas. This approach is evident from many initiatives during the Thatcher decade. The new right attack concentrated mainly on local government[41], bringing a centralised curriculum without any reference to multiculturalism[42], forcing local authorities to sell their houses, even though black and ethnic minorities were over-represented on waiting lists, fuelling the welfare debate time and again and linking it with immigration[43]. These changes clearly indicate that the Conservative Party, influenced by the new right philosophy, has written off its black and ethnic minority constituency. Even the institutions which do take on board the race equality issues tend to fall prey to ambivalence. Young (1981) captures the ambivalence[44] of such British institutions to programmes aimed at race equality:

Behind the ambiguity of such programmes lies a complex of psycho-cultural factors which bear upon the decision-making process in central and local government, in firms and in public agencies. These sometimes take the form of ambivalence about the explicit identification of ethnicity, or reluctance to shed established notions of ethnic assimilation; at worst, these take the form of covert or overt hostility towards Britain's black population.

This ambiguity manifests itself in an unrelated and badly co-ordinated allocation of responsibilities in various central government departments with vaguely defined briefs. When endeavouring to

353

present some sort of diagrammatic representation for responsibility on race equality in the Home Office or the DoE, the author was met by amusing comments about the problem of locating such people, let alone providing an organisational diagram. Both urban and immigration policy, particularly the substantive race dimension of urban policy, are handled mainly by the Home Office and partly by the DoE, which meant that even a rudimentary interdepartmental approach did not develop until the late eighties and had to do so without tangible political commitment or support[45]. The connection between immigration control, urban development, race policy and policing - which are all elements embodied in the Home Office overseeing brief - remains indicative of the social control dimension of urban policy[46].

In the past decade, the Conservative government has been rather reluctant to use the term 'race' in urban policy debates. Thus, the term 'inner city' has become a euphemism for race. In the late eighties, the government launched a range of initiatives that were aimed, for the most part, at releasing private sector resources in the inner city. These included Urban Development Corporations, city technology colleges (CTC) and Task Forces. By the early nineties, however, most of these initiatives had clearly failed or made marginal or transient impact on poverty.

For example the CTCs never really took off and failed to unlock the expected levels of private sector money[47]. The garden festivals launched by Heseltine failed to generate employment and most agencies working to support black enterprises were struggling to survive[48].

If one takes stock of the government responses to race equality across the board, it is clear that some of its initiatives were developed as part of it's dual race relations policy of keeping immigration issues on the boil at the same time as making concessions on other fronts (see Chart 8.6).

Chart 8.6 Key central government responses to race

Gov	Year	Corp. Arrangements Organisation/INIT	Legislation	Committees/ Key Reports
L	1962			Nat. Committee for Commonwealth Immigration
L	1965	Race Relations Board	RR Act 1965	
L	1966		LG Act 1966 (S.11)	
L	1968	CRC established, Home Office - UDP unit	RR Act 1968	
C	1971	Home Office adviser		
L	1973	DES - Educational Disadvantage Unit Centre for Educational Disadvantage		
L	1976	CRE established, DE - Race Relations Advisory Service	RR Act 1976	
C	1978			Home Affairs Select Committee on Race Relations
C	1980	Jnr Minister for Racial Equality appointed		Scarman Report Police training report
C	1983	Brunel Centre established to train police	CRE code of practice on employment (voluntary)	
C	1985	Swann Report		
C	1988	HO appoints 2 consultants →Inner City Directorate →Task Force →City Action Team →City technology colleges Section 11 Review	LG Act 1988 CRE code of practice (social landlords)	Local Govt Act contract compliance powers of local authorities Lane Report (Education)
C	1989	City Challenge launched		
C	1991	Urban Programme abolished	Asylum Bill	No action at European level
C	1992	UK Presidency of Europe	Substantial cuts in housing budget continue. Section 11 budget cuts and tapering	
C	1994	Single Regeneration Budget	Absorbs large proportion of Section 11 funding and urban programme	

Key: L - Labour. C - Conservative. RR - Race Relations. LG - Local Governments. CRC - Community Relations Commission. DES - Department of Education and Science. CRE - Commission for Racial Equality. DE - Department of Employment.

Programmes, initiatives and public expenditure in the late eighties

On her last election victory Mrs Thatcher indicated a passing interest in the inner cities. The problems of poor co-ordination of inner city initiatives were being highlighted at the top to which Mr Major attended as he became PM through a leadership contest. The government outlined its two major objectives in relation to the inner city policy in *Action for Cities* (1988). The first aimed to ameliorate the creation, maintainance and improvement of inner city firms. The second objective included moves to eliminate physical dereliction, improve the infrastructure, develop housing and prepare sites for economic development. Although the emphasis was very much on regenerating urban environments, *People in Cities* (1990) and *Getting People in Jobs and Targeting Urban Employment* (1990), both published by the DoE, indicated a shift in policy towards partnership in the inner cities. That shift came despite a deep recession in the property market and considerable strait-jacketing of local authorities[49]. Central govern-ment modified its stance on non-intervention to acknowledge its intermediate distributional role (i.e. to provide resources to deal with social malaise, long-term unemployment, hopelessness and lack of enterprise), as well as its responsibility to act as a buffer against market defects (i.e. the drop in property values, high urban wage rates) until such time as they settle in proportion to the appropriate level of risk required in inner city investment[50]. The appropriate level remains undefined.

The government's inner city policy objectives raised two other important issues. First, among the range of programmes and initiatives that fall within the scope of the *Action for Cities* programme, there are specific programmes relating to, for example, the Urban Programme Enterprise Zones, Urban Development Corporations and Safer Cities schemes. Second, a number of national programmes have been steered towards the problems of inner city areas and might sensibly have been included in the *Action for Cities* programme which was launched as a co-ordinating initiative in 1988.

Chart 8.7 Inner city policy in the eighties

Programme	Evaluation in relation to ethnic dimension	Comments
Urban Programme	Survey in 1985 by DoE	EMG under-represented in funding allocation
Section 11	No impact evaluation, the programme was supported by Teachers Unions and professionals	Home Office scrutiny report looked at emphasis and focus but did not evaluate impact
Ethnic Minority Business Initiative	No independent evaluation	Some impact on major banks in particular
Race Relations Advisory Service (Dept of Employment)	No evaluation hitherto but appeared prominent in a survey of employers by CRE who had developed EOP policies	Being market tested
Enterprise Agencies	No specific evaluation - Ethnic Enterprise Agency struggling	'One stop' shops developed from it
Task Forces	Evaluations showed varied impact	Cannot correct market defects. Long-term viability of projects questionable
TECs	Ethnic minority representation on TEC boards poor	Civil service secondments created all white TECs. Cannot correct market defects and counter discrimination
Urban Development Corporations	Not known	
SRB/City Challenge	1st round - SRB only 20% applications had ethnic dimension. Ethnic minority projects less likely to get shortlisted (2nd round)	Voluntary sector organisations accepted by the civil service as applicants but main thrust on private sector gearing

Source: Luthra, M. (1995) literature survey.

To these should have been added the programmes and objectives of relevant local authorities, other agencies and the private sector. Government policy was targeting some 14 million people, in particular those 7 million who lived in inne city areas, including approximately 2 million black and ethnic minorities.

Chart 8.8 shows six central government departments responsible for some thirty inner city initiatives and programmes that were encompassed within the Action for Cities programme. The DoE remains the dominant department for broader inner city policy and has several key programmes targeted specifically at inner cities. These include the Urban Programme, Urban Development Corporations, City Grants and City Action Teams. Ten of the 26 enterprise zones are located in inner city areas, as are two of the garden festivals, and may reasonably be regarded as targeted on inner cities. The incidence of derelict land grants and other DoE programmes is coincidental.

Moore (1992) calculates that the total public expenditure associated with the Action for Cities programme was about £3 billion in 1989/90; of that sum the DoE accounted for £1.13 billion, the DE for £1.12 billion, the Department of Trade and Industry (DTI) for £220 million, the Department of Transport for £250 million and the Scottish and Welsh Offices about £300 million combined. Less than £1 billion out of the £3 billion public expenditure that benefits inner city areas was specifically allocated in favour of the inner cities, according to Moore.

He identifies only £400 million (excluding TECs and Section 11) as 'high incidence' in 1981 doubling to £800 million in 1991. Most of this could be traced to the cuts in the rate support grant and increased expenditure on regional policy in the past decade[51].

Two DTI programmes - the English Estates Managed Workshop Programme and 16 inner city Task Forces - are targeted specifically on inner cities. The incidence of the Enterprise Initiative and Regional Selective Assistance in inner cities is again coincidental, although the activities of the Race Relations Employment Advisory Service are almost entirely concentrated in inner city areas.

Chart 8.8 Inner city and race equality programmes in the eighties

HM Treasury

Departments and National Programmes

Home Office	Transport	Education	Environment	Employment	Trade & Industry

Scottish and Welsh Offices (SDA and WDA)

Regional Offices
TEED/TECS
Regional Offices

Action for cities programmes

Local Authorities
- Economic Development Units
- Enterprise Boards

- Safer Cities
- Section 11 Grant
- Ethnic Minority Business

- Transport Supplementary Grant

- City Tech. Colleges
- Inner City Open Learning Centres

- Urban Programme
- Urban Dev. Corps
- City Grant
- City Action Teams
- City Challenge
- Derelict Land Grants
- Housing Corps
- Land Registers
- Housing Action Trusts
- Estates Action
- Garden Festivals

- Job Clubs
- Loan Guarantee Schemes
- RR Employment Advisory Service
- Small Firms Service
- Enterprise Training
- Enterprise Allowance Scheme
- Employment Action
- Compacts
- Youth Training

- English Estates Workshop
- Task Force
- Enterprise Initiative
- Regional Selective Assistance

Non-Govt Organisations
- Trade Unions
- Unity Bank
- Community Business
- Cooperatives
- Enterprise Agencies
- Business in the Community
- Inner City Enterprises
- British Urban Development Phoenix
- Local Business Leadership Teams

OBJECTIVES

Improving housing quality | Removal of dereliction | Enterprise | Employment creation

Improving transport links & services | Site preparation | Reducing crime | Skills improvement

Note: Recently the All English Development Agency has been developed.

The Home Office's diminished role in race issues since 1977 is further evidenced by the department's lack of initiatives in the past decade. Only one Home Office programme, Safer Cities, is targeted at the inner city, although the very small Ethnic Minorities Business Initiative impinges mainly on inner city areas.

As we show later, independent evaluation suggests these programmes have had a mixed impact. An analysis of the job creation programme suggests that a two-year job was created for every £10,000 spent on Task forces[52]. The Task Force programme, although constituting a small proportion of the overall budget[53], was nevertheless quite relevant to inner city ethnic minority residents. Simpson (1988) collected data on the Nottinghamshire Task Force operation and highlighted its inability to fund black and ethnic minority projects[54].

The UDC development, which was led substantially by the property and consumer credit boom of the eighties, in most cases failed to deliver long-term, genuine jobs as opposed to displacement jobs, as the property market collapsed. However in some cases UDC, according to Christie (1991), unlocked an impressive amount of private sector money at the height of the boom[55]. In addition, declared donations from companies to charity doubled from 1977 levels[56]. This level however still remained a miniscule 0.2% of the overall corporate profits. Christie et al also note the lack of well-developed community investment policies amongst private sector firms[57].

Overall, evaluations of these programmes suggest poor co-ordination across government departments and poor dialogue with local authorities who have built up considerable expertise in this area. Robson et al's (1992) examination of urban areas from 1983 to 1990 suggests that the inner city programmes failed to tap local creativity by virtue of inflexibility in budget headings[58]. The net result has therefore been that the core areas fared less well than other areas[59]. The authors also emphasise the positive relationship between expenditure and positive impact, although such expert observations are at odds with the perceptions of residents. Residents singled out crime, health care and the cost of living as key areas of concern, yet urban policy hitherto has lacked both a substantial crime prevention[60] and a health dimension[61].

Two thirds of the urban programme areas studied by Robson et al had mainly positive or mixed outcomes in respect of the government's envisaged goals. The study concludes that spending per head under both the Urban Programme and Regional Selective Assistance had a significant impact on tackling unemployment between 1986 and 1990. Evidence however failed to support discernible improvement in the creation of new firms and migration of young adults seeking jobs, nor could the study find evidence of greater corporate commitment to the inner city. The study also observed that the Urban Programme and visible environmental improvements, which were made during the period, had little effect on the profound pessimism of the residents.

As to the specific implications for ethnic minority groups, the PSI evaluation of urban policy[62] came to the conclusion that if judged by classic urban indicators, there was no structural shift between 1982 and 1992 and that the benefits to ethnic minorities were poor. Insofar as the specific impact of these programmes on ethnic minorities in different areas is concerned, there is scattered evidence of minorities benefiting to the same extent as indigenous communities in some areas. However, the absence of a big business sector among the ethnic minorities and a lack of contract compliance means that they tend to be short-changed by developers and large players, including business[63]. Housener et al (1993) conclude in their analysis for the DoE that the absence of[64] ethnic minority programmes, the lack of awareness of ethnic minority needs and the barriers faced by them, coupled with the misguided belief in the permeation theory, hampered the development of meaningful strategies aimed at ethnic minority groups. Gray et al's (1990) analysis of youth unemployment concludes that simply living in the inner city adds to disadvantage[65], which is then further perpetuated by discrimination.

Much of the urban policy analysis is influenced by the

establishment perspective, partly reflected in the organisational arrangements to manage major programmes. Section 11, EMG grants and the Ethnic Minority Business Initiative all remain Home Office funded, while the Urban Programme and the Race Relations Employment Advisory Service are managed by the DoE and the DE. This means that whilst urban policy at large may have moved into the hands of the DoE, the Home Office remains in charge of race relations work, continuing to link it to immigration control and law and order issues[66].

Until its curtailment in 1990, the Section 11 programme had been the major programme aimed at ethnic minorities, a large proportion of which was subsequently absorbed into a wider non-specific programme called the Single Regeneration Budget. At the same time, the emphasis of the dwindling Section 11 programme was shifted towards cultural integration[67]- an action which destroyed many well-established positive action and race equality projects. That destruction was accelerated in part by the increasing inability of rate-capped urban local authorities to find the necessary matching funds. The Urban Programme, meanwhile, was abolished quietly in 1992. These changes combined almost completely to destroy the black and ethnic minority voluntary sector also depriving the black communities of a voice and creating a set-back for many race equality initiatives[68].

The advent of local management in schools, the creation of trusts and TECs, and the splitting up of central government agencies has created a new magistracy in which black and ethnic minorities tend to be under-represented and there is little concern over egalitarian issues amongst this group[69]. There is little evidence that TECs have done much to carry the mantle of race equality forward. They may have endeavoured to assist minorities by getting them to come off the unemployment register, but have not been successful in placing ethnic minority groups in jobs. TECs have come up with a kite mark for employers who are good trainers, but nothing has been pioneered in relation to a kite mark on equal opportunities training. They have done even less to specifically prepare ethnic minority groups to enter

362

and survive the minefield of the new contract culture. Local TECs remain elitist, have closed cultures, and adopt network employment policies in which the larger consultants can develop parasitic relationships with local communities.

Overall, the creation of a purchaser/provider split in the absence of contract compliance has led to the wholesale flouting of equal opportunity codes (historically adopted by the parent organisation, such as regional health authorities or councils at corporate level) in what is the new, often casual job sector[70] where ethnic minorities are over-represented[71]. Years of development in terms of monitoring and institutionalising race equality policies and racial harassment policies in some pioneering authorities has been rolled back. In many ways we have returned to the days of the seventies.

Despite the injection of market and contract culture into the health service it has belatedly tried to catch up with other sectors. Since 1988 it has increased the number of somewhat junior and rudderless equal opportunities advisers to 30 from a handful of people in the mid-eighties[72]. It has generated some research and is beginning to record good practice[73]. The evidence of disadvantage in service delivery to ethnic minorities and discrimination in employment continues to emerge. To what extent the contract culture is adding to this disadvantage by hindering race equality development remains a moot point (see Chapter 6)[74].

To deal with the proliferation of regeneration initiatives, two recent government initiatives - the City Challenge followed by the Single Regeneration Budget - are aimed at improving co-ordination. The former involves the 'top-slicing' some £82.5 million per year off the housing budget and some eight inner city funding programmes. Urban Programme authorities are able to make competitive bids for this funding and there is a responsibility to develop a strategy that encompasses the local area and the wider city economy and includes a wide range of local organisations. These programmes have been criticised for being overly political, lottery-like and for placing an excessive emphasis on presentation.

The principle of the City Challenge programme was extended to create the Single Regeneration Budget (SRB) which was based on absorbing a large chunk of Section 11 and Urban Programme resources together with top-sliced resources from some twenty other programmes. During the SRB's first run, according to the CRE's analysis (1995), only 19 per cent of the bids had an ethnic minority dimension. Local authorities and the TECs were on the whole most likely to lead with less than 5% of resources going to voluntary sector-led projects.

A recent analysis of British urban policy on regeneration identified a lack of a bottom-up approach, specifically they identified poor links between housing and other regeneration arrangements, poor corporate input, little focus on inter-sector neighbourhood approach, and poor inter-sector links between neighbourhoods. Overall, the government's strategy lacks a coherence, failing as it does to link housing, training, regeneration and employment. City Action Teams have tried to rectify the fault and this has recently been followed by the City Challenge and the SRB programmes (supported by regional offices), although they still squeeze out community groups.

There are poor links between housing associations (which are successful developers and fundraisers but remote, in accountability terms, from local communities), local authorities (over-regulated, poor, but with land and building availability), banks (unwilling to lend and take risks in the inner city), TECs (arrogant and unaccountable; historically they were training agencies, but have been converted into regeneration agencies) and the corporate sector, which does not see community investment in the inner cities as sound business on top of its tax burden. Attempts at urban regeneration often tend to degenerate into cosy agreements between top players. This results in top-down development and leaves little room for input from local residents. The emphasis on presentation and deadlines continues. The community development scene is dominated by technocrats, quangos and groups with large resources who oust citizens from the decision-making arena. As shown in Chapter 1, given the underdevelopment of the community capacity and the absence of technocratic and well-funded organisations

364

amongst black and ethnic minority groups, there is little in the way of a force that is able to engage on an equal footing with these large players at local level, to ensure the removal of barriers faced by ethnic minorities.

Disadvantage and discrimination in the nineties

The evidence of racial disadvantage persists, albeit at a reduced level in the case of older, well-established communities, and ethnic minority women in some communities have made significant headway in catching up with their white counterparts[75]. Overall, however, unemployment and redundancy among some black and ethnic groups is many times that of whites[76], and a disparate impact on ethnic minorities is evident in the context of poverty[77]. There is little evidence that racism or its manifestation in terms of exclusion of minorities has abated. Indeed it has taken an increasingly violent form with at least 7000 racial attacks[78] each year, and reported violence appears to be increasing, with ethnic minorities at a higher than average risk from crime[79]. The number of employment complaints to the CRE has been increasing gradually despite the decline of the voluntary sector which picks up such complaints[80]. The evidence of discrimination against young black ethnic minorities continues to emerge in training, careers advice and access to jobs[81].

Insofar as institutional permeation is concerned, there has been some progress over the last decade which needs to be evaluated in the light of the widely varied average length of residence and compositional factors of different groups, and the hurdles they face, including racism, (Luthra forthcoming), although problems of recruitment continue in some areas such as teaching, social work and many other public service areas - an exception being medicine and nursing[82] where ethnic minority recruitment has been targeted historically. This picture is likely to improve as the data suggests that ethnic minorities are now over-represented as students in the higher education sector (see Chapter 5). At school level, most ethnic minority groups have enjoyed improvement with the exception of the

Caribbeans and Bangladeshis (see Chapter 5). Education is seen as one way of countering disadvantage and overcoming discrimination, although the evidence on access to the labour market does not fully bear out this optimism[83].

The split in purchasing and providing roles and the development of autonomous units in public services means that a centralised, executive-driven, model of promoting equal opportunities on a regional basis is less workable than it used to be. It would be a tall order to market such concepts to a large number of emerging organisational and casualised units, particularly as black and ethnic minority workers feel vulnerable in a contract culture setting, in which they are last hired and first fired. As a number of studies have shown, the new contract culture has hit ethnic minorities very hard, increasing their vulnerability to casualisation and unemployment. The increasing wage differential between some ethnic groups, such as Bangladeshis, and white people in inner London is further evidence that race inequality is being maintained[84].

Self-employment, enterprise and unemployment: comparative reflections

There has been considerable debate in the eighties about the role of small business in generating income and contributing to economic growth as well as the rise of the so-called enterprise culture. Research suggests that the evidence for the former proposition is stronger. However it is less convincing in relation to the latter proposition[85] on enterprising tendencies. In fact, most of the entrepreneurs appear to be either reluctant or opportunistic entrants to self-employment and small business. In any case as we later show, ethnic minority businesses developed and grew without any substantial support from the Thatcherite ethos.

The number of small businesses, according to the DTI in 1996, has doubled to a figure of 2.3 million, of which 95% are small businesses with less than 20 employees, providing around 20% to 35% of jobs with 400,000 new start-ups each year containing 1.8 jobs per start-up. During the period 1970 to 1990, self-employment amongst ethnic minorities increased at a higher rate than amongst whites. However during this period they also faced an increased risk of unemployment. It is also notable that a particular increase in the self-employed among the Asian population appears to have taken place in the seventies. To what extent this was due to the arrival of the East Africans (East-African Asians) is difficult to distinguish from the role which rising unemployment may have played. The figures suggest that the white population's self-employment rate tends to be less affected by fluctuations in unemployment, as is also the case with Caribbean communities (Luthra forthcoming). Generally, it appears that there is little relationship between unemployment and self-employment when we analyse the data across ethnic groups (see Table 8.1); although there may be a converse relationship - i.e., when unemployment is low then self-employment goes up as people feel confident to take the risk of establishing businesses, particularly in the case of ethnic minority business[86]. It seems that the minorities are more likely than their white counterparts to respond to such a trend. This assertion is further supported by an analysis of regional levels of long-term unemployment and its impact on self-employment[87].

The decline of the inner city appears to have contributed to the availability of cheap shops, accelerating self-employment. Lock-up shops, often without good will, and shops with accommodation above them were ideal for retailers or for restauranteurs, who frequently had workers who were in need of accommodation. Ward (1985) in his analyses of such inner city locations, developed an ecological model and a hierarchy of response of the inner city to ethnic enterprise. The former suggests that the variety and number of ethnic minority shops were dependent upon the proportion of ethnic residents, while the latter emphasised that there was a hierarchy of shopping centres catering for an identifiable pecking order of customers' purchasing needs[88].

In a study of retailers in Greenwich by Luthra and Bajwa, 12% of the respondents gave redundancy as a reason for self-employment[89]. Further analyses of redundant workers however showed that most failed to utilise their redundancy money for setting up businesses. Ward[90] has argued that self-employment among Asians varies from area to area and tends to be concentrated in areas of long-term unemployment (in Newcastle, 31% were self-employed in 1977, while the figure was 2% for Birmingham, where he argues that well-paid jobs were still available). The size of differing levels of unemployment, or the degree of long-term unemployment on their own do not explain the magnitude of levels of regional self-employment.

Table 8.1 Self-employment and unemployment among ethnic minorities   (1984 and 1987-89)

Gender	Employment	White %	West Indian/ Guyanese %	Indian %	Pakistani/ Bangladeshi %
Male	Self-employed	13 (16)	8 (10)	21 (27)	17 (23)
	Unemployed	11 (9)	28 (18)	13 (11)	14 (25)
	Number	14,613	153 (168)	229 (261)	109 (151)
Female	Self-employed	6 (7)	2 (5)	10 (12)	6 (18)
	Unemployed	10 (8)	17 (11)	18 (13)	20
	Number	10,229	14 (151)	142 (253)	19 (138)

Source: *Labour Force Survey*, OPCS, January 1984-1987 averages.
( ) = 1987 to 1989 averages.

Arguably, in this sense, self-employment could be regarded as family job creation which can absorb highly vulnerable and de-skilled women workers and inexperienced young adults and tap their potential behind the counter. The relatively high figures of Asian women who are self-employed is likely in some measure to be due to the increase in the number of homeworkers, as unemployment and increased redundancies [91] have severely hit Asian women. It may also be partly due to the way the census asks a question on business, not representing owners and family businesses.

Table 8.2 Self-employment, industry and ethnic groups

	1976 (PEP)			1982 (PSI)			1988-1990 (LFS)#		
	W %	WI %	A %	W %	WI* %	A %	W %	WI* %	A %
M	21	14	12	14	18	10	11	10	10.5
D/C	26	2	61	26	21	67	23	19.0	62.3
S	36	30	18	26	14	21	-	-	-
C	17	46	2	28	47	2	23	34	5.7
O	0	8	7	6	0	0	-	-	-
Total	100	100	100	100	100	100	-	-	-

M = Manufacturing
D/C = Distribution and Catering
S = Service
C = Construction
O = Other
- Data not available

W = White
WI = West Indian
A = Asian

Sources: PSI (1982), PEP (1976), LFS (1988-1990).
* Small samples less reliable. # No Bangladeshis in sample; not exactly comparable with PSI.

Catering and retailing have been two major areas of enterprise developed amongst ethnic minorities over the past two decades. In this sector there were two competitors in low-priced ethnic catering during the last two decades: the Asians and the Chinese. The Chinese never really appear to have considered entrance into retailing, partly due to their relatively low proficiency in English compared to the Asians. The other most notable feature of ethnic enterprise of the period is the entry of West Indians into self-employment (see Table 8.1), although the overall figure is too small for it be of major significance. Ward's (1984) survey of small businesses showed that West Indian firms were concentrated in hairdressing, travel and estate agents, fashion shops, etc.[92]. Recently Caribbeans are beginning to make inroads into music and sports shops, as well as youth-oriented outlets. In addition a few Caribbean restaurants have sprung up, albeit confined mainly to London. Asians on the other hand have diversified into second-hand furniture shops, highstreet electronics shops, videos, pharmacy, optics, finance and insurance consultancies. Manufacturing seems still to elude Asian entrepreneurs (except in textiles), although in commerce there have been a considerable number of inroads in terms of penetrating employment in building societies and banks in the city.

As evident from the *National Dwelling and Housing Survey* (1978), settlers of Bangladeshi, Chinese and Turkish origins earned their living in the late seventies by providing personal services, mostly in catering [93]. Over the past decade, some communities - the Indians particularly - have diversified their businesses (e.g. in metals, chemicals, hotels, commodity trading and vehicle parts)[94]. In the eighties the number of Indian restaurants increased substantially[95].

Research based on the period 1979 to 1984 develops an alternative perspective[96] and points out that, despite the growth in self-employment amongst ethnic minorities of New Commonwealth origin, they only comprise 10% of all self-employed. According to this study, Asians did not show a higher propensity for self-employment than whites, or groups such as the Mediterraneans or the Irish who became well- established during the early eighties, despite

Table 8.3 Proportion of employed engaged in small business ownership (SBO) and self-employment workers (SEWs) by ethnicity and gender, for GHS 1979-82 combined

	SBOs		SEWs		N	
	Male%	Female%	Male%	Female%	Male%	Female%
White British	3.0	1.3	6.0	3.2	25,478	19,785
Irish	2.9	0.3	8.0	2.2	724	579
Asian[1]	4.4	2.7	6.4	2.7	639	291
Afro-Caribbean	0.4	0.4	3.7	1.1	273	267
Mediterranean	18.8	3.3	9.4	6.6	96	61
Europe/Rest of World	5.6	2.8	7.2	4.4	414	360

[1] = Indian, Pakistani and East African.
Source: Curran and Burrows (1988), *Enterprise in Britain: A National Profile of Small Businesses*, p.68.

high Asian business formation during 1982-1984[97]. Mediterraneans are still more likely to be self-employed business owners compared with Asians (see Table 8.3 and Table 8.4). Nevertheless, the resilience of Asian business is evident from a recent study by McVoy and Aldrich, who found that in the period 1978-1984, Asian retail business had better survival rates than its white counterparts [98]. From 1984 until 1986 goodwill for shops in the inner city escalated. Subsequently however, erratic fluctuations in property value, increasing business rates, and crime pushing up insurance costs, have all acted as motivating factors for high street stores to move out into cheaper suburban sites. These sites are primarily able to cater for the car-owning shopper, leaving Asian retailers in the inner cities to cater for the poor and the less mobile.

The ethnic minority shopkeeper is finding it hard to keep prices down to compete with supermarkets whilst providing for the elderly, for single parents and council tenants, the very people who do not have cars and who are least likely to do bulk buying. This can create

371

tensions between such family businesses and the local disadvantaged customers[99]. There has been a considerable amount of pressure due to recession on retail, textile and construction sectors affecting the ethnic minority small business sector. Nevertheless, as shown in Tables 8.1 and 8.5, Pakistani and Bangladeshi self-employment has caught up with the Indian figure with some improvement in West Indian and Guyanese performance, although there is evidence to suggest that, in terms of self-employed with employees, there may have been little improvement in the latter two groups. Another interesting feature which emerges from Table 8.5 is the increase in the proportion of Bangladeshi/Pakistani female self-employed and the sustaining of female West Indian business with employees, which requires attention. This is in contrast to an overall decline in the proportion of self-employed people with employees, which possibly suggests the increasing number of solo entrepreneurs or homeworkers.

Table 8.4 Proportion of employed white, Asian and African-Caribbeans engaged in small business ownership and self-employment by gender, for GHS 1983-4 combined

	SBOs		SEWs		N	
	M	F	M	F	M	F
White British	3.6	1.7	8.5	4.4	11338	8473
Asian*	10.7	5.6	10.7	8.3	196	108
Afro-Caribbean	0.0	0.0	6.2	1.1	97	02

* Includes those with Indian, Pakistani, Bangladeshi and East African origins.
SBO = Small Business Owner. SEW = Self-Employed Worker.
Source: GHS (1983-4)

Table 8.5: Change in proportion of self-employed by ethnic origin (%)

	Self-employed as proportion of all in employment		Those with employees as a proportion of all self-employed	
	Average		Average	
All	1979-83	1987-89	1977-83	1987-89
White	8.8	12.6	39.2	32.7
Ethnic minority groups of whom:	10.3	16.4	45.5	39.2
West Indian/Guyanese	2.6	6.7	29.4	18.9
Indian	13.8	21.2	42.2	41.9
Pakistani/Bangladeshi	17.4	22.3	51.4	47.8
All other origins	10.8	16.3	53.0	38.4
White - **Male**	11.6	16.5	40.1	33.7
Ethnic minority groups of whom:	13.0	21.5	48.2	40.5
West Indian/Guyanese - **Male**	4.0	10.4	26.4	13.5
Indian - **Male**	16.2	27.5	44.6	44.6
Pakistani/Bangladeshi - **Male**	18.3	23.3	54.4	49.2
All other origins - **Male**	13.3	21.1	58.0	39.7
White - **Female**	4.7	7.3	36.0	29.6
Ethnic minority groups of whom:	5.7	9.0	35.1	34.4
West Indian/Guyanese - **Female**	1.0	3.0	42.0	37.3
Indian - **Female**	9.3	11.7	34.3	32.4
Pakistani/Bangladeshi - **Female**	11.1	18.1	21.5	40.3
All other origins - **Female**	6.8	9.9	37.8	34.7

Note: It is usual practice to quote results for ethnic minority groups as averages of three surveys, in order to give more reliable figures. The need to do so arises partly from the relatively small numbers of respondents from ethnic minority groups in the overall sample, but also from the tendency of the ethnic minority population to be clustered in particular geographical areas. In this table, figures are given for the average of the latest three surveys (1987, 1988, 1989) and the average of the 1979, 1981 and 1983 surveys.

Source: *Labour Force Survey, Employment Gazette*, (1990).

Two factors could significantly explain the overall increase in the level of self-employment in general, without taking into account employees of all ethnic groups such as the Asians. These include the population growth and age distribution effect. Both Tables 8.6 and 8.7 indicate that, in the case of Pakistanis and Bangladeshis, population growth appears to have contributed considerably to growth in self-employment, while the reverse is true of 'other' ethnic origins. In the case of Caribbeans the age factor appears to count very little towards the increase in self-employment while the Indians have been most influenced by this factor. Clearly there has been a substantial increase in self-employment among Caribbeans and Pakistanis/Bangladeshis, except in the case of self-employed with employees.

Table 8.6 Effect of population growth on self-employment by ethnic origin increase between average 1979, 1981, 1983 and average 1987-1989 (%)

	Total % increase	Of which population component*	Self-employment component‡
All ethnic origins	53.4	5.2	48.2
White	51.5	4.8	46.7
Ethnic minority groups of whom:	94.6	19.1	75.6
West Indian/Guyanese	178.8	5.7	173.1
Indian	83.9	11.1	72.9
Pakistani/ Bangladeshi	68.8	37.6	31.2
All other origins	108.9	24.0	84.9

* The percentage increase that would have occurred, had the proportion of each age/sex group in self-employment remained constant.
‡ The residual, that is that part of the overall increase attributable to increasing proportions in self-employment.

Table 8.7 Effect of age distribution on self-employment by ethnic origin 1987-1989 average

	Age distribution effect‡	Within age-band effect*	Overall self-employment percentage (%)
White - **(All)**	0.0	12.6	12.6
Ethnic minority groups of whom: **(All)**	1.1	15.2	16.3
West Indian/Guyanese	-0.2	6.9	6.7
Indian	3.1	18.1	21.2
Pakistani/Bangladeshi	-0.2	22.5	22.3
All other origins	0.2	16.0	16.2
White - **Male**	0.0	16.5	16.5
Ethnic minority groups of whom: **Male -**	1.3	20.1	21.4
West Indian/Guyanese	-0.2	10.5	10.3
Indian	3.4	24.1	27.5
Pakistani/Bangladeshi	-0.3	23.6	23.3
All other origins	0.7	20.4	21.1
White - **Female**	0.0	7.3	7.3
Ethnic minority groups of whom: **Female -**	0.7	8.2	8.9
West Indian/Guyanese	-0.2	3.2	3.0
Indian	2.7	9.0	11.7
Pakistani/Bangladeshi	0.1	18.0	18.1
All other origins	-0.5	10.4	9.9

* That is the overall self-employment proportion which would have been observed, had the age distribution been identical in all ethnic groups.
‡ The residual, that is, the effect on the overall % of the age distribution of that particular ethnic group.

Source: *Employment Gazette*, (1990).

There is however a twist in the tale - Bangladeshis fare very badly if one examines the data where they are categorised separately from the Pakistanis (see Charts 8.9 and 8.10 for the last decade). It is quite evident from Chart 8.9 that the Bangladeshis have not been able to sustain their catering-based economy as well as their Chinese counterparts whose catering economy has been more resilient than that of the Bangladeshis. The Chinese also have been able to sustain a lower level of unemployment throughout the last decade.

Chart 8.9 Self-employment rates by ethnic group (%)

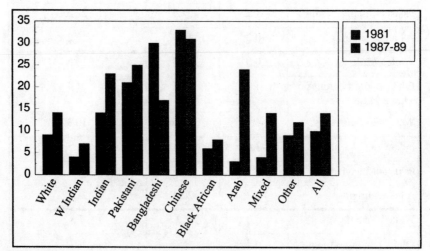

Source: *Labour Force Survey* (1981,1987-1989).

As stated earlier on, the one reliable indicator of enterprise development is the growth in business owners. Caribbean business has not grown despite half-hearted central and local government's attempt during the last decade to support such business, as shown later. It is too short a period to establish a business environment in a community which does not have the starting point of a cultural enterprise, lacks historical experience in business, and has not been supported by its own ethnic minority or indigenous banks.

Chart 8.10 Relative unemployment rates 1981-1988

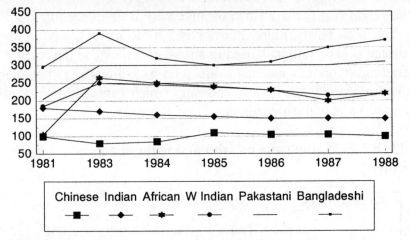

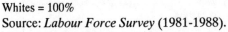

Whites = 100%
Source: *Labour Force Survey* (1981-1988).

The overall picture which appears to emerge from this survey is that there has been an increase in self-employment in the case of all ethnic minority groups, except Bangladeshis, over the last decade, with the Pakistanis catching up with the Indians. Both business ownership and self-employment with employees have been sustained well over the last decade by most ethnic minority groups, except in the case of Caribbeans (see Table 8.8).

Phizacklia (1990) has argued that the reason why some communities are better placed to develop an enterprise culture is due to their strong patriarchal value systems which are often described as the family value systems. These patriarchal value systems, she argues, coupled with the fact that some groups migrated as family units, is a substantial contributing factor in the development of ethnic enterprise in textiles[100] where the Cypriots and Asians have taken over from the Jews whose children have moved on to other occupations[101]. The difficulty with this perspective is that, while it explains the limited success of the Caribbean community in terms of business development, it does not explain why the Irish failed to

377

become textiles entrepreneurs, nor does it explain why the Asian Muslims in Glasgow are successful in areas such as retail despite the observation that the women contribute very little to the running of the business. Furthermore, Phizacklia fails to make the point that marriage is less contractualised in an Asian context, so the benefits, including status enhancement, are seen as collective rather than individual, strengthening a relationship which generally transcends normal contractual partnerships.

Table 8.8 Self-employment with and without employees by the decade

Ethnic Group	Self Employed		Self Employed with Employee	
	1981	1991	1981	1991
White		12.8		4.3
Caribbean	2.6 (1.8)	6.7	1.0 (0.1)	1.3
African	-	6.0	-	2.3
Indian	6.2 (4.9)	26.3	5.0 (2.0)	8.7
Pakistani	} 5.4	23.9	} 2.4	9.2
Bangladeshi		18.6		13.6
Chinese	-	27.2	-	15.8

Source: Owen (1992) OPCS Special tabs (1990) Warwick University tabs for CRE.
( ) = Brown, C. (1982) *Black and White Britain,* PSI.
1981 figures without brackets are from NDHS tabs, DoE.

Another explanation of the success of Asian business is offered by Ward (1984). He suggests that the dense clustering of old terraced housing in many predominantly Asian areas helps form an ethnic niche which is difficult to form in the case of Caribbeans who face a diverse population in older working class areas and council housing[102]. Yet the retail outlets on such estates are often run by Asian retailers and Caribbean retailers often complain about a lack of West Indian customer loyalty and stiff competition from Asians. Nevertheless in areas such as Lambeth, Brent, Hackney and Manchester, Caribbeans have had limited success in establishing clothing, hair and beauty, record sales and travel businesses[103].

State responses

The government's first major initiatives to enhance small enterprise in the eighties were: to establish a loan guarantee scheme (1982) introduced as a last resort scheme, and a business expansion scheme (1983) aimed at increasing investment in small firms. As Woodcock pointed out in *The Guardian* (16, May 1995), the benefits of the 100 initiatives launched remained questionable. These schemes have been somewhat irrelevant to ethnic minority business partly due to their focus on medium-size firms and also due to preference given to areas such as new electronic technology[104]. They were generally unknown to small business and in financial terms comprise less than 5% of the total amount of monies lent by banks to small business in the UK[105]. In addition, a small firms service was established by the Training, Enterprise and Education Department (TEED) which was also largely unheard of by the ethnic minority communities. In view of this neglect of small business, some specific state responses were made to assist their development. These included:

- Some 60 enterprise agencies supported by an umbrella organisation called BIC. Most acted as loan packaging or training or business advice agencies. Of these ten were black-run business agencies. They struggled to stay in business as they were unable to raise the private sector funding needed when government withdrew its funding. Recently they were taken over by the One Stop Shops set up by the TECs [106].

- Business Incentive Schemes (up to £5,000) were established to provide start-up loans for black businesses.

- Prince's Youth Trust offered loans and grants for people under 25, although not exclusively aimed at ethnic minorities, a substantial proportion are allocated as such.

- In November 1990, the Department of Employment launched Greater London Enterprises, a low interest rate loan scheme supported by Barclays and then by Midlands offering loans of up to £10,000 [107] for three years.

- The Ethnic Minorities Initiative was established in 1989 by the Home Office to encourage banks to employ more ethnic minority staff and to help them to shape responsive policies to achieve improved economic development for minorities.

- The City Challenge project has sometimes awarded a lump sum for minority business development as in the case of East London TEC which awarded £1.7 million (for Bangladeshi residents in Tower Hamlets)[108].

- Several banks developed marginally low interest loan schemes for black and ethnic minority businesses for a short period.

Several council economic development departments offered help with loan packaging, fundraising and often guaranteed loans for small businesses in the late eighties, but this disappeared in the nineties as the role of local government in economic development was curtailed and councils were rate-capped[109]. The emphasis of such councils on co-ops, and small-scale job creation programmes meant that wider joint development with the business sector never really emerged thereby affecting macro local economic development[110]. Local government in the eighties was characterised by the ethos [111] that local government intervention on free enterprise should be minimised, i.e. an arm's length approach was developed (Robinson 1979, Mills and Young 1979) although labour councils engaged with small business issues for the purpose of supporting disadvantaged groups. The TECs which have inherited the small business development brief short-changed small businesses of the £32 million spent by TECs, less than 1.2% of which was spent on small business (*Financial Times*, 19 May 1995, 'TECs services show benefit').

Most of these measures were an attempt to offset banks' unwillingness to lend to Caribbeans particularly and also Africans[112]. The banks' reluctance was based on negative assumptions made about their business skills and experience. These measures have been criticised for being aimed at the very small end of the business spectrum, their impact has been limited to increasing self-employment rather than ownership amongst Africans and Caribbeans with the exception of increased activity in areas like Brixton. The decline of the construction industry, an area of Caribbean self-employment, suffered heavily from recession. Government initiatives have also coincided with the recession making both the lenders and business starters reluctant. The emphasis in public policy on start-ups has now been shifted to consolidation and expansion.

Ethnic enterprise: commercial group domination

The business activity of the Asian community, particularly the Indian community has generated some corporate clout[113]. The pundit's view is that despite the problem of expansion the prognosis in relation to Asian businesses is positive as they tend to aim at the white market[114]. Ram (1993) has recently argued that despite lack of training, the recession and racism, Asian businesses have been able to survive primarily due to family support[115], and the fact that a substantial number are cultural enterprises and still retain an ethnic enclave link, i.e. they can rely on ethnic loyalties to survive during difficult periods[116]. In the case of larger businesses, of which there are estimated to be 300, financial protection comes from the overseas and international links of the Indian businesses.

Most such businesses are essentially controlled by traditional merchant castes amongst Asians although other caste groups are making headway in areas such as retail[117]. In the absence of Bengalis who dominated catering in England (up until recently until challenged by the Punjabis), and Gujeratis (who dominate retail), the Punjabi Hindus, Sikhs and Muslims in Scotland have carved up the local retail and catering sector amongst themselves (Luthra forthcoming). Some studies (Mullins 1979) based on too small a sample, assert that Muslims from the Indian subcontinent are trapped in the service sector more so than other Asian groups[118]. In fact as a group, despite low literacy rates and lack of business tradition, the business owner profile in terms of education amongst Asian Muslims now resembles other Asian counterparts[119]. Indeed they have overtaken the Indians (mostly Hindus and Sikhs) in terms of business establishment. This could partly be attributed to the unleashing of the enterprise culture in their countries of origin (particularly Pakistan) during the post-independence[120] period which also provided links with UK business communities, and partly due to the catching-up effect. The Pakistani Punjabis have, over the past decade, been able to establish ethnic enterprises to cater for a growing Pakistani population. They have now particularly challenged the domination of Bangladeshis[121] in the retaurant sector (who still control most of the restaurants) by opening regional cooking cafes such as the Balti and Karahi*, and in textiles by establishing textile units, particularly in the north, for instance in Manchester and Glasgow[122].

Networks within and across communities continue to play a crucial role. As Phizacklia (1990) has shown, the rag trade is now considerably dominated by Asians, most of which remains peripheral sub-contracting involving considerable homeworkers and part-timers in a high mark-up industry in which many people in a long chain take a cut[123]. In catering, having one's own wholesalers and distributors has helped nurture the notion of realistic mark-ups

* Specialist single dishes cooked on a larger scale with a regional emphasis

between traders. These links have helped develop new large cash-and-carries as well as the emergence of some Asian medium-sized stores such as Dadus and chains such as Azad Videos in Scotland, and Royal and Ambala Sweets. Proliferation of electronic retailing led by Gujeratis has paralleled the development of Asian electronic firms such as Binatone, while penetration of young Asians into the city has helped sustain the Asian financial sector. These networks also help sustàin and provide a cushion during periods of recession as experienced groups pioneer new lines which others then follow. Property ownership is a crucial factor in developing Asian business [124] because it is used as a source of collateral.

The constant diversification of skills in the Asian community, i.e. the emergence of financial lawyers, accountants and city operators, all provide role models and link the Asian economy with the mainstream economy. Given this organic model in which different ethnic trading groups have a symbiotic relationship in the pecking order with business leaders, the division notion of Muslim and non-Muslim, used by people like Rafiq (1990) for analysis is highly simplistic, particularly when some communities such as the Sikhs, who have relatively limited experience of trading, as do the Muslims, are interlocked in the business networks with other Asian groups. Furthermore, attempts to organise business around religion have been a failure[125]. Despite the highly pluralist nature of the Asian community they have been able to form chambers of commerce in some areas, for example in Bradford, while it is local government initiatives which have brought them together in areas such as Glasgow. National organisations have, however, failed to emerge to represent the interests of ethnic minority business (see Chapter 1), although white conglomerate-based organisations such as BIC and the Percent Club have been quite effective in helping equal opportunities work.

Conclusions, issues and challenges

Total central government expenditure on race equality issues remains small as a percentage of GDP, but not insignificant. It has, however, increased in real terms over the last two decades. A lot of it has been creamed off by local government as has been the case with Section 11 funding or it has failed to unlock the resources of local government. Although urban local government has shown some flair and has been successful to a limited extent in developing equal employment policies, its other policies in relation to services remain largely unimplemented. Central government lags behind local government in terms of initiatives on race equality, and there appears to be little evidence of a move towards a corporate strategy on race equality. The situation is made worse by the reluctance of the government to openly debate race issues. The decreasing influence of local government on the local scene means that minorities have to penetrate new structures such as TECs to retain their influence.

Despite US influences in a number of policy areas[126] including innercity policy, the government refused to extend its role in a substantial manner to enhance economic development and employment provision for black and ethnic communities. This ignores overwhelming evidence of discrimination and the significant success of measures such as contract compliance and the establishment of Minority Business Development Associations (MBDA), Small Business Administration (SBA), and set-aside arrangements* in the USA[127]. In fact government intervention during the Thatcher years in areas such as contract compliance has been malign in nature (see Chapter 4). The race equality issue became party-politicised in the cold war between central and local authorities.

Scarman's consensus view has not been taken forward to any significant extent. As evident from post-Scarman developments, initiatives proposed to tackle race inequality generally appear to take a considerable time to be followed up, if at all. Unlike local

---

* These involve the state setting aside a proportion of contracts for ethnic minorities.

government, there is little evidence of the presence of policy entrepreneurs within central government who are prepared to challenge resistance and bring about sustained action. Consequently, race as an issue, slips down the agenda as soon as the pressure is eased.

In the phase of atomisation and the emergence of a new independent sector it will be very hard to influence and monitor changes or apply executive thrust to push for race equality, particularly as ethnic minorities are under-represented in the new magistracy. The state has, in the values domain, leap-frogged to connect with the nativism and nationalism of the working classes by by-passing liberals, while handing over the guardianship of consumer interest to magistracy who carry the torch for moulding the world in the image of a bygone age of the British empire. The new scenario, in which the public sector is fragmented and subject to a purchaser/provider split and decentralisation, presents a challenge as the loci of power are shifting within the organisations, often away from professionals and bureaucrats to managers.

The private sector, although coaxed a little, has not been pushed at all or offered any incentives to take on equality issues. The relative success story has been in the creation of a municipal middle class among black and ethnic minorities in urban areas with some penetration into the professions, which has been somewhat undermined by the recession. The major failure in urban policy insofar as race equality is concerned has been not only on the economic side but also any kind of community capacity building. Despite the rhetoric of economic regeneration in the eighties, little emerged as a sound regeneration policy co-ordinating various sectors and involving local people on a partnership basis.

Insofar as the impact of these programmes on ethnic minorities is concerned, there is scattered evidence of minorities benefiting on a par with indigenous communities, although the absence of a big business sector amongst ethnic minorities and a lack of contract compliance means that they tend to be short-changed by large developers and business. Lack of awareness of needs and the barriers faced by local people coupled with the belief in the permeation theory have all hampered development of meaningful strategies aimed at ethnic minority groups.

Conditions such as poor links between housing associations, local authorities' banks' unwillingness to lend and take risks, TECs and a corporate sector tendency not see community investment in the inner cities as sound business, all contribute to occasional and opportunistic project-based development rather than systematic long-term programmes. Regeneration attempts often degenerate into agreements between top players leading to top-down development. Neither the Single Regeneration Budget nor City Challenge have dealt with this issue. The emphasis on presentation and meeting deadlines continues with local authority, TEC and private sector schemes preferred.

With the exception of few cases, regeneration has been dominated by technocrats and quangos and developers which have large resources, ousting the citizens and small groups. As shown in Chaper 1, given the lack of community development and the emergence of large organisations amongst ethnic minority groups, there is little by way of a force on the scene which can engage with such powerful players on an equal footing which is able to ensure that, in addition to creating opportunities, large players also remove the barriers faced by ethnic minorities. As Nicholas and Deakin (1993) cogently argue, the emphasis of government-led regeneration needs to shift to people-led regeneration[128]. Programmes, in my view, should pass the test of community capacity building and long-term benefits and should aim to unlock latent skills and energy of the local communities including its voluntarism. As the task force evaluation concluded, even if such measures were successful they cannot correct labour market defects.

As we have shown, there is persuasive evidence to support the notion that the entry of ethnic minorities into self-employment, has grown in the case of most ethnic groups. Also the number of small business owners and employers with employees is expanding. The Bangladeshis are the exception to this rule. In the case of Pakistanis this growth could be explained to some extent by population growth. Traditionally it was thought that the decline in employment opportunities tended to increase self-employment amongst entrepreneurs while the entrepreneurs flourished during 'good times'. It is possible that the decline in unemployment gives impetus to the tendency of ethnic minorities, particularly Asians to seek shelter in self-employment, i.e., ethnic enterprise acts as a welfare sector.

There is also some evidence that Asian business formation has sustained itself very well from 1982 to 1984, and Asian self-employment has tended to be quite independent of economic fluctuations. The evidence of an increasing proportion of owner managers and some diversification of the Asian economy is strong during the last decade despite recession. This could be attributed to family support, overseas investments of the Indian elite, and late enterprise development amongst some groups such as the Pakistanis. On the whole, different ethnic minority groups are at varying points of economic development and integration.

Generally, successful groups share common features such as unpaid family labour, extended kinship and a pre-capitalist business background including the Africans, albeit to a lesser extent as the African family appears to be fragmenting in Britain. The Caribbeans have a matriarchal kinship with a weak pre-capitalist experience of business and a fragmented family with a large proportion of single parents and relatively low equity base (see Chapters 1 and 6). These factors, combined with poor access to lending by banks, militate against business formation in a patriarchal capitalist society. Asian enterprise is sustained by continuous small-scale diversification, together with a bifurcated Asian economy with overseas links at the apex of a business pyramid of networks, which are underpinned by family links.

The Asians, however, still lag behind the Mediterranean, Cypriot, Arab and Chinese groups in terms of business ownership, although their economy is becoming increasingly diverse. The Pakistanis have caught up with the Indians in terms of self-employment over the last decade. Considering that Pakistani Punjabis are not historically a commercial group or a very westernised community, this is a remarkable achievement. The explanation that the development of ethnic enterprise is related to patriarchy and why some communities do better than others is a useful notion, but presents a problem in explaining the success of some communities such as the Pakistani and Bangladeshi communities in which women tend to be relatively economically inactive in the labour market or in business.

A related issue is the rise of, and resilience of, female entrepreneurs including female business owners within the ethnic communities. This warrants further analysis. To what extent these women perceive themselves to be part of the business as owners or co-workers is a moot point. Further, is it a mechanism of retaining multiple roles by ethnic minority women and an alternative to the oppressive British labour market which forces many women to choose between family contact and security, and an insecure job often at the margins of the economy?

It is likely that people of Indian origin are following the Jewish route of entering mainstream corporations and the city institutions in addition to establishing a business elite with international networks. Already the children of self-employed Asians are more likely to be either self-employed professionals (opticians/pharmacists) or business professionals, similar to the early Jewish experience. Caribbeans have made limited headway into self-employment particularly into self-employed ownership during the last decade, supported by very patchy state assistance. In fact the proportion of owner managers and those with employees has declined over the last decade with Caribbean women resisting the decline.

As we have shown from the case study of Asians, the picture of ethnic groups as such being enterprising is somewhat incomplete or even false, as it is the traditional elite within such communities who are at the apex in the hierarchy of business ownership. This is not to say that there are no joiners in the enterprise dream. Indeed both the Muslim and Sikh Punjabis have now a fairly well-developed commercial base. The Bangladeshis appear to have reached their saturation point partly due to excessive reliance on textiles and catering. In contrast the Chinese have done well despite their excessive reliance on catering over the last decade, by distributing their business. Like the Chinese-Americans, second generation Chinese will probably abandon this sector to enter the professions.

Hitherto, analytical models based around extended family and niche market (the inner resources model) or exclusion (discrimination) or the less studied ecological model, on their own paint a partial and somewhat static picture of ethnic enterprise put forward by some authors such as Ward (1988) and a more recent model of reluctant entrepreneurs (Centre for Employment Research 1990)[129]. The actual picture is quite complex with a hierarchy of segments in the ethnic minority economy in which the most diversified commercial and mainstream enterprises lie at the top controlled by traditional groups with commercial experience, good education and international links with the elite in the country of origin. The second layer is comprised of chains such as Pathak and Royal, or those who own several restaurants and are breaking into the mainstream markets, this also includes video chains such as Azad Video in Scotland. This is followed by small shopkeepers in electronics and professionals such as pharmacists and dentists, and there is the ordinary grocer or newsagent. These layers are interlinked through horizontal and vertical networks between different communities with established groups providing leadership.

All of these have various vertical and horizontal links with other sectors within the mainstream economy. One could argue that the Asian ethnic economy is following a model of family and communitarian capitalism stratified on conventional lines prevalent in countries such as Italy, amidst a more individual and corporate form of capitalism. The Chinese appear to follow a similar model but it is very vertically integrated showing little sign of stepping out of the catering business. The Caribbeans on the other hand show an affinity towards an autonomous individual model of enterprise led by women in the community who also appear to be doing better in the labour market than the men. The development of African business probably falls between the two models. Education and westernisation are likely to push many individuals, particularly the next generation of ethnic minorities, to leave the 'family model' and seek integration into mainstream business.

To what extent the ethnic minority business base will continue to be able to offer jobs to members of their respective groups remains a moot point, although clearly the ethnic minority small business sector has acted as a welfare buffer absorbing unemployment as well as under-employment. Cashmore (1990) has, however, recently shown that medium-sized black and ethnic minority businesses are increasingly having to employ white middle managers and sales persons in order to survive, i.e. they tend to kick the ladder away from underneath them under pressures of discrimination[130].

On the state assistance side, a holistic model of local economic development with genuine partnership with local communities with well-established links across sectors and institutional mechanisms for ethnic minorities to contribute as a major player is needed. Players need to be given funding on the precondition that they have a brief not only to regenerate the local economy, but also to tackle discrimination.

The absence of focus on ethnic minority business development in public policy, perpetuated by malign action in contract compliance by government has meant a loss of opportunity to develop a medium-size business sector, as well as the chance to offer jobs to local ethnic minority people and to influence local development. Worse still, the government has failed to insist that local organisations be created which can represent the interests of disadvantaged groups and local communities, and maintain the balance between physical short-term regeneration and long-term community regeneration. The situation has been made worse by the curtailment of community development and the sidelining of local government. The regeneration story is littered with failure to tap the entrepreneurial energy of ethnic minority people in areas of concentration such as Southall in Ealing and Soho Road in Birmingham, in contrast to the US experience

390

where they have been able to develop such towns into cultural assets.

References

1   The figures for UK-born vary from community to community, with people of Caribbean origin having the highest proportion whilst Africans and Bangladeshis have the least (OPCS 1991) in a report by SAUS (1994). Effects of socio-demographic change in the innter city (SAUS) concluded that there was little evidence of dispersal.
2   Hall, S. (1978) *Policing the Crisis*, Hutchinson, London.
3   Howe, cf. Bridges, 'Keeping the lid on British social policy, 1975-1981', *Race and Class*, winter 1982.
4   Bridges (op.cit.).
5   Seabrooks, J., 'The war on jingoism', *The Guardian*.
6   Bridges (op.cit.).
7   As we have shown in Chapter 3 it destroyed the only tool it had to have a social dimension to procurement.
8   Birch, D. et al. (1985) *The Job Generation Process*, MIT Programme on Neighbourhood and Regional Change, Cambridge, Mass.
9   DoE (1984) *Urban Programme. A Report on its Operation and Achievements in England.*
10 Williams, G. (1988) *Inner-city and Black Minorities*, NCVO.
11 See Home Office Scrutiny Report (1988).
12 Bridges (op.cit.).
13 The evidence on government's bashing of the so called 'loony left' and anti-racism is well documented; see *Searchlight* August-December issues. See also Mang, N. (1986) 'Race and the press in Thatcher's Britain', *Race and Class,* no. 3, IRR.
14 For criticism of the Swann Report see CRE (1985) *A Response from the CRE* and Parekh, B. in Verma, G. (ed.) *Education for All, A Landmark in Pluralism*, Falmer, Brighton.
15 DES (1990) *A Survey of the Local Education Authorities.*
16 Nixon, J. (1982) 'The Home Office and race relations policy', *Journal of Public Policy*, vol. 29, no.4, pp404-20.
17 See Chapter 5.
18 Ibid.
19 Gallagher, P. (1981) 'The role of race relations advisors', MA dissertation, Stirling University.
20 Labour Research Group (1988) 'Internal report'.
21 The CRE investigation into Hackney Council (1988).

22 *The Guardian*, 3rd August 1978.

23 Authorities such as London Authority, West Midlands, Leicester City Council and Bradford have all done well as evident from their ethnic minority data. Equal opportunities in the Civil Service for ethnic minorities, Cabinet Office (1994).

24 As the above report suggests in fact the Civil Service was not doing too badly.

25 An example is Flew, A. (1986) *Power to the People,* Sherwood.

26 Greenstreet, R., *The Republic*, 25th March 1985.

27 'Conservative funds and British minority groups', *New Statesman*, 29th May 1978, cites the evidence of connections between Tories and the far right.

28 Seldon, A. (1986) *Agenda for Free Society*, Hutchinson, London, for Institute of Economic Affairs.

29 Nozick, R. (1974) *The State and Utopia,* Oxford, Blackwell.

30 Hayek (1984) 'The road to serfdom', in Seldon (op.cit.).

31 Sowell, T. (1981), *Minorities and Markets*, Basic Books, New York. Murray, C. (1984) *Losing Ground*, Basic Books, New York.

32 Scrutton, R. in Palmer (ed.)(1986) *Anti-racism: An Attack on Values and Education,* Sherwood.

33 Cohen, G. et al. (1986) *The New Right, Image and Reality*, Runnymede Trust.

34 'Parliamentary debates', *The Guardian*, 13th March 1985.

35 *The Financial Times*, 12th December 1985.

36 'Parliamentary debates', *The Guardian*, 13th December 1985.

37 Ibid.

38 Gamble, A. (1974) *The Conservative Nation*, RKP. Moufle, C. (1981) *Democracy and the New Right.*

39 Cohen, G. et al. (eds) (1988) (op.cit.).

40 Ibid p159. See Basquenet in Cohen, G. et al. (op.cit.).

41 Wilding, P., 'Legacy of Thatcherism', *Policy and Politics*, vol. 20, no. 3, July 1992, pp201-12.

42 Multiculturalism is not explicitly mentioned in the DES Cross-curricular themes although Richardson et al., from Runnymead Trust have shown the scope for interpretation of these themes widely. See Chapter 5

43 Home Office (1982) *Racial Attacks*, HMSO.

44 Young, K. (1982) *The Role of Race Relations Advisors*, PSI.

45 See Moore, B. in Mitchie, J. (ed.)(1993) *Thatcherism - The Economic Legacy*, Academic Press, UK.

46 The lead has never been given by the minister for Racial Equality.

47 Only six CTC's have been set up and little money has emerged from the private sector.

48 I discovered this in a seminar of London agencies at GCRE Woolwich. They

have been subsumed into the one stop programme.

49 Wilding, S. (op.cit.).
50 DoE internal documents. I am thankful to Derek Whyte Head of Policy at London Borough of Ealing for his assistance with summary papers.
51 See Moore, B. (op.cit.) and also variety of Action for Cities Reports, DoE, (1988-1992).
52 DoE (1988) Task Force Evaluation, Action for Cities Reports.
53 Less than 1.9% of the total urban policy budget of £1237m in 1991 of which 50% was spent on training and 16% onactual job creation and even less on environmental improvement, P.A. Cambridge Economic Consultants (1991) *An Evaluation of the Government's Inner Cities Task Force Initiative.*
54 Simpson, A. (1988) *Cuckoo's Nest*, CRC, Nottingham.
55 Christie, J. (1991) *Profitable Partnerships*, PSI.
57 In London, with the exception of London Borough of Greenwich and Waltham Forest, no council retains its race advisor in the Chief Executive's Department.
57 See Moore (op.cit.).
58 Robson, R.T. et al. (1994) *Assessing the Impact of Government Urban Policy*, CUPS, (Manchester University), EIUA (Liverpool John Moore's University and Mori.
59 Ibid.
60 Ibid.
61 Regenerating the inner cities, July 1990, Committee on Public Awards, HMSO.
62 Wilding, P., *Policy and Politics*, vol. 20, no. 3, July 1992, pp. 201-12.
63 Housener, V. et al. (1993) *Economic Revitalisation of Inner Cities: The Urban Programme and Ethnic Minorities*, DoE.
64 Ibid.
65 Gray et al (1990) cited in Chapter 5
66 Recently Home Office officials have been accused of being too liberal, hence a restructuring has been suggested.
67 The scrutiny led in 1986 to Lord Lane's criticism of the lack of co-ordination of DES, DoE and Home Office programmes. See Lane's Report on Brent Development Program for Racial Equality, HMSO (1988).
68 In London, with the exception of the London Boroughs of Greenwich and Waltham Forest, no council retains its race advisor in the Chief Executive's Department, Section 11, Home Office Circular 1988, barred expenditure on multicultural and race equality programmes.
69 In the trusts, for instance ethnic minorities are under-represented in the political structure of AHA (See Chapter 6) and trusts. The national figure for the TECS is less than one percent (NCVO, 1995, cited from *Community Care*, 25th-31rd May 1995).

70 Many council employees have been rehired by the contractors to do the same job with little protection and lower wages - for example, cleaners in Ealing library (interview with Peter Jones, Head Librarian).

71 Casualisation is the highest for ethnic minority groups according to a TUC report published September 1990.

72 See Hicks, C., 'NHS colour blindness', *Health Services Journal*, 26th May 1988, pp.590-91, for the position in 1987; the progress is charted in regular articles by Mark Johnson in *New Community* (1988-1995).

73 For an update on sporadic and limited action by the central government, see Johnson, M., *New Community*, January 1989, vol.15 and Johnson. M., *New Community*, 1991, vol. 17, no.4. Also see *Survey of Social Services* (1990), CRE, for current position.

74 See the case of two doctors who sent identical forms for appointment, one with Asian names and other with Anglo-Saxon names (*BMJ*, 1993). See Chapter 6 for details.

75 Men are more disadvantaged than women in some groups, e.g., Caribbean men in relation to unemployment (OPCS, 1991 data).

76 Kaushika, A. and Oppenheim, C. (1994) *Poverty in Black and White: Deprivation and Ethnic Minorities*, CPAG.

77 A recent report in the British Crime Survey (1992) put the figure to 70,000 acts of harassment a year.

78 CRE Annual Reports 1988-1994.

79 Mayhew, P (1988) *British Crime Survey*, Research Study No. 111 and Menny, A. and Mirlees-Black, C. (1994) RAPU Paper No 82, both by Home Office.

80 See Chapter 3.

81 Class composition and community orientation towards a sector or a profession is an important and crucial variable.

82 Over-representation in some sectors such as medicine and nursing does not mean that access is easy for second generation. See Chapter 6.

83 Five percent of newly qualified social workers are from ethnic minorities (CCESTW, 1988). Seare, P. and Stibbs, 'The under-representation of ethnic minority students in post-graduate training', *New Community*, 14th January 1983, vol. 15, no.2, pp253-60.

84 Escott, K. and Whitfield, C. (1995) *The Gender Impact of CCT in Local Government*, EOC.

85 For detailed analysis of this see Hakim who cites the 1987 BSA which does not show a great deal difference between self-employed and the others in relation to enterprise culture. Subsequent BSA surveys show disenchantment.

86 Bovenkirk, cited in Luthra, M. (forthcoming).

87 Story, J and Johnson, *Scottish Journal of Political Economy*, May 1987, vol.

34, no. 2, May. There is much debate about the relationship between rise in self-employment and unemployment in different European countries. See Bogonhold, D. and Staber, U. (1993) *Self-Employed Dynamics in Work Employment and Society,* 7,3, 462-72. See also *The Rise and Decline of Self Employment and Society*, 5,2, 223-9.

88   Ward, R. and Jenkins, R. (1984)(eds) *Ethnic Communities in Business,* Cambridge University Press.

89   Luthra, M. and Bajwa, M. (1988) *Asian Retailers in Greenwich,* IWA.

90   Ward (op.cit.).

91   Brown, C. (1986) *Black and White Britain,* p.51, PSI.

92   Ward, (op.cit.).

93   NDHS 1978, DOE. Select Committee Report 1981, HMSO.

94   Wilson, P. and Stanworth, J. (1984) 'Growth and change in black minority enterprise in London', *ISBJ,* 4, 3.

95   Currently there are 2,000 Indian restaurants (1,500 in London), *The Guardian,* 8th October.

96   Curran, J. and Burrow, R. (1988) *Enterprise in Britain - A National Profile of Small Business Owners and the Self-employed,* CBR Trust, 'Asian business on the move', *The Times,* 1st June 1983,

97   Ibid.

98   McEvoy, D. and Aldrich, R. (1985) 'Survival rates of Asian and white retailers', *ISBJ,* 4, 3. The 1971 Census also indicated the Cypriots were twice as likely to be self-employed than Asians.

99   Ward, R. (1985) 'New shops in old areas; Patterns of inner city business', paper presented to the UK National Small Firms Policy and Conference, University of Ulster. Harrison (1987) makes this point in *Inside the Inner City,* Penguin. See also Home Office report on racial attacks on retailers, HMSO.

100   Phizacklia, A. (1990) *Unpacking the Fashion Industry,* RKP.

101   Luthra, M. (forthcoming) *Asian Retailers in Glasgow.*

102   Ward, see ref. 125.

103   Basu, D. (1991) 'Afro-Carribean business in Britain. Factors affecting business success and marginality', unpublished PhD, Manchester Business School.

104   Stanworth, J. and Grey, C. (eds) (1990) *Bolton, Twenty Years on,* CBR Trust, London.

105   Banks themselves have taken a number of initiatives. See Stanworth et al above.

106   These were inspired by GLEB experience. I discovered the difficulties faced by the enterprise agency at a meeting held at the GCRE in 1992.

107   *The Financial Times,* 29th December 1992.

108   *TES,* 3rd June 1992.

109 Councils such as Greenwich and Ealing.

110 I am thankful to Gurbux Singh the Chief Executive of Haringey for this comment.

111 Mills, L. and Young, K. (1982) 'LAL Economic Development: A preliminary analysis', in *Critical Issues in Urban Economic Development*, vol. 1, Clarendon Press, Oxford.

112 Not willing to lend to Asians. See Soar, H. (1989) Heads of the Home Office Unit on Ethnic Minority Business Initiative Annual Report of the EMBI.

113 *Independent on Sunday,* 1992, p.13, article by Nick Fielding.

114 *Financial Times,* 1995, p.15, effect on black unemployment.

115 Ram, M., 'Coping with racism; Asian employers in the inner city', *Employment and Society*, 6th December 1993 (4).

116 Merger, M., 'East Indians in business', *New Community*, July 1990.

117 The key names were Varsani (607), Aggrawals (567), Bhudia (585), Mehta (2767), Kakhani (866), Gosh (583), Hirani (934) Sood (582), Popat (1013), Thakrar (99), Shah (1680). Database group cited in *Today*, 6th February 1993, mean wealth 20K.

118 Mullins, D., 'Asian retailing in Croydon', *New Community*, 1979, 7 (3), pp403-405.

119 Rafiq, M. (1988) 'Asian business in Bradford', Ph.D., Bradford University. Werbners, P., 'Business in trust', in Ward and Jenkins (op.cit.).

120 Ahmed, S.H. (1981) 'Entrepreneurship and management practices amongst immigrants from Bangladesh', unpublished thesis, Brunel University.

121 Rafiq, M. (op.cit.).

122 This had led to many Banglaeshis renaming their restaurants.

123 Phizacklia (op.cit.).

124 Islamic Funds floated on the Stock Exchange in 1993 was a failure, and it shelved its share offer.

125 Ward, R. (1984) *Resistance, Accommodation and Advantage. Strategic Development in Ethnic Business*.

126 Waltman, J. and Studler, D. (ed) *Political and Public Policies in Britain & USA*, Mississippi University Press.

127 For a wider debate on setting aside, see Chapter 3.

128 Deeken, N. and Edwards, J. (1994) *The Enterprise Culture and the Inner Cities*, RKP.

129 Ward (op.cit.). I am thankful to Professor Storey for the term 'reluctant entrepreneurs'. Cashmore, R., 'Room at the top', *New Statesman*, 17th August 1990, vol. 3, no. 114, pp10-14.

Conclusions to section IV and the way forward

As we have shown in Chapter 7 there are major differences in accumulation of equity in different ethnic minority communities. Although most of this equity is concentrated at the lower end of the spectrum and in a poor state, nevertheless it has probably enabled some communities, such as the various Asian communities who have used it as collatoral to establish small-scale business over the last decade. On the whole, however, ethnic minorities remain consumers of housing with hardly any building societies or banks owned by them. In urban policy terms two major issues flow from this. First, the emergence of negative equity and drying up of funds such as repair and improvement grants would have long-term implications for the future development of enterprise. Second, this demise in the level of equity would mean that there would be reduced opportunities to take the traditional opportunistic route to enterprise for ethnic groups who have have increasingly found themselves in the casualised secondary labour market.

Given the above scenario the opportunities for single parents, concentrated on council estates with no equity, are likely to be next to nil. Here the housing associations' provisions such as part-rent part-buy need to be developed on a much larger scale if this avenue is to be sustained. Similarly, the very small self-build and cooperative movement needs explicit support for young people to build equity in the inner city areas. In this respect the black housing association movement has a major role to play tapping historical orientation of some communities towards construction. This movement along with the local authorities need to press the building societies to lend on an interest-only basis to the unemployed and part-timers as well. Similarly local contract compliacnce restricted to the inner cities should be part of any housing expansion which may take place. There are enough black and ethnic minority small-scale building firms which need to be supported to be able to participate in the expansion of the housing market.

The shrinking public sector housing provision restricts mobility in terms of employment adding to the barriers to opportunities in a market ridden with discrimination. Current housing allocation policies have no employment dimension - an option which should be considered. Clearer and more detailed guidance in all allocation categories and publication of a model allocation system would minimise discrimination in the area of discretion and enhance opportunities for victims of racial harassment.

Clearly despite the lack of support from banks who have been less than generous to small business, ethnic minority businesses have sustained themselves quite well over the two recessions, probably with the support of the extended family and probably at the top end due to their links with their country of origin. In the case of some communities such as Pakistanis there has been significant growth in business, albeit restricted to the cultural enterprise sector. Overall the concentration of medium-size and mainstream business still remains in the hands of an historically experienced elite, whilst others remain concentrated in retail and in cultural enterprise. A concerted effort is needed to support expansion and diversification of ethnic minority business in addition to offering lending facilities for start-ups. In this respect the government has failed to recognise that banks such as BCCI did good business as they were able to cater for small ethnic minority businesses in respect of all these areas. Unlike the US which has some twenty black owned banks and a set aside facility for ethnic minority businesses, no such provision has been developed in Britain.

Another major failure of urban policy has been to encourage racial desegregation which on the whole has remained unchanged. In fact many local authorities through their housing policies dump refugees and homeless families in areas of ethnic concentration due to their low cost rent, catalysing a spiral of decline and enhancing segregation. The policymakers have failed to capitalise on the tourist and novel attraction of ethnic minority business concentration on American lines. They have failed to develop their infrastructures and tap the energy of ethnic enterprise for local economic development. A more imaginative urban policy taking housing, employment and educational aspects into account with a mechanism for community development and input at local level, acknowledging discrimination as a key barrier, is now needed.

9 What next? Strategies, discourses and agendas

Despite frequent moral panics about immigration, the actual number of ethnic minorities as a percentage of the population remains small. There is increasing evidence of falling birth rates as well as loss of the elderly section of the ethnic minority population who oftenreturn to their country of origin as they find Britain hostile in their later years. The overall black and ethnic minority population is unlikely to increase beyond 8% by the turn of the century. Extrapolating from the current figures and drawing upon recent experience of ethnic minorities in the arena of party politics, these figures are unlikely to translate into a significant increase in parliamentary representation over the next decade.

Consequently, a variety of strategies are needed to compensate for the relative lack of political parliamentary muscle of ethnic minorities. To this end, Smith[1] outlined and evaluated a variety of courses of action open to ethnic minorities. Unless there is a radical, but unlikely, change in the electoral system, the increase in representation of ethnic minority MPs will inevitably be a gradual process. Political strategists will have to take into account the emergence of composite and new identities such as the British Muslims, as well as bear in mind the major distinction between how the first generation perceives itself as compared to the second generation of black and ethnic minority communities.

Progress and the politics of identity

As argued in Section I, in terms of intergenerational progress, the second and third generation ethnic minorities have made considerable gains over the last three decades. This can be observed when their position is compared with the first generation arrivals, education and literacy being two specific examples. If one takes an optimistic view, this should, in the not too distant future, translate into economic mobility and hopefully into social mobility too. There is also some evidence of representational gains in some sectors, for instance in the legal profession in the private sector, and in urban local government as well as in the health sector and the civil service. The latter two are also conventional areas of ethnic minority participation for the first generation (Asians in the civil service and Caribbeans in the health sector - excluding medicine).

A large number of ethnic minority young people born in families with no literacy have made impressive gains in education against all odds. In many cases those who were relatively destitute in their country of origin have felt empowered by virtue of strengthening their economic position through migration. Others have made economic gains yet suffered in terms of loss of status. However, in many cases the social cost of such educational or economic gains, at least as perceived by first generation settlers, has been enormous - an area which warrants some research.

As I have explored in Section I, the majority of the black and ethnic minority population in the long-established communities is now UK-born. They have to live the 'politics of identity' debate which has emerged over the last decade, partly fuelled by the British ruling elite's insecurity of being swallowed up by a pan-European identity and partly by the anxiety which flows from the rapidly diminishing *global leader* status of Britain. The developments in Ireland and Scottish rumblings about belonging to the wider Europe whilst conservative England remains a reluctant player - have all contributed to this insecurity, often manifested in the form of nostalgia in either the curriculum or in the debates about values.

From the academic side, it is the discussion of post-modernism which has contributed to the identity debate. In dealing with this issue in the literature on post-modernism, there has been a tendency to present self-representation as a voluntary choice implying that young people imitate consumer behaviour in choosing their own identity. Furthermore, the literature tends not to make a distinction between the first and second generations. To this end I have endeavoured to evolve a more complex and less static model of identities in Section I.

Section I also charts how, in the last three decades, in addition to the experience of racism, a variety of other forces, such as secularisation, westernisation and Ashrafisation, have all interacted with racism to shape the identity of ethnic minority people. In the case of ethnic minority young people it appears to have become situational and composite, and also remains dynamic. As research by Carrington et al (1995) suggests, even primary school pupils' including Scottish pupils, are having to resort to hyphenated identities to express the duality of their cultural identity[2].

In my view a good case can be made for the use of hyphenated identities in the next census, as well as in a variety of ethnic monitoring forms, as a set of useful categories of self-identification. The hyphenated identity would also be beneficial to the Scots who are known in a variety of surveys to express dual aspects of their identity. Another useful alternative expression worth exploring would be to rely on the notion of heritage rather than ethnicity for self-description and for the description of others. For instance (and of course only if it is acceptable to all concerned) those from Africa might describe themselves as African heritage people.

In the long run the above-mentioned forces would continue to jostle with each other, with different groups resisting the force of secularisation and westernisation at different paces. If the Jewish experience is anything to go by, and given the evidence of physical relocation of the better off from their original place of settlement, the influence of the clergy and that of religious institutions on young people is likely to decline in the forthcoming years. Ethnic minority youth is more likely to be influenced by a leadership which is English speaking and able to build a bridge between faith and rationality, its folk (cultural) aspects, and contemporary issues related to living in the west.

Some of the Asian communities are evolving a religious-ethnic nationalism with a global dimension and are expressing affiliations across traditional boundaries of nations and ethnicity. In the case of the Muslim community this is significantly accentuated by the arrival of African Muslims in the UK. That is to say, Islam is less likely to be perceived as a Middle Eastern or Asian faith. Although the conflict will continue between some universal notions and western egalitarian notions (such as those of human rights and gender equality), and some religious practices and beliefs held by ethnic minority groups, overall there appears to be a trend towards 'reformation'. This is manifested in the separation of the personal and the public on the one hand as well as the cultural and the religious on the other, in the minds of young Asian people, including young Muslims.

Tragically, neither this process of reformation nor a dialogue between young people of different faiths has been encouraged by the British state through the education system or through youth work. Over the last decade the conservative position has developed in a way that is highly narrowly-nationalist and backward-looking. Recently the ideal of British education has been described as embracing classicism in literature, royalism in politics and Anglo-Catholicism in religion (see Dr Tate's[1] statement in *The Independent* on Sunday 23 July 1994)[3]. This is a notion based on T.S. Eliot's essentialist, monarchist and Tory ideology. Such a nostalgic view of education and citizenship is unlikely to equip young British people of any colour and ethnicity with appropriate life skills or provide an intellectual framework relevant to the rapidly changing world.

Historically the notion of long-distance and hyphenated ethnic identity, such as that evolved by the Chinese and the Jews, have served communities well. For people from the Indian subcontinent the term 'Asian' is obviously emerging as one most frequently used

404

by Asians in Britain. It remains, however, at odds with the American description of people from the Indian subcontinent as 'East Indians' and the Canadian description of them as 'South Asians'. As regards Africans and Caribbeans, Gilroy urges historians 'to produce' a complex unit of analysis by taking the diasporic and transnational idea of the 'Black Atlantic' to which all African and Caribbean people could belong without falling prey to race-related essentialism, Afrocentricism and uniformism (Gilroy 1994)[4]. Gilroy's analysis boldly insists upon hybridity, and relies on the imagery of openness of identity, which is mobile and heterogeneous. In so doing, he takes his stand against those who emphasise the enduring manifestation of their roots in black culture and their return to such roots.

If we think about identities and points of similarity and difference as things that are always being negotiated and challenged, we may think more about the ways in which these categories depend upon the particular purpose of those who create and maintain them (Spellman 1988)[5]. Laclau and Moufflé (1994) argue that identities are formed by the exercise of power in oppressive ways, but the oppressed themselves can also contribute to this process[6]. They suggest that the political system never achieves a total closure in the development of new identities articulated in the social arena.

The optimistic view is that identity politics is a project of building new political groupings as an attempt to mobilise people, with the discourse on quality rights providing a`forum in which the ensuing struggle and debates involving newly-emerging identities can take place (Williams 1991, Herman 1993)[7,8]. A less optimistic, although no less valid, view would be that identity politics is also an expression of reactionary, quasi-feudal forces which continue to assert themselves to maintain their hegemony by fragmenting the larger group and thus weakening its bargaining power to negotiate with the system. Over a period, state-defined identity categories dialectically interact with these categories constructed by the categorised to formulate new often transient identities. None of this, however, helps the policy-makers' needs to develop an overview of disadvantage and discrimination through the process of categorising people.

As to the emerging sectarianism amongst the ethnic minority young, particularly amongst Asians in Britain, the demise of a secular (although in many cases what was an ethno-centric) youth provision in the inner cities has left a gap which is increasingly occupied by ethnic and religious nationalists' fringe groups. Furthermore, the weakening of the anti-racist movement has meant that there is no focal point nor any analytical framework to enable the ethnic minority young to translate and interpret their own experience or the history of their heritage through shared political analysis.

The manifest energy and enthusiasm amongst ethnic minority young people as they search for their roots, or seek an affirmation of their identities, need to be harnessed and located in a wider intellectual and internationalist framework. To this end, like the European cultural awareness programme, an internationalist awareness programme is needed which addresses issues such as identity, critical multiculturalism, fundamentalism, sectarianism and racism. It is no longer intellectually tenable to focus on any of the above-mentioned issues or to bestow essentialist or prescriptive qualities on any one of the above in isolation from the others.

Social and economic integration

As part of the global trend, the gradual movement of black culture towards the centre of mainstream youth culture in Britain over the last two decades appears to have had little impact as yet on the level of discrimination which young blacks face. Ethnic nationalism, albeit quite popular amongst the fringe groups within the black community, is likely to be eroded rapidly in Britain by the integrationist tide in the case of long-term resident communities such as the Caribbeans.

The presence of a legal framework to deal with discrimination has also created an ethnic consciousness amongst the Irish and the Scots who, along with the newcomers, are asking for the establishment of their own categories in censuses and ethnic monitoring forms in use by various institutions. These groups are also increasingly resorting to legal remedies to counter the discrimination they face. The number of monitoring categories will inevitably increase, and there appears to be a need to include religion as part of the monitoring process.

Despite increasing codification of recruitment processes in employment and training in the eighties (which have been rapidly undermined in the nineties), networks remain very important for young people in terms of co-option and access to the system, particularly as racial discrimination continues to be a major barrier and employers continue to exclude young minority people. Those who network, or integrate culturally or phenotypically, are likely to be in a better position to surmount discriminatory barriers than those who are not so situated. Groups which are reluctant or slow to integrate are likely to continue to rely significantly for survival on the route of the small business sector, which will probably remain as a kind of 'welfare sector' for young ethnic minority people in the near future.

The economic trajectories followed by young people of different ethnic origins and their affinities towards different sectors and professions are as likely to be shaped by the exclusions imposed by the majority community as they are by the historical traditions and preferences within the respective communities. A more sophisticated analysis of the interplay between disadvantage and discrimination, and between the social and cultural capital of different ethnic minority communities is needed in charting the trajectory of economic progression and prospects of an ethnic group (Luthra forthcoming), taking future developments into account[9].

Pundits project that managerial jobs will grow at a rate of almost three times that of professional jobs (Brown 1995)[10], although this is unlikely to be the case in relation to the care sector. Generally skills acquired tend to have approximately a seven year shelf-life and need to be updated. Given the above situation, a national training strategy needs to be hammered out for the ethnic minority young with the consortium of TECs. It has to be done in a very targeted way given the failure of the modern apprenticeship scheme to engage ethnic minority young people (*The Guardian*, 25 May 1996)[11].

Furthermore, the pace of economic development in the respective countries of origin of different ethnic groups will also be a crucial variable in shaping the economic opportunities which become available to the ethnic minority young at the turn of the century. The more developed the economy of the country of origin, the better the scope of opportunities for ethnic minority groups originating from those countries to network. In this way they can widen their commercial base which, historically, has been limited to the traditional business elite within different ethnic communities.

The economic success of a community, however, is not likely to lead to the lowering of the level of racism directed against an ethnic group (Harrison 1984)[12]. Only a major community education programme can assist in this direction. Generally, large-scale community education programmes aimed at countering racism have been distinctively lacking in Britain in the last decade - the recent campaigns in football, as well the poster campaign involving Saatchi and Saatchi, being two major successful exceptions. Other education programmes, such as the European Awareness Programme, also need to address issues related to diversity and equality. In fact, a similar large-scale social awareness programme is needed at European level.

The poor access of the ethnic minority young to the European Union's culture and its languages is an issue which also warrants serious action over the next decade, just as the teaching of English is an issue for the visible ethnic minorities across Europe. This is essential if ethnic minorities are to enjoy a reasonable degree of mobility within the market, as well as to participate in Brussels' developing Eurocracy in which ethnic minorities remain under-represented.

Limits of the law

The concept of such freedom of movement is being undermined in the European Union by some of its leading nations who pander to narrow nationalism and xenophobia and are replicating the traditional British strategy of stronger immigration control together with assimilative policies. Nevertheless, as part of the latter policy, a number of states, particularly north European states, have developed anti-discrimination measures which in some cases are a variation of the UK model. Any further developments on anti-discrimination law at EU level are likely to be shaped by the attitude European governments may take to EU-level initiatives. The speed at which these could develop into effective pieces of legislation over the next decade depend upon the political alignments at European level and the political will to resolve the issue of competency in the Treaty of Rome.

Even if guidance is produced and a target date is established, by way of a directive from the EU, to pass an anti-discrimination law, such developments are likely to vary considerably from state to state. Current arrangements across the EU appear to be poor, particularly in the southern European countries. The same appears to be true of legal arrangements on racial harassment in the European Union. The UK debate about a specific anti-racial harassment law needs to be expanded to Europe, so as to argue for building an expertise in the area amongst both lawyers and the judiciary as well as to enhance its scope. As argued in Section I, the systemic, social and psychological analysis of conversion of grievances into complaints is needed in assessing the effectiveness of various anti-discriminatory systems emerging in Europe.

In Britain, recent legal precedences which have restricted employers' liability for harassment to the workplace (*Tower Boot Ltd* v. *Raymond Jones* 1996), the refusal of the courts to grant permission to Satpal Ram to appeal in a case of self defence (despite the fact that interpreters were not used to take evidence during the course of the trial), and the rejection of the High Court to grant permission to Stephen Lawrence's parents to pursue civil litigation on behalf of their murdered son (where police prosecution had failed), are all major setbacks. Such cases need to be assessed and their outcomes challenged at European Court level. Similarly the failure of a number of local authorities to intervene effectively in situations of racial harassment needs to be legally tested. The cost of such litigation is prohibitive and a benevolent fund is needed for pursuing such cases.

As evident from the case of Marshall, the fate of the Race Relations and the Sex Discrimination Acts are inextricably intertwined - hence a regular dialogue between the lawyers of the two bodies (the EOC and the CRE) is needed. As to the recent observation that there has been an increasing number of complaints during the last year from men to the EOC (which constituted the majority) and from white applicants to the CRE (which constituted 10% for the CRE applicants' pool), this phenomenon warrants further analysis and needs to be expressed as a positive trend in the public domain to show that the CRE and the EOC are not only promoting the rights of ethnic minorities and women respectively (Almuhajir 1996)[13].

Continuing with the positive side of the legal equation, damages being awarded by tribunals for racial harassment have been increasing (e.g. the *Johnson* v. *Armitage* prison service case 18510/93/LS awarded £24,000 in damages). The level of settlements in discrimination cases as well as, to a lesser extent, the level of damages awarded by tribunals has also gradually been going up. However, the evidence of the impact of legislation on the organisational culture of discriminatory organisations remains somewhat disappointing.

As I have argued, the reliance on the law as a main tool of social and organisational change is unlikely to pay large dividends unless the issues thrown up by a particular case lead to an instruction to the discriminator by the tribunal to conduct an audit and publish a report using an independent-approved analyst. The onus should be on the company to show that it has taken the necessary measures in good faith to rectify the situation. This is particularly important given that the Prestige case has restricted the ability of the CRE's to investigate organisations unless it can show belief in the existence of discrimination, and in any case the CRE resources are limited. Furthermore, there is a need to argue for a provision similar to the one enshrined in the Fair Employment Act in Northern Ireland which has a requirement beyond the elimination of discrimination.

On the issue of legal responses to the cultural issues, the British response is pragmatic in comparison with the exclusionary or segregative responses by other European states, and warrants further analysis. Gordon (1994) in his analysis of domestic and foreign divorce law has optimistically argued that it should be possible to incorporate some aspects of Islamic law into English law[14]. In Britain the legal distinction drawn between an ethnic group (common descent and shared language) and a religious group (evangelical history of conversion, *Hampson and Mendella* v. *Lee*) is intellectually untenable and appears to be spurious. The same applies to the distinction between those who are of Jewish *faith* and those who belong to the Jewish *race*. EAT (523/91) went as far as to emphasize the distinction between the small number of Jews who keep the Sabbath and the majority who do not. Thus the detriment suffered by disallowing Sabbath leave could not fall under indirect discrimination. Yet at the same time in *Azam and others* v. *J H Walker Ltd* (COIT case no. 411161/92) the tribunal accepted that the feelings of the employees in relation to the festival of Eid were so strong that the employer's refusal was not justified; hence the employers' action constituted indirect discrimination.

Overall, the CRE's reviews of the Race Relations Act have been ignored by the Conservative government although there has been some progress through case law and some incorporation of the proposals into mainstream legislation. The trend of European courts in setting the agenda on equality is likely to continue unless, as favoured by the current government in Britain, the role of the ECJ is curtailed.

Social policy: a few steps forward and a few steps back

As I have shown in Section III, clearly in all four areas of social policy I have surveyed developments have taken place at different times, and some sectors came late to the race equality debate and were not aided by funding pools such as Section 11 - health being one example. As my survey shows, there is a mixed balance sheet, with some gains and some losses over the last decade.

Education for all

In education there has been a marginalisation of anti-racist and multicultural policies, whilst at the same time there appears to have been gains in terms of improved educational performances of ethnic minority pupils at school level as well as in terms of their access to the universities. The Caribbean young people, particularly males, still remain an exception. There is also further scope for pushing the attainment levels of pupils of Bangladeshi and Pakistani origin.

To what extent such progress can be attributed to the multicultural policies of the last decade or to ESL teaching remains a moot point. One thing, however, is clear: old-fashioned, backward-looking multiculturalism is unlikely to appeal to the young. To this end, critical multiculturalism explored earlier on, has an important contribution to make in addressing the criticisms of the left and the right as well as the segregationists. In addition to the need to disseminate some excellent materials produced by academics to schools, there is a need to intervene in schools using approaches (exhibitions, drama, art, etc) which do not rely solely on the rationalist's paradigm.

Sadly, educational qualifications remain a poor protection against discrimination. The disproportionate representation of ethnic minorities in the urban space means that a large proportion of ethnic minority students are still not reaching their full potential at school or in the post-school phase. There is little evidence that the TECs are able to counter both the 'urban effect' and race discrimination in

412

terms of getting ethnic minority young people into employment.

As I have argued, a broader analysis of the strategic options, including open schools, is needed if the issue of under-performance of the Caribbean young is to be tackled. There is some evidence that, unlike Asian peoples, the Caribbean male pupils fail to catch up with their peers as they move from Key Stage 1 to Key Stage 4 during school years. The situation with regard to improvement in Asian attainment is not homogeneous either. It varies considerably between pupils, say, in Southall, Waltham Forest and Bradford, even when restricted to groups such as the children of parents of Pakistani origin. Attainment levels at primary stage remain poor for Asian pupils, primarily due to English language handicap. Here, there is obviously a clear agenda for educational interventions targeted at different ethnic groups at different key stages during the course of schooling. On the issue of behaviour in schools, there is a need for a wider debate about strategic options followed by evaluated trials (open schools, schools with attached youth workers, city in schools*).

The demise of programmes which targeted ethnic minorities, such as the Section 11 programme (now drastically reduced and spread very thinly) which was well supported by the education profession and parents alike, has particularly eroded the expertise base developed over the years and has also adversely affected the representation of ethnic minority teachers in the education system. In slashing the Section 11 programme, the government has also failed to take into account the arrival of new ethnic minorities, such as the Somalis. The demise of mother-tongue teaching is a serious loss considering the general agreement among academics that to have a knowledge of two languages other than English can improve competence in English[15]. This is evident from English language GCSE results at secondary level in 1995 in London. The social value of communication between the young and their grandparents in terms of transmission of family values is incalculable. Here there is scope for a partnership fund to which parents, embassies, and local religious institutions could contribute to continue mother-tongue

* City in schools is a programme aimed at pupils at risk or with behavioural problems who are given attention while they remain at school.

413

teaching in a professional framework.

As a backdrop to this, the overall trend in education appears to be towards the creation of a credit economy in higher education in the public sector, whilst a notion of 'pay as you learn' develops in the independent sector. As has been pointed out[16], the middle classes will invest heavily in getting their young into premium and elite institutions to retain their historical advantages, as their security is somewhat threatened by the undermining of the public (professional) sector. Given the serious under-representation of ethnic minorities in the elite higher education institutions and their affinity towards new universities, steps are needed to redress the imbalance through introductory schemes, mentoring and work placements at such institutions for black and ethnic minority young people. Substantial scholarship schemes aimed at enhancing access to post-graduate institutions are also needed.

Community care and care in the community

Social services, like education, have suffered set-backs in the area of training, although the gains in terms of an increased number of black and ethnic minority social workers have not been reversed. Over the last five years, the commitment of social services, professional body to race equality has weakened. On the other hand, the separation of quality assurance from service provision presents an opportunity to use both the Social Services Inspectorate and local inspectors for the purpose of weaving quality and equality assurance together. Similarly, care in the community under the Community Care Act can be a helpful notion for institutions to connect with disengaged communities. Yet at the same time the ethnic minority population with little savings and poor advocacy support, and with a lack both of English and of a knowledge of rights and services, is likely to be short-changed. Institutions such as the SSI need to incorporate the inspection of bilingual provision and adequate advocacy provision into their quality assurance inspections.

So far the impact of the Community Care Act on ethnic minorities

414

remains unassessed. This needs urgent action given the complexity of provision which flows from the mixed economy model which the government has tried to put into practice at individual level, with great variation from one local authority to another. The ageing ethnic minority population also presents a serious challenge to service-providers in the inner cities, as well as in terms of provision for those who may want to make their meagre pensions go further by returning to their country of origin, as they see the British welfare state diminishing.

On the academic side, more writing is needed on various specialist aspects of social work rather than the continuation of broad-based analysis, which is of limited use to practitioners. The ongoing debate about the crises concerning the role of social workers in society needs to be accompanied by a simultaneous examination of the role of social workers in a multiracial society and the kind of competencies which may be necessary for well-defined social work roles.

The health of the nation's minorities

As discussed earlier, in the area of health there has been some sporadic developments at a time when the health system has been undergoing major reform. In health there have been government attempts to lay the foundation of some sort of policy, albeit without a convincing strategic framework. Training and curriculum development on race equality and diversity remains under-developed and patchy, particularly in areas such as nursing, midwifery and medicine.

Variations on the basis of ethnicity in health confronts us with formidable challenges. Why is hypertension more common in black people, whilst coronary heart disease is more common amongst Asians, than in others? Though levels of hypertension and diabetes are both higher in black people, coronary heart disease on the other hand is significantly lower than expected in these communities. These questions not only focus on issues centred on ethnic minority populations but also provide opportunities to understand both the aetiology and the pathogenesis of disease in general - although there are ethical issues about using these populations for experimental purposes.

There are also ethical issues surrounding the targeting of populations for screening, treatment or isolation who are statistically known to be more susceptible to some diseases than the general population. This is particularly an issue when a moral agenda has been introduced into a medical debate and the folk or medical discourse pertaining to the disease has been racialised - AIDS is one example of this. In health, the issue of genetic marking, as well as the establishment of norms for each ethnic group (for instance on blood pressure, taking morphological and physiological features into account), is likely to be an integral part of the building of a comprehensive picture of risk and needs assessment. Ethical committees need to address these areas and to come up with guide-lines for issues which fall into this category.

On the prevention side, the promotion of healthy lifestyles among respective ethnic minority groups, as a means of preventing major killers such as coronary heart disease and stroke, requires a focused and targeted approach. There is no reason not to set targets for these and for, say, perinatal mortality for ethnic minority populations, based on both evidence and good practice. To date, approaches to developing appropriate, relevant and clear messages that are placed in the context of cultural, religious and social norms are just beginning to emerge, but are often stifled by the present framework of short-term project culture.

Variations in food and dietary habits amongst different ethnic groups provide a significant challenge to those involved in health promotion and the management of obesity, hypertension and diabetes, diseases that are more frequent in some ethnic groups than others. Other aspects are the challenges these provide for both secondary and tertiary prevention. The burden of hypertension on black communities is a case in point. Do we adopt screening targeted specially at these populations, and if so in what modality? Should it be an opportunistic approach as advocated in the Health of the Nation strategy in England, or is there another model that would be more effective? What are the cost implications of such approaches? These are challenges not only for the health economists but also for those involved in the allocation of resources.

For the clinicians, ethnicity provides challenges presented by some esoteric diseases, though these are rarer events in comparison to the variations in the clinical presentations of less rare diseases. Besides variations in the stages of the natural history of diseases, such as an advanced malignant lesion or a fulminating coronary, there are challenges in the diagnosis of common disorders, such as depression, in their varying presentations in different cultural contexts. The presentations are often related to the varying perceptions of illness, their social stigmas, value systems and associated behaviour patterns, all of which require an understanding of the cultural and social milieu of ethnic groups. There is a need for a more formal consideration of such issues in the curriculum both of doctors and of other health professionals. A multi-agency unit involving the British Medical Association, the General Medical Council and other edu-cationalists, is needed to train academics in diversity and equality issues so that they can impart such analysis, at both undergraduate and post-graduate levels, in medicine. Similar initiatives are needed for nursing and allied health subjects by boards such as the English Nursing Board.

Despite acrimonious debate, in some areas of race ethnicity and health, as is the case with mental health, little has emerged as to why some groups continue to bear a disproportionate burden of illness, and worse still, how this could be prevented. Research needs to shift its focus to referral links and cohort studies in order to analyse institutional inclusions and exclusions of certain sub-groups within the black and ethnic minority communities. To this end I have endeavoured to create a model which could be developed further.

A well thought-out national strategy on research and evaluation in race equality and health is needed to replace the piecemeal and *ad hoc* approach which has led to duplication and poor quality research.

An evaluation culture based on large, reliable studies needs to be developed, together with systematic and regional approaches to funding. Comparative and collaborative work across continents can be rewarding in this area, particularly in relation to aetiology. There are indications that coronary heart disease, for example, is becoming a major issue in the Indian subcontinent, and disease related to eating and lifestyle may very well be issues for the future in urban India. The demise of the ethnic minorities unit established in Leeds, aimed at ethnicity and health, is regrettable. A considerable amount of work is needed in relation to employment and redundancy in the health service.

Quality and equality assurance

Clearly in both health and social services, quality assurance approaches have been developed. It is, however, unclear whether the current structures aimed at ensuring quality assurance, which in some cases are also entrusted with auditing equal opportunities aspects in the new audit culture, actually do so effectively. During the course of writing this book I had considerable difficulty in finding strategic or policy development material on the issues even in the case of a centralised system such as the Social Services Inspectorate. Currently, analysis of equality or initiatives related to the issue are often found in *ad hoc* confidential papers which are not brought explicitly to the public domain, nor are the results of inspections collated and published. In health, since quality assurance roles are scattered and poorly defined, equality aspects of such assurance often appear to be missing in what are highly varied and *ad hoc* arrangements.

Contract culture, policy enterprise and partnerships

On the policy responses side, both in health and social services, it would appear from the foregoing survey that policy development on

418

race equality and diversity has shifted from the institutional framework model developed in the eighties to the policy enterprise and voluntaristic model. Consequently it is likely to burden those individuals (particularly black and ethnic minority people) with a reform agenda, probably and usually at some personal cost in terms of upward mobility. This is made worse by the fact that new organisational configurations which have emerged from a contract and audit culture, do not as yet contain effective mechanisms for equality assurance, and there is severe under-representation of ethnic minorities amongst staff in such outfits. Given that networking and partnerships are becoming major modalities of governance, the issue of role models within services and networks of black and ethnic minority people, both within and between different sectors and institutions, is likely to be a major one over the next decade.

In a contract culture setting, the auditing of equality and diversity, and their relationship with efficiency, needs some attention. Here some theoretical work on organisational economics is needed, together with the production of detailed good practice guidelines on successful experiments in equality and diversity. The issue of language and ethnic (cultural) competency and appropriate rewards for such skills needs to be addressed by the Institute of Personnel Development, as indeed does the issue of ghetto-ising black workers in 'ethnic minority-type' jobs. There is also a research agenda on the issue of ethnically mixed and competent teams and their effectiveness, which needs attention.

On the whole it would appear that there has been some significant successes in the area of attainment in education (excluding the area of multiculturalism), some good but poorly strategised attempts in health, and some retraction from earlier gains in social services. As both political parties begin to undermine the cradle to the grave social covenant [17] negotiated on the welfare state, and given the unanimous political commitment to restrict the public sector borrowing budget to 3% of the GDP - there is a need to analyse and project the implications of such a shift for black and ethnic minorities.

419

At another level, the issue of having an adequate number of careers for multi-ethnic provision, as well as role models in public service for the young ethnic minority population (which is ageing at one end and moving into the 16-25 age-band at the other end of the spectrum), warrants further attention by bodies such as the TECs, health trusts and the English Nursing Board. There is also likely to be severe shortage of teachers at large at the turn of the century.

Urban policy: segregation and community regeneration

On the housing front there remains considerable segregation and entrapment of ethnic minority groups in poor housing, although the situation has improved over the years in relation to some indicators such as amenities and overcrowding. Some ethnic minority groups have also been able to improve their equity base, as well as the quality of their housing to a higher extent than others. The Asians in particular have utilised their equity well to develop housing and ethnic enterprise. On the whole, ethnic minority influence on the supply side of housing remains marginal, with the exception of the black housing association movement which is struggling to sustain itself. The movement is nevertheless a good example of government-supported and professionally-led incremental development, with good technical back-up and training facilities. The replication of this model could be a feasible option for development in other areas.

The combination of the absence of cheaper loans for house building or buying, together with the rise in rents in a ring-fenced budget for the public sector, has added to the housing difficulties of unemployment-prone ethnic minority young, particularly for people who are trapped in poor housing and are suffering racial harassment. Housing can be a crucial element in the development of collateral leading to the growth of ethnic enterprise. In one sense, the development of the black housing association movement and owner occupation in housing is a good example of self-betterment by black and ethnic minorities in the face of adversity, challenging the victimology model. Nevertheless, there appear to be hardly any

420

major programmes aimed either at enhancing the equity base of ethnic minority communities or at tackling segregation within public sector housing. The emergence of CCT has been a distraction and is unlikely to improve services. In the process of preparing for competition, many housing departments have undermined the provision for racial harassment work over the last couple of years. The government's recent proposal concerning the creation of a single register for housing allocation, and extended powers for the Secretary of State to intervene in regard to local eligibility criteria, is likely to hit ethnic minorities disproportionately as they tend to be over-represented among the homeless. Another proposal to deal with unsocial behaviour on the part of tenants through probationary periods and other sanctions is welcome.

None of these measures, according to a recent survey, are likely to make any significant difference to the problem of housing provision (Roof 1995, c.f. Blake 1995, Crawley 1994), and furthermore, they are unlikely to make any impact on the reduction of racial tension in public sector housing or enhance mobility for victims[18,19]. Both of these issues warrant a major housing investment dovetailed with an estates-based community safety programme. A national strategy is needed, developed on the lines of the priority estates programmes targeting multi-ethnic estates, with a strong community safety dimension to tackle racial harassment. On the equity development side, building for sale or part-rent and part-sale schemes, coupled with self-build programmes, could be effective. There is no reason why local authorities cannot build affordable housing for sale, similar to the model of 'build for sale' practised by many housing boards in developing countries.

Turning to the wider urban policy context, the issue of the domination of public space and amenities in the current inner city development framework by the developers and major players, remains a central issue. The ousting of minority interests from the local arena, and its focus on bricks and mortar, is another form of under redevelopment. To this end, community regeneration councils, which are suitably empowered to challenge the technical muscle of the large players, need to be established, using Lottery and SRB funds. The absence of an equal opportunity brief amongst TECs means that they tend to turn a blind eye to the attitude of employers whom, in many cases, they know to be discriminating against ethnic minorities. Equality targets need to be made a mandatory precondition for the TECs. Market correction pertaining to discrimination through various positive action programmes should be one of the key functions of the TECs. The tendency to use compliant consultants and develop hit-and-run equal opportunities work is unlikely to pay dividends.

The notions of 'public service' and that of the importance of local non-governmental organisations (NGOs) has been seriously undermined in Britain at a time when there is an increasing recognition of such a role at international level. The new magistracy may be able to play the guardian of the public purse, but its ability to play the watchdog and represent the public interest, including ethnic minority interest, remains highly questionable. Overall it would appear that the demise of targeted programmes, such as Section 11 and the urban programme, together with the emerging focus on joint development, tends to militate against ethnic minority community groups and blunts their role as local critics.

Given the increasing domination of the social agenda by the notions of a free market and a contract culture, as well as by the increasing complexity of legislation, local NGOs have to be equipped and aided by specialist staff with the appropriate expertise to survive in such a complex arena. Here the challenge lies in using community development, historically aimed at seeking concessions from the local state, to bring about the innovative integration of different ethnic minority communities who may be in conflict with each other over the issues of identities, or access to resources or local amenities. In the inner city areas with diverse communities, the need for NGO development should be regarded as part and parcel of legitimate expenditure on local democracy. The new managerialism must not be allowed to undermine democracy.

There is also a need to construct research agenda which are able to challenge the channelling of some ethnic groups into an entrapped position of marginalisation with a diminishing ability to escape from such a position. To this end, the role played by referral agencies such as the police, schools, the health service and the social services in funnelling young people into deviancy or psychiatric institutions, warrants further analysis. I have endeavoured to evolve a basic conceptual model around this which needs further development.

The government's current supposition that local quangos such as the TECs should not bear the cost or responsibility for local community development, or should not have a brief for enhancing good community relations or deal with issues pertaining to equality and diversity, needs rigorous intellectual interrogation. After all, like any other market corrections the government endeavours to make, whether it be the exclusion or disengagement of some groups in such markets (private or social), the publicly-funded quangos cannot argue that they do not need to make an attempt to correct discrimination.

As the current situation stands, despite the patchwork development approach to regeneration through programmes such as the SRB, the government's hostility to a locality-based (if not ethnicity-based) contract compliance appears to be incomprehensible. Similarly the absence of local coordination of training and education (given the proliferation of providers) has been highly detrimental to the inner city young, particularly as a lot of it has lacked any quality assurance provision. Overall, social policy approaches have lacked an urban or inner city dimension, thus linking very poorly with urban policy.

The absence of contract compliance and European tendering legislation makes it very difficult to offer contract work to local companies who in turn would employ local people in the local regeneration process. This is an issue which needs to be taken up at European Union level in the context of regeneration. Unlike the US and Canada, where local government has been able to convert ethnic towns into major tourist attractions by linking arms with foreign banks and private business, this kind of approach has failed to emerge in the UK, leading to the failure on the part of local authorities to tap the energy of ethnic entrepreneurs. A programme focusing on development of such towns is needed in the SRB framework.

Although recently there has been a backlash against a 'bricks and mortar' type of development, and an attempt to involve ethnic minorities in the bidding of the SRB, the latest data (Gahagan 1996) suggest that there is very little relationship between successful bids and the concentration of ethnic minorities, with only a small proportion of project bids having an ethnic dimension[20]. Currently it is not a requirement in the SRB bidding process to reflect the needs of the local population. Two issues are clear. Firstly, the private sector leverage requirement is detrimental to ethnic minority projects, as such a tradition does not exist in the private sector *vis-à-vis* the funding of ethnic minority projects. Secondly, ethnic minority groups which tend to be smaller cannot in practice bid for projects themselves, as the emphasis tends to be on large projects. SRB managers need to create a small fund for innovatory projects which can be led by small NGOs, as well as develop a pre-condition that there must be an ethnic dimension if the population profile (of an area from which the application emanates) is such that it is warranted. Furthermore, a capacity building and/or community development fund is needed. Even in rural areas, projects aimed at ethnic minorities are needed.

Much of urban policy ends up dealing with bricks and mortar aspects or training programmes which rarely lead to jobs. This is often at the expense of a real social agenda. Furthermore, various players are increasingly being given resources in different frameworks to run their own programmes with little or no reference to those of others. Apart from this lack of any co-ordination or dialogue between various agencies, there is little accurate analysis of local communities or of their relative strengths and needs. Too often projects are cobbled together in a hurry relying on poor information and even poorer understanding of the diversity and history of the local communities and economies.

Equality, diversity and contemporary discourses

Over the last decade a number of debates have informed public policy to varying extents. For instance, throughout the eighties the cumulative model of discrimination and disadavantage has been prevalent, with new additions such as sexual orientation and ageism. There is not an overarching theory which can do away with having to deal with such issues separately and cumulatively using different models. To this end, the models which can explain discrimination, disengagement and disadvantage across the board need to be developed. Paradoxically, the cumulative disadvantage model aimed at tackling disadvantage can also create a state-sanctioned static victimology, which in turn could damage the capacity of individuals in a particular ethnic group to pull out of adverse circumstances. In this sense, using a more interactive model, an analysis of the social and economic mobility and progression of various ethnic groups, in terms of periodic and intergenerational changes, is likely to produce a better picture than the cumulative topping-up of disadvantage indicators.

In addition to the analysis of demographic and social indicators, an examination of barriers and other factors need also to be taken into account when approaching strategic planning of public policy pertaining to ethnic minorities. As Fu Yama (1995) has recently argued, both the social and cultural capital of an ethnic group and, in my view, the nature of their economic experience as well as the discrimination encountered, need to be taken into account when charting the progression of an ethnic minority group[21]. In other words, what is going on within ethnic minority communities, and its dialectical relationship with what is external to the communities, needs to be subjected to analysis. In so doing, however, both researchers and policy developers need also to be cautious about falling prey to exoticism and pathologisation of ethnic minority communities.

One recent example which illustrates this point is DeSouza's sensationally entitled book *The End of Racism* (1995)[22] (which is similar to Gilroy's equally sensational title of an article, 'The End of Antiracism', 1994[23]). In this book, De Souza grossly overstates the case in relation to the role of culture in shaping educational and economic disadvantage. Such titles do not add much to the debate but instead transmit selective and sometimes distorted strands of analysis into the racist folklore, contributing to the pool of racism. Another incident which illustrates this point is the recent Home Office research unit's observation which followed media assertions that there was a growing criminalised underclass of young Asians who had become alienated from their local communities (Fitzgerald 1995, *The Independent,* 22 July 1995)[24,25]. This was quickly challenged by the subsequent involvement of the same young people (in Bradford) in the cleaning-up of their areas from illicit sexual activities, as well as by the observation that most of them were living at home with their parents.

Similarly, although the discourse on post-modernist debate has opened a space for dialogue between cultures, the extent to which it applies to developing non-European nations and the cultures which emanate from these nations via immigration, remains a moot point. Another danger of the debate on post-modernist debate is its capacity to generate complacency through the notion of indeterminacy, i.e. societal analysis is now so complicated that one cannot make sense of it using traditional social science tools. Furthermore, its perpetuation of choice of identity, almost as though it were a consumer product, wreaks of voluntarism. Aimed at countering essentialism, such a view discourages analysis of social phenomenon from a sociopolitical or from a political economy position. After all, in developing nations such as India there has always been scepticism of modernist rationality, and a pastiche of old aspects of cultures has always blended with the new or lived alongside it. Social sciences in pluralist societies have always had to struggle with a variety of movements and multiple cleavages other than class.

The British discourse on identity, to which I alluded earlier on, also has a European dimension which is likely to be a major issue for a large number of black and ethnic minorities young. At a theoretical level, the manner in which some ethnic groups may become visible and victim minorities in one part of Europe, yet may be perceived as part of the scene elsewhere, or may even be the oppressing dominant group themselves, presents further problems for current terminology and prevalent paradigms of analysis of majority/minority relations and visibility.

At a policy level, issues pertaining to graded citizenship and the exclusion of newcomers leading to a fortress Europe, appear to be as much driven by moral panics in response to what has been described as the twin crises of the Keynsian economy and the welfare state, as it is by the re-emergence of Euro-racism and fascism. Most of the current legislation aimed at reducing asylum seekers and the refugee's access to various benefits is likely to affect the black and ethnic minorities adversely and turn urban gate-keepers into *de facto* immigration officers - a situation similar to the one observed in the seventies.

Studies are needed to establish the contributory and cushioning effect of immigration on economies of different host countries (Spencer 1994)[26]. At a practical level, a European-wide programme is needed to counter racism with a well-defined focus. Recent ARA efforts to develop a European-wide network with the possibility of holding summer youth camps, are commendable. But a more comprehensive programme of activities is needed with a focus on youth work and education in order to make an impact.

As I have shown, most of the international and European treaties, as they stand, tend to offer limited and varied protection against racial discrimination, partly because little specific legislation has been enacted by various states. With the exception of Belgium, there is even less by way of established cultural rights - for instance, the right to be taught your parents' mother tongue, or your right to a certain kind of burial facility, or the right to interpretation. In Britain this is particularly important in the context of the current debate on the Bill of Rights which needs to address the issue of some fundamental cultural rights. Given the diversity of Europe, it is likely that such an

427

issue would get a better hearing at European community level. The issue of conflict between cultural rights, human rights and egalitarian rights needs to be addressed with a view to developing some concensus on which elements should remain in the public domain (Rex 1985)[27]. The segregationists and particularists (Gutman 1992) must not be allowed to hijack the cultural rights debate[28]. The purpose of education as a crucial factor in enhancing democracy must not be distorted.

It also remains to be seen to what extent the debate on communitarianism (Etzoni 1994), with its emphasis on change of heart and on long pre-policy development discourses and its reliance on uniformity of local communities to create the community spirit in the neighbourhood, will address the issue of racism[29]. Historically, neighbourhood nativism has been too readily converted into local racism (Luthra 1988)[30], occasionally to be challenged in some cases by the relatively enlightened central state. Hallesten (1995) has also argued that the promotion of communal values and common good degenerates communitarianism towards cultural relativism, which in real life can translate into promotion of moral indifference[31]. Furthermore, the communitarian notion of having very long discourses running into decades prior to implementation of controversial policies, does not take into account the dialectical relationship between morality, legal sanctions and policy development.

Turning to organisations, a related discourse which has developed over the last decade is the relevance of new managerialism and its implications for race equality. The shift observed in the dominant nomenclature from equality to equal opportunities, and now to diversity, has coincided with the development of new managerialism rhetorically committed to democratic ideals of management, but in practice driven by efficiency and delayering drives. The new managerialism has driven the race equality issue to the margins of personnel departments and obfuscated it in the realm of equal opportunities, performance indicators and quality assurance, making them somewhat invisible. Here the agenda would be to make them

428

explicit and to highlight them.

Two arguments are often marshalled in attacking the idea of enhancing race equality in organisations. Firstly, that equality and diversity are incompatible, i.e. how can one expect all ethnic groups to progress at the same rate considering that there would be diversity in their performance? In the case of this argument, the counter argument is that the notion of equality in organisations cannot simply be reduced to statistical parity. Furthermore, as is often done in the case of many other policy implementation programmes, the aspirations and targets for achieving equality and diversity have to be translated into practical tasks, using the 'art of the possible' management techniques. Statistics are mere tools to assess the management competency of the managers in meeting their goals.

Secondly, an argument for using diversity (which has been much influenced by the American emphasis on diversity being good for corporate profits and public relations) as a key concept to replace the notion of 'equality' (which replaced historical compensation as an explanation for preference for ethnic minority groups) as justification to market it to the British private and quasi-private sector organisations such as the TECs, is beginning to establish itself (Kandola 1995)[32]. It is also permeating the British personnel fraternity. One major problem with this argument is that, unlike the US where the historical compensation argument has been deployed by the US courts and affirmative action targets are enforced by federal and local agencies, in a British setting, where voluntarism has prevailed, the borrowing of such a notion of diversity could become a bit like peddling the old-style multiculturalism of the sixties. That is to say, it may be comfortable to talk about diversity, but it does not address the issue of majority/minority power relationships and exclusions in society or in organisations. Here there is a definitive agenda for organisational theorists to grapple with as to what terminologies can be used and what concepts should underpin such approaches to make significant inroads into, and to catalyse, the permeation of race equality in different sectors. The broad concept of 'equality and diversity', both enshrining critical multiculturalism and counter-racism, can be useful in dealing with a spectrum of concerns.

At the level of implementation, it would appear that any approaches to race equality aimed at the public sector have to deal with the challenge of highly fragmented hollowed-out local and central state (Rhodes 1995)[33]. The new governance has eroded the distinction between civil society and the state, putting a diminishing number of ethnic minority activists and NGOs at large into a compromising position. This, on the one hand, has created a poorly-utilised opportunity to integrate a lot more ethnic minority people into a spectrum of emerging agencies. On the other hand, the hollowed-out local and central state presents a tremendous and time-consuming challenge to reformers as the loci of power have become numerous. Hence, it is difficult to identify these loci for the purpose of seeking change in relation to equality and diversity.

As to the affirmative action discourse, the advantages of targets are now well conceded by the large corporate sector in the US. Edwards (1994) has convincingly argued that intellectual merit *per se* does not present a major intellectual obstacle to the establishment of affirmative action targets[34]. It is the compensatory justice argument (rarely deployed in Britain) which presents a difficulty. If carefully constructed, Edwards argues, well-targeted and time-limited preferential policies can be useful tools for the creation of mentors as well as pioneers for disadvantaged ethnic minority groups.

So what next? Some key strategic issues

As we have shown, young people need adult support and good local social provision in order to mix with their peers and understand each other's culture and faith and construct a dialogue. Youth work appears to have slipped off the the local government agenda over the last few years. It needs to be recast and framed in a different manner to deal with a variety of issues including counter-racism and sectarianism as well as sexism. With the current emphasis on economic access rather than social access and community

430

understanding, we may be sowing the seeds for discontent and fundamentalism.

At European level, clearly the issue for legal reformers remains whether there is competency enshrined in the Treaty of Rome to issue a directive with a time-limit to pass anti-discrimination laws. Should we be concentrating on the amendment of the Treaty, or should the focus be on arguing that there is competence - hence the need to campaign for a directive? Closer to home in Britain, there is considerable scope for improving the effectiveness of anti-discrimination law to enhance incentives for complainants; in addition to this some effort is needed to develop effective systems of support to assist the victims of discrimination and racial harassment.

The current system of complaints on discrimination needs a thorough examination in this respect, particularly in relation to enhancing advocacy and support for the complainants. In the case of discrimination, innovative ways of enhancing accountability of organisations without litigation are also needed to catalyse organisational change in a positive way, such as the enhancement of follow-up powers for tribunals or the automatic removal of discriminatory personnel officers.

Public interest litigation and community lawyering

The limited community lawyering tradition built up in Britain in the seventies has been weakened even further in the nineties, and has not been able to generate public debate on race equality issues. The radical lawyering community has become a victim of the tradition of lawyer/client relationships, with their focus on rule underpinned by court-centred thinking. Both the voluntary sector and the CRE have become appendages to this quasi-market lawyering and have adopted the professional modality of a 'take it or leave it' attitude, thus maintaining an emotional distance from the pain of discrimination.

The enfeebled trade unions and voluntary sector movements have both failed to contribute significantly to the arena of community lawyering or to translate the idea of individual legal rights into collective struggles around public interest litigation. Young lawyers need opportunities and locations to realise the scope of law through legal mobilisation. The CRE remains a cautious repeat player, taking only very safe cases. The role of a 'risk player' could be filled by an independent regionalised National Law Centre which could also offer specialist advice on racial harassment, law and strategies. The CRE also needs to link arms with the trade union movement as well as with universities, to tap this energy with a view to reviving the radical lawyering and victim support tradition which can counter the culture of victimhood. This requires the development of programmes such as university-based law clinics or partnership clinics. One example of this is the Community Advice Programme run by the Ealing Council for Racial Equality in conjunction with the Society of Black Lawyers and Thames Valley University. The enthusiastic approach of the Society of Black Lawyers in pushing the frontiers of change can serve as a model for other staff associations and trade unions.

Organisational change and race equality strategies

Returning to the theme of organisational change, the managerial class in organisations has become a facilitator creating limitations for the executive thrust approach to change. Furthermore, it has become apparent that such a variety of agencies cannot be governed centrally. The situation is further complicated by the fact that new managerialism publicly exhorts the virtue of democracy, but is poor on partnership management (Metcalf and Richards 1991)[35]. It is public sector managers who have been much better at developing the latter skill and who have contributed to local regeneration. Another feature of the new managerialism is that it is highly imbued with the old notion of management by objectives, yet the application of this to race equality is rarely to be seen. Furthermore, in the public sector the split in purchasing and commissioning, and in assessment and provision which is in addition to the separation of quality assurance and provision - all warrant a revision of the conventional approaches to managing change.

Given the above scenario and in the light of the foregoing, is it possible to have a sense of direction and a strategic national framework for managing change on race equality? One realistic proposition in current circumstances could be to develop broad guidelines, and then establish good practice models and let such practice permeate the system of networks. Such an approach has to be based on opportunistic partnerships based on alliances between policy entrepreneurs, albeit blessed by the hierarchy in agencies and organisations, and has to be accompanied by funding and personnel incentives for implementation, as well as some sanctions. Such an approach can also be made more effective in the public sector, at least by establishing good regulatory regimes embedded and explicit in the quality assurance and customer care policies.

Regulatory and good practice approach

On the issue of quality assurance, at least in the public sector, embedding equality assurance targets along with quality assurance can enhance the above approach. Furthermore, to this end a guide describing evaluated and effective projects needs to be compiled by agencies such as OFSTED, the SSI and NHS Executive. The debate about whether there should be a section in the report about equality aspects or whether it should be integrated is a distraction, as both are needed, as indeed is an annual report pulling all the findings together on an annual basis. Both the SSI and OFSTED need to deal with the mistaken and yet prevalent view developing (Batra 1996) amongst the institutions that they (the SSI and OFSTED) regard equal opportunity issues as of secondary importance[36].

Given the fragmentation of housing provision, and if the evaluation of the regulatory model of equality pursued by housing associations is successful, there is no reason why housing departments could not follow suit. All quality assurance outfits also need to develop programmes to enhance the number of paid and lay inspectors and of inspectors/quality assurance employees who originate from ethnic

433

minority backgrounds through secondments.

It is not intellectually untenable to weave equality targets into contractual arrangements, given the emergence of the contract culture involving large sums of public monies. Current arrangements leave the economic integration of ethnic minorities to the whims of market forces and to the goodwill of local authorities and TECs. Furthermore, the current British contract compliance legal position appears to be duplicitous, given the government's stance on this issue in Northern Ireland. In the light of *The Economist*'s caution that such compliance discourages small companies from employing minorities, there is no reason why large companies at least should not have a social audit along with companies who get public sector resources or contracts[37].

Such an approach does not preclude arguing the case for public service idealism, which should embrace equality and diversity whilst at the same time arguing for the private sector to be accountable to local communities. Neither does it mean that we should not aim to press the government to develop a national strategy for racial equality which is led by the government, and is more interventionist in nature, for instance through some form of contract compliance of audits by the major quality assurance and other audit bodies. It is important to argue and campaign for a qualified exemption from EU contracting rules (which insist on large contracts being free of any restrictions) in regard to pursuing local social goals.

Towards a national strategy

A national strategy on race equality could have the following strategic components, i.e. information- and data-gathering, educational provision, public education, welfare provision, urban policy and community development, employment and positive action, as well as legal support. A series of documents on each of these themes and options available are needed to clarify the government's position comparing it with what needs to be done.

434

Currently, little exists by way of a coherent system to monitor and generate data for a public policy analysis of race equality, let alone take development work forward. To this end, the success of the Home Affairs Committee, as well as the Interdepartmental Racial Harassment Working Group needs to be subjected to analysis to assess its effectiveness in making change. The failure of bodies such as the CPS in dealing with perpetrators warrants attention by way of setting up special units with committed staff which can assist with racial harassment and violence cases. At the same time, development on community safety programmes needs to embrace racial harassment as a community safety issue. To this end, trade unions and staff associations, which have considerable resources at their disposal, need to be pressed to develop legal support provision on anti-discrimination law, including 'phone lines and quick response legal opinion facilities for individuals and service providers.

In addition, each government department responsible for a variety of government agencies should be presssed to produce an annual report on race equality measures, on service delivery and on the employment situation. Currently, barring the Department of the Environment and the Home Office, even basic information is lacking, and in all cases there are very few evaluations of programmes and projects. An external focal point is needed in the form of an organisation charged with evaluations of government measures taken to counter racial inequality. Such an outfit could have a brief to maintain critical vigilance on such measures and to publish a kind of 'state of ethnic minority Britain' report on a three-year cycle basis. Internally, departments need to be pressed to have a senior civil servant responsible for race equality affairs.

Finally, the British database is extremely poor on race, whether it be government departments, public sector agencies, or even major surveys including the OPCS, Labour Force Survey and General Household Surveys. All these tend to rely partially on ethnicity to varying extents, but offer only limited scope for meaningful analysis, with no data on religion and language. Some surveys, such as the Family Expenditure survey, do not have an ethnic dimension at all.

435

The local job centres do not collect data on ethnicity and unemployment, making it impossible for the TECs and other players to build a clear picture of the local economy. There is no requirement for either the public or the private corporate sector to collect data on ethnicity. This needs to be remedied, although the Conservative government has resisted such data collection on a compulsory basis, including data on education. Furthermore, most of the data produced tends to be standardised by class, which can be shown to be somewhat irrelevant in the case of some ethnic 'groups' (Smith 1974, Carhill 1995) who do conform to the British modality of stratification[38,39]. Overall it would make sense to develop a race equality interdepartmental group in the government on the lines of the one evolved for coordination of initiatives for racial attacks (RAG) to improve coordination between various government departments.

Towards durable multi-funded NGOs

Yet at another level, good national and regional ethnic minority NGOs are needed to represent the Racial Equality Councils (RECs) and the black and ethnic minority voluntary sector. An anti-discrimination litigation centre which also focuses on racial harassment work and is able to take risks, a monitoring agency on quality and equality assurance, and a major centre for international promotion similar to the European Central Bureau, are some of the possibilities. There is also a desperate need for an ethnic minority youth bureau with a budget to develop a national strategy and with the aim to tap the energy of the ethnic minority young.

These agencies could complement the role of the CRE, which at the moment is rather too wide and vague. Perhaps it needs to concentrate on litigation, on audits of key agencies, on the establishment of codes of practice, and on offering advice to an increasing number of central government agencies. It also needs to develop an overall strategy for different sectors. The desire on the part of the CRE to use local RECs as its litigation arm is likely to pay

436

poor dividends in the near future due to the skills gap from which RECs suffer. Instead, regional offices would be more helpful in the support of litigation work at local level.

The review of the 80 RECs commissioned by the CRE needs to take into account that the RECs in many cases are the sole ethnic minority interest organisations in some areas. They perform a multitude of tasks in an environment in which power is increasingly diffused and the local ethnic minority voluntary sector has quite often been devastated. Social indicators continue to suggest a high degree of vulnerability of ethnic minorities to poverty, with the situation in many areas requiring considerable old-fashioned support for victims of disadvantage and discrimination - a situation almost similar to the one I myself encountered as a Community Relations Officer working for an REC in the early seventies.

Turning to the challenges which RECs face, these include having to manage a variety of programme funding exercises, having to develop litigation skills as part of the CRE funding requirement, and having to cope with a diminishing commitment from local authorities who have traditionally contributed financial resources to the RECs. Furthermore, partnership and development through fundraising are new challenges for which RECs have not been equipped and they face a bewildering spectrum of agencies in the new magistracy sector, including the trusts and the TECs. Here again regional specialist support to the RECs in relation to regeneration and litigation would be the way forward.

There is also a need to evolve agencies and strategies which can assist and enhance the co-ordination of various elements of a very fragmented local state so that these can work together with - and are accountable to - local people, particularly the young. Current multi-agency approaches which have been tried in relation to community safety need to be replicated for urban regeneration. To this end, a programme such as the SRB needs to foster partnership through a community development fund to empower local voluntary sector groups and actually engage in what is called community capacity building. Yet this needs to be undertaken without making small organisations dependent upon the big players and without compromising their autonomy and position. In this respect, organisations such as the JCWI are good working models. A list of ten strategic organisations within the state structures and ten outside would be one way of developing a community development agenda.

Profits, diversity and equality

A slightly different strategy for private sector organisations is needed with a focus on the benefits of a diverse work force, implications for profits, and good business practices - i.e. the need to reflect a spectrum of shareholders and customers and the notion of investment in the community. It is, however, unwise to rely solely on such arguments to engage people in this sector. Senior managers in the corporate world are well able to comprehend the social cost of unrest and waste and indeed are better positioned than a decade ago to empathise with the anger and frustration of marginalisation (now that most people in Britain are economically unsafe). An analysis of the political economy of racism still needs to be put across as part of any training engagement with the private sector.

Large companies need to be encouraged to produce visible evidence of their commitment to racial equality by publishing data on the recruitment of ethnic minorities in their annual reports. An annual social audit based on a yearly questionnaire needs to be produced, naming names. At the beginning of the millennium it is estimated that there will be some 15 million shareholders, of which 1 million are likely to be from ethnic minorities. These shareholders, along with those from the white community who believe in ethical investment and equality of opportunity, can have considerable clout in terms of changing corporate policies. Institutional mechanisms and databases need to be developed to extend the horizons of the ethical investment movement.

No business like one's own business

The issue of the poor development of a business base amongst some ethnic minority communities can partly be addressed by launching sizeable low-interest schemes or good guaranteed loan schemes. There is no reason why schemes such as the Grameen bank scheme (in Bangladesh) could not be adapted and piloted in a European setting. Some of the US banks, particularly black-owned banks, need to be encouraged to open up in Britain. There is no reason why lottery funds could not be utilised to develop a business support fund in conjunction with major banks and building societies to support ethnic minority business development.

Currently, small business incubation provision and small business loan packaging, as well as trouble-shooting expertise, is just not available for ethnic minority business. To this end, the experience of the American Minority Business Development Association and Small Business Administration is worth revisiting. The issue of the development of equity is also tied up with housing equity which forms collateral for business and which, as I have argued, has been differentially available to different groups. Availability of equity can be a crucial determinant of economic mobility and ethnic enterprise (Luthra, forthcoming)[40].

In addition to the new business development strategy for people of Caribbean origin, a business diversification strategy for the Asian communities is needed to enhance access to the mainstream business opportunities. There is also an absence of rescue facilities for ethnic minority communities which could be helpful in sustaining the Asian business.

Looking ahead on mobility

Historically, the availability of intermediate rungs of economic mobility (e.g. apprenticeships and manufacturing jobs) and access to education, over generations have been two key vehicles for ethnic minority groups to work through to acquire a better life. Such

439

Chart 9.1 Sector-based approaches to race equality in Britain

	I Market model	II Inner city local authority model	III New governance model
Causal analysis	• Newness of groups leads to disadvantage and discrimination • Racism - a market distortion - might need correction	• Racism - historical and exclusionist in service delivery • Racial disadvantage - part and parcel of inner city dimension	• A mixture of I and II, *often poorly understood and conceptualised* • *Very limited*
Ethos	• Market ethos • Some acknowledgement of business interests in the community • Voluntarism	• Professional/bureaucratic • Accountable via local politicians • Project development orientated • Minorities are consumers and ratepayers	• Public relations - *blurred identity* • Minimalist provision - autonomous • Improve access to service delivery to all groups • No accountability to people
Approach	In theory: • Limited positive action • Business development • Enhance access	• Some executive thrust • Top down and bureaucratic • Performance outputs	• Minimalist, highly subservient to commercial and professional interests • Ad hoc short-term project development

	I Market model	II Inner city local authority model	III New governance model
Key concepts	• Diversity • Consumer-conscious minimalistic intervention • Voluntaristic • Emphasis on disadvantage *as opposed to discrimination* • Business incentives • Enhance access	• Cumulative disadvantage • Quality assurance - little equality assurance • Equal opportunities policies and procedures • Inner city development through SRB projects • Diversity, equality and multiculturalism	• Diversity (*a little*) • Equal opportunities (*a little*)
Key players	• CRE - anti-discrimination law • LAs - S.71 of the Race Relations Act (1976) using own resources • TECs - through training	• CRE, LAs, TECs plus voluntary sector • Plus development elite • Service providers • Politicians	• White-dominated government-appointed boards • Development elite (*some*) • New magistracy
Problems	• Minimalist • Cosmetic	• Splitting into elements such as purchaser/provider or provider/assessor • Shift from earlier commitment to symbolic commitment • Emphasis on SRB development	• Fragmented - difficult to influence and target • Quality assurance and equality assurance not linked • Autonomous - dominated by business ethos or interests • Remote

441

intermediate rungs have now disappeared and education is likely to be less a vehicle for countering inequality than in the post-war years. Furthermore, education, as evidence from ethnic minority graduate unemployment figures suggests, offers little protection against discrimination in employment or promotion.

Clearly, a spectrum of education and training institutions such as the TECs have a major role to play in facilitating the access of ethnic minority graduates to the labour market. Although school performance profile data substantially explains the representation of different ethnic minority groups amongst university student entrants, it does not fully explain the severe under-representation of ethnic minorities amongst staff (*The Guardian* 25, May 1996)[41].

Even in the inner cities and progressive universities, such as Southbank University, with a large proportion of ethnic minority graduates, the ethnic minority under-representation amongst staff is severe in comparison with the student ethnic profile, and this is particularly so for senior administration staff. Universities need collectively to monitor, and at the same time to launch, regional positive action programmes, as well as to engage in secondments of black and ethnic minority people from other sectors, to remedy the current prevalent imbalance. Otherwise, the university recruitment profile will continue to resemble the police employment profile.

Whilst higher education is held in high esteem so far, the faith of ethnic minorities in British comprehensive education has been weakened a great deal with an increasing number of pupils being sent to independent [42] schools, including schools in the subcontinent, and the increasing demand for Islamic schools. This, in my view, is partly due to the fact that the prevailing rationalist and individualist slant of the British educational system is perceived as partly an enabling, rather than a wholly enabling and ennobling, experience in terms of introspection or socialisation in collective living.

Given the disproportionate level of constraints in the housing and labour market on ethnic minority working class people, it is unlikely that they would be able to compete in the social market of admissions with selection policies. Such trends are likely to

442

intensify the need for independent (from local education authorities) advocacy provision. Recruitment of ethnic minority teachers, and in particular heads of schools, would be another way of ensuring that community contact and access is retained equitably.

To sum up, we have outlined briefly in Chart 9.1 the prevailing race equality strategies in a construct using three models which can be observed to be underpinning the thinking of organisations in the various sectors. In reality, it is possible to find all three models inhabiting one organisation. As we have argued elsewhere, given the ethos and organisational culture of different sectors, different strategies are needed based on the analysis of organisations (Luthra et al 1988)[43]. To some extent, in the light of increasing amounts of awards and compensations in tribunal cases, the legal arguments are likely to be more effective than they have been in the past. One major area which remains underdeveloped and needs to be investigated is the use of moral arguments for challenging racism in organisations.

Clearly the new governance sector comprised of TECs and health trusts warrants that a coherent approach is developed on the basis of its emerging interprofessional culture. This presents a formidable challenge to race equality policymakers and academics alike. Three possible and overlapping strategies could be helpful in this sector. One option could be to argue for guidelines to be produced by the consortia organisations which represent, for instance, the health trusts and the TECs. Another could be to argue for targets to be established as a precondition embedded in the funding regimes. Thirdly, one could target the inner city bodies intially to create good practice models. Fourthly, intervention at curriculum level in this sector increasingly necessitates that race equality is located within an inter-professional framework (Leiba 1996)[44].

Programmes such as the SRB have, on the one hand, enabled local people to participate in development directly; on the other hand, they undermine local democracy by reducing the constructive tension and autonomy of local groups who are often obliged to fall behind the big players in the process of bidding for resources. A quasi-market ideology of resourcing is increasingly shaping development in which the regeneration elite and the private sector procure the consent of the local people to bid for money without actually dealing with the underlying causes of inequality, including race inequality. The race equality movement needs to develop long-term, multiple-funded and robust organisations which can build experience and acquire technical skills to participate in the new modality of development as part of a wider programme of community development. They should be able to carry on their very important work irrespective of governments, as well as tap the energy of people who want to contribute, voluntarily or otherwise, to the project of challenging race inequality.

As I have raised earlier, a cumulative or triple jeopardy model of discrimination and disadvantage (race, class and gender) has been applied to target social provision as well as being used as a tool of analysis. This model has considerable limitations within the context of the services discussed. Academics need to work toward an underpinning of the cumulative model of disadvantage and discrimination with a common, if not a unified, theory of discrimination which can go some way towards explaining what is now an increasing number of 'isms' (ageism and fatism being the latest 'isms').

On the spectrum of developments on equality over the last decade, the class element has been least supported in terms of identity, monitoring and positive action. This, together with poorly explained race equality policies, has often created a backlash amongst white working class youth, underpinned by the resentment that there is no one to champion their cause. This points us in the direction of development of ethnically-integrated programmes with an explicit ethnically-targeted dimension. Such an approach to development, supported by strong regulatory mechanisms which in turn are underpinned by good databases available in the public domain, coupled with the establishment of resilient multifunded and specialised NGOs, can make a significant contribution towards enhancing the effectiveness of current measures. This, however,

444

needs to be supported politically. There is a need to make a serious effort to remedy the disengagement of the ethnic minority young from the mainstream political culture. Programmes such as university summer schools, camps and challenge programmes need to be developed with a view to enhance leadership and political skills.

The focus of the anti-racist struggle relying mainly on the idea of the black identity has been aimed at sensitising social provision by local government and improving representation of ethnic minorities amongst staff, now has to shift to a wider concept of counter-racism embracing issues related to Europe and the new governance sector, as well as ensuring that energies are channelled into community development and community capacity building. A set of specialised institutions aimed at specific areas of public policy with clear objectives need to be developed within the state structures, as well as outside, to pursue race equality goals in a different climate than the one in which the anti-racist struggle of the eighties was conceived.

Finally, although I have by way of an illustration outlined some options, a commission on race equality composed of a variety of eminent people needs to be established to take evidence and plan a strategy for the turn of the century, as we journey into the next millennium.

References

1   Smith, S. (1989) *The Politics of Race and Residence*, Polity Press. Smith alluded to extending representative democracy by reorganising the Select Committees, and reforming party structures by changing the electoral representation system. She preferred the development of black groups as a more effective and symbolically better option for the future development of race equality.

2   Carrington, B. and Short, G. (1995) *Ethnic Identites Amongst Primary School Children,* Education Studies, vol. 21, pp217-38. Carrrington et al have also carried out some more recent work with white children from Scottish community and found them toalso have a bifurcated identity .

3   *The Independent on Sunday*, 23rd July 1994.

445

4   Gilroy, P. (1993) *The Black Atlantic*, Harvard University Press.

5   Spelman, E. (1988) *Inessential Woman*, p158, cited from *A Postmodern Constitutionalism: Equality Rights, Identity Politics, and the Canadian National Imagination*, cf. Stychin, Department of Law, Lecture at Institute of Education, 1993.

6   Laclau, E. and Moufflé, C. (1985) *Hegemony and Socialist Strategy*, cf. Stychin.

7   Williams, J.C. (1991) 'Dissolving the sameness/difference debate: a post-modern path beyond essentialism' in 'Feminist and Critical Race Theory', *Duke Law Journal*, 296, 307.

8   Herman, D. (1993) *Beyond the Rights Debate*, 2.1 Social and Legal Studies 25. On the relationship of equality rights in Canada and the new social movements.

9   Luthra, M. (forthcoming)

10   Brown, P., 'Culture capital and social exclusions', W*ork and Society,* March 1995, vol 9.

11   *The Guardian*, 25th May 1996.

12   Harrison, P. (1982) *Inside the Inner City*, Penguin Books. The author details the jealousy experienced by the indigenous population in relation to self-employed Asians.

13   Al-Muhajir, 'Everyone's accusing everyone else of racism', 1st July 1995.

14   Gordon, D. (1988) *Foreign Divorces, English Law Practice*, Avebury, Aldershot.

15   AMA research on GCSE results cited in *Sunday Express*, 7th May 1995.

16   Brown, P. (op.cit.).

17   Donovan, P. and Ryle, S., 'Stocking-up for winter', *The Finance Guardian*, 25th May 1996.

18   Blake, J., 'The great council house comeback', *Society*, 28th June 1995 reporting on the roof survey, *The Guardian*.

19   Crawley, J., 'No room for racism', *The Guardian*, 24th December 1994.

20   Gahagan, M. (1996) *Into the Third Round of SRB - a Government Perspective*, QMW Public Policy Seminars, 8th May 1996.

21   Yama, F. (1995) *Trust: The Social Virtues and the Creation of Prosperity*, Hamish Hamilton.

22   DeSouza, D. (1995) 'The end of racism', lecture at Institute of Education sponsored by the *Sunday Express*, 2nd May 1995.

23   Gilroy, P., 'The end of anti-racism', *New Community*, October 1990, vol.17, no.1, pp71-83.

24   Fitzgerald, M. (1995) *Race and Crime Facts*, Home Office Research Unit. The figure of Asian inmates increased from 2.3% to 3.1%.

25   *The Independent*, 22nd July 1995.

26   Spencer, S. (ed.)(1994) *Immigration as an Economic Asset: The German*

Experience, Trentham Books Ltd, Stoke on Trent.

27 Rex, J. (1985) *The Concept of a Multi-Cultural Society*, Centre for Research in Ethnic Relations. Rex attempted to separate the two domains locating 'family issues' and religion in the private domain.

28 Gutman, A. (1992) paper on multicultural education, conference in Jerusalem on education and democracy.

29 Etzoni, A. (1994) *The Spirit of the Community*, Simon and Schuster.

30 Luthra, M. and Oakley, R. (1988) *Approaches to Race Training,* Ethnic Relations Unit, Warwick University.

31 Hallesten, S. (1995) *Liberals, Communitarians and Supression of Will*, University of Helsinski.

32 Kandola, R. and Fullerton, P. (1994) *Managing the Mosaic: Diversity in Action,* IPD.

33 Rhodes, R. A. W., 'The hollowing out of the state: the changing nature of the public service in Britain', *Political Quarterly*, April-June 1994, pp138-51.

34 Edwards, J. (1995) *When Race Counts*, RKP.

35 Metcalf, L. and Richards, S. (1991) *Improving Public Management*, Sage, London

36 Batra, S. (1996) AEO, London Borough of Waltham Forest, wrote a paper to this effect to counter the frequent misinterpretation of OFSTED's position by the LEA schools.

37 'A question of colour', *The Economist*, 15th April 1995.

38 Smith, D. and Whalley, K. (1974) *Racial Minorities and Housing*, PEP noted that there was poor correlation between housing ownership and class amongst Asians.

39 Carr-Hill, R. (1995) at the Institute of Education noted that there was little relationship between class and other variables in the case of data he had analysed on Asians.

40 Luthra, M. (op.cit.).

41 *The Guardian*, 25th May 1996.

42 'Why Patel has gone to the top of the class', *Daily Mail,* 9th May 1995.

43 Luthra, M. and Oakley, R. (op.cit.).

44 Leiba, T. (1996) 'Interprofessional and multi-agency training and working', *British Journal of Community Health Nursing*, 1, 1.

447